Becoming a
LANDSCAPE
ARCHITECT

Other Titles in the Series

›Becoming a
LANDSCAPE
ARCHITECT

A Guide to Careers in Design

Kelleann Foster, RLA, ASLA

WILEY

John Wiley & Sons, Inc.

Copyright © 2010 by John Wiley & Sons, Inc. All rights reserved.

Published by John Wiley & Sons, Inc., Hoboken, New Jersey

Published simultaneously in Canada

For general information about our other products and services, please contact our Customer Care Department within the United States at (800) 762-2974, outside the United States at (317) 572-3993 or fax (317) 572-4002.

Wiley also publishes its books in a variety of electronic formats. Some content that appears in print may not be available in electronic books. For more information about Wiley products, visit our web site at www.wiley.com.

Library of Congress Cataloging-in-Publication Data:

Foster, Kelleann.
  Becoming a landscape architect : a guide to careers in design / Kelleann Foster.
      p. cm.
  ISBN 978-0-470-33845-2 (pbk.)
  1. Landscape architecture--Vocational guidance. I. Title.
  SB469.37.F67 2009
  712.023—dc22

                                                                    2009006813

Printed in the United States of America

10 9 8 7 6 5 4 3 2 1

To my family,
for their steadfast and encouraging support;
in particular, to my parents, for trotting us kids
all around North America to numerous cities,
and state and national parks and forests,
where the seeds for my love of the land
and its diversity were sown

CONTENTS

FOREWORD

Perry Howard, FASLA, RLA, 2008 ASLA President

MOST LANDSCAPE ARCHITECTS find out about landscape architecture by accident. It is not a profession that is the subject of much media attention; nor does it have a deep or long history. The term "landscape architect" was first used in the mid-1800s by Fredrick Law Olmsted, the designer of Central Park in New York City. Our professional association, the American Society of Landscape Architects, was founded in 1899, and the first School of Landscape Architecture was started in 1900 at Harvard University. Landscape architects do not often make it into the limelight, as do doctors, lawyers, engineers, firemen, teachers, the clergy, or even architects. The hope is that this book and other efforts like it will help illuminate the profession of landscape architecture, because we need more landscape architects today. Why is this so critical now?

Simply, we need more landscape architects to help restore the damage we humans have been causing to our planet, in particular over the last 50 years. To cite just one statistic, the human population has more than doubled in those 50 years, adding untold stresses to an already overburdened and highly complex ecosystem, further weakening the life-support systems of planet Earth. It is said that we cannot solve even the poverty problem for the world without first repairing our damaged ecosystems.

We in the profession of landscape architecture are equipped with the tools to help repair our shared home. Through research, planning, design, and management of our landscapes, we have been turning out cutting-edge works that both promote environmental awareness and encourage ethical design practices. With the help of a multitude of scientific and allied disciplines, we are making headway in finding solutions to the air, water, and soil problems, and putting those solutions into action. We are at the forefront in demanding green and blue infrastructure, at all costs, in our old and new urban areas. We are beginning to find ways to provide food and housing for everyone on our planet, and to grasp and appreciate diversity and, thereby, become an integral part of the restoration of our ecosystem. We are raising our voices as advocates for all people and creatures everywhere, and in doing so becoming stewards of land, humanity, and culture. We are focused on designing and building walkable and livable communities, demonstrating that all our human needs can be met "in the neighborhood," in order to conserve energy. We are focused, too, on ensuring privacy, even in the face of great population density in our urban centers.

Through these works we are healing the earth and the human spirit. We are addressing global issues through issues on the home front. We are "walking the talk," and "thinking globally and acting locally." Our works are celebrating the spirit of individual places, adding to—rather than taking away from—the continuous landscape mosaic, and doing so in an artful manner. Expressive forms are being generated from user and ecosystem needs. More responsive and creative site details are installed at all levels of design. There is a rich blending and contrasting of the natural with highly refined man-made machined objects and materials.

All of this is apparent in *Becoming a Landscape Architect*. Included in this book is a very wide-ranging group of people, who represent the best of the profession. Through their voices and experiences, readers will gain a comprehensive snapshot of the practice.

I grew up in New Orleans but spent my summers near my birthplace of Morganza, Louisiana, a rural wonderland of levees, lakes, wetland areas, seafood harvesting areas, and farmland. New Orleans, in contrast, is probably the first true urban community of the so-called New World. When I grew up there, all the neighborhoods had corner stores; barber shops, bakeries, and hardware stores were close at hand. But there were open spaces, too, room enough for a football game in the middle of the streets between parked cars.

It was the combination of those two environments from my childhood that stoked my inner fire to study landscape architecture, which I discovered my first day on the campus of Louisiana State University, where I had gone to study architecture. After reviewing the landscape architecture curriculum, which just so happened to be on the page opposite the one describing the architecture curriculum, I decided to change my major. It was the best decision I ever made.

PREFACE

I HAVE BEEN TEACHING LANDSCAPE ARCHITECTURE for nearly 20 years and enjoy helping students explore the many career paths open to them in this exciting and expanding profession. I wrote this book in large part as a reflection of my passion for this profession coupled with the need to increase the number of individuals going into landscape architecture. One of my roles as assistant department head at Penn State has been student recruitment, and I have given a great deal of thought about how to raise awareness about landscape architecture as a rewarding career choice for creative individuals who care about humanity and our planet. I also wrote this book because I am concerned, as are many in the profession, about the need for greater diversity within our ranks. Therefore, another of my goals in writing this book is to present a broad cross section of career opportunities. To achieve that objective, I interviewed more than 50 noted landscape architects from a broad range of backgrounds and ethnicities and representing all sectors of landscape architectural practice; in addition, I included the "voices" of a number of landscape architecture students, both undergraduates and graduates, from schools across the United States. All these men and women share their thoughts: why they went into landscape architecture, what they feel the future holds for the profession, and what their work means to them. They also offer tips on the job search process, among other issues.

Chapters 2 and 3, which form the core of the book, are structured to emphasize the variety inherent in the profession. Chapter 2 focuses on the myriad types of design (broadly defined) in which landscape architects practice; Chapter 3 describes the broad scope of professional practice settings available to landscape architects—public, private, nonprofit, and academic. Reading these two chapters will make it abundantly clear that this profession truly can offer something for just about anyone interested in design.

Becoming a Landscape Architect also features 15 Project Profiles, containing the details of specific designs, most of them built. One of my express purposes with these profiles was to dispel the all-too-common narrow perception of landscape architecture; therefore, the profiles I selected for inclusion are intentionally diverse and broad, and located throughout the world. You'll read, for example, about a zoo, an urban waterfront park, and a major land plan in China. Many of these projects are award winners, including one completed by university undergraduate students.

Several of the topics covered in this book I derived from a course I have taught for many years, "Professional Practice." As such, the book will be of great interest not only to those curious to learn what landscape architecture has to offer as a career, such as junior high and high school students and anyone seeking a career change, but also to those currently studying landscape architecture in college. This book can serve triple duty: one, as a solid overview for a first-year introductory course; two, in a professional practice course, providing essential information on marketing and professional ethics and licensure issues; and three, as a valuable resource for students reaching the end of their studies and seeking more information about career options and advice about interviews, portfolios, and the job search process (these topics are covered in Chapter 3 under "Marketing Yourself: Finding a Job"). The book concludes with additional references and resources, to further aid your understanding of the profession of landscape architecture.

It is my sincere desire that this book be of great value in helping to clarify and illuminate the unique and inspiring world of the landscape architect. This is a very exciting time for the profession, and I encourage you to explore it thoroughly, as there are many ways in which your interests and future goals can find a very satisfying home in this multidisciplinary, creative profession.

A portion of the proceeds from this book will be donated to the Landscape Architecture Foundation to assist in their mission of attaining sustainable landscape solutions through research and scholarship.

— KELLEANN FOSTER, RLA, ASLA

ACKNOWLEDGMENTS

THIS BOOK WOULD NOT HAVE BEEN POSSIBLE without the insights offered by the wonderful professionals and students I interviewed. I thank you all for your generosity and encouragement. With each interview my enthusiasm for this profession grew; you inspired me, and I am sure readers will feel the same. I am also grateful for the unending support of my colleagues at Penn State's Department of Landscape Architecture. In particular: Tim Baird, your suggestions regarding professionals to interview were helpful in getting me started; Brian Orland, your encouragement, insights, and support were essential; my dear friend and colleague Bonj Szczygiel, your feedback and critique at key times during my writing were invaluable.

I was also extremely fortunate to have a fantastic student assistant, Mary Nunn: Mary, your perspective on which projects to feature, followed by your detailed research and writing of the initial drafts of all the profiles, was terrific. You were an integral part of this book and I am grateful for your involvement.

At John Wiley & Sons, I truly appreciate the patience, kindness, and timely assistance provided by Lauren Poplawski, senior editorial assistant. And thank you Margaret Cummins, my editor, for your interest in this book and belief in me. Your perspective was always valuable.

1 Introduction to the Profession of Landscape Architecture

The profession of landscape architecture has a client, the earth and its creatures. In order to meet this challenge, to respond to our client in a sustainable manner, the profession must ensure that it forms an alliance with the environmental sciences and that we come to be seen by them and the public as their agents for achieving felicitous, ecological adaptations.

—IAN L. MCHARG, *To Heal the Earth*[1]

Overview of Landscape Architecture

Those less familiar with landscape architecture tend to think of the profession in relatively basic terms, involving plantings around a building or in a park, for example. The reality is quite different; much broader, richer, and far-reaching. The profession of landscape architecture is much more diverse than the public may imagine. So wide is the range of opportunities, in fact, that people with a variety of interests and from many different types of backgrounds are able to fit comfortably under the title "landscape architect" and build exciting careers for themselves. Landscape architects do, however, no matter what their specialty, have a number of important things in common: a deep appreciation for the environment, a commitment to the highest standards of design and planning, and pride in knowing that their work directly enhances the quality of people's lives.

Gold Medal Park, Minneapolis, Minnesota. Designed by oslund.and.assoc. Photographer: Michael Mingo.

Landscape architecture can be thought of as a 360-degree profession because there are literally hundreds of different directions one can go with a degree in this field. Landscape architects design at many scales, ranging from a tiny roof deck terrace to thousands of acres of National Forest lands; from the private realm of a corporate office courtyard to the public realm of a neighborhood park and playground; from the specialized creation of a healing garden at a hospital to a customized rehabilitation of a native wetland. The next few chapters will highlight in greater depth the diversity of practice types, along with the professional possibilities available to someone with a background in landscape architecture.

Eighty-three percent of the earth's land surface has come under the influence of humans.[2] It is now recognized that much of that influence has not been positive, for either humans or the natural environment. However, every time humans interact with the land—whether to solve a problem, to move between places, or to build—there is an opportunity for landscape architects to become involved and assist in producing a positive outcome. A growing understanding of the capabilities of landscape architects and the value they bring to many types of projects accounts for the ongoing expansion of the profession.

The Many Definitions of Landscape Architecture

Many landscape architects would agree it is anything but straightforward to define their profession. The inherent diversity of the field is both an advantage and a disadvantage. The disadvantage is that, in being so broad, it is not easy to define, which makes it difficult for those outside the profession to understand it fully. The advantages are that its diversity enables so many people to benefit from the work of landscape architects, and, as mentioned above, allows individuals with a variety of interests and strengths to find a satisfying career in landscape architecture.

Perhaps a good place to start to define the field is with the American Society of Landscape Architects (ASLA), the national organization that represents the profession. It offers this definition of landscape architecture:

> Landscape architecture encompasses the analysis, planning, design, management and stewardship of the natural and built environment through science and design.... It is a profession that is broad in scale and scope. Landscape architects receive training in site design, historic preservation, and planning, as well as in technical and scientific areas such as grading, drainage, horticulture, and environmental sciences. With this diverse background, landscape architects possess a unique blend of abilities to help address important local, regional, and national priorities.[3]

> *How do you define landscape architecture or a landscape architect?*

❯ A landscape architect is *one who designs outdoor environments.* * When asked that question by clients, we typically tell them it's conceivable that our scope of work could be anything outside of a habitable structure.

Jeffrey K. Carbo, FASLA
Principal, Jeffrey Carbo Landscape Architects and Site Planners

❯ Landscape architecture is *truly an art that integrates the idea of the built environment with nature* and, most importantly, how it relates to the individual—what a person feels like in a space is critical to the success of our profession.

Frederick R. Bonci, RLA, ASLA
Founding Principal, LaQuatra Bonci Associates

*Author's emphasis added throughout.

❯ Landscape architecture is a discipline where design and research intersect, and more specifically, it is the *hybridization of art, science, economics, and politics* at different scales.

Julia Czerniak
Principal, CLEAR; Associate Professor of Architecture, Syracuse University

❯ Landscape architecture is about trying to find something that's really wonderful about the environment around you, and something that's really unique about the culture around you, and *combining all those things into a rich experience.*

Kofi Boone, ASLA
Assistant Professor, Department of Landscape Architecture, North Carolina State University

How do you define landscape architecture or a landscape architect? (Continued)

❭ Design of the exterior environment that benefits humans, animals, and the planet.

Ruben L. Valenzuela, RLA
Principal, Terrano

❭ I often quip that it is "any modification of the surface of the planet," but I find that definition too restrictive because it doesn't adequately address issues of landscape preservation. By defining the profession this broadly, *creative work can be found in areas not historically considered* within the bounds of the profession, such as mined land reclamation and end-use planning.

Kurt Culbertson, FASLA
Chairman of the Board, Design Workshop

❭ Landscape architects work at the interface of cultural and natural issues. Landscape architecture is a unique profession in that *it houses a very wide range of scales and environments*, allowing for designers to work at the micro scale of designing playground equipment or benches, to macro considerations of urban development or environmental restoration.

Mikyoung Kim
Principal, mikyoung kim design

❭ Landscape architecture is *planning and designing the structure of the land, human-made and nature-made*. Nature-made is a green infrastructure of living things, including plant communities and their landforms. Nature-made infrastructures are remade by where and how we place them. Human-made constructions are things we design or place. They form a mosaic of circulation corridors, both animal and machine, buildings for shelter and gathering, utilities and familiar site amenities that grace the communities where we live.

Edward L. Blake, Jr.
Founding Principal, The Landscape Studio

❭ I think that, finally, the economic and cultural climate is such that landscape architects can really prevail in design. Landscape architecture offers an opportunity to meld creativity with a love of the land and *the ability to create places that are everlasting* in a way that is not detrimental to the ecology and the quality of a community's life.

Roy Kraynyk
Executive Director, Allegheny Land Trust

❭ A landscape architect is more like *a sculptor who manipulates the earth, and the grade and horizon*. It is more of an art form versus a service. The work that we tend to do in landscape architecture has a much more sculptural bent to it.

Thomas Oslund, FASLA, FAAR
Principal, oslund.and.assoc.

❭ A landscape architect is more of a *holistic coordinator of many things that take place in spaces*, to create a harmonious and, ultimately, long-term sustainable whole.

Juanita D. Shearer–Swink, FASLA
Project Manager, Triangle Transit Authority

❭ Landscape architecture has a very broad agenda.… It taps in to issues of infrastructure, ecology, and environment, of urbanism and metropolitanization. Our approach deals with how you *set in place a framework that may evolve and be acted on over time*. These are not closed systems—ecological process, social process, even political process—it's very open-ended. The goal of landscape architecture is to develop strategies that can respond to some of these conditions through time; whatever we're making can have vibrancy and relevance for many, many years to come.

Chris Reed
Founding Principal, StoSS

❭ Landscape architecture is the acute awareness of natural systems and their function within built and nonbuilt environments. It is *the systematic comprehension and integration of these systems* with cultural program, social overlays, and design that enables large-scale and small-scale landscapes to exist for multiple uses.

Gerdo Aquino, ASLA
Managing Principal, SWA Group

❯ Landscape architecture is the restoration of the community, or humanity, with nature. It is *the opportunity to reconnect us as human beings with what happens out there that is generally considered nonhuman*. We have that unique privilege of making spaces or places for people to reconnect with the outside world in a way that they might not normally do in our contemporary culture.

Jacob Blue, MS, RLA, ASLA
Landscape Architect/Ecological Designer, Applied Ecological Services, Inc.

❯ Landscape architecture is the creation of spaces that improve the ability for people to use and enjoy the land.

Kevin Campion, ASLA
Senior Associate, Graham Landscape Architecture

❯ Landscape architecture is the coming together of the arts, natural sciences, and culture. It is a *design of place that connects land and culture*. And, it has many applications, from small-scale design projects to more large-scale urban design and regional planning.

Robin Lee Gyorgyfalvy, ASLA
Director of Interpretive Services & Scenic Byway, USDA Forest Service: Deschutes National Forest

❯ Landscape architecture is the design of space outside the façade of any piece of architecture—from the plaza, the streetscapes, the roadways—*everything outside the building is what we can help create, at any scale* from a backyard garden all the way up to a brand-new city.

Todd Kohli, RLA, ASLA
Co-Managing Director, Senior Director, EDAW San Francisco

❯ One of the things that we say in our office is, "The sky is mine." Landscape architecture isn't just confined to dirt and bushes, *it is all the things that are under the sky*. Landscape architecture is the places that people occupy, whether they are private locations or public locations. But they're often part of someone's life experiences in moving through space, being outdoors.

Jennifer Guthrie, RLA, ASLA
Director, Gustafson Guthrie Nichol, Ltd.

❯ I started out as an architect. In school, during the design of a theoretical new town, I decided I was much more interested in the space between the buildings than the building itself. So *I define landscape architecture as dealing with the space between buildings*.

James van Sweden, FASLA
Founding Principal, Oehme, van Sweden & Associates, Inc.

❯ It's very broad but it has a really specific core for me and that is resanctifying the earth. Landscape architecture deals with the earth in a stewardship manner. So, to me, it's almost like taking the earth and bringing it back into a human context. It is the only profession that does this; *it is the only design profession that is a steward of the land*. We do other things that engineers and architects do, except they do not do it with this stewardship value.

Stephanie Landregan, ASLA
Chief of Landscape Architecture, Mountains Recreation & Conservation Authority

❯ There are a lot of hats under the landscape architecture umbrella: landscape planning through to graphic design. Landscape architects create designs and produce *solutions that make memorable spaces*.

Eddie George, ASLA
Founding Principal, The Edge Group

❯ It's an application of science to art *and it goes beyond problem solving to creating new opportunities and regenerating biological integrity*.

Nancy D. Rottle, RLA, ASLA
Associate Professor, Department of Landscape Architecture, University of Washington

❯ I define [landscape architecture] as *the planning, design, and management of the landscape, which is external space*. As landscape architects we need to look beyond what Peter Walker talks about as the iconic landscape, which is only 2 percent of the designed environment. We need to look at forest and agriculture and apply the principles we learn to basically the whole landscape, as it is, both natural and managed.

Gary Scott, FASLA
Director, West Des Moines Parks & Recreation Department

How do you define landscape architecture or a landscape architect? (Continued)

❯ I have a simple definition of landscape architecture, and that's the design and construction of the outside world with plants.

Meredith Upchurch, ASLA
Green Infrastructure Designer, Casey Trees Endowment Fund

❯ Landscape architects are like the glue between several professions that deal with the development of the land—the transformation of the lithosphere. *We are like renaissance people in that we need to be good at many things but not a master of any particular one.* That makes it more exciting because we deal with architects, engineers, land managers; we need to understand what the natural scientists are telling us because our medium involves all those disciplines. Landscape architecture is the consummate multidisciplinary profession in that it is related to managing the resources of the planet.

Jose Alminana, ASLA
Principal, Andropogon Associates, Ltd.

❯ Landscape architecture is one of the design disciplines, together with urban design, planning, and architecture. Landscape architecture primarily deals with the design of open space: from the residence to the community park to urban spaces and city form to the regional level of land uses and environmental planning. Luis Barragán, (a great Mexican architect and landscape architect) used to *define landscape architecture as architecture without roofs.*

Mario Schjetnan, FASLA
Founding Partner, Grupo de Diseno Urbano

❯ I would say it's the ability to manipulate our environment in order to *create places where people can connect to nature* through the aesthetics, functionality, or spirituality of the spaces created.

Emmanuel Thingue, RLA
Senior Landscape Architect, New York City Parks Department

❯ Landscape architecture is a profession that helps shape, by design and definition of activities, cities, and other places, and includes the highest respect for the natural and human-made elements that are *brought together in a mutually supportive manner.* Landscape architects should help shape public policy to achieve these designs and activities.

Tom Liptan, ASLA
Sustainable Stormwater Management Program, Portland Bureau of Environmental Services

❯ The profession of landscape architecture falls alongside Ian McHarg's intent—*to place mankind's impact softly upon the earth.*

Karen Coffman, RLA
NPDES Coordinator, Highway Hydraulics Division, Maryland State Highway Administration

❯ Landscape architects encourage their clients to think about what it is they want—we provoke them to think deeply about that. We then help interpolate those ideas into a solution that matches not only the client's needs with the capabilities of the land, but *does so in a way that it is a positive for both the client and the earth.*

Douglas Hoerr, FASLA
Partner, Hoerr Schaudt Landscape Architects

❯ *We're a combination of art people and engineering people*—civil engineers and artists. To give a really good idea of what it takes to be a landscape architect, get a civil engineer and an artist together and get them married and have children, then the children would be a perfect fit to be landscape architects.

Scott S. Weinberg, FASLA
Associate Dean and Professor, School of Environmental Design, University of Georgia

❯ Landscape architecture is about helping people to have and build relationships with the landscape by creating spaces for outdoor use. It has also *broadened to become a sustainability and an earth-care profession*, at least in parts of the field where restoration for the other beings on the planet is really important.

John Koepke
Associate Professor, Department of Landscape Architecture , University of Minnesota

❯ Landscape architecture is the design and planning of outdoor spaces. Actually, *the definition of landscape architecture is less of a challenge than defining the term landscape.* If you look back at its Dutch origin, it was literally "making land" or "making territory." In German and Scandinavian, it is sort of a synthesis of natural and cultural processes. Then there is the other meaning, which is basically a view, or what you can see with a single glance, which became more prominent with the English landscape movement. So the definition gets tricky not in the term of what a landscape architect is, but in defining what landscape means.

Frederick R. Steiner, PhD, FASLA
Dean, School of Architecture, University of Texas

❯ *Landscape architecture is placemaking*, which I understand as the act of designing outdoor environs that hold significance to people because of societal, ecological, and/or spiritual implications.

Nathan Scott
Landscape Designer, Mahan Rykiel Associates

> How would you characterize the difference between landscape architecture and allied professions, such as architecture, planning, or engineering?

❯ I've worked with many architects and engineers on teams. The biggest difference is a focus on the natural environment. There is an interface between the natural and built environment, which landscape architects are really adept at. All three professions look at the bigger picture, but landscape architects are more in tune to the natural processes, and also pay more attention to the social components and the people who use these places.

Robin Lee Gyorgyfalvy, ASLA
Director of Interpretive Services & Scenic Byways, USDA Forest Service: Deschutes National Forest

❯ The primary distinction is that landscape architecture always deals with process, and architecture doesn't necessarily deal with process. We deal with systems that continue to grow and change, that are affected by everything from climate to tectonic movement. Architecture generally deals with defining something that is more discreet, more self-referencing.

Mark Johnson, FASLA
Founding Principal and the President, Civitas, Inc.

❯ Landscape architecture is, in some ways, more what people imagine planning to be—designing communities, and parks, and so on. The major difference is, until fairly recently, design has been marginalized within planning. Planning education has emphasized social sciences and law. Engineering education is very narrow. Engineers end up doing a lot of things that they really don't have an academic background in, but they are very well prepared in an analytical tradition. A lot of landscape architects get involved in site engineering, and many get involved in city and regional planning.

Frederick R. Steiner, PhD, FASLA
Dean, School of Architecture, University of Texas

❯ The medium we work with is endless. It is the thing that connects all the engineering and buildings together. In addition to that, it is a living system. It is putting plant materials in the ground and being able to understand what they will do in the next 10 to 100-plus years. It grows. One of my mentors said, "When a building is built, it looks

How would you characterize the difference between landscape architecture and allied professions such as architecture, planning, or engineering? (Continued)

best when it's first built. When a landscape is built, it's at its worst, and it only gets better." I think that is definitely the difference between architecture, engineering, and landscape architecture. And one more thing: landscape is experiential. You touch it, you move through it; it touches all of your senses; it is seasonal; it is a memory maker.

Jennifer Guthrie, RLA, ASLA
Director, Gustafson Guthrie Nichol, Ltd.

❯ Architects—not all, but most—do not think as much in a contextual context. They tend to be more "object oriented." They often do not come from as strong an environmental orientation. Architects are working hard, however, to catch up. The New Urbanist movement is one example of a reclaiming of community planning lost to landscape architects. Engineers, in my experience, do not aspire to lead a project as often, but rather want to concentrate on the details of their field. In many ways, landscape architects are leading civil engineering toward more environmentally sensitive design in such areas a stormwater management and roadway design.

Kurt Culbertson, FASLA
Chairman of the Board, Design Workshop

❯ Landscape architecture, architecture, and engineering are similar because they all require the ability to synthesize numerous ideas and follow the same procedures to achieve a project. The main difference is that landscape architecture deals with a final product—nature—that continually evolves. Although buildings age, it's a static change, which shouldn't be considered a true evolution. Nature is anything but static. The landscape architect must be able to design spaces in anticipation of the evolution of nature and its impact on the programming and functionality of the spaces created.

Emmanuel Thingue, RLA
Senior Landscape Architect, New York City Parks Department

❯ I started in architecture, so I have just as much of an interest in architecture and engineering as I do in landscape architecture. I think the understandings and the influences are very similar. The one difference is that we as landscape architects have control of the horizon, whereas architects have control of the vertical. Philosophically, that's one of the bigger differences, but the principles are the same in terms of inspiration and approach to how you solve design problems.

Thomas Oslund, FASLA, FAAR
Principal, oslund.and.assoc.

❯ We are the most collaborative of all our sister professions and are the ideal bridge between the professions—having the expertise and knowledge base to marry site, building, nature, and technology into an integrated and sustainable solution. The design professions have become too focused on solving only their issues. This is the single largest detriment to creating great places. We all need to be more collaborative and engaging. Our profession's rich history, from landscape preservation and urban design to parks and public open spaces, legitimize us and make us equal players. Ours is the one profession that deals with the quality of outdoor spaces and the ability to create meaningful places that enhance life. No other profession can claim this.

Frederick R. Bonci, RLA, ASLA
Founding Principal, LaQuatra Bonci Associates

❯ Architecture is to structural engineering as landscape architecture is to civil engineering.

Karen Coffman, RLA
NPDES Coordinator, Highway Hydraulics Division, Maryland State Highway Administration

❯ Part of the equation that doesn't figure into the other professions is time—growth, maturation, aging. In outdoor environments there are rooms of different sizes and scales that will be defined by a landscape component, such as trees, hedges, and so on, but much of what you are trying to accomplish will be created in time, as these things grow and evolve. That is the most satisfying part, but potentially the most frustrating.

Jeffrey K. Carbo, FASLA
Principal, Jeffrey Carbo Landscape Architects and Site Planners

❯ The similarity is that we are all problem solvers; however, each of these allied professions tries to solve problems within the building industry in different ways. The difference between architecture and engineering is function versus image. I would go out on a limb and say engineering is more focused on making things functional, while architects and landscape architects are always challenged by making a place functional and making it into the image we've envisioned.

Kevin Campion, ASLA
Senior Associate, Graham Landscape Architecture

❯ Whereas our colleagues in architecture are focused on form, usually a building, and our engineering colleagues are more supportive of the way things function, we are the ones that bind all of those together. Because of landscape architecture's integrative approach, we look at ways to deal with, for example, stormwater and runoff, instead of just getting rid of the water, as engineers have done. We look at how we can use that end product. We carry the responsibility of making sure that the natural systems work, as opposed to just applying the built

systems. That's a difference between engineers and landscape architects.

Juanita D. Shearer-Swink, FASLA
Project Manager, Triangle Transit Authority

❯ Architecture, very simply, deals with habitable structures. Engineering structures are not necessarily habitable, and engineering represents a wide range of systems—environmental, structural, information. Landscape architecture is about issues pertaining to the management and inhabiting of the land.

Elizabeth Kennedy, RLA
Principal, EKLA Studio

❯ Landscape architects generally have a greater sensitivity to the overall picture. Landscape architects can easily slide into the profession of planning, and go back and forth between that larger picture and the specifics, much easier than the architect or the engineer can. A lot of times the engineer has been charged with such specific problem-solving functions that he or she kind of loses sight of the whole picture. A lot of architects that I run into are keyed in on satisfying the client's concerns about making sure that the building has certain features, but they are not so much concerned with what the impacts of the building might be on the overall site. So I think the landscape architect tends to have this general awareness of the larger picture.

Jacob Blue, MS, RLA, ASLA
Landscape Architect/Ecological Designer, Applied Ecological Services, Inc.

Background on the Profession

Terrace of One Hundred Fountains, Villa D'Este, Tivoli, Italy, circa 1550.

As long as humans have roamed the earth, they have been modifying their environment. The term *landscape architect* was coined in the mid-1800s; however, many contend that the design of the landscape—in other words, purposeful, meaningful manipulation of land—began occurring well before that. In ancient Egypt and Central America, for example, ceremonial events and processions occurred in landscapes specifically arranged and designed to accommodate these special activities, or to draw the users' attention to a particular place, such as a sacred tomb. There are also numerous examples over the centuries and around the world of walled or meditative gardens, ceremonial courts, villas, and hunting grounds that illustrate the determination of humans to creatively change their environment to meet their needs and desires.

In the early 1800s, most notably in England and Europe, a shift occurred in landscape design: No longer was it just for the well-to-do; it began to include expansive parks for the public. This shift can be attributed to growing concerns about the deteriorating quality of living and working conditions among the public-at-large, many of which were brought on due to advances in the Industrial Revolution.[4] These public parks were designed in the pastoral "English landscape garden" style, whose designers sought to create places of respite from the increasingly congested and polluted city environs. These public landscapes had a tremendous influence on a young Frederick Law Olmsted, who visited them when he traveled abroad. It was Olmsted who first used the term "landscape architect" after he and architect Calvert Vaux won a competition for what would become New York City's world-renowned Central Park. To this day, many believe that Central Park is simply land that was never built upon; however every acre of it was, in fact, carefully designed. Thousands of trees were planted; lakes created in low areas; and the landform underwent major contouring. All this was designed with the express purpose of providing outdoor social spaces, to accommodate both large gatherings as well as intimate settings—to create a sense "of enlarged freedom" in contrast to the cramped conditions of the city streets.[5] The landscape architecture profession was thus founded on the idea that nature is an "ameliorative force," which should be employed to guide design for the public's welfare.[6]

The profession became official in 1899 with the founding of the American Society of Landscape Architects (ASLA), the national organization that advocates for the profession. Shortly thereafter, in 1900, Harvard became the first school to offer formalized training toward a degree in landscape architecture.

During the early decades, those interested in this budding profession followed two main directions, both rooted in concerns about the problems of the nation's growing cities and a belief that the built environment had the power to improve people's lives.

One direction emerged following the 1893 World's Fair in Chicago, specifically its Columbia Exposition. There visitors could view a full-scale example of desirable civic design—a stark contrast to the look of most U.S. cities at the time. Called the City Beautiful Movement, landscape architects taking this direction worked to improve living conditions in cities. These landscape architects were also engaged in town planning and community design. An offshoot of the City Beautiful Movement,

Aerial view of Central Park, New York City, in 1938. New York City Parks Photo Archive.

often called the Country Place Era, featured the design of large metropolitan park systems and college campuses, as well as estates for the wealthy. While having a more formal flair, this group took on a stewardship role toward the land because of mounting concerns about the widespread development of the countryside.[7]

The second important development, which coincided with the birth of the landscape architecture profession, was the creation, in 1872, of Yellowstone National Park, the first such park in the nation. Landscape architects were instrumental in helping to establish these early parks. As the number of national parks grew, the federal government formed the National Park Service (NPS), which eventually included its own Division of Landscape Architecture. One of the many responsibilities for NPS landscape architects was to design and maintain a master plan for each park.[8]

The Great Depression brought changes to the profession of landscape architecture. One aspect of President Roosevelt's New Deal, his national recovery program, was the establishment of the Civilian Conservation Corps (CCC). The CCC employed thousands of young men in conservation efforts, such as reforesting logged areas. The program also called for the construction of park facilities, such as scenic byways, lodges, roads, trails, and picnic pavilions. Hundreds of state parks were established through the CCC, and many national parks were enhanced. This translated into jobs for many professionals, including landscape architects, who served as designers and supervisors of the work. Involving landscape architects ensured that the park designs would meet a high-level of craftsmanship, and that the work fostered respect for the natural environment.

In the last half of the twentieth century, following the Second World War, landscape architecture continued to grow and diversify. For example, with more people attending college, there was an increasing need to program and design college and university campuses. And, with changes in mobility due to the popularity of the automobile came the need to design suburban communities, out of which evolved a "new towns" movement. Many corporations likewise began relocating to the outskirts of cities, giving landscape ar-

The Blue Ridge Parkway in North Carolina. Photographer: Timothy P. Johnson.

chitects the opportunity to design expansive headquarters campuses. Shopping center design also became a growing area of professional practice, with the most innovative offering an inviting setting focused on the pedestrian. The interest in providing unique shopping experiences also took place in some cities as part of urban revitalization efforts. "Festival marketplaces," for example, were developed to reinvigorate waterfronts and create new uses for old industrial areas.

With the advent of the first Earth Day in 1970, which followed closely on the heels of the publication of Ian McHarg's seminal book *Design with Nature* (Garden City, NY: Natural History Press, 1969), landscape architecture professionals refocused on the importance of ecology in the design process. Then, during the last decades of the twentieth century, and taking cues from innovative work being done in Europe, the urban landscape once again came more sharply into view. The profession continued to expand throughout the closing decades of the twentieth century, to include landscape conservation, preservation, restoration, and the reclamation of despoiled land called brownfields.

Now, in the first decade of the twenty-first century, landscape architects are increasingly involved in projects around the globe. There is also a growing public recognition of the important role the landscape plays in human health and well-being, which brings us back to the origins of the profession and Olmsted's ideas behind early park designs. Today, as principles of sustainability take hold, it seems that landscape architecture has never strayed too far from its roots. The sense of "nature in peril," a strong theme in earlier eras, is once again informing the practice of landscape architecture. [9]

Note: To learn more about the history of landscape architecture, refer to the references listed in Appendix B.

What does it take to become a successful landscape architect?

The landscape architects who addressed this question cited a number of characteristics and skills they regard as essential to achieve success in the field. These include:

- Business sense
- Curiosity and lifelong learning
- Design and aesthetic sense
- Team player, collaborator, and negotiator
- Stewardship of the environment and understanding of natural resources
- Commitment to people and communication skills

- Perseverance, persistence, and patience
- Integrity
- Passion, dedication, and conviction
- Balance
- Ability to synthesize information and/or be a big-picture thinker

Business Sense

❯ A knowledge of the realities of business and politics. You need to understand what people are talking about in terms of politics and business.
Roy Kraynyk
Allegheny Land Trust

What does it take to become a successful landscape architect? (Continued)

❯ It takes a business sense, especially if you are going to be in private practice, because it ends up being a business.

Nancy D. Rottle, RLA, ASLA
University of Washington

❯ In a recent conversation with a colleague about her business, she was begrudging all of the work that it took to run the business. I told her she should get out of business or embrace that. If you're going to lead a firm in private practice, you either have to have the business skills, or find those skills and rely on those people to put them in the right position for your venture to succeed.

Patricia O'Donnell, FASLA, AICP
Heritage Landscapes

❯ You have to be a good salesperson. A lot of times we're selling our ideas, and it's hard to sell ideas. I've found that people don't really understand what's on paper, so what you're doing, in essence, is selling yourself. You're selling a belief in your skills.

Scott S. Weinberg, FASLA
University of Georgia

❯ You have to know how to make a successful business—very important. It is unusual to find a really a good designer who understands the business part as well.

James van Sweden, FASLA
Oehme, van Sweden & Associates, Inc.

❯ You have to have a good sense of business. Whether you work in the public sector or the private sector, you have to use money in a way that makes things work, not because you're spending it but because those are the best choices. So, you have to have a reasonable understanding of business.

Juanita D. Shearer-Swink, FASLA
Triangle Transit Authority

❯ I'll admit to being a landscape architect first and a businessman second. But I could not have had my own practice for over nine years now without some business skills.

Ruben L. Valenzuela, RLA
Terrano

Curiosity and Lifelong Learning

❯ Landscape architecture is a creative endeavor that requires an interest in lifelong learning and growth. Each project brings new challenges into our office and asks us to listen, invent, and learn with our clients and the sites they bring to the table.

Mikyoung Kim
mikyoung kim design

❯ A never-ending quest for knowledge.

Mike Faha, ASLA, LEED AP
GreenWorks, PC

❯ The most important thing is an almost insatiable curiosity, because to be a good landscape architect you have to know so much about so many different things. Landscape architects, more than other professions, are the ones that sit in the middle and have to understand what everyone else is doing, and how it all comes together.

Jim Sipes, ASLA
EDAW

❯ Always look at your current project as a stepping stone to the next one and always strive to do better and better on every job. Learn from every job and don't feel that you've ever mastered this profession, because it's impossible.

Frederick R. Bonci, RLA, ASLA
LaQuatra Bonci Associates

❯ Constantly being an observer, to be humble, and study how things come together in mutually beneficial ways. So I think it's a really, really careful observation of the world around you.

Kofi Boone, ASLA
North Carolina State University

❯ You have to be willing to continually build your skills, continually be aware of what's going on socially and culturally, and gain new knowledge about the natural environment, as well as of new technologies.

Nancy D. Rottle, RLA, ASLA
University of Washington

❯ Landscape architects have to get out of the box almost on every project, and then decide whether they should get back in the box. Many professions count on something that has been done before. I think if you are really a responsible landscape architect, you have to step out and say, "Okay, Liptan did it like this, but is that really the best way to do it? Or the code says I have to do it this way, but is that really best?" You need to ask the questions.

Tom Liptan, ASLA
Portland Bureau of Environmental Services

❯ The ability to continue to learn is the most important thing—the ability to be a reflective practitioner so that you learn from your projects; you learn from your successes and failures.

Frederick R. Steiner, PhD, FASLA
University of Texas

Design and Aesthetic Sense

❯ A measure of success is the mark you've left on the landscape and the quality of built work: Are people enjoying what you have designed? Is the environment performing better and healthier after you've left than before you got there?

Kofi Boone, ASLA
North Carolina State University

❯ An important aspect of the profession is the way we as human beings form, shape, and interface with the evolving systems of the environment.

Mikyoung Kim
mikyoung kim design

❯ Obviously, I think they need good design skills and they need to know what those are.

Gary Scott, FASLA
West Des Moines Parks & Recreation Department

❯ To be successful in landscape architecture you have to have the design, talent, and aesthetic sense.

James van Sweden, FASLA
Oehme, van Sweden & Associates, Inc.

❯ It is good for a landscape architect to have a degree of understanding about the multisensory qualities of space. It's also important to have good three-dimensional perception and a sense of perception through movement—we often talk about a sequence and choreography and the intended effects.

Patricia O'Donnell, FASLA, AICP
Principal, Heritage Landscapes

Team Player, Collaborator, and Negotiator

❯ Successful landscape architects are team oriented; working with other design disciplines throughout the project.

Joanne Cody, ASLA
National Park Service

❯ To be really successful we need to concentrate on understanding allied professions very well—visual arts, performing arts, and architecture, in particular. I think we really need to learn how to collaborate.

Frederick R. Bonci, RLA, ASLA
LaQuatra Bonci Associates

❯ A landscape architect who is a team player stands a better chance of producing relevant, successful projects.

Cindy Tyler
Terra Design Studios

❯ Interpersonal skills are critical. You have to be able to negotiate in a way that is diplomatic and to the point where you are not sacrificing your values and your integrity. You need to have the personal skills to be able to compromise and not offend people, and stand up for what you think is the right thing from a professional perspective and from a design perspective.

Roy Kraynyk
Allegheny Land Trust

What does it take to become a successful landscape architect? (Continued)

❭ I think they need good facilitation skills, because a successful landscape architect often brings together people from multiple disciplines. He or she needs to be able to manage those people and facilitate their input and synthesize it into a solution.

Gary Scott, FASLA
West Des Moines Parks & Recreation Department

❭ A successful landscape architect needs to be a collaborator. That is a really important factor—a collaborator with a sense of art, science, technology, and ecology or nature.

Tom Liptan, ASLA
Portland Bureau of Environmental Services

Stewardship of the Environment and Understanding of Natural Resources

❭ See the adjacencies and complexities of the earth: To become a successful landscape architect, you have to realize that connectivity.

Stephanie Landregan, ASLA
Mountains Recreation & Conservation Authority

❭ You have to have a good understanding of natural systems. You need to be aware that the consequences of what you see on the land is the result of years of evolution; that doesn't mean you have to be an expert in geology or an expert on soil, but you need to know enough to ask questions and find out where to get those answers.

Jose Alminana, ASLA
Andropogon Associates, Ltd.

❭ To be a landscape architect one has to act as steward, engage and change the planet in a manner that shifts with each new environment and context that we work in.

Mikyoung Kim
mikyoung kim design

❭ Passion for nature.

Mike Faha, ASLA, LEED AP
GreenWorks, PC

Commitment to People and Communication Skills

❭ The most important thing is to be a really good listener, because what people say and what they mean are two different things. You have to listen to what they are really saying, not what their words are, and understand their concerns, their objectives, and the constraints being placed on them. If you can listen, you can go forward a lot faster because you are able to respond to the real issues and not the perceived issues.

Jacob Blue, MS, RLA, ASLA
Applied Ecological Services, Inc.

❭ A love of people, because a very important thing that we do is help others realize their visions for the places they want to be. The only way that we can understand their vision is to get to know them and feel very comfortable with them like you would a good friend.

Edward L. Blake, Jr.
The Landscape Studio

❭ Passion for people.

Mike Faha, ASLA, LEED AP
GreenWorks, PC

❭ It takes clarity of thought and speech, to be able to think through a story that makes sense and that is explainable to others—whether they are on your immediate team or in other disciplines working with you to develop an idea—and of course to the client itself.

Jennifer Guthrie, RLA, ASLA
Gustafson Guthrie Nichol, Ltd.

❭ To draw the best ideas from our team, we must be able to communicate our ideas and listen to theirs.

Cindy Tyler
Terra Design Studios

❭ The ability to promote your ideas and your work.

Frederick R. Steiner, PhD, FASLA
University of Texas

❯ The ability to communicate verbally and in writing, and using visual language skills, I think has made many landscape architects really quite successful.

John Koepke
University of Minnesota

❯ An ability to communicate with clients through good listening skills, quick sketches, and understandable dialogue.

Joanne Cody, ASLA
National Park Service

❯ In working with clients and other professionals, being a good listener and a good communicator (graphic, verbal, and written) are important attributes.

Douglas C. Smith, ASLA
EDSA

Perseverance, Persistence, and Patience

❯ It is time and patience and insight and intuition.

Kofi Boone, ASLA
North Carolina State University

❯ Perseverance.

Gerdo Aquino, ASLA
SWA Group

❯ It takes that ability to kind of move across barriers. I always talk about thinking like water. When you come to a barrier, you can either go over it, around it, under or through it. You have to be able to sort of back up and figure out what the next tact should be in order to address the problem or issue, or whatever it happens to be, successfully.

John Koepke
University of Minnesota

❯ To become a successful landscape architect, it takes a lot of patience.

Dawn Kroh, RLA
Green 3, LLC

❯ A landscape architect needs a lot of perseverance.

Gary Scott, FASLA
West Des Moines Parks & Recreation Department

❯ Persistence, persistence, persistence. In our work, it often takes so long to be realized.

Edward L. Blake, Jr.
The Landscape Studio

❯ You have to have a lot of patience to be a landscape architect, especially when you're in school. You're learning all the steps to be a landscape architect but you really don't get to do it until you get an internship and see something that you've designed being built, or when you get out and see your first project being built.

Scott S. Weinberg, FASLA
University of Georgia

Integrity

❯ You need to develop and grow a reputation as someone who has integrity and is trustworthy and fulfills his or her promises.

Roy Kraynyk
Allegheny Land Trust

❯ You have to be willing to hold on to your core values while adapting to the changing world that surrounds you.

Juanita D. Shearer–Swink, FASLA
Triangle Transit Authority

❯ I say diligence, because I believe you really feel principled about what it is you're doing.

Jeffrey K. Carbo, FASLA
Jeffrey Carbo Landscape Architects and Site Planners

❯ Practicing landscape architecture with passion, while being balanced, automatically makes one successful. The balance that I refer to is the ability to prioritize one's values in order to achieve a greater good. Compromise is not a bad thing, if the alternative will deny the community of a much-needed amenity. Having said that, there are times when one has to take a stand. Use your judgment, because only you can truly evaluate if you're successful; not others.

Emmanuel Thingue, RLA
New York City Parks Department

What does it take to become a successful landscape architect? (Continued)

Passion, Dedication, and Conviction

❭ You have to find what your passion is. We're lucky enough to do that and get paid for it. We're discriminating with the kind of work that we take so that we're not swimming upstream trying to convince somebody who is not interested in what we're about to do. The hardest thing is trying to define what you're about and what your practice wants to be about. If you make that decision and define that and stick to it and not try to change it with every new fad that comes through, you will be successful. Be genuine to yourself.

Thomas Oslund, FASLA, FAAR
oslund.and.assoc.

❭ Energy, enthusiasm, and initiative are what's necessary.

Chris Reed
StoSS

❭ If you make landscape architecture part of your soul, if you take on responsibility, if you promote the profession, and you want to push it further—if you have that passion, you will be successful.

Todd Kohli, RLA, ASLA
EDAW San Francisco

❭ Success for any professional is achieved through finding your passion for what you do, and then feeding that passion.

Cindy Tyler
Terra Design Studios

❭ It is a passion for what you focus on, and what I mean by that is there are so many different kinds of practices. I know landscape architects who do people's gardens; they're almost horticulturalists, they know so much about plants; but that is not me. My passion is as much for research as it is for design, and my practice reflects that, so it is really identifying your niche within both the discipline and the profession.

Julia Czerniak
CLEAR

❭ To be truly successful you have to be passionate; to view it as a calling rather than a profession. It requires an enormous amount of hard work, discipline, and commitment. To assume that success can come from anything else would be misguided.

Kurt Culbertson, FASLA
Design Workshop

❭ It takes passion for what you do, probably above all else. It takes tenacity; you have to be competitive and you have to want to win.

Dawn Kroh, RLA
Green 3, LLC

❭ You really need to be passionate about what you are doing, and in order to be passionate, you better really love it so it doesn't feel like work.

Jeffrey K. Carbo, FASLA
Jeffrey Carbo Landscape Architects and Site Planners

Balance

❭ There are probably two pathways to being successful. One is being exceptionally talented and the other is being exceptionally driven. Probably most people who would be regarded as successful have some measure of both. Each of those people finds a way to balance the relationship between their talent and their drive to pursue what they are particularly good at.

Mark Johnson, FASLA
Civitas, Inc.

❭ There are two answers, and it all comes under the umbrella of balance. First is balancing a number of skills, aptitudes, and knowledge sets that you need to be a good landscape architect—horticulture, geology, art history, and so on. Then you also have to balance the practical versus the creative. You need to have a business hat and a creative hat and you need to know when to put each one on, and that's not always easy.

Kevin Campion, ASLA
Graham Landscape Architecture

❯ Great landscape architects are good at engaging both sides of the brain—they are really good at this translation of science into an art. People who are able to continually make that translation are the people who end up being really great.

Nancy D. Rottle, RLA, ASLA
University of Washington

❯ They have to have what I would call a pragmatic sense of how things go together in the environment. You can't just have an idea—how does it actually get built, how does it come together, and how does it get created?

Gary Scott, FASLA
West Des Moines Parks & Recreation Department

Ability to Synthesize and/or Be a Big-Picture Thinker

❯ A successful landscape architect is someone who is like a hub and provides a connection to all the moving parts. A successful landscape architect can, as a generalist, take a lot of different opinions and actually forge them into something better: a better design, a better place, a better way for people to interact with the land. It's someone who not only pays attention to the details and the process, but can see the bigger picture and has a vision for how it all fits together and continues.

Robin Lee Gyorgyfalvy, ASLA
USDA Forest Service: Deschutes National Forest

❯ Systems thinking: to translate or to apply knowledge or findings to create solutions. To be able to synthesize, integrate, and apply information for people and places to solve problems.

Barbara Deutsch, ASLA, ISA
BioRegional North America

❯ The ability to lead clients toward designs that exceed their vision, goals, and expectations.

Ignacio Bunster–Ossa, ASLA, LEED AP
Wallace Roberts & Todd, LLC

❯ Vision.

Gerdo Aquino, ASLA
SWA Group

❯ At some point in the future the success of a landscape architect won't necessarily be building landscape architecture or physical stuff, but it will be the thinking about how the world works and how to really find the best of all opportunities for all of us to share this place; that will be the measure of success.

Kofi Boone, ASLA
North Carolina State University

❯ The ability to bring all of that information in, organize it, synthesize and figure out what to do with it—that's the essence of what we do.

Jim Sipes, ASLA
EDAW, Atlanta

2 Landscape Architectural Design

FEW WOULD ARGUE THAT THE EARTH is a highly complex environment, so if you are going to design on this planet, which is what landscape architects do, you will have to consider a great many factors. Most obvious, initially, is the surface of the land itself, which raises a number of questions, among them:

- Is the surface flat or rolling? How it is contoured?
- What covers that surface—plants, paving, water, buildings, other?

There also are questions about what is under the surface.

- What makes the surface look as it does? Is it the soils, the underlying geology, underground utilities?

Of course, you must look at what happens upon the surface, as well.

- Are people using it? How?
- What about wildlife?
- It is a place for transportation? For cars, trains, bikes?
- Is it a place for contemplation? Or for celebration?

All of this is just skimming the surface (if you'll excuse the pun). Designing upon the earth must also take into consideration the weather, seasonal changes, safety, beauty, history, and the overriding fact that all things on earth are interconnected. When you actually think about the job of the landscape architect and designing on the earth, you begin to have some idea just how complex it is; at the same time you also become aware how very exciting the potential is.

Bird's-eye view of pergola on roof at 900 North Michigan Avenue, Chicago, Illinois. Photographer: Scott Shigley. Courtesy of Hoerr Schaudt Landscape Architects.

Landscape architecture is commonly characterized as being both art and science. It is rooted in solving problems and resolving issues, but in the most creative, responsible ways possible. Landscape architects create imaginative outdoor environments that are sensitive to both aesthetic and ecological issues, and to economic and social concerns and opportunities. The purpose of this chapter is to provide an overview of the breadth and depth of landscape architectural design. It begins by discussing the diverse interests of those working in the profession, then highlights the different realms within which landscape architects work. This leads to a synopsis about the multitude of scales at which a landscape architect can design, which addresses the importance of green design, systems thinking, and human involvement. The chapter concludes with an outline of the many modes of communication valued by the landscape architecture profession.

Diverse Interests: From Creative Expression to Ecology to Construction Techniques

One reason it is such fun for me to teach landscape architecture is the great joy I find in helping students realize the many directions they can take within this profession. I always point out to them that as they begin to think about what they want to do to make a living, it is important to understand the difference between having a career and having a job. A career is usually described as a person's lifework, a continuous progression through specialized training. In selecting a career, you want to find something you can stick with and grow with; therefore, it is very important to seek a career that is rooted in activities you enjoy, in topics that interest you, and in beliefs you hold dear—in sum, it should resonate with you.

It also is fun to show students how they can accommodate their particular interests, usually in a variety of ways, in the profession of landscape architecture. For example, if you have an artistic and creative flair, you might want to investigate the design side of landscape architecture. If you are a more left-brained, nuts-and-bolts-type individual, you might be intrigued more by the detailed, how-things-get-built aspect of landscape architecture. If you are interested in plants, nature, and ecology, the profession will provide many outlets for your talents. If you are curious about how people behave and interact, or why people use spaces the way they do, there is a place in landscape architecture for you, too, because much of what landscape architects design involves human use and mitigating human impacts.

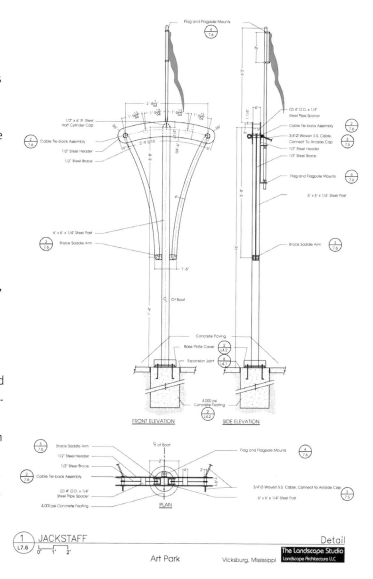

Construction details of Wheelhouse Jackstaff in Art Park at Vicksburg, Mississippi. Park Designer: The Landscape Studio Landscape Architecture LLC.

Students come into landscape architecture from many different directions—agricultural science, architecture, engineering, graphic design, art history, computer science, and environmental studies, to name only a few. Yet all can find a home in landscape architecture and build a satisfying career as a landscape architect.

Creating Places with Purpose

JENNIFER GUTHRIE, RLA, ASLA

Director

Gustafson Guthrie Nichol Ltd.

Seattle, Washington

Landscape architect Jennifer Guthrie. Gustafson Guthrie Nichol Ltd.

Why did you decide to pursue a career in landscape architecture?

〉 My course to landscape architecture, like many, was not direct. I had intended to be a math major. On a study-abroad program to England, I fell in love with the notion of architecture. The funny thing is, looking back on it, I decided I wanted to pursue architecture while I was sitting in a beautiful garden outside of a castle. When I was a few years into it, I realized I was spending more time outside the buildings. I found my way to the University of Washington's landscape architecture studio and was sold. I ended up getting degrees in both landscape architecture and architecture, but I pursued landscape architecture. I grew up with a strong gardening family in southern California. It was a part of my life, but I hadn't put all of those things together until I got into school.

How would you characterize the work of your office?

〉 We aim to create places with purpose. The most exciting part about designing in this office is the amount of attention that goes into the initial phases. We to do a ton of research into what makes that place we're designing special. We don't want to create icons or objects in the landscape; we want to come up with a landscape design that says something about the space of that site—creating a contemporary design that extracts all the qualities that are special about that place, because every site is special.

What is the size of your office and what is your role in it?

〉 We're currently at about 28 people. Eight of those are licensed landscape architects and one is a licensed architect, though many people in the office have multiple disciplines as part of their experience. We have people whose first degrees are in ecology, atmospheric science, architecture, and engineering. All those backgrounds are fantastic [for us], in that they allow us to approach a design or a problem in a varied way.

We still have a small-office mind-set here. I'm a director; I'm an owner; I'm a managing partner; I'm a partner in charge—I'm all of those things. But my job, as is Kathryn's and Shannon's, is to oversee the development as well as the management of projects.

Civic plaza at Seattle
City Hall, Seattle
Washington. Gustafson
Guthrie Nichol Ltd.

Whether that's contracts or financial management, I make sure that we are not only getting a good design out of a project, but since we are a business, to make sure we are meeting the targets we set.

What has been your most rewarding project to date?

❯ It's a project in Costa Mesa at a shopping center. It's called the Bridge of Gardens, a pedestrian bridge that goes up over the parking lot and a street to a building across the way. I was young, I was cocky, and I took on way more than I should have. I was responsible for leading a team of architects, engineers, landscape architects—the whole group—without ever having done that before. It is probably one of the highest-grossing shopping malls in the world. The level of finish, detailing, and materials for the bridge was extremely high.

[The bridge] is encased by bougainvillea planting and has wings that extend from both sides of the bridge, where the bougainvillea will grow out and create a carpet in the air. It has warped walls and very complicated detailing. Being able to figure out all that in the timeframe we had, and at the level of design the client expected, and then to see it built, gave me great pride and really convinced me that this was the profession for me. It is also how I met my partners, Kathryn Gustafson and Shannon Nichol. In doing that project we knew that we were the right group to form our own office.

What role do new technologies play in your design process?

❯ This is probably one of the most exciting components about design right now. As far as technologies go, digital modeling really shortcuts answering a lot of the questions we have in designing space. We've also been using 3D printing to help communicate form. The form of the earth captures light and human experiences in such subtle ways that it's really

View of detailing, underside of Bridge of Gardens, Costa Mesa, California. Gustafson Guthrie Nichol Ltd.

hard to show on a 2D drawing or on a flat screen. 3D modeling is extremely important in communicating that, so we do a lot of modeling, whether with the computer or with clay models. Technology has also made communication more accessible so we're able to interact with others on projects all over the world. You can tap into resources globally now, and that makes for more sophisticated science.

We've also been experimenting with new technologies for construction document communication. Sometimes it's so hard to describe your intent in a two-dimensional document. We haven't quite moved to sharing three-dimensional drawing files yet, but we're heading in that direction. Many contractors are excited and interested about taking on new things. But being able to translate what that new thing is, through document form to the contactor, is a gray area.

You believe people with varied interests and skills can be landscape architects. Please explain.

〉 It is an exciting time to be in this profession; it's an evolving profession. It's a profession that supports the scientific mind of someone who is really interested in the technology and science of landscape architecture. It also appeals to the design mind, someone who is interested in creating sculpted spaces and excels at three-dimensional thinking. It also supports people who are really pragmatic and have an appreciation for the arts and are able to think with both sides of their brain. I feel it's a pretty vast profession that can suit a lot of different people.

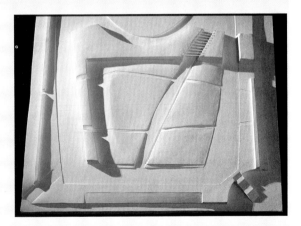

Plaster study model of the design for Lurie Garden. Gustafson Guthrie Nichol Ltd.

Pride in Public Spaces

EMMANUEL THINGUE, RLA

Senior Landscape Architect

New York City Department of Parks and Recreation

Flushing Meadows–Corona Park, New York

Landscape architect Emmanuel Thingue at work on a design.

Why did you decide to pursue a career in landscape architecture?

❯ I became a landscape architect quite by accident. I started out as an architect and was unfamiliar with landscape architecture as a profession. Paul Friedberg, who initiated the Landscape Architecture Program at City College, recruited me and convinced me that a dual degree was more advantageous in the job market. I have both degrees; however, I practice only landscape architecture because I enjoy the flexibility it offers far more than the rigidity, I perceive, in the architectural field.

How would you characterize your work ?

❯ I work for the New York City (NYC) Department of Parks and Recreation, and the work we do is extremely thoughtful and user-friendly. The primary goal of all projects is to satisfy the end users while maintaining the unique identity of the NYC park system. We will not design a park simply to make it look beautiful, at the expense of comfort, function, and usability. These are public spaces and we take great pride in balancing aesthetics, functionality, and usability.

What is the size of your organization? How many landscape architects and other professionals are on staff there?

❯ There are approximately 330 employees in the Capital Division, whose function is to reconstruct existing parks and create new ones as they are acquired; they include some 40 to 50 landscape architects. Most of them are in charge of managing their own in-house projects, from conception to construction; however, some are also in charge of managing consultant projects. The remaining employees have tasks relating, in one way or another, to helping achieve project completion. They include the administrators, our specification division, our legal team, our in-house engineering staff, our budget section, our architectural section, and our construction division.

What is your role in the office?

❯ I am a senior landscape architect. I supervise a group of four people and mentor some of the newcomers to the Parks Department. I have some knowledge of engineering and a great deal of experience in construction detailing. This allows me to

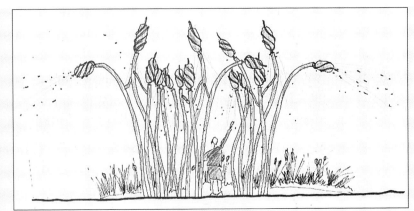

Initial sketch of cattails spray water feature for South Oxford Park. Courtesy of City of New York Parks and Recreation.

View of spray feature and playground at South Oxford Park, New York City. Courtesy of City of New York Parks and Recreation.

help those with less experience in those aspects of our profession. It also allows me to work on some of the more complex large-scale projects.

What is the most exciting aspect of your work?

❯ I would have to say designing. There is nothing more exciting to me. I sometimes design at home, free of charge, as a way to relax. It is very addictive. I don't think I am unique, because I don't believe designers can just shut off the de-

sign "valve." If you need to resolve a design issue, you will continually think about it until you have figured it out.

What has been your most rewarding project to date?

❯ My most rewarding project is a park called Hamilton–Metz [in Brooklyn]. It's neither the most beautiful nor the most interesting of my projects; however, it's the most gratifying in terms of the change, I perceive, that it brought to the park in question. It was supposed to involve the simple in-kind reconstruction of two basketball courts. I convinced the parties involved that it could be more if we added a garden area and a small plaza. There is a lot of gratification in providing more than what is expected. Although, upon completion of the project, I realized I could have extended the work even further; still, it remains a special project to me.

Which aptitudes, traits, and skills do you see in most landscape architects?

❯ A landscape architect should:

■ Have the ability to visualize nature and the subtle nuances of its beauty.

■ Have the ability to sell ideas. It is not enough to create great designs; one must be able to convince others that they are great designs. One might say great design sells itself;

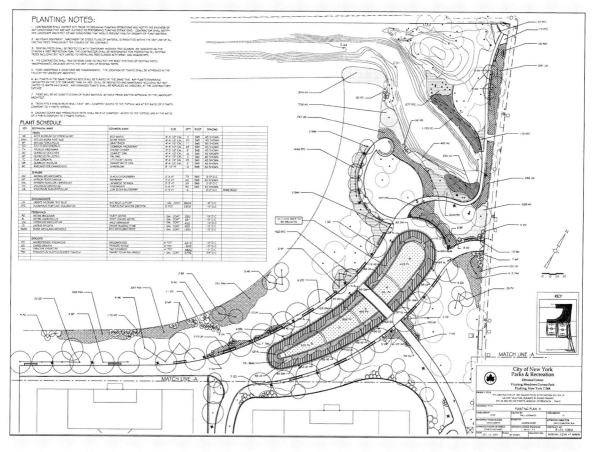

Planting plan of main entry garden for a 73-acre waterfront park. Courtesy of City of New York Parks and Recreation.

that's not always true. When one pushes the envelope, he or she must be skilled at convincing others to accept the unusual.

■ Be well-rounded and skilled in a variety of fields. This will help when presenting your ideas to others because you will be able to discuss a variety of topics. This will also allow you to have a bigger source from which to tap design ideas.

■ Be able to relate well with people. The success of your project depends so much on convincing other people of its validity; and to achieve this, one has to work well with other people.

■ Be able to synthesize numerous ideas. This is critical in design because there are so many possibilities and so many aspects to think about simultaneously. It requires the ability to prioritize and think of all aspects at once and separately. It seems counterintuitive but that's the nature of designing.

■ Be flexible. He or she must be able to see other people's point of view while being faithful to him- or herself. So much of what we create is for public usage, therefore we should be flexible in incorporating their ideas during the review process. We shouldn't be presumptuous and assume that only designers can generate great ideas.

■ Have the ability to grow and evolve. Design should analyze cultural changes and respond accordingly. Stagnation is the killer of all creativity.

■ Be observant. There is so much to learn, just from paying attention to your surroundings. When something attracts your attention, you should take the time to understand why and how you can repeat that experience.

What tips can you offer someone regarding the job search process?

❯ I would say an internship is extremely important. It gets you one foot in the door. That's how I started, and I've seen numerous students get hired at the Parks Department through that process. Given the choice, people would rather work with someone they already know, provided that person shows a certain level of competence.

Plant-Savvy Landscape Architect

DOUGLAS HOERR, FASLA

Partner

Hoerr Schaudt Landscape Architects

Chicago, Illinois

Landscape architect Douglas Hoerr. Photographer: Charlie Simokaitis/Charlie Simokaitis Photography.

Why did you decide to pursue a career in landscape architecture?

❯ I was not the book-smart kid in the family, and I hated school. I didn't plan to go right to college. I thought I would continue to work in construction for a couple years. In my senior year of high school my uncle showed me plans for a gravel pit he owned. It was a place I knew well; I used to go there to fish and hunt. He said, "You want to see a landscape plan?" He had hired a landscape architecture firm from Fort Wayne, Indiana, to look at a feasibility study. I saw toboggan hills, camping sites,

ice skating ponds, and fishing piers. I thought, wow, there are people who actually predetermine the use of land. I realized I would like to do that, because I loved building things and being outdoors.

How and why did you choose the school you attended to earn your degree?

❯ I chose Purdue because they teach you how to think. Everything was very purposeful. It was not as radical as some people would like, but they taught you the craft, and they taught you a strong focus in engineering and horticulture.

Which aspect of your education had the greatest influence on you?

❯ My first plant identification course resonated with me, and it has held true that I am a plant-savvy landscape architect. That is not necessarily always the case; other people find joy in other things. But that has been a constant through my career— the desire to learn and use plant material.

How would you characterize the work of your office?

❯ Our work tends to be carefully crafted. It is very site-sensitive and client-oriented. We want to work with people who appreciate the design process. We do a variety of types of projects that need very careful design consideration. We work all over the country doing parks, college campuses, streetscapes, and high-end residential projects.

What is the size of your firm and what is your role in it?

❯ We are a group of about 45, and three-quarters of those are landscape architects. My partner, Peter, is an architect and landscape architect. We have peo-

Hoerr used a Midwestern plant palette to unify the campus at North Park University, Chicago, Illinois. Photographer: Scott Shigley. Courtesy of Hoerr Schaudt Landscape Architects.

ple with art and horticulture degrees, arborists, and people with experience in land management. My role has changed, and I now focus on setting a design direction on certain projects. I sort of launch the boat properly so it stays the course regarding our response to the site. I help market, and I am also on-site. I love to be on-site during the critical stages of layout that require subjectivity.

Your early practice and experience in England is unique. Please explain.

❭ I started off in design/build for eight years. Then I realized I needed a change. I didn't like school, but I thought there had to be another way to excel in

this profession without getting a master's degree, so I chose the working-man's route. I wrote a cold-call letter to the most famous gardener I had heard of in England. I said I would come to work for free if I could learn about plants. I quit my job, and moved to England, and went to work for The Blooms of Bressingham. I apprenticed myself to these English gardeners. I call this experience my real-life masters. After eight years of trying to figure it out, being able to work with these people every day, it all came together; I finally understood what I was doing.

What role do new technologies play in your design process?

❭ We try to be as cutting-edge as possible, especially in the sustainable movement and green roof design. I chair Mayor Daley's Green Roof Committee. I am very proud of 900 North Michigan, which is one of the largest green roofs in Chicago. The changes in green roof technology in recent years are staggering. We strive to come up with something that works well and is not just a gimmick. But you have to keep in mind that while new technologies can be good, they have not always been tested.

A "rooftop prairie" grows 10 floors above Chicago's Magnificent Mile. Photographer: Scott Shigley. Courtesy of Hoerr Schaudt Landscape Architects.

What role can landscape architects take in making our world better?

❯ To start, we will make it better if we think like landscapes architects and not try to think like architects. We should be very proud of what we do. We should bring our talents, wisdom, and efforts to the table, and make sure the landscape is "heard." We will end up making a kinder, more beautiful, site-sensitive world if we stick to our guns.

Spanning a Range of Project Types and Scales

EDWARD L. BLAKE, JR.

Founding Principal

The Landscape Studio

Hattiesburg, Mississippi

Landscape architect Edward L. Blake, Jr. Photo: DC Young.

Why did you decide to pursue a career in landscape architecture?

❯ I was enrolled in premed and did not like it. I talked with my father and he suggested I look into landscape architecture. I grew up with my father on 60 acres in the country. It had been heavily grazed and row-cropped. We set about restoring it to get things growing there again. When he made that suggestion, though I'd never heard of landscape architecture, I immediately knew what he meant because that's what we had been doing together. I spent my whole youth growing up preparing for it. I just didn't know it.

How would you characterize the work of your office?

❯ Our office is a small studio. I call it a studio practice because there is a strong design orientation, and it's very collaborative. When I chose the title for the office, The Landscape Studio, I wanted it to be an umbrella where people of like minds, who wanted to explore landscape issues that are very timely, had a place to do that. Our work ranges in all scales. We've worked as small as fractions of an acre up to over 50,000 acres in size for larger land planning inventories. Our work also spans a range of project types, from fine garden design to institutions. We've done a lot of work for museums—art museums as well as botanical gardens. We've worked with university campuses, with cemeteries, and with parks and playgrounds.

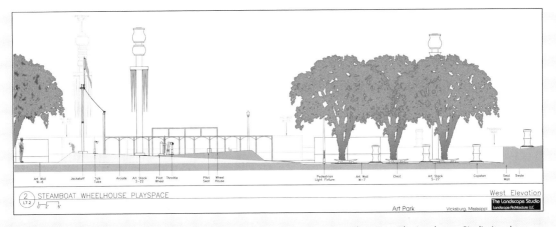

Elevation of Sprague Wheelhouse Playspace, Art Park at Vicksburg, Mississippi. Park Design: The Landscape Studio Landscape Architecture LLC.

What role do new technologies play in your design process?

❯ We just bought a GPS handheld device so we can go out and flag in pathways or roadways on a site. We walk the desired layout and pick up the coordinate points and then design the alignment around those. We are also linking that up with Google Maps and what's available from the aerials. But let me also say this: With all of that, I still consider pens, colored pencils, and watercolors to be technologies, too. It has taken us a while to learn to work with computer technologies the way we do, but generally what works best with us is to do all of our conceptual and most of our schematic and design development work by hand on sketch paper. It's very easy, once we get ideas, to scan them quickly and then to lay those scans over digital topographies to firm them up. We've found a way to work using the older technologies with the newer ones, and the synthesis works really well for us.

Who are some of the allied professionals you consult with? What role do they play in the design process?

❯ I have worked in collaboration with architects, structural and mechanical engineers, lighting engineers, and with specialty consultants such as a fountain designer. I've worked with ecologists, horticulturalists, arborists, and interior designers. For some of the projects where we've been the lead consultant, I've hired those consultants to work with us. At the front end we work very hard to develop the conceptual framework of the design based on understanding a place—the cultural structure as well as the biological structure. I ask all of the consultants who work with us to do the same in the work they do.

Catfish Fountain in the Art Park at Vicksburg, Mississippi. Photographer: Ed Blake, The Landscape Studio.

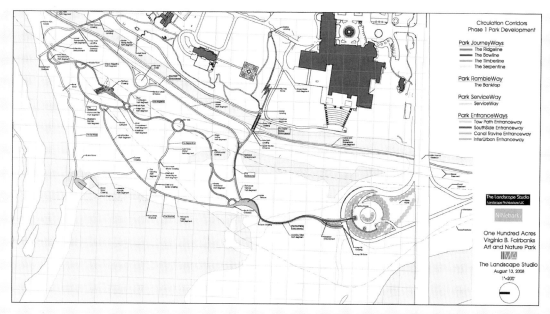

Circulation corridors for One Hundred Acres at Virginia B. Fairbanks Art and Nature Park, Indianapolis Museum of Art, Indianapolis, Indiana. Park Planning and Design: The Landscape Studio Landscape Architecture LLC. Local landscape architect: NINebark, Inc.

Which aptitudes, traits, and skills do you see in most landscape architects?

❯ The most important thing is an empathy for nature—a sense of knowing that if you're going to shape the home of people, plants, and animals, you do that in an empathetic way. To do it in that way requires incredible knowledge and a skill base that spans scientific endeavors such as geology, ecology, and biology, as well as zoology and everything in between. It also requires the skills to reassemble all of this on a landscape scale. When I say landscape scale, I don't mean just the scale most of us are familiar with in our own backyards; it might be hundreds or even thousands of acres.

When hiring a student for an internship or entry-level job, what types of questions might you ask in the interview?

❯ You need an incredible amount of self-confidence and a mastery of technique. I don't necessarily ask students what their goals are. I ask them what their

purpose in life is, and what makes life worth living for them. I ask them what they are reading. I ask them what music they are listening to, and I ask them about where they grew up. I ask them about their experience in education; what stands out and what teachers did that they feel made a big impact on them. And then I will look at their work to see how it fits with all of this.

What role can landscape architects play in making our world better?

❯ I go back to an old seventies expression, "Think globally and act locally." Really learning the place you live and understanding it as a community, and then working from that understanding. I don't think it's going to be models that solve the problems. Those will give insights, but we've got to have a diversity of solutions that fit each locale on this planet for this to work. We are going to need more people who are more and more familiar with specific places.

Project Profiles

SIDWELL FRIENDS SCHOOL

Showcasing Unique Working Environments

▼ Annotated illustration shows terraced wetland, rain garden, and pond. Illustration: Andropogon Associates Ltd. and Kieran Timberlake Associates. Courtesy of Andropogon Associates Ltd.

DRAWING BY ANDROPOGON ASSOCIATES LTD AND KIERAN TIMBERLAKE ASSOCIATES

1. EXISTING MIDDLE SCHOOL
2. MIDDLE SCHOOL ADDITION
3. TRICKLE FILTER WITH INTERPRETIVE DISPLAY
4. WETLANDS FOR WASTEWATER TREATMENT
5. RAIN GARDEN
6. POND

▶ Detailed view of wetland terrace's stone walls and plantings. Photo courtesy of Andropogon Associates Ltd.

▼ Diagrammatic section illustrates details about the constructed wetland. Photo courtesy of Andropogon Associates Ltd.

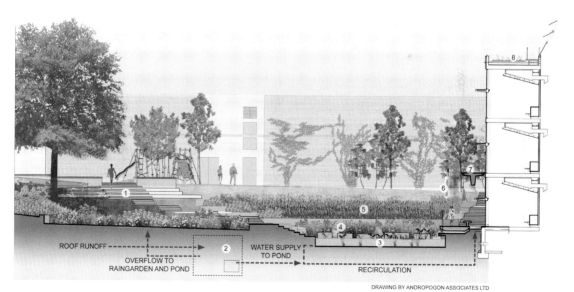

ROOF RUNOFF

OVERFLOW TO
RAINGARDEN AND POND

WATER SUPPLY
TO POND

RECIRCULATION

DRAWING BY ANDROPOGON ASSOCIATES LTD

1. OUTDOOR CLASSROOM
2. CISTERN
3. POND
4. RAIN GARDEN
5. WETLANDS FOR WASTEWATER TREATMENT
6. TRICKLE FILTER WITH INTERPRETIVE DISPLAY
7. RAMP TO SECOND FLOOR ENTRY
8. GREEN ROOF

PROJECT OVERVIEW

Date: 2006

Type: Institutional/Ecological

Location: Washington, DC

Client: Sidwell Friends School

Firm: Andropogon Associates Ltd., Philadelphia, Pennsylvania

Awards: U.S. Green Building Council LEED Platinum Rating; Top 10 Green Projects–AIA 2007; Award for Excellence, National Committee for Architecture on Education–AIA 2007; Honor Award–Sustainable Design Awards, Boston Society of Architects 2007; 2007 Craftsmanship Awards–Special Construction and Landscaping, Washington Building Congress

Web link to project: www.andropogon.com

We started out designing a building, which turned into a green building, and that green building ended up transforming the whole school, culturally and operationally.

—Mike Saxenian, Assistant Head of the Sidwell Friends Middle School[1]

A Multifunction Landscape

The centerpiece of the new addition to the Sidwell Friends Middle School is a constructed wetland, the first in the District of Columbia. It is designed to recycle wastewater from the building for reuse on site. The wetland, an active "laboratory for learning," uses biological processes to clean water, providing students with a vivid example of how such systems work in nature. Sewage is given primary treatment in an underground tank before being circulated through a series of terraced reed beds. Microorganisms provide an efficient breakdown of contaminants; a trickle filter and sand filter provide further treatment. The wetland system will receive up to 3,000 gallons per day, and the high-quality outflow is recycled into the building for reuse in lavatories.[2] One hundred percent of toilet water is expected to be reclaimed effluent.

A green roof on the new building addition slows the flow of stormwater runoff, the excess of which is diverted by transparent roof leaders to an underground cistern. The stored cistern water is then used in the biology pond in the courtyard.

To achieve improvements in water quality, the site's overland flow of runoff is routed from paved areas and lawn through a water-quality storm filter to remove suspended solids and excess nutrients. Runoff from other landscape areas flows to a vegetated drainage swale. Water, from both the swale and the filter, flows into an attractive rain garden, which then cleanses and infiltrates water back into the groundwater table.

While the landscape design is heavily rooted in water reuse, making it a working landscape, it also considers other components of good environmental design. In terms of energy, 78 percent of the material products used are from the region (within 500 miles), to decrease the amount of embodied energy for the project. Additionally, 60 percent of the waste from the construction phase of the project was recycled, rather than placed in a landfill. Not only is Sidwell Friends School an environmentally sensitive design, but at every stage of the design and construction, the environment was given priority.[3]

Student Interaction with the Design

In addition to functioning as a "working landscape," the site design for the school integrates educational opportunities into the redesign of the campus landscape. Deeply committed to practicing and promoting environmental stewardship, the school requested environmentally responsible stormwater and wastewater management systems to be designed as educational and awareness-building tools, highly visible in the landscape. Jose Alminana, Andropogon Associates' landscape architect project manager, feels strongly about the student/ landscape interaction. He said, "I can only hope that what we've done there in that project, after the students move through it for four years…[will]…change their minds. They are going to realize the whole water cycle, plants and filtration, and how animals and aquatic inhabitants interact. How we live and interact with atmosphere and the climate and how we take advantage of the sun…. How do we use materials in ways that are the least damaging possible?"[4]

Green Design

The project landscape architects, Andropogon Associates, and architects, Kieran Timberlake Associates, alongside a variety of engineers, consultants, and specialists, were able to create an award-winning LEED [Leadership in Energy and Environmental Design] Platinum design. Sidwell Friends School was awarded this honor by the U.S. Green Building Council as a measure of their success in sustainable development. This award is tremendous; not only was Sidwell the first LEED platinum building for the District of Columbia, but the first school in the United States for grades K–12 to receive such a high ranking.[5]

Project Profile

MESA ARTS CENTER

Landscape Architecture as Contextual Artistry

▲ Digital 3D model illustrates all the components of the site design. Illustration: Martha Schwartz Partners. Courtesy of ASLA

▼People enjoying a "flash flood" in the Arroyo water feature. Courtesy of ASLA. Photograph: Martha Schwartz Partners.

▶ Color is infused through the use of translucent glass panels and cactus in crushed glass. Courtesy of ASLA. Photographer: Shauna Gillies-Smith.

PROJECT OVERVIEW

Date: 2005

Type: Civic/Institutional

Location: Mesa, Arizona

Client: Mesa Arts Center

Firm: Martha Schwartz Partners, Cambridge, Massachusetts

Award: 2007 ASLA Professional General Design Honor Award

Web link to project: www.marthaschwartz.com/prjts/commercial/mesa/mesa.html

It sustains so much color and culture in one place and has transformed the area. We love the energy and that it looks beautiful with water or not.

—ASLA 2007 PROFESSIONAL AWARDS JURY[6]

Identity for Mesa

Mesa, a rapidly growing commuter town near Phoenix, Arizona, is considered to be one of the largest suburban cities in the United States. Given the nature of bedroom communities and the rapid growth of the area, much was lacking in terms of a city core or an interesting civic space where residents could gather. The Mesa Arts Center is the largest in the state, and with the unique and highly skilled influence of the architects, landscape architects, and artists, it is anticipated to attract tourism to Mesa.[7]

The Mesa Arts Center is intended serve as a catalyst for urban regeneration and to act as a focus for culture and the arts, including elements such as performing arts venues and exhibit spaces. Thus, while the center's outdoor space responds to the interior uses, it also seeks to achieve a larger goal of reconnecting the city and adjacent sites through the creation of a central hub for meeting, activity, and leisure. The location of the site at the intersection of Main Street and Center Street (two of the main roads in Mesa) gives the space an opportunity to become the basis for a new civic core and a strongly imaginable destination for the community.[8]

Addressing the Context

In the Southwest United States, a significant environmental constraint is the sun. Mesa averages 300-plus days of sun a year; so, naturally, shade became a core element of the site design.[9] The project features a "shadow walk," a walkway filled with canopies, flora, trellises, and shadow patterns. The space provides a place for art exhibitions, a point of respite for city dwellers, and both small and large gathering spaces for visitors.

Water is also a key element in the design. The "Arroyo" functions as a unique water feature that extends 300 feet along the shadow walk and emulates a dry creek. To symbolize a flash flood, a common occurrence in the Southwest, it is periodically inundated with a rapid rush of water. During the artificial flash flood, visitors can rest by the Arroyo, dipping their feet in the cooling water feature. Combined with the shadow walk, this becomes a grand promenade that provides a refreshing contrast to Mesa's intense heat.[10]

Considering the setting and the goal to create a vibrant public plaza, water is further integrated into a key site feature. Unique banquet tables are designed with an open slice in the center, for running water, along the entire length. They are meant to capture, on a smaller scale, the water table idea made famous at Villa Lante in the Italian countryside.[11]

Materials Selection

Martha Schwartz and Partners has long been distinguished as a firm known to challenge the idea of traditional landscape architecture. The firm's passion to create landscapes that are truly pieces of art is visible in this design's forms, style, colors, and mixture of materials. The firm's creative approach is visible in a few standout features: the stainless steel and glass shade canopy, the bed of crushed red glass with cactus emerging, and vibrant-colored translucent glass walls. While environmental factors and programming are significant informants for the design, the true beauty of the space is the artistry in bold and unique details. The patterns of shapes on the horizontal and vertical planes, as well as the textures and colors in the design, are evidence the landscape is most definitely a work of art on its own.

Project Profile

LURIE GARDEN

A Rooftop Abstracted from the Past

◀ Plantings capture seasonal displays; here the Light Plate during spring. Courtesy of ASLA. Photograph: Gustafson Guthrie Nichol Ltd.

▲ Site plan shows the two "plates" bisected by the "Seam" and surrounded by the "Shoulder Hedge" on the left and top. Courtesy of ASLA. Illustration: Gustafson Guthrie Nichol Ltd.

▲ The Seam-wide walkway, casual seating, and shallow water feature. Courtesy of ASLA. Photograph: Gustafson Guthrie Nichol Ltd.

PROJECT OVERVIEW

Date: June 2004

Type: Urban Design/Green Roof

Location: Chicago, Illinois

Client: Millennium Park, Inc., City of Chicago Illinois

Firm: Gustafson Guthrie Nichol Ltd., Seattle, Washington

Awards: 2008 ASLA Professional Design Award of Excellence; 2006 AIA Institute Honor Awards for Regional & Urban Design (Millennium Park); 2005 WASLA Professional Award of Honor; 2005 Green Roofs for Healthy Cities Intensive Industrial Award; 2005 Travel + Leisure Magazine Best Public Space Award

Web link to project: www.ggnltd.com/frame-sets/portfolio-fset.htm

The Lurie Garden is a design inspired by Chicago's distinct natural and cultural history.

—KATHRYN GUSTAFSON, Gustafson Guthrie Nichol Ltd.[12]

Designing on a Rooftop

Green Roofs for Healthy Cities lists Millennium Park, a total 24.5 acres in size, as one of the largest roof gardens in the world. The park sits on top of Chicago's Lakefront Millennium Parking Garage (4,000 parking spaces), a transit hub, and an indoor theater.[13] Roof gardens are always interesting projects due to restrictions and requirements that often create more challenging situations than a typical landscape. One significant issue for Millennium Park was the load restrictions dictated by the parking structure. In the case of Lurie Garden, a 3-acre garden within the park, lightweight geo-foam underneath the soil was used to create undulations in the landform. This material provided a substitute to excessive heavy soil material.[14]

Lurie Garden provides a calm escape from the city and the adjacent playful park. Nestled between two structures, a band shell and the workshop addition to the Chicago Art Institute, Lurie Garden is designed to accommodate both large and small crowds. It stands out from the rest of the park because of the unique textures and tones of the plant material.[15] The garden's design provides not only an exciting environment to visit, but one rich in style, materials, and meaning.

Design Components

Gustafson Guthrie Nichol Ltd. (GGN), a landscape architecture firm based in Seattle, Washington, won the internationally invited design competition for the design of Lurie Garden. The concept for the project established four key parts to the site's design. These were named the Seam, the Shoulder Hedge, and the Dark and Light Plates. The two plates cover the interior of the site. They are elevated and filled with plant material. The Dark Plate is representative of the site's history—a loose shoreline. Plant material on the Dark Plate is cool, strong, and robust; combined with the undulations in the landscape, the plate creates a sense of immersion for visitors. In contrast, the Light Plate is vibrant in color and presents an array of interestingly textured plant varieties. It is representative of the city today and in the future, an artistic and creative "control of nature." While the Dark Plate creates a feeling of enclosure for visitors, the Light Plate promotes a feeling of openness and can be explored by several walkways that spread across it. The Seam creates a diagonal slice between the two plates, symbolizing a point of intersection for the site's history and its contemporary state. It is composed of a wall, a walkway, and a linear pool of water, which runs parallel to the walkway. The Seam serves as the main corridor through Lurie Garden. Surrounding the plates is the Shoulder Hedge, named to reflect Carl Sandberg's famous description of Chicago as the "City of Big Shoulders." The Hedge encloses the garden on two sides and also creates a protective barrier between the band shell and the perennial garden.[16]

Materials Selection

The materials used in the project are reminiscent of the midwestern landscape. GGN used native plant species and local stone gathered from a nearby quarry. In collaboration with perennial planting design expert, Piet Oudolf, the team carefully selected plants suitable to the soil and climate conditions present on the site. In terms of stone selection, two types were used: limestone and granite. Limestone is used for curbs, stairs, and landings, and the wall's coping and cladding, and granite is used as pavement and for the wall veneer in the water feature.[17]

Other materials used in the project include Forest Stewardship Council (FSC) certified Ipe for the wood benches and the boardwalk; and patinized naval brass, patinized architectural bronze, and powder-coated steel for the metal plates, handrails, and the Armature, respectively.[18]

Site Evolution

The history of the site provided a basis that inspired much of the design for the garden. What began as the shore of Lake Michigan was filled and built up to become the Illinois Central rail yard, which evolved into a parking garage, and has now become a park. While this waterfront location functions far greater as a civic space for cultural and social events, it stands as a constant reminder of the evolution of place.

Design Variety: Living, Working, Playing, Learning, Healing, Protecting, Restoring

Throughout this book are interviews with more than 50 professionals. The diversity of their work serves to illuminate how wide ranging a landscape architect's job can be. The American Society of Landscape Architects conducts a biannual survey of its members, which lists nearly 50 types of work in 6 service areas. A representative sampling of these project types includes: urban revitalization, college campuses, transportation systems, landfill and mine reclamation, farmland preservation, stormwater management, waterfronts, state and county parks, sports facilities, and streetscapes. The six service areas, which refer to the type of professional service provided on a project, are: design, planning, preservation, public policy, management, and research.

Landscape architects are engaged in the design and planning of environments where people live, work, learn, and play. Living environments include everything from the yard of a single-family house to entire residential communities. Projects that relate to where people work include court-

yards and public plazas, office campuses, transit facilities, schools, and museums. Recreational design encompasses sports fields, linear parks and trails, golf courses, botanic gardens, resorts, playgrounds, even national parks and forests. Landscape architects are also increasingly involved in protecting and restoring both culturally and naturally significant places, where their work ranges from conducting detailed investigations and preparing design proposals for restoring a historic site to larger-scale planning to protect an entire watershed from overdevelopment. Whatever the project, however, landscape architects consider both aesthetic and functional factors and always seek to improve the sites on which they work.

Campus quadrangle at the University of Pennsylvania, Philadelphia. Designed by Andropogon Associates, Ltd. J Totaro Photography, © 2002.

Inherently Sustainable: Historic Preservation

PATRICIA O'DONNELL, FASLA, AICP

Principal

Heritage Landscapes, Preservation Landscape Architects & Planners

Charlotte, Vermont

Landscape architect Patricia O'Donnell (in hat) with colleagues, on site. Courtesy of Heritage Landscapes.

Why did you decide to pursue a career in landscape architecture?

❭ I grew up in Buffalo, New York, a city that was shaped by Olmsted and Vaux. It had the very first park system, both parks and parkways. In my mid-20s I was leading a youth conservation group program in Buffalo, which was focused on parks. So I came at landscape architecture through historic parks and youth programs. I realized there were a bundle of values in having a city shaped by parks and parkways, but that those resources were becoming threatened. It seemed to me that landscape architecture and planning were professional paths that could help with those problems.

How and why did you choose the school you attended to earn your degree?

❭ I got my undergraduate degree in environmental design. I got two masters degrees: an MLA (Master in Landscape Architecture) and an MUP (Master in Urban Planning), both from the University of Illinois. I was accepted at six schools, but Illinois gave me a fellowship; plus, I had made a personal visit to each school and thought the community there would be more supportive. I had a seven-year-old daughter at the time, so the fellowship and the character of the community were pretty critical. My landscape architecture degree focus was in applied behavioral research, and I use that knowledge all the time.

How would you characterize the work of your office?

❭ We are a private consultancy. Our expertise is specifically in landscapes of heritage value. A lot of our work is landscape-centric, meaning we're the only discipline on the contract, and landscape is the main focus. We endeavor to understand the aesthetics, the function, the motivation, and the design ideas of some place of the past that is valued. We are interested in coming to a thorough understanding of a place and its evolution. We work at varying scales and do strategic planning through construction documents. We also do management planning and interpretation, where we look at how best to present the resources to people.

Renewing Historic Parks-Keystones of Livability

City Identity
Livability
Linkages
Connections
Presence of Parks

Quality of Experience
Diverse Uses
Use Conflicts
Programs

Park Maintenance
Functionalities
Basic Services
Public Safety
Perceived Security

Historic Preservation
Park Character
Legacy & Uniqueness
Adaptability & Innovation
Aesthetics

Sustainability
Natural Resources
Conservation
Ecological Stewardship
Habitat Diversity

Community Awareness
Heighten Sense of Value
Partnerships
Volunteerism

Principles and benefits of historic park renovation. Courtesy of Heritage Landscapes.

What role do research techniques and best practices play in the projects you're commissioned to undertake?

❯ We love to be able to research and understand traditional practices because a lot of them have been forgotten, but they are often rooted in sustainability. As an example, we're working with bound gravel specifications instead of concrete. We are trying to be authentic at the same time that we're sustainable. At Lincoln Cottage we just did a bound gravel drive and a cobbled gutter, to match the historic. We were really excited, because we anticipated there would be this cobbled gutter, from what we knew from historic documentation. When we excavated to build it, we found a fragment of the historic block.

We try to keep up with the literature on the latest advances. For example, we've been very interested in soil. In a historic place, when you're going to intervene, you have to consider soil as a resource because it is not replaceable. We recently researched excavation equipment to decide what size and weight equipment we would allow on a historic site. Sustainability is very important to us, and it's our position that historic preservation is inherently one of the most sustainable practices we can undertake.

What has been your most rewarding project to date?

❯ We have had the good fortune for the last 11 years to work with the Pittsburgh Parks Conservancy on 1,400 acres of parks that serve 4 areas of the city and 10 different neighborhoods. We were able to do some good planning and establish an overall signage design system, as well as guidelines for park furnishings and lighting. These are pieces that get implemented over time. We have also done some detailing for implementation. At Highland Park we designed a public garden that was in scale and continuity with the evolution of that park entry, which had become quite degraded. These projects take patience, but are very rewarding.

You engage in a lot of professional volunteer work. What has that service meant to you?

❯ I've always felt it's very important to be involved in your profession through bringing your expertise to volunteer efforts. Most of my professional volunteer work is for the ASLA; for the International Federation of Landscape Architects, IFLA; and for ICOMOS, the International Council on Monuments and Sites. I also am on the board of the Cultural Landscape Foundation and I've just finished service on the board of the National Center of Preservation, Training, and Technology. Through my involvement on these boards or as committee chair, I am sometimes asked to attend and participate in expert meetings for the World Heritage Center. A number of years ago, for ICOMOS, I participated in a 10-day planning charrette in Cape Coast, which is one of the most historic cities in Ghana. Meeting colleagues and sharing information at these events is very enriching. Occasionally we do pro bono projects for special situations. We have a role in the international team on Finca Vigía, which is Ernest Hemingway's house in Cuba. Under the direction of the Hemingway Preservation Foundation, we have been the landscape architect on the team aiding our Cuban colleagues in the preservation of Hemingway's property.

What tips can you offer someone regarding the job search process?

❯ Ask people for an informational interview. Be clear what your purpose is, and respect their time. A 20-minute informational interview with several different professionals can really help you figure out where you want to go. Find out if they have a desired interview process. We have an interviewing process where first we ask for portfolio and writing examples. We review them. Then we do a phone interview; after the phone interview, those who seem closest to what we need are asked to come for a half-day office interview. We want to know more about them, and they need to know more about us to make a decision.

Highland Park (Pittsburgh, Pennsylvania) project rehabilitated the grand nineteenth-century entry fountain basin and gardens. Courtesy of Heritage Landscapes.

Designing for Outdoor Natural Play and Learning

CINDY TYLER

Principal

Terra Design Studios

Pittsburgh, Pennsylvania

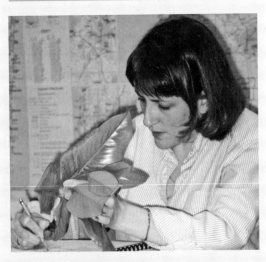

Cindy Tyler during a design workshop drawing southern magnolia leaves for an exhibit idea. Courtesy of Terra Design Studios.

Why did you decide to pursue a career in landscape architecture?

❯ My choice was pure luck. I graduated high school in the era of guidance counselors who looked up career opportunities in a book. In my case, he cross-referenced my stated love of drawing with my love of the outdoors. I still remember when he said, "Hmmm, here's something. Have you ever heard of landscape architecture?" It sounded great on paper, so I decided to give it a try. I went to Penn State because it was one of two schools that offered land-scape architecture in my region.

Much of your work focuses on designing for children and youth; why have you chosen that as a career direction?

❯ I grew up with the freedom of roaming the woods behind our house with my sister and friends. In the mid-1990s, as a young professional and mother, I became troubled with the lack of time children were playing freely, unstructured, and spontaneously out-doors. I worried we were raising a generation that might fully understand how to master the keyboard or television remote but would not grow to know,

A re-created pond in the Healthy Earth, Healthy You section of the Children's Healthcare of Atlanta Children's Garden at the Atlanta Botanical Gardens, Georgia. Photographer: Geoffrey L. Rausch.

Springmelt Stream

Sketch for interactive stream at the Mordecai Children's Garden at the Denver Botanic Gardens, Colorado. Courtesy of Terra Design Studios.

love, and protect their green world. I saw an opportunity through my profession as a landscape architect to be part of the solution.

I was an associate with a national firm whose focus was public garden design. We had just been awarded the design for a children's garden at the Atlanta Botanical Garden. There were only two or three such gardens in the country at that time. I was asked to lead the design and fell totally in love with this unique segment of our profession. I have never looked back. I have grown since then to focus more fully on family environments that not only are a great place to visit and learn, but are user-friendly and inspirational. By that I mean, it is my hope to inspire the grownups who come with the children to re-create these kinds of outdoor natural play and learning spaces in their own backyards, schools, and parks so children find it easier to immerse themselves on a daily basis in the green world. Designing family gardens has given me a voice that

would otherwise go unheard, and it has made landscape architecture relevant for me.

What is the most exciting aspect of your work?

❯ I love the thrill of competing for a commission and getting it. I cherish the relationships and friendships I have made along the way; many of my clients have become great friends. I really enjoy helping new organizations get started. And I love that our work at Terra Design is relevant, meeting a dire social need and hopefully making a difference, however incremental.

Who are some of the allied professionals you consult with? What role do they play in the design process?

❯ We typically assemble a team of educators, horticulturists, water feature designers, sculptors, artists, architects, and engineers to contribute to the design of our family gardens. Given our public garden client base, often the early education specialist and horticulturists are also our clients. This team process begins with us in master planning, and ends with the construction administration phases. Though they are not professionals, their opinions are important—we try to involve children in some aspect in early phases of the master plan.

What has been your most rewarding project to date?

⟩ The adaptive reuse of Washington's Landing on Herr's Island, was extremely rewarding. When I visit this project now, I am pleased to see so many people using the river trail and park. It used to be a brown-

field site, and now hundreds of people live, work, and play there. It is one of the first projects I directed, and after 20 years, it has stood the test of time and remains quite true to its vision (see p. 176).

What role can landscape architects take in making our world better?

⟩ Landscape architects are destined to save the world. In part, I am joking. But in part, I think we are one of the professions that focuses its passion on honoring the earth's natural systems. Our world needs to do that in a big way. Landscape architects create places that we naturally seek as humans, but are fast disappearing: green, calm, sensory, and the like.

Middle school class explores plants and nature in Wegerzyn Children's Discovery Garden, Dayton, Ohio. Courtesy of Five Rivers MetroParks, Dayton, Ohio.

Creating Restorative, Sensory Experiences

JIM BURNETT, FASLA

President

The Office of James Burnett

Houston, Texas, and Solana Beach, California

Landscape architect James Burnett. Courtesy of The Office of James Burnett.

Why did you decide to pursue a career in landscape architecture?

❭ I went to school enrolled in an environmental design program, but I was leaning toward architecture. I was at LSU (Louisiana State University) and I took an introduction to landscape architecture class. I got bitten by the whole idea that it would be more fun to design places where people could get outside than it would be to design buildings. I was fortunate that LSU had landscape architecture, so I switched into that program.

You founded your firm to address the "humanization of healthcare." Why have you chosen restorative and therapeutic design as one of your primary career foci?

❭ One of the first big jobs I went after, with the architect I was renting space from, was a hospital. Prior to our interview I did some research and I found that, at that time, there had not been much emphasis on getting patients out of doors and giving them a positive environment, a restorative healing experience. From that point on I got to thinking there was a real opportunity to make a difference in the healthcare environment by designing gardens that are sensitive to the needs of those recovering from surgery, facing a life crisis, or perhaps even celebrating a happy experience, such as the birth of a child.

Shortly after that, my mother was diagnosed with cancer. We chose the hospital pretty quickly and learned firsthand how bad that experience could be—there was no place to take her out of doors, to get good daylight, or to look at something interesting. It just was not a pleasant experience. She died about 90 days later. The whole experience reinforced the idea that it really would be good to take this approach. Having started the firm in a direction of healthcare has been positive because we take time to address all aspects, the whole sensory experience, whether it's a healthcare project or something else.

What has been your most rewarding project to date?

❭ The Campus Heart central garden for Exxon's Brookhollow campus, because it taught us is that good ideas can come together in a very short time.

We designed the project in about three weeks and then started building it in about a month and a half, which is very rare. It was a renovation project that had been mostly concrete; we ripped it all out. Exxon wanted to create a center court for their employees where they could gather and have special events or just eat their lunch. In a way, it was like a restorative environment project. We took all the hospital concepts for healing gardens and put them into a corporate environment, and it worked very well.

What is the most exciting aspect of your work?

❯ The most exciting aspect is seeing our work built. To go from the early stages of formulating the design and then seeing everything we put down on paper being constructed is great. With two offices, one in California and one in Texas, we have four or five projects being built at any one time, and it's great fun for me to go out and see things come alive.

▲ The Park at Lakeshore East, Chicago, Illinois. Photograph: © David B. Seide/www .DefinedSpace.com

❯ Paving pattern detail at an entrance to the 5-acre Park at Lakeshore East, Chicago, Illinois. Courtesy of The Office of James Burnett.

Water feature and outdoor seating at the Brochstein Pavilion, Rice University, Houston, Texas. Courtesy of The Office of James Burnett.

What tips can you offer someone regarding the job search process?

❭ Working in the summer as an intern is really key because we know they understand the whole experience of working in a firm. It is important they have good work habits; and no matter what position we are looking for, that they present their work in a beautiful way. The presentation part of our profession is huge to us. Then, of course, when we meet them, their attitude is very important. We can teach most people anything, but if they have a positive attitude, are willing to work hard, and are passionate about what they are doing, then all those other things will come.

What role can landscape architects take in making our world better?

❭ We are trying to make things that inspire people, and we tell our clients this. When we are done, our clients have had a bit of an education in landscape architecture. They understand how things work and why we are doing what we're doing, and they can tell the story to their team or to their family or whoever is experiencing that space. Spreading the understanding about what we do, how landscape architects are making a difference on the planet, and are helping to change people's lives, is important.

Applying a Land Ethic to Large Estates

KEVIN CAMPION, ASLA

Senior Associate

Graham Landscape Architecture

Annapolis, Maryland

Landscape architect Kevin Campion at his office.

Why did you decide to pursue a career in landscape architecture?

❯ When I was growing up I was curious about how things were built. I spent most of my childhood outside. When I came to college, related to my interests in building, I started as an architectural engineering major. After one year I decided I had to make a decision between that and architecture and landscape architecture. I found landscape architecture through architecture at Penn State, and I was very happy that I did.

How and why did you choose the schools you attended to earn your degrees?

❯ I lived in Pennsylvania and I chose the school before I chose the profession. My graduate degree is a different story. I waited for seven years until I really understood what I wanted to study in greater detail. I chose a school, the Edinburgh College of Art in Scotland, for a number of reasons. It made sense with the body of work I was studying; but also I chose a place where I knew I could remove myself from the life I had in order to think about the life I want to have.

Which aspect of your education had the greatest influence on you?

❯ Travel, and community or real-world projects my professors worked hard to bring to us. I thought these were very valuable in connecting the work I did in college with the real world, and realizing that what you do is important. Presenting our ideas to actual members of a community was fundamental. Travel lets you see how different people live, and see so much more design—especially world travel that allows you to engulf yourself in a rich layering of cultural history and details.

How would you characterize the work of your office?

❯ We are focused on the high-end residential market and other aspects associated with that, such as work in academia and institutions where our clients send their kids, and we have a few projects in some high-end resorts. Our work is estate planning and design, but we don't just design gardens, we look beyond them. With big pieces of land we feel compelled to help landowners understand their land asset and to appreciate it and conserve it. With estates that are 300 to 500 acres, there is a real opportunity to do some planning on a small scale, but for residential projects it's a very large scale.

Tell us about your ecological metrics approach.

❯ This was partially an outgrowth of my master's degree research, especially on large pieces of land and how to improve them. I'm working with interns this summer to develop this list of measuring devices for the land, whereby you can go in at the beginning of a project and ask, what are the metrics of this land, what are the aptitudes, what does this land have to offer, how is it struggling, and then do a site analysis of the land in a very quantitative way. Then, when the project is finished, come back and look at those same metrics and start to develop a way to measure—did I leave this site better than I found it? If we can finish projects leaving the site the same or better than we found it, then that's a success. This is closely aligned with the ASLA's Sustainable Sites Initiative. Seeing what they are doing, I thought, I can apply this idea directly to my projects.

What has been your most rewarding project to date?

❯ The project that inspired my master's degree research and that has been the most rewarding is called Wye Hall, an estate developed in the eighteenth century on an island in the Chesapeake Bay called Wye Island. It was built by William Paca, who was a signer on the Declaration of Independence and a governor of Maryland. The reason this project is so rewarding is because the clients are true patrons. You come across many different kinds of clients and there are the very few we call patrons, who are really, truly appreciative of what we are doing. These clients really raised the bar on how to conserve the land.

We brought in archeologists to try and retell the story of this very important piece of land, so were been able look at it from an archeological perspec-

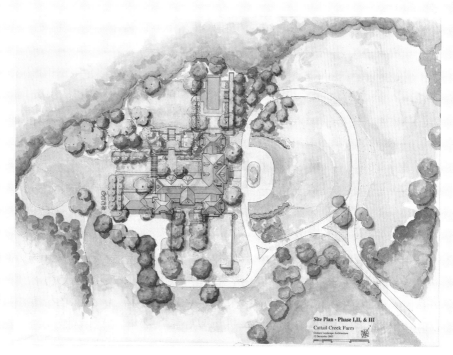

Watercolor of detailed design plans for the garden at Cattail Creek Farm, Maryland. Illustrator: Kevin Campion.

Employing ecological metrics to blend the lines between garden and site at Tidewater Farm, Maryland. Photographer: Auther Batter.

tive. We designed beautiful gardens; but most importantly, we've been able to heal the land and do a lot of great conservation projects that are making the aesthetic of the land more sympathetic with the history. We designed more open space, and more space for wildlife while still keeping the balance of agriculture.

What is the most exciting aspect of your work?

❯ The whole process: the genesis of the idea through to the manifestation of the built work. Seeing things built, that always brings a sense of appreciation. Working with clients is also very exciting—dealing with people and their homes, their aspirations, and helping them to create a very special place that is meaningful to them is very fulfilling. It's also fulfilling to think about creating something that will be left behind, that will live beyond your career; something that you will leave for the next generation.

Which aptitudes, traits, and skills do you see in most landscape architects?

❯ The most important aptitude is the ability to solve problems. Fundamentally at the end of the day, landscape architects are problem solvers. I also think you need to be creative, and that goes with being a problem solver—figuring out creative ways to solve the problem. Last, sensitivity and awareness, especially to the land—kind of listening to the land, is the way I would describe that.

What role can landscape architects take in making our world better?

❯ We're in a profession that gives us the opportunity to be experts where our expertise is really needed, in this whole green spectrum and environmental movement, which is the largest movement in the history of the world perhaps. We need to be vocal and really curious for the knowledge and the understanding of what it will take to sustain the world in the future.

Project Profile

ERIE BASIN PARK

A Contemporary Approach to Preservation

Ferry arrival plaza and bosque at the Erie Basin Park waterfront promenade. Photographer: Colin Cooke.

Historic concrete blocks, called "chalks," salvaged and reused in the site design. Photographer: Colin Cooke.

Site plan design for Erie Basin Park, Brooklyn, New York. Courtesy of Lee Weintraub Landscape Architecture, LLC.

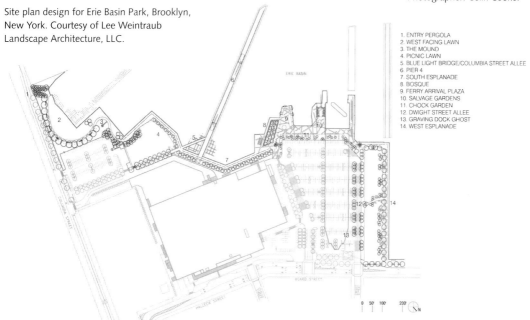

1. ENTRY PERGOLA
2. WEST FACING LAWN
3. THE MOUND
4. PICNIC LAWN
5. BLUE LIGHT BRIDGE/COLUMBIA STREET ALLEE
6. PIER 4
7. SOUTH ESPLANADE
8. BOSQUE
9. FERRY ARRIVAL PLAZA
10. SALVAGE GARDENS
11. CHOCK GARDEN
12. DWIGHT STREET ALLEE
13. GRAVING DOCK GHOST
14. WEST ESPLANADE

PROJECT OVERVIEW

Date: 2008

Type: Preservation Design

Location: Red Hook, Brooklyn, New York

Client: IKEA

Firm: Lee Weintraub Landscape Architecture, LLC

They didn't have to do 90 percent of what they did....This is a situation where you had a client, IKEA, that really wanted to make a difference and leave a lasting legacy..., and we had a landscape architect who really put his heart and soul into keeping after the essence of what he wanted to achieve.

—AMANDA BURDEN, Chair, New York City Planning Department[19]

The Site

Red Hook, Brooklyn, is just south of Governors Island and Manhattan. Historically, Red Hook was recognized as the home of Todd Shipyard, a major 22-acre ship repair facility for New York Harbor.[20] The ship repair business was vacated over a decade ago. A lack of public transportation from Manhattan to Red Hook, combined with the predominance of public housing, meant the neighborhood was unattractive to developers. While much of the waterfront property in Manhattan and Queens is occupied by retail, residential, and linear parks, Red Hook's waterfront space was left abandoned: functionless shipyards, in a state of industrial decay.[21]

IKEA's Role

IKEA chose Red Hook's waterfront as the prime location for a new 346,000-square-foot big-box store, in spite of the site's condition. This decision was controversial given the site's history as a grand shipyard, juxtaposed with the retailer's potential to help improve the neighborhood.[22] Big-box projects of this scale, if successful, can rapidly and drastically transform neighborhoods, by encouraging sister businesses and other retailers to move into the area.

IKEA's first step involved working with the city planning department to obtain needed zoning code changes to build retail in the place of former industry. The city planning department decided that in order to grant this redevelopment IKEA would have to provide access to the waterfront and build, as well as maintain, a public promenade. The role of the promenade is twofold: to give the public access to the waterfront and to preserve some reflection of the site's history.[23]

The Process

Given the controversial nature of the project and IKEA's hopes to change the zoning regulations, the client sought out Lee Weintraub, a landscape architect practicing in Yonkers, New York, to quickly develop plans for the waterfront promenade park.[24] Weintraub has a reputation for working in challenging situations and producing results that respect the place while providing a catalyst for change.[25] One of Weintraub's many project challenges was IKEA's request to produce a schematic design in only six weeks.

Although the park had not been the client's first priority, it became so when IKEA realized it was essential to securing the zoning change needed to build on the site. Weintraub's office had to balance many factors in preparing the design, as well as satisfy many constituent groups.[26]

Incorporating Historic Preservation into Design

Weintraub's office was keenly interested in referencing the site's past while making this a contemporary waterfront park. In order to better understand the site history and the story of the place, Weintraub consulted with Pino Deserio, a former shipyard foreman. Deserio helped move equipment around to uncover industrial artifacts on-site. He also explained to Weintraub the function of various spaces and equipment and the role these artifacts played. Weintraub incorporated Deserio's stories and historical knowledge into the site's design through graphic signage, photographs, and historical relics retained for display. Additionally, due to a limited budget, materials on-site were recycled and reused in the project.[27]

The design also commemorates elements of the site that were lost to construction of the IKEA building and parking lot. A graving dock, previously on the Preservation League of New York's list of "Seven to Save," was filled in during construction. The graving dock no longer remains, but traces of it are revealed in the landscape. Salvaged and recycled cobblestones were inlaid within the pavement to permanently inscribe the graving dock's outline. Large concrete blocks used in ship repairs at the graving dock, called "chalks," were salvaged and reused to create a buffer between the linear park and IKEA's parking lot. Also maintained, and now illuminated at night, are several tall gantry cranes.[28]

Some may argue that, in the strictest sense, Todd Shipyard was not preserved, but it is hard to disregard the preservation-based components of Erie Basin Park. The park showcases the history of the place, while opening up waterfront access that had been inaccessible to the community for a century. As development inevitably continues to filter into the lost historic reaches of our urban environments, it is essential that we look to precedents like Erie Basin Park, where revitalization, preservation, and social well-being are intertwined.

Project Profile

COASTAL ISLAND RETREAT

Preserving Ecology through Residential Design

◀ Selective clearing reveals the beauty of native live oaks and opens up views to the distant marshland. Courtesy of ASLA. Photographer: Richard Felber.

◣ After three successive, controlled burns, a meadow is replanted in the clearing. Courtesy of ASLA. Photographer: James van Sweden.

▼ House and decking are raised to protect the sensitive ecosystem and accommodate changing tidal floodplain patterns. Courtesy of ASLA. Photographer: Richard Felber.

PROJECT OVERVIEW

Date: 2008

Type: Residential Design

Location: Spring Island, South Carolina

Firm: Oehme, van Sweden & Associates, Inc., Washington, DC

Awards: 2008 ASLA Professional Design Award of Honor

Web link to project: www.ovsla.com/ovsnews.htm

Each project is as unique as the individuals we work for and the sites we encounter. Coastal Island Retreat was special nonetheless; a project in which the architect and the landscape architect worked in tandem from the very beginning.

—SHEILA A. BRADY, FASLA[29]

Site Ecology

Contrary to the typical landscape of an American single-family home, Coastal Island Retreat capitalizes on ecological restoration and sustainability. Shelia Brady, the lead landscape architect with Oehme, van Sweden & Associates, Inc., explained that, "Despite the relatively large scale of this residential project, the landscape architectural and architectural interventions were few and the human impact on the land and its systems minimal."[30] The marshy site and surrounding context was at one time a rice plantation. The area is now a private community, whose intent focuses on preserving and sustaining the existing maritime forest.[31]

Since the site is within a fragile ecosystem, the community established special guidelines for development. In an effort to meet the *Habitat Review Guidelines* set forth by the community, Oehme, van Sweden & Associates, Inc. worked with staff naturalists on the island. These guidelines require a maintenance strategy that includes prescribed burns to regularly restore and regenerate the meadowlands.[32]

The plant palette, similar to all other aspects of the design, was selected based on the surrounding maritime forest. Some plants were relocated on site; others were selected based on their occurrence elsewhere on site and in the surrounding forests. Folk Land Management, a naturalist consultant, was hired to make recommendations regarding which areas should be cleared and which plants could be reintroduced.[33]

Residential Design

Residential projects may at the surface appear the easiest, but that is not the case. They vary drasti-cally, depending on the client, and often demand an intense site inventory and attention to detail. The Coastal Island Retreat landscape spans 65 acres and is a place greatly inspired by the sur-rounding environment. Several ecosensitive methods were implemented in an effort to preserve the ecological patterns and processes on-site. All of the surficial hard materials are pervious, such as gravel and pine straw. Hardwoods, used for the construction of the terraces, were reharvested and certified, and designed to blend into existing tones and colors.[34]

In regard to the architecture, a rainwater catchment system is built into the dwelling. It diverts water from the impervious rooftop into the meadowlands. The dwelling itself, designed by architects William McDonough + Partners, further promotes the idea of not tainting site systems. The elevated first floor stands 8 feet above the existing grade. This preserves wildlife habitat and provides a flex-ible space for the ever-changing tidal floodplain patterns.[35]

Challenges

The retreat has been described as an ecological and aesthetic gem, "reveal[ing] calming views of sky, grass, and water."[36] Creating this rich and diverse vegetative aesthetic was one of the greatest challenges for Oehme, van Sweden & Associates, Inc. In addition to selecting and planting vegeta-tion, the firm analyzed the large site to select special view corridors to enhance. The goals were to highlight certain plant species and to capitalize on distant vistas beyond the site's boundaries. Because vegetation is by far the most dynamic element of this landscape, it was essential for the landscape architects to find the precise balance between creating a jungle, in terms of density and variety, and a sanctuary, in terms of aesthetic and function.

Working with Clients

Clients have the ability to make or break a project, especially in residential design. In the case of Coastal Island Retreat, Oehme, van Sweden & Associates, Inc. had worked with this client on previ-ous projects and thus had established a good working relationship. However, throughout the life of the project, the designers continued to meet with the client at least once a month to review the design process and ideas.[37]

The client's overriding goal aligned with that of their neighbors—to preserve the lowland iden-tity of the site, rather than establish a series of lush gardens. Programmatic elements were deemed less important in the design, giving full focus to the experiential nature of the space. The client had studied and greatly appreciated Japanese gardens. They requested that the landscape architects incorporate the Japanese concept of *ma* (the harmony of light and dark) into the project. For this reason the end result is very Zenlike and minimalistic in appearance, encouraging the naturalistic beauty of the existing environment to emerge.[38]

Nested Scales: From Intimate Spaces to Expansive Wildlife Preserves

Landscape architects like to refer to the realm beyond a building's walls as our profession's domain. That covers a lot of ground—literally. The short explanation I often give to describe my profession to those outside the field is: We can design anything from a small, secluded meditative garden to thousands of acres of public lands, such as a national forest, and everything in between. As designers, planners, and managers of outdoor environments we landscape architects have the distinct privilege to be able to work at any number of scales, from a small children's "tot-lot," to helping plan and design entire new cities in countries around the world.

There are landscape architects who are captivated by the fine details of plant palettes and enjoy working with individuals to improve their private property. Others delight in working on projects that will be used by large numbers of people; for example, designing the amenities for a new city park. Still other landscape architects thrive at the neighborhood design scale, deciding where new roads, parks, schools, shopping areas, and housing should be placed, with a goal of creating a sustainable, walkable community setting. There also are landscape architects who prefer to work with corridors, to help establish connections. They create trail systems or enhance the riparian edges along a network of streams, for example. Some landscape architects direct their focus on preserving and enhancing large tracts of land for the benefit of wildlife and other natural resources, such as the protection of water quality.

A landscape architect may choose to specialize in one area or on a specific scale, whereas another prefers diversity, seeking project variety to ensure plentiful design opportunities. The point is, as a landscape architect you will have many choices for how and where you want to work—truly, thousands of opportunities from which to choose.

Consilience

KURT CULBERTSON, FASLA

Chairman of the Board

Design Workshop

Aspen, Colorado

Kurt Culberston (middle) in the Republic of Georgia for the Bakhmaro Area Recreational Study. Courtesy of Design Workshop.

〉 Why did you decide to pursue a career in landscape architecture?

I grew up in rural Louisiana spending every moment running through the woods. I originally thought I would study architecture because I loved to draw and design. However, when I went to Louisiana State University (LSU) I was underwhelmed by my architecture professors. My freshman year I took Introduction to Landscape Architecture, taught by Dr. Robert S. Reich ("Doc"). I had never seen someone so turned on about his profession. Over the next five years, I learned from Doc that landscape architecture is not a profession; it is a calling. I loved the breadth of

the profession, I loved the environmental and social purpose, and I loved its relationship to nature.

How and why did you choose the schools you attended to earn your degrees?

〉 For undergraduate school, I realized I bled "purple and gold." My parents went to LSU, as did much of my extended family. I was fortunate to find one of the best landscape architecture programs in the same place.

I also define my university education broadly. I learned a tremendous amount from the landscape architecture program, but also in student government, my fraternity, the rugby team, and volunteering for the crisis hotline. I can't urge students enough to drink in the entire university experience!

I also have a Master of Business Administration with an emphasis on real estate from Southern Methodist University in Dallas. I am a fierce believer in lifelong learning. I read about a book a week, on average, in a very wide range of topics. I emphasize to students and our staff that their education does not end with the receipt of their diploma; rather, they must commit to a process of lifelong learning.

How would you characterize the work of your office?

〉 We have tried to create a practice that realizes what we enjoy about the profession—its diversity. We believe that an ability to work at a planning scale can make you a better designer. In a similar way, we believe being a good designer can also make you a better planner.

At Design Workshop we have evolved a concept we call "Legacy Design." Edward O. Wilson used

High Desert community in Albuquerque, New Mexico. Photographer: D.A. Horchner. Courtesy of Design Workshop.

Digital terrain model used for public workshops in Flathead County, Montana. Courtesy of Design Workshop.

the term "consilience" to describe a coming to-gether of bodies of knowledge. Legacy Design is related in many ways to this notion. It is based on the premise that the best projects succeed environmentally, economically, artistically, and from a community perspective. We believe the true challenge is in synthesizing all of these elements into one solution.

What has been your most rewarding project to date?

❯ The nod for "most rewarding" goes to our work for the Albuquerque Academy and its wholly owned real estate development company, High Desert Investment Corporation. We have planned two master communities for this client, High Desert and Mariposa, in Albuquerque,

New Mexico. Both have been excellent models of sustainable development and were innovative on a national level at their time. They are highly valued within the community. Most important, their economic success has helped the operations of the Albuquerque Academy, an extraordinary private school, 40 percent of whose students are minorities. The design involved the collaborative participation of students and faculty.

How often do you involve the community and/or end users in the design process? In what way?

⟩ I would say not enough, but we are working at it. Consistent with the idea of Legacy Design, community is an essential part of the process. I have tried to learn from the work of Randy Hester, a good friend of the firm, and others with far more experience than I, to be mindful of the need for true community engagement.

One example was our master plan for Flathead County, Montana, which involved 170 public meetings of all kinds, surveys, and television and radio interviews over a 12-month period. We employed a wide variety of user engagement including such things as cognitive mapping, weighting of GIS factors based on public values, and visual preference surveys.

How do new technologies and more traditional approaches interface at your firm?

⟩ We have always been early adopters of technology, jumping very early into GIS and visual simulation. We continue to strive for new ways to innovate, and are fierce believers in the value of technology in a variety of forms, not just computers. We are also firmly committed to hand drawing, the construction of physical models, and other traditional visualization techniques. These offer different ways of seeing than a computer can provide.

Which aptitudes, traits, and skills do you see in most landscape architects?

⟩ The primary distinguishing feature is the ability to synthesize complex information from a variety of sources. In my experience, landscape architects are often team leaders because of their ability to see the points of view of many disciplines and bring them together in a meaningful way.

What tips can you offer someone regarding the job search process?

⟩ I tell students, "Include your BEST work in your portfolio; I know you can do worse!" Students often feel compelled to include every project they did in school. It is far better to show your very best work. Edit.

Explain what makes you special—what distinguishes you from your peers? If you can communicate your leadership, discipline, work ethic, and interpersonal skills, your odds of finding employment go up dramatically. Individuals who have been president of their sorority or fraternity, active in student government, or in volunteer organizations or their place of worship often turn out to be exceptional practitioners. Sadly, these experiences are often overlooked by candidates in communicating their qualifications.

What role can landscape architects take in making our world better?

⟩ Landscape architects have been present, and often leaders, from the very beginning of the environmental movement. Where the greatest need lies today is in issues of social justice and equity. I believe if we can help to lift up all people, we will simultaneously solve many of the planet's environmental challenges as well.

Sustainable Gardens

JAMES VAN SWEDEN, FASLA

Founding Principal

Oehme, van Sweden & Associates, Inc.

Washington, DC

James van Sweden (right) and Wolfgang Oehme review plans on-site. Courtesy of Oehme, van Sweden and Associates. Photographer: Volkmar Wentzel.

Why did you decide to pursue a career in landscape architecture?

❯ I have quite a varied career, starting with architecture, then city planning and urban design; finally I ended up designing gardens and building landscapes because I realized I had to build. The way for me to build was to get out and plant gardens and that's why I pursued a career in landscape architecture. We used to build all of our work ourselves—even all the digging. That's a great way to go through life, seeing results everyday.

How and why did you choose the school you attended to earn your degree?

❯ My first degree was in architecture. I became interested in landscape architecture and my professor suggested I study landscape architecture to get a handle on urban design. I did a year of graduate work at the University of Michigan. Then I decided I would go to Europe because I always wanted to explore my roots, which are in The Netherlands. Studying at the University of Delft really changed everything about my life. The Dutch are so liberal; my politics changed, and the way I looked at design and the land. The Netherlands have centuries of planning because land is very scarce.

Garden and landscape design in Mabley, New York. Courtesy of Oehme, van Sweden and Associates. Photographer: Richard Felber.

The Atlantic Pavilion, World War II Memorial, Washington, DC. Courtesy of Oehme, van Sweden and Associates. Photographer: Roger Foley.

How would you characterize the work of your office?

〉Our office is famous for a particular kind of landscape called the New American Garden. Wolfgang Oehme and I started doing so-called sustainable gardens 35 or so years ago; we called it low-maintenance. We're most famous for the way we use plants and perennials. These gardens are very interesting because they change dramatically with the seasons and they take very little water. It is natural, inspired by the American meadow and prairie.

Our work is at a whole range of scales. We've done hundreds of Georgetown (a historic neighborhood in DC) townhouse gardens—they're really outdoor living rooms—up to great estates on the ocean. We are just finishing an immense garden in Kiev, in the Ukraine. We did Oprah's farm in southern Indiana. I love going from designing, for instance, the World War II Memorial, to designing a small balcony on an apartment building. Moving from one scale to the other just in an afternoon is so satisfying and makes our design careers so interesting.

You are practicing into your seventies. Can you talk about longevity in the profession?

〉In some professions you are obsolete when you are 50, but in landscape architecture you just keep learning and getting better. I have back problems and problems walking. I'm sitting in a wheelchair but you can do landscape architecture in a wheelchair, and this is great! So that is certainly a positive part of the profession.

How often do you involve the community and/or end users in the design process?

〉We're always involving the community when we can, and I think the community is much more interested in the design process and being involved. It's very important to bring along the community. A few years ago we finished the World War II Memorial here on the Mall, and I'd never been through so many meetings. Finally, it all got ironed out and the memorial was built and almost everybody loves it, and it's working extremely well. It was worth all the trouble, as the design is definitely better due to that process.

Gardens of the Great Basin, Chicago Botanic Garden, Glencoe, Illinois. Courtesy of Oehme, van Sweden and Associates. Photographer: Richard Felber.

Who are some of the allied professionals you consult with?

❯ I am a great believer in collaboration. I think everybody learns. Because I'm an architect as well as a landscape architect, I get along well with architects. I always say I know how they think, and that's important. We work with engineers and fountain specialists. Landscape architecture is a very complicated field, incredibly complex, and nobody can know it all. So I believe in pulling people in who are experts in a particular field. One thing that makes our office work so well is that Wolfgang Oehme is a horticulturist and landscape architect, and I'm an architect and landscape architect. It's a kind of magical partnership because we bridge so many different disciplines.

When hiring a student for an internship or entry-level job, which aspects of their education do you find to be most important?

❯ We look for people who have a good design sense. We want to see a lot of drawings; and not only computer drawings, but also hand drawing, and any artwork they've done. This is the way we can tell that they have an aesthetic sense. We need people who understand the computer, and can work with it right away and have that talent. We are always interested if they know anything about plants or have worked in nurseries. If we find somebody who has plant knowledge, we will hire them immediately.

Working across Multiple Continents

GERDO AQUINO, ASLA

Managing Principal

SWA Group

Los Angeles, California

Gerdo Aquino in SWA Group's Los Angeles office.
Photographer: Goran Kosanovic. © 2007, SWA Group.

Why did you decide to pursue a career in landscape architecture?

❯ I started in architecture and was fascinated by the spatial consequences of buildings within a landscape. After two years in school, my fascination broadened to include the spaces outside the buildings, which led me to examine a larger scale and the larger systems that form the overall structure of a community, a city, a region.

How and why did you choose the schools you attended to earn your degrees?

❯ I attended the University of Florida for my BLA (undergraduate degree) and Harvard University

Graduate School of Design for my MLA (master's degree): Florida, because of its proximity to home and its reputation in the Southeast for architecture; Harvard because it has the most history and influence in the profession of landscape architecture.

How would you characterize the work of your office?

❯ SWA Group is a world leader in landscape architecture. As a firm of more than 170 professionals, our work stretches across multiple continents and addresses complex issues of watershed protection, land and resource conservation, preservation, infrastructure, housing, and open space creation. Individual SWA studios have a unique identity, partly due to their geographic locations but also due in larger part to the contribution of the professionals who work within the various offices, and the critical insights and points of view they offer. Approximately 130 of our staff are landscape architects/planners. Other professionals include CPAs (certified public accountants), photographers, graphic designers, and office managers.

What is your role in the office?

❯ I am the managing principal of SWA Los Angeles and Shanghai. In our Los Angles studio, we have a staff of 16 people, and 1 person full-time in Shanghai. In this role I oversee all aspects of professional practice—the work, marketing, promotional, outreach, administrative, design leadership, mentorship, and financial viability.

How often do you involve the community and/or end users in the design process? In what way?

❯ A certain percentage of our work is in the public realm. Public projects always involve the local constituents in an active outreach effort to gain their consensus. Some communities are passionate about the process of involvement and are as much a stakeholder in the final design as the landscape architects. City agencies often look to the leadership and experience of landscape architects to shepherd a project through, from beginning to end, and to bring the public along every step of the way.

What role do new technologies play in your design process?

❯ Technology is critical to the profession of landscape architecture. GIS (geographic information systems) are satellite-based software mapping systems that allow planners to assess thousands of acres of land via complex mapping software that digitally maps topography, vegetation, and waterways. Other technology, such as laser-cutting machines, are used in making three-dimensional models. Students of landscape architecture would be wise to learn three primary software programs: computer-aided drafting software such as AutoCAD for basic plan, section, and elevation drawings; 3D software such as SketchUp for visualization; and Adobe Photoshop for montage, graphic layouts, and presentations.

Zobon City Villa pedestrian overlook at reflecting pool, Pudong District, Shanghai, China. Photographer: Gerdo Aquino. © 2002, SWA Group.

Laser-cut model of Downtown Jebel Ali (Dubai), Zone 1, Central Plaza. Model Makers: SWA Group LA. © 2007, SWA Group.

Who are some of the allied professionals you work/consult with? What role do they play in the design process?

❯ Landscape architects do not work in isolation. The success of our work is contingent upon the involvement of many consultants such as architects, civil engineers, environmental engineers, ecologists, lighting designers, irrigation consultants, hydrologic engineers, transportation engineers, geotechnical engineers, and other specialists. Everyone has a specific role in any given project. Often, the landscape architect is the glue that holds the project together. It's the landscape that stretches across boundaries and ties places to places, buildings to buildings, water to drainage outlets, and people to various destinations.

When hiring a student for an internship or entry-level job, which aspects of their education do you feel are most important?

❯ It is important to have the ability to keep an open mind to the process of design. In other words, an intern/entry-level person is in an office to learn from whatever task is placed in front of them. They need to learn how to learn, in some cases, learning all over again.

What role can landscape architects take in making our world better?

❯ We can take a leadership role in addressing sustainability at all scales and all levels of detail.

PPG Plaza, located in the central business district of downtown Pittsburgh, Pennsylvania. Photographer: Tom Fox. © 2003, SWA Group.

New Ways to Engage the Landscape

MIKYOUNG KIM

Principal

mikyoung kim design

Brookline, Massachusetts

Mikyoung Kim and a colleague in her Brookline, Massachusetts, studio. © 2008, mikyoung kim design.

Why did you decide to pursue a career in landscape architecture?

> I came to landscape architecture from the fine arts and music. I studied piano performance at Oberlin Conservatory while developing an interest in sculpture and art history in the college. The idea of public engagement that is a natural part of music and performance drew me to landscape architecture and the public arena. The aspect of sculptural design interfaced with natural materials and cycles drew me to study landscape architecture in graduate school.

How and why did you choose the school you attended to earn your degree?

> I attended a summer program at Harvard and found the focus of the program was a perfect confluence of my interest in environmental art and social issues in public space. After having a positive experience, I decided to continue studies in Harvard's Graduate School of Design. Another reason for going to Harvard was my ability to take visual arts classes at MIT and create a hybrid education between design and the visual arts.

How would you characterize the work of your office?

> Our work spans a very wide range of design, from sculptural installations to citywide planning. In

Sculptural "FLEXfence" at Farrar Pond residence, Lincoln, Massachusetts. © 2007, Charles Mayer.

Perspective of outdoor lab and rain garden, Stamford Environmental Magnet School, Stamford, Connecticut. © 2008, mikyoung kim design.

both, we address design innovation and problem-solving issues—ultimately that is what differentiates design from the fine arts. While creating plazas and gardens, we look at the aesthetic vision of the project, and the safety, code, and human use requirements.

The smaller-scale work we do focuses on exploring new materials and creating innovative landscapes—our smallest project is a kaleidoscope lighting project on the Potomac River in Washington DC. In our larger projects we address structural and systemic issues. In one example, we look at how a mile-long streetscape in Chapel Hill can develop a cohesive plan over a period of 20 years.

What is the size of your office and what is your role?

❭ I am the principal of the office and oversee all design work and implementation of the design. I am also involved in all of the interviewing processes for jobs and the financial aspect of maintaining the office. We have eight designers, one accountant, and one computer tech staff member.

How often do you involve the community and/or end users in the design process? In what way?

❭ Each project is different; in some, we start off by meeting the community and developing initial design directions with them before coming back and brainstorming at our office in Boston. In other work, we are brought in to create a strong vision and present our ideas to community groups after we have finalized the concept design. In all of our work, we are interested in learning how the public interfaces with the site currently and helping them understand new ways to engage their landscape through our work.

What role do new technologies play in your design process?

❯ Technology plays a very big role. We are constantly trying to push and find innovation in every project we work on—it is the spark that keeps this profession interesting. In landscape architecture, one is constantly working with, or sometimes against, time. All materials degrade, evolve, and transform. We are interested in how new materials and lighting technologies can be integrated into the landscapes we design.

Who are some of the allied professionals you consult with? What role do they play in the design process?

❯ We usually work with structural engineers, civil engineers, architects, urban planners, lighting designers, soil scientists, horticulturalists, and fountain designers. All of these professionals are part of the dialogue in our design process. Usually we develop an initial concept design for our project and then start to bring in these consultants to aid in the realization of this vision.

What tips can you offer to someone regarding the job search process?

❯ Clearly communicate your strengths. Listen well when you are interviewing and develop a strong dialogue with the team.

Urban park and fountain celebrate the source of an underground canal, ChonGae Canal Park, financial district, Seoul, Korea. Taeoh Kim Photography.

What role can landscape architects take in making our world better?

❯ Landscape architects can act to create a more sustainable environment—teaching stewardship of the natural systems during this age of global warming. Landscape architects also create environments that are memorable and shape the public imagination.

Project Profile

METRO SKATE PARK

Innovative Public Recreation

▼ Drawings showing overview
of entire park design. Courtesy of
space2place design, inc.

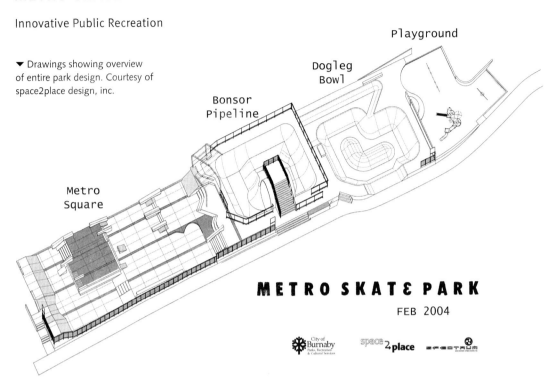

Playground

Dogleg
Bowl

Bonsor
Pipeline

Metro
Square

METRO SKATE PARK

FEB 2004

City of Burnaby
Parks, Recreation
& Cultural Services

space2place

◀ Local youth participate in workshop
to design the new skate park.
Courtesy of space2place design, inc.

▲ The Dogleg Bowl area at Metro Skate Park,
Burnaby, British Columbia, Canada. Courtesy of
space2place design, inc.

PROJECT OVERVIEW

Date: 2004

Type: Recreation Design

Location: Burnaby, British Columbia, Canada

Firm: space2place design inc., Vancouver, British Columbia

Awards: 2007 CPRA Award of Excellence for Innovation

Web link to project: www.space2place.com/public_bonsor.html

An engaging design process coupled with environmental construction materials has made Metro Skate Park innovative, successful, and unique.

—2007 CPRA AWARDS AND RECOGNITION PROGRAM[39]

Skate Park Design

In the past few decades, skateboarding has grown dramatically in popularity across North America. Due to this trend, cities and towns without skate parks have suffered. Landscape elements, particularly low walls within public spaces, have in many cases been destroyed from unanticipated use by skaters. Initially, as parks and public space faced destruction, alterations were made to those landscape elements so that they would not appeal to skaters.

More recently, landscape architects have taken a different approach to resolve this issue. The potential of skate parks has been recognized for their capability to function as areas for active play and socialization. Today, skate parks are emerging in cities and towns across the country, providing durable environments for skaters to practice while encouraging intergenerational interaction.

Metro Skate Park, located in Burnaby, British Columbia, is an example of a recently designed, successful skate park. It is conveniently located within Bonsor Park, close to several skytrain stops, allowing young visitors to easily access the park via public transportation.[40]

Process

Space2place, the landscape architecture firm that designed Metro Skate Park, worked closely with industry consultants and local skateboarding youth to understand the keys to successful skate park design. The firm held a series of workshops with community children from a local elementary school. The young students were given modeling clay and colored markers to develop sketches and 3D models of their visions for the skate park. Additionally, the firm asked students broad questions about the skate park, such as: How would they get there? What would they like in the design? What kinds of space do they enjoy? The workshop results gave space2place a better understanding of the user group for which they were designing, and helped the firm gauge which items were most important for inclusion in the design.[41] Another important aspect of involving local youth in the design is that they will then develop a sense of ownership and pride in the facility. This helps with maintenance, in that people tend to respect something more if they were involved in its creation.

Design and Materials

In terms of the park's design, the site is divided into three areas: the Dogleg Bowl, Bonsor Pipeline, and Metro Square. Each space caters to the varying needs of skaters, from beginner to highly advanced. Additionally, the skate park provides areas to rest and socialize, as well as walkways and viewing areas. The space is accommodating not only to the skaters, but also to others within the community who enjoy watching the free public theatrics.[42]

While the design of Metro Skate Park is beneficial to the community from a social and cultural standpoint, it also considers the environment through the use of ecofriendly materials. Since the project is a skate park, the dominant material needed for its construction was concrete. High-volume fly ash concrete was used as a replacement for standard concrete. This material is considered stronger, has a smoother finish, and ages better than standard concrete. The main difference between fly ash concrete and standard concrete is that fly ash concrete has a variable amount of recycled fly ash within the concrete.[43] Additionally, both high-volume fly ash concrete and the additive implemented, Hard-Cem, were used to minimize carbon dioxide emissions.[44]

Metro Skate Park is an exciting example of how landscape architecture expands far beyond the realm of traditional park or garden design.

Project Profile

NEW TERRAIN FOR THE NORTH LAKE REGION OF CHONGMING ISLAND

Sustainable Strategies

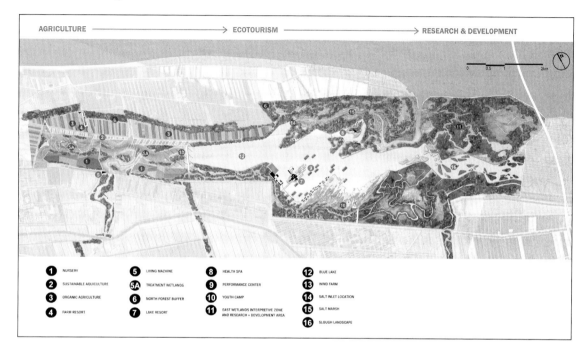

AGRICULTURE ————————————→ ECOTOURISM ————————————→ RESEARCH & DEVELOPMENT

1 NURSERY	**5** LIVING MACHINE	**8** HEALTH SPA	**12** BLUE LAKE
2 SUSTAINABLE AQUICULTURE	**5A** TREATMENT WETLANDS	**9** PERFORMANCE CENTER	**13** WIND FARM
3 ORGANIC AGRICULTURE	**6** NORTH FOREST BUFFER	**10** YOUTH CAMP	**14** SALT INLET LOCATION
4 FARM RESORT	**7** LAKE RESORT	**11** EAST WETLANDS INTERPRETIVE ZONE AND RESEARCH + DEVELOPMENT AREA	**15** SALT MARSH
			16 SLOUGH LANDSCAPE

▲ The master plan illustrates how the landscape structure provides an economic framework. Courtesy of ASLA. Illustration: SWA Group, Los Angeles.

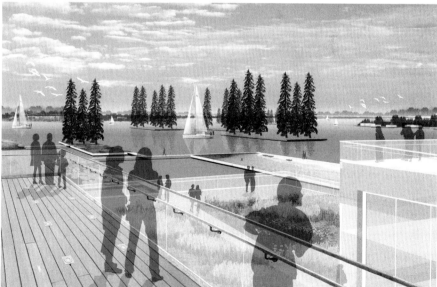

▶ Proposed view of coastal wetlands, part of the large-scale landscape development. Courtesy of ASLA. Illustration: SWA Group, Los Angeles.

The creation of coastal wetlands and upland habitats reintroduces globally important landscapes. Courtesy of ASLA. Illustration: SWA Group, Los Angeles.

PROJECT OVERVIEW

Date: 2004

Type: Analysis and Planning

Location: Shanghai, China

Client: Shanghai Urban Planning Administrative Bureau

Firm: SWA Group, Los Angeles California

Awards: 2008 ASLA Professional Design Award of Honor for Analysis and Planning

[A] landscape oasis [to] serve these urban pods and…allow people to get away and get out of the urban context…and…to provide mitigation for all of the pollution that's going to be happening within these urban pods.

—Patrick Curran, SWA[45]

Large-Scale Sustainable Development

New Terrain for the North Lake Region of Chongming Island is a large-scale master plan project that aims to create an environmentally sensitive redevelopment strategy for 34.5 square kilometers (13.3 square miles) of land. Chongming Island is 20 minutes to the north of Shanghai by high-speed rail, and an hour outside the city by car. It is at the crux of urban growth, with the development of several new urban centers within a 350-square-kilometer (135-square-mile) radius of the island, each one accommodating up to a million residents. Given this context, SWA's approach to the project was to provide a "landscape oasis," one that would consider adjacent development and aim to improve air quality, water quality, and quality of life. It will serve as a nearby point of respite for the surrounding urban dwellers.

The approach of the firm is manifested through a series of design components. These include a farm resort and agriculture research facility, an organic and sustainable agriculture operation, an aquaculture operation, a biological wastewater treatment facility, a 20-million kWh wind farm, a saltwater lake and lake resort, and a wetlands interpretive zone. These design components exemplify a contemporary self-sustaining landscape and, in turn, work to educate visitors on a unique living system in the midst of rampant development.

Landscape as an Economic Generator

As we continue to hear about increased development in China, it is surprising to find a project of this scale that has such little urban development. However, since development is minimal, the landscape must act as the primary financial generator. Due to the surrounding urban context, the project's capability to treat and reuse wastewater from nearby cities is extraordinarily beneficial. In terms of location, the site borders the Yangtze River. Water in the river is being polluted upstream from construction and development; therefore, the potential for this site to treat it and return it to the larger water system, with a higher water quality, is tremendous. Additionally, the implementation of wind and solar energy generators, which can offer more than the energy needs of Chongming Island, all contributed to give the client and community further incentive to embrace the project.

The landscape also acts as an economic generator in terms of agriculture. Prior to the project, a portion of the land in the floodplain was used for agriculture. When the levies and dams were removed, the land became inundated. While rice can no longer be harvested, a new type of farming is possible: wetland farming. This can create more jobs for the community, as well as potential products that can further contribute to the local economy.

International Work and Collaboration

Given that the project is in Shanghai, accessibility to the site and project details were considerably more complex. The team visited the site three to four times in a six-month time span, but the project would not have been possible without the help of others. SWA has several office locations (Sausalito, Laguna Beach, Houston, Dallas, San Francisco, Los Angeles, and Shanghai), so while the project and team were based in the Los Angeles office, Koi Chi Ma of the Shanghai office also worked on the project. Her location enabled her to regularly visit the site and meet with the client. Additionally, in terms of expertise, EOS Ecology, an ecology team based in New Zealand, helped SWA gauge an understanding of the native plant species, aquatic species, and edge conditions.

Aside from accessibility, working abroad sometimes raises other challenges. Within the United States, it is relatively easy to gather information pertaining to geographic regions or site-specific conditions. China, however, has a much different government system, making information gathering a more difficult and time-consuming process. Conversely, in terms of design and strategies for development, the rules and restrictions abroad are, in most cases, not nearly as strict as in the United States. So, at the same time working abroad causes some problems, it also provides rare opportunities for design innovation.[46]

Green Design: Sustainability, Biodiversity, and Recycled Materials

The notion of creating designs with environmental impacts in mind—so-called green design—is not new to landscape architects. Designing with respect for nature and ecological systems, while balancing human needs and desires, has always been a hallmark of the landscape architecture profession. What is new is the growing recognition by the general public and government officials that green design is important, that how we design with respect to the earth and its resources has merit; more, it can be said to be a global imperative. Thanks to the profession's history and long-term experience in sustainable design techniques, the landscape architecture profession today stands poised to be at the forefront of the expanding green movement.

Environmental factors are always key criteria in a landscape architect's work. These factors continue to expand, and now include such undertakings as designing green roofs, accessing the embodied energy in the materials selected for use in a design, considering the viability of reusing materials found on-site, and selecting elements for use in the design that have been manufactured from recycled materials or produced in a nonpolluting way. Understanding the full range and value of services derived from natural processes is another aspect of green design that is drawing attention. In sum, designing to enhance the effectiveness of these ecosystem services and showcasing their aesthetic appeal illustrates how green design will continue to be an integral feature of the practice of landscape architecture.

Urban Ecological Design

MIKE FAHA, ASLA, LEED AP

Founding Principal

GreenWorks, PC

Portland, Oregon

Landscape architect Mike Faha. GreenWorks Landscape Architects.

Why did you decide to pursue a career in landscape architecture?

〉 I appreciated the profession's blending of the arts and sciences. When I took an introductory class on landscape architectural theory from Chuck DeDeurwaeder, at Oregon State University, I found my calling: a blending of applied art and science that I knew would challenge me for a lifetime.

How and why did you choose the school you attended for your degree?

〉 I was a military dependent and moved frequently all over the country and overseas (16 moves in 17 years; 5 high schools in 4 years). I decided to attend Oregon State University, where both my parents attended, and I could be near both sets of grandparents. I did not discover landscape architecture until the summer after my freshmen year, when I studied the course catalog from cover to cover. I was also introduced to a new notion about statewide land-use planning in my intro to LA course, and I have been hooked on Oregon's progressive approach to natural resource protection and environmental quality ever since.

How would you characterize the work of your office?

〉 GreenWorks is a full-service private office that plans and designs individual sites, neighborhoods, communities, and regions. We are recognized for our knowledge and experience in urban ecological design, wide-ranging economic development project experience, and our focus on creating livable communities under current land use mandates for increasing urban density. In addition to sustainable design, we aim to work in a sustainable manner. GreenWorks encourages healthy, inexpensive, and fun ways to get to work.

How often do you involve the community and/or end users in the design process? In what way?

〉 Frequently we work with local neighborhoods and community groups to review project goals and concept alternatives and have them play a role in selecting preferred alternatives. We do this for community parks, downtown redevelopment, and public streetscape improvement projects.

◀ Tanner Springs Park, Portland, Oregon. Designed by GreenWorks, PC, and Atelier Dreiseitl. GreenWorks Landscape Architects.

▼ Photo visualization of University of California–Davis West Village. Designed by GreenWorks, PC, with Moore Ruble Yudell, and SWA Group. GreenWorks Landscape Architects.

What role do new technologies play in your design process?

❯ In our everyday work environment, digital technology has increased our productivity at all levels of design. Most recently, 3D technology has become an important tool for conceptualization and will play a stronger role in construction documentation.

Which aptitudes, traits, and skills do you see in most landscape architects?

❯ Landscape architects are typically curious about the world around them and how to make it better. They are creative and have the imagination to envision change. They must have good communication skills in writing, speaking, and drawing.

▶ Green roof on Beranger Condominiums, Gresham, Oregon. GreenWorks Landscape Architects.

Ecosystem Service Design

JACOB BLUE, MS, RLA, ASLA

Landscape Architect/Ecological Designer

Applied Ecological Services, Inc.

Brodhead, Wisconsin

Landscape architect Jay Blue doing a site assessment. Photographer: Lee Marlowe. © 2009 Applied Ecological Services, Inc.

How and why did you choose the schools you attended to earn your degrees?

❯ I didn't really choose the school, but I benefited by the school that was selected for me, so I got lucky from an undergraduate position. For graduate school, I went after the program. My graduate degree is in ecology so I targeted two programs I felt had the strongest ecology degrees in the nation.

Which aspect of your education had the greatest influence on you?

❯ Two things had a great influence on me. One was the design process we learned at Penn State. It focuses in on helping people understand what design really means and how you take these ideas and turn them into 3D tangible spaces. The other influence Penn State played was that it got me interested in natural resources. It ultimately led me to a postgraduate degree in ecology and understanding how natural systems really work as a whole, as a group.

How would you characterize the work of your office?

❯ The type of work we do is ecosystem service design. When we are charged to participate in a project, we conduct a natural resources inventory, or an NRI, where we evaluate the site's ecological conditions. From there we develop what we call a program suitability plan. We want to help identify whether the program proposed for the site fits the site's constraints. And very often it doesn't. So we do the critical analyses up front, and then the output results in maximizing the protection or restoration of ecosystem services of a site. The intent is that our client ends up with a better product because it has had less impact on the planet, and it also typically costs less money because they have reduced their construction costs.

We work on something as small as a rain garden, which might be only 200 square feet, to a project as large as 2,000 acres. As the landscape architects, we are involved in projects near our home base in the Midwest, to Philadelphia, Texas, and India. We also have projects in Costa Rica, so we are charged with understanding ecosystems all over the world.

Prairie landscape behind the main offices of Applied Ecological Services, Brodhead, Wisconsin. © 2009 Applied Ecological Services, Inc.

What is the size of your office—how many landscape architects and other professionals?

❯ The office I work in is the corporate headquarters, which also has a contracting and nursery division. In our organization as a whole, we have about 150 permanent employees. We have landscape architects, GIS (geographic information systems) specialists, cartographers, stormwater engineers, and ecologists. We have three licensed landscape architects and four we call ecological designers, which is the title for someone who hasn't passed his or her LARE (Landscape Architecture Registration Exam) yet.

What is the most exciting aspect of your work?

❯ The projects we work on are cutting-edge. We are part of a team that's solving some of the most interesting problems that are out there from a design perspective, like free petroleum in soils—how do you control that? Or maximizing carbon sequestration, or starting to look at setting up really large carbon banking projects; and things like that.

What is a BMP?

❯ A lot of BMPs, best management practices, tend to be related to stormwater; that seems to be where the bulk of the research has been to date, although it's not necessarily a stormwater-only type of idea. A BMP, for example, would be to take your corporate headquarters and convert 25 acres of mowed lawn into prairie or something like that, which has much lower maintenance costs and can provide greater habitat, aesthetic value, and also carbon sequestration. A stormwater-related BMP might be something as simple as a rain garden in someone's yard.

When hiring a student for an internship or entry-level job, which aspects of their education do you find to be most important?

> In their portfolio, do they demonstrate they understand design? I remember a lot of portfolios where the student got lost in the concept; the concept never became more than iconic, and that icon maybe was carried too far, and I could see they probably didn't quite get the design process. It's important that they understand the principles of grading design. We are going to give students an opportunity to do grading design here, and they are going to have me looking over their shoulder and helping them understand how to do grading better. A strong portfolio is key, and it should be a mix of stuff. We want to see that they can render drawings by hand, but we want to see that they can do AutoCAD and Photoshop, too.

What role can landscape architects take in making our world better?

> Landscape architects can take a stronger stand on understanding that we don't have to accept bad design, which can be one of two things: poor design technique or poor understanding of the existing ecosystem services. As a profession, we have gotten the back of our wrists slapped a little when the architects beat us to the punch with LEED. So landscape architects need to take a stronger role; and they have to some degree—ASLA is doing

The use of native plants at a private residence. © 2009 Applied Ecological Services, Inc.

that. Landscape architects have to take a stronger role in identifying what good design is about. It's about preserving farmland where appropriate and stopping development when it shouldn't happen; and it's about championing development where it should take place. We can play a larger role in helping the public in general, and our sister professions, understand the responsibilities we have from a design position.

Environmentally Sensitive Economic Work

TOM LIPTAN, ASLA

City of Portland Bureau of Environmental Services

Sustainable Stormwater Management Program

Portland, Oregon

Landscape architect Tom Liptan giving a tour of Portland Green Streets. Courtesy of Stuart P. Echols and Eliza Pennypacker, Penn State University.

Why did you decide to pursue a career in landscape architecture?

❭ I became a landscape architect by accident. I did not hear the term "landscape architecture" until I was 24 years old. I had a job at the City of Orlando Florida Parks and Forestry Department as an apprentice draftsperson. I always loved drafting and drawing. I thought, "Wow, I wish I had known this when I was high school because I would have pur-

sued a career in landscape architecture." It struck me this was very coincidental because at the same time I had become a Buddhist, and that philosophy teaches the interconnectedness of everything. I wanted to go back to school, but due to personal circumstances—the single parent of a 12-month-old son—I could not. So I decided that since I was an apprentice at this, I would stick with the City of Orlando and get as much training as I could and then pursue a more formal education later.

As it turned out, I was so interested in it I studied on my own. One of the first books I read was *Design with Nature* by Ian McHarg, and it was fascinating. I continued my personal education by studying on my own as well as learning anything I could from the various landscape architects I would run into. I became a sponge. I never did make it back to college. When I moved to Oregon, I took the exam for licensure and I became the first landscape architect in the state to pass the exam without a college degree of any kind. I had to work for 12 or so years under a landscape architect to be eligible to sit for the exam. It is not necessarily the route I would recommend, although for some people it might be the best way to go.

How would you characterize the work of your office?

❭ I work for the City of Portland, and I am in a design group, which I would characterize as environmentally sensitive economic work. I work for a city agency that is trying to better manage stormwater, but at the same time, we are also trying to produce numerous other benefits associated with that, such as enhancing parks, reducing the urban heat island effect, reducing energy consumption, and creating jobs.

Daylighted stream runs through the Headwaters development project, Portland, Oregon. Courtesy of Stuart P. Echols and Eliza Pennypacker, Penn State University.

What is size of your office and what is your role?

❭ The Bureau of Environmental Services has more than 500 people. Within that, our group, the Sustainable Stormwater Group, has 12 staff members. Of those, five are registered landscape architects. The others are environmental science majors, planners, a civil engineer, and a horticulturalist.

My position is what's called an environmental specialist—I'm like a senior design nerd. I manage projects that relate to our mission of addressing watershed issues and stormwater. But associated with that, we have a broader prospective of trying to enhance the livability of the city. So, I do all kinds of things related to that. What's been really good about this as a place to work is that there has been a lot of latitude to explore areas that might help address the problems.

What is the most exciting aspect of your work?

❭ When we make a breakthrough. Just to give you an idea: I had heard about ecoroofs or green

roofs in 1990. I started actually gathering serious information about them in 1994. I built my home garage ecoroof in 1996, and it wasn't until somewhere around 1998 when one of the city commissioners said, "I'm interested in this ecoroof idea you guys have been talking about." It was eight years, and for me, it was this watershed moment. It doesn't always take eight years, but making those breakthroughs is exciting.

What has been your most rewarding project to date?

❭ Headwaters is a project where a stream was daylighted. I did very little design, but I did have influence in the whole project coming about. It was a 3-acre site, and the creek was in a pipe underneath the site. The site was being redeveloped. The developer had a choice about rebuilding the pipe and leaving the creek in the pipe—the City did not require daylighting the creek. He chose to daylight the creek and decided it would run through his development. The City said, "If you daylight your creek, we will daylight the creek in the right-of-

Artist weir as part of stormwater management, adjacent to Headwaters, Portland, Oregon. Courtesy of Stuart P. Echols and Eliza Pennypacker, Penn State University.

way." For us to do that, we had to remove a street; we took it out and we put in the creek. It was a wonderful private/public partnership. Headwaters also has ecoroofs, stormwater planters, and porous pavement. It has almost everything you hear about in terms of low-impact development on this one project. It did cost him more money, but it turns out his property is the highest-valued property in the area now. This relates to our goal of connecting environment and economics.

You advocate "thinking outside the box" as part of the design process. Can you explain?

❯ The "box" represents accepted conventions. Sometimes the box is okay; but I think you have to step out of it, look at it, and then decide whether it is good. For example in the Headwaters project, who removes public streets? That just doesn't happen very often. I asked the question, "Do we need that street? And everybody said check with

Transportation (another city department). We asked, and they said, "Of course we need the street." But I asked again: Do we really need that street? And they said, "You know what, we don't really like that street and if it wasn't there, that would be okay as long as the intersection over here was improved." It's a matter asking good questions by getting out of the box and looking for other ways to do it.

What tips can you provide to someone regarding the job search process?

❯ Persistence, endlessly applied persistence. And volunteer. If you volunteer, you can start meeting people and networking. Then it's a matter of going around and visiting all the design firms. When I moved here, I would make the circuit. Portland's not a really big city, so I would hit everybody and then I'd just go back and touch base with everybody again. It was three months before I got a job, but eventually I got hired because of my management skills.

Project Profile

NE SISKIYOU GREEN STREET

Sustainable Stormwater Retrofits

▲ Portion of parking lane removed and
converted into landscaped curb extension.
Courtesy of ASLA. Photographer: Kevin
Robert Perry.

▶ Checkdams made of packed earth and
river rock slow and retain stormwater runoff.
Courtesy of ASLA. Photographer: Kevin
Robert Perry.

Illustration of planting scheme given to neighbors during the public outreach process. Courtesy of ASLA. Photographer: Kevin Robert Perry.

PROJECT OVERVIEW

Date: 2003

Type: Infrastructure/Environmental Design

Location: Portland, Oregon

Client: Sustainable Stormwater Management Program, City of Portland, Oregon

Firm: Kevin Robert Perry, ASLA, Portland, Oregon

Awards: 2007 ASLA Professional General Design Honor Award

[T]his is a great example of stormwater management in residential settings. It gains a lot of environmental mileage for very little and sets a prototype for designers, policymakers, and neighborhoods.

—2007 PROFESSIONAL AWARDS JURY COMMENTS[47]

Catalyst for Change

The cities of Portland and Seattle have played important roles as leaders in the recent sustainable stormwater design movement. As Portland's Willamette River continued to face pollution from urban runoff, the City searched for innovative stormwater catchment solutions. In 2003, the City of Portland's Environmental Services Sustainable Management Team initiated the NE Siskiyou Green Street project, in an effort to evaluate various methods and techniques for stormwater management. Kevin Robert Perry was selected as the lead landscape architect for the project.[48]

First of Its Kind

NE Siskiyou Green Street is the first retrofit of an existing street in the effort to take a more sustainable approach to stormwater management. The 80-year-old street was transformed from a typical suburban residential street into a major collector of storm event runoff. Portions of the street were demolished on each side to make way for two vegetated curb extensions.[49] Rather than traditional stormwater inlets into piping, the planted curb extensions create a point at which the runoff can infiltrate back into the soil.

Because it was the first of its kind, finding a good location was key. The low-traffic flow typical of a residential setting made the design possible. This meant that changes to the streetscape would not affect traffic patterns. At 28 feet in width, the two extensions narrowed the road to 14 feet in width, for a length of 50 feet.[50] This narrowing of the street also serves a "traffic calming" function—slowing vehicle speeds at the intersection.

How It Works

Rather than using storm drains to capture polluted runoff, the NE Siskiyou Green Street retrofit relies on curb cuts and a vegetated area that is lower than the adjacent road surface. Stormwater from the surrounding 10,000 square feet of impervious surfaces flows to where the edge of the curb and street meet. The water runs along the curb until it hits the curb extensions (each one measuring 50 feet in length and 7 feet in width). As the water enters the vegetative curb extension, by way of an 18-inch curb cut, it encounters a string of three stone checkdams. These checkdams decrease the speed of the stormwater flow and provide water storage for various levels of storm events. The checkdams and vegetation then work to help infiltrate 3 inches of stormwater each hour back into the ground. The stormwater system treats nearly 225,000 gallons of street runoff annually.[51]

This complex process is visible only during and following a rainfall, therefore small interpretive signs educate neighborhood visitors about the system. The signs are placed facing the sidewalks, within the vegetated area.[52]

A Streetscape Model

NE Siskiyou Green Street has served, and will continue to act, as a model for future residential street retrofits because of its expedient construction, affordable cost, and secure maintenance strategy. In October 2003, construction crews in the City of Portland built the project in two weeks. Moreover, the total fee for the curb extension retrofits was $1.83 a square foot; about $20,000 total.[53]

The maintenance strategy has two parts. For the initial two years, from 2003 to 2005, the retrofits were maintained by Portland Parks and Recreation, to nurture the establishment of the vegetation. After this two-year period, the neighborhood residents agreed to partner with the city in the maintenance responsibilities.[54]

The NE Siskiyou Green Street retrofit is minimal, efficient, and affordable. The community acceptance and appreciation for the project has resulted in a waiting list of residents in the City of Portland who would like a similar system installed on their streets. The design has educated the community, inspired landscape architecture and engineering students and practitioners to think creatively about green solutions, and has led to the application of many other retrofits on existing streets throughout the Northwest United States.

Systems Thinking: Natural, Social, Political, Infrastructural

A critical part of a landscape architect's training is the development of holistic thinking skills. Landscape architects realize that no site is isolated—everything is interconnected. These interconnections occur across a continuum of time and space, and at multiple levels. These are characterized as *systems*, which may include:

- Human/social
- Hydrology/natural processes
- Cultural/natural history
- Infrastructure/utilities
- Transportation/circulation
- Political/regulatory
- Visual/spatial setting

To comprehend the complexity of the issues and opportunities associated with a site or a project, landscape architects study and organize the information in relation to the various component systems. Initially, a project may seem overwhelming, but by looking at its individual components and then considering how these overlap and interact, the task becomes more manageable. This approach also makes it possible to weight the various factors and systems for the purpose of assigning priorities; it also helps to ensure that all the parts are understood separately as well as their contribution to the whole.

Throughout the design or planning process, landscape architects will regularly move back and forth across the continuum of each system, as well as between the various systems. It is a push-pull process that seeks to balance the multiple factors toward achieving the desired outcome. This is both challenging and exciting, and the richness that emerges from responding to all systems is evident in a successful result. A full recognition of the role of all the systems produces designs and plans that exhibit an appropriateness and connection to place and to its larger context. More and more often, that larger context is considered to be a global one. There is increasing recognition that the accumulation of what occurs, even on the smallest sites, has consequences well beyond the site, or even regional boundaries. Many believe that addressing the issue of global climate change must be an integral component of thoughtful design on each and every site. A saying from the 1970s captures the idea perfectly: "Think globally. Act locally."

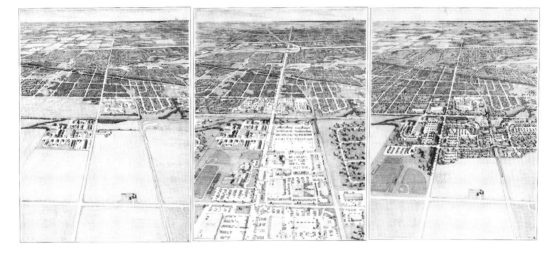

Three aerial perspective drawings of existing conditions, along with typical and recommended future development scenarios for New Lenox, Illinois. Regional Planning & Design: Dodson Associates, Ltd., with Tony Hiss. Illustrator: Jack Werner.

Designing Systems on the Land

BARBARA DEUTSCH, ASLA, ISA

Associate Director

BioRegional North America (One Planet Communities)

Washington, DC

Landscape architect Barbara Deutsch.

Why did you decide to pursue a career in landscape architecture?

❭ My first degree was in business, by default, because I didn't know what I wanted to do, but I like working with people. I went to work for IBM for almost 10 years as a systems engineer. As I became more environmentally aware, I discovered new urbanism. I began thinking about architecture, but several people suggested landscape architecture, if I wanted to design communities and really solve the complex environmental issues we face today. I got a master's in landscape architecture, so now

instead of designing computer systems, I'm designing systems on the land. I love what I do and I've been enriched in more ways than I could have imagined.

How and why did you choose the school you attended to earn your degree?

❭ My second degree is a Master of Landscape Architecture from the University of Washington in Seattle. I chose that school primarily because the department focused on urban ecological design, which suited my interest in working in cities and working with people.

How would you characterize the work of your organization?

❭ My organization is a nonprofit, based in London, and I'm its first employee in the United States. I would characterize the work as landscape planning. We have a key program called One Planet Living. We're aiming to design communities and cities that utilize one planet level of resources. It's all based on ecological footprints. Right now in Europe they're operating at three-plus planets; in North America we are at five-plus planets. But we only have one planet. We work with developers or cities to come up with strategies for how to implement our 10 design guidelines.

What is your role in the office?

❭ I'm the associate director for the One Planet DC Program and my job is to create a One Planet Community here, and make Washington, DC, a One Planet City. I am working to build partnerships to make it happen. I feel like I'm doing a lot of marketing to sell the program. This is a start-up business; a start-up organization.

A green roof in springtime, at 1425 K Street, Washington, DC. Courtesy of Barbara Deutsch.

Rendering of Sonoma Mountain Village Town Square in Rohnert Park, California, illustrates aspects of sustainable lifestyles. Courtesy of BioRegional North America and its One Planet Communities Program.

What has been your most rewarding project to date?

❯ It was very rewarding to put the first green roof on a commercial building here in DC. The really rewarding part was that we partnered with a non-profit, DC Greenworks, as part of a green-collar jobs training program. We trained 12 at-risk youth in how to build green roofs. There was so much interest generated from our demonstration project that DC Greenworks was able to employ several youth, at least part-time, for the year. Casey Trees, where I used to work, was a tenant of the building and helped to acquire $60,000 in grants for the project.

Who are some of the allied professionals you consult with? What role do they play in your process?

❭ A key part of our method is to have a charette process with the developer and the master planning team. The professionals we work with are real estate, finance, and development consultants who also understand sustainability and can speak the real estate finance language with the developers. We've worked with different energy companies, in different technologies, whether they be geothermal or using biomass. Some of these are standard operating procedure in Europe. Because my organization is based in London, we have access to consultants who are experts in those technical solutions.

Which aptitudes, traits, and skills do you see in most landscape architects?

❭ First is systems thinking—being able to understand natural processes, resources, people, and places, and then optimize for all of them, to meet all objectives. Also, being able to communicate technical information in a friendly, easy-to-understand manner, whether it be verbally or graphically. And being able to work with people is essential, as it is in many fields. A love of travel is good, too. Since becoming a landscape architect, I have traveled more and in more enriching ways than in my wildest dreams.

When hiring a student for an internship or entry-level job, which aspects of their education do you find to be most important?

❭ I look for their critical thinking ability, their ability to resolve issues through form, and to be consistent with their concept. And being pragmatic but creative; creative but pragmatic. I want to see that they listen and understand the client; that they are sensitive to place; and astute in their perceptions of what the essential issues are.

What role can landscape architects take in making our world better?

❭ They can take a leadership role. Because the complex environmental issues we face today are so interrelated, there's no one thing that's going to solve it. As far as I'm concerned, it's all about context, and landscape architects are all about context, so there certainly is an opportunity for them to lead. A landscape architect has expert skills in site planning and landscape systems, in being able to see the big picture and then break it down and figure out how to put it together so it works.

Grant Writing Accelerates the Process

DAWN KROH, RLA

President

Green 3, LLC

Indianapolis, Indiana

Landscape architect Dawn Kroh at her office. Courtesy of Green 3 LLC.

What is your background and how did you get into landscape architecture?

❯ My undergraduate degree is in fine arts, painting and printmaking, from San Diego State University. For my undergraduate degree, I wanted a totally new experience, so I drove out West. As far as choosing landscape architecture, I didn't really choose it; it chose me. I was attracted to it because of the relationship with the environment. My graduate degree is a Master of Landscape Architecture from Ball State University.

How does your art background affect your landscape architecture design work?

❯ You don't think of the design you do as a landscape architect as art, per se. You tend to think of it as a visual representation of problem solving. Doing a design doesn't make you feel the same as painting a picture. You to have some objectivity about your design work. You expect the critique. You don't get all invested in things like, "It's my design and I'm a great designer." It becomes about the actual act of developing the design. The design is a reflection of what nature told me or people told me. It's not art, per se. That's good because it gives you a real ability to be more creative when you're not so invested in it.

How would you characterize the work of your office?

❯ We have a small office; there are four of us, and two are registered landscape architects. We do a very broad spectrum of work. Things are generally very fast-paced, with many things going on at once. The projects on any given day could range from graphic design of an interpretative sign to reading through geotechnical reports to giving a presentation on native species to doing traditional CAD work. Most of the work in our office is public sector work. We do a little bit of everything almost all the time.

Many years ago you developed a strategy for a trail system in your state. Explain how that works.

❯ For the past 13 years I have been chugging along getting people connected, getting these 10 miles built there and those 5 miles here, and then starting to link all of it. We now have some of the biggest long-distance trails either in process, getting ready

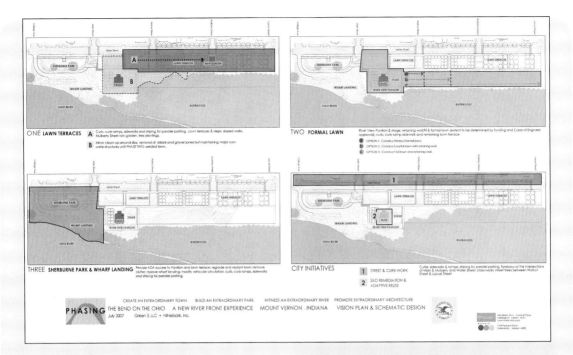

ONE **LAWN TERRACES** A   Curb, curb ramps, sidewalks and striping for parallel parking. Lawn terraces & steps, sloped walks. Mulberry Street rain garden, tree plantings.

B   Minor clean-up around silos; removal of details and gravel zones but maintaining major concrete structures until PHASE TWO; seeded lawn.

TWO   **FORMAL LAWN**   River View Pavilion & stage; retaining wall/fill & formal lawn (extent to be determined by funding and Corps of Engineer approval), curb, curb ramp sidewalk and remaining lawn terrace.

A   OPTION 1: Construct limited formal lawn.
B   OPTION 2: Construct partial lawn with retaining wall.
C   OPTION 3: Construct full lawn and retaining wall.

THREE   **SHERBURNE PARK & WHARF LANDING**   Provide ADA access to Pavilion and lawn terrace; regrade and replant lawn; remove clutter; repave wharf landing; modify vehicular circulation; curb, curb ramps, sidewalks and striping for parallel parking.

CITY INITIATIVES

1   STREET & CURB WORK

2   SILO REMEDIATION & ADAPTIVE REUSE

Curbs, sidewalks & ramps; striping for parallel parking, forebays at the intersections of Main & Mulberry and Water Street; cross walks; street trees between Walnut Street & Locust Street.

CREATE AN EXTRAORDINARY TOWN   BUILD AN EXTRAORDINARY PARK   WITNESS AN EXTRAORDINARY RIVER   PROMOTE EXTRAORDINARY ARCHITECTURE

PHASING   THE BEND ON THE OHIO   A NEW RIVER FRONT EXPERIENCE   MOUNT VERNON . INDIANA   VISION PLAN & SCHEMATIC DESIGN
July 2007   Green 3, LLC + NINebark, Inc.

▲ Vision and phasing plans for riverfront improvements, Mt. Vernon, Indiana. Illustrators: Eric Fulford and Ann Reed. Courtesy of Green 3 LLC and NINebark Inc.

▶ Scott Starling Nature Sanctuary observation deck. Courtesy of Green 3 LLC.

to start, or almost done, to make the whole system jell. It is kind of a body of work. I tend to think ahead and say, "This trail is going to end there, and the next place down the line is city B." So I go to city B. and say, "If you will let me help you, I can make this happen for you." I have been able to do that, and so I just keep moving down the line. We do grant writing, so I can come to the table and say, "I don't need money. I need you to let me go find you money." It changes everything. We superaccelerate the process because they aren't waiting for pennies to fall from heaven. It makes me feel good to know the strategy I thought would work, did work—I just keep moving down the line and getting people fired up; sometimes that's all it takes.

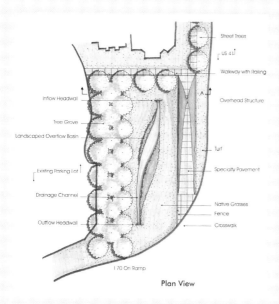

Street Trees
US 41
Walkway with Railing
Inflow Headwall
Overhead Structure
Tree Grove
Landscaped Overflow Basin
Turf
Existing Parking Lot
Specialty Pavement
Drainage Channel
Native Grasses
Fence
Outflow Headwall
Crosswalk
I 70 On Ramp

Plan View

Plan view drawing of preliminary gateway concept at U.S. I–70 and U.S. 41, Terre Haute, Indiana. Illustrator: Dawn Kroh. Courtesy of Green 3 LLC.

What has been your most rewarding project to date?

❯ When I worked for the Department of Natural Resources, I started the Hoosier Riverwatch Program here in Indiana. For the last 15 years it was the most popular environmental education program in the department. I figured out the program, wrote a grant, and got funding. I set up all the training materials and launched the program. I left DNR a couple of years after that, but it's still going gangbusters. The program has sustained itself in a state where we don't have fabulous landscapes in the same dramatic way others do; but we have rivers. The idea that we could get an education program up and running in a way that made people look at these resources and really love them is meaningful to me.

How often do you involve the community and/or end users in the design process? In what way?

❯ There isn't a single project where we don't have the public involved from beginning to end. Due to my background in government, I truly believe that with public projects we need to listen to what people say. Throughout the whole process of project development and fundraising, it's a constant dialogue. Sometimes we work with volunteers and they go out and rally the troops; in other cases, when it's a little more high-profile, we carry the ball.

❯ What tips can you offer to someone regarding the job search process?

Never take no for an answer. If they say, "We're not hiring," the experience of going though the interview is still beneficial. I would encourage you to ask if you can come in to visit with them. You never know when a few months after they met you, they might have something and you might be a good fit. I always ask for is a writing sample. I need people who know how to convince me with the written word. Share something about yourself that makes you different from others. Maybe it's a photograph of you volunteering in the boys' and girls' club. Anything that shows your character is helpful in figuring out if you're a good fit in any given office.

What role can landscape architects take in making our world better?

❯ Landscape architects can become more active. If we would all just volunteer a little bit of our time and try to make real change happen, it would have a big effect. Landscape architects are particularly well-suited to do that because we to have a holistic sense about the environment. There are lots of opportunities when you understand it in that way.

Synthetic Thinking across Boundaries

MARK JOHNSON, FASLA

Founding Principal and President

Civitas, Inc.

Denver, Colorado

Landscape architect Mark Johnson.

Why did you decide to pursue a career in landscape architecture?

❯ I was in engineering school and found that the methods were prescribed, and everything was measurable in one way or another. I looked around at the world and saw that it is not that well defined, and it's not easy to find the answers. I came upon landscape architecture through an elective course and thought I should pursue it.

How and why did you choose the schools you attended to earn your degrees?

❯ While at the University of Minnesota I took a class called "Introduction to Landscape Architecture" because it satisfied a humanities requirement. The professor who taught it was very inspirational. The next year he moved back to Logan, Utah, to teach. I went to Utah State because of the people—it was the inspired nature of the teachers. I also eventually went to the Harvard Graduate School of Design to get my master's degree.

How would you characterize the work of your office?

❯ Civitas integrates architecture, planning, urban design, and landscape architecture. We are focused on making lasting change that benefits people, while trying to protect or enhance how people interface with natural places, even if it's in the middle of a city. We work at a broad range of scales. We are currently working in Kansas City doing a park on top of a freeway, and in St. Louis on regenerating economic and social vitality in 400 blocks of downtown.

What is your role in the office?

❯ I'm the CEO. More specifically, I am the primary thinker and inspiration for the firm. My most important role is growing the capabilities of people in the firm: coaching, teaching, supporting them with access to resources, helping them find project opportunities, and bailing them out when they screw up. In the last seven years I have specifically extracted myself from the office to force others to take over. I'm only in my office about one day a week.

What is the mix of design professionals in your firm?

❯ We have about 30 people in two offices. Of the 30, probably 20 are landscape architects, and about 6 are architects. However, I can define it in ways that add

◀ Belmar Village central plaza, Lakewood Colorado. Photographer: Frank Ohms.

▼ Curved walkway in Denver Commons Park, Colorado. Courtesy of Civitas, Inc.

up to more than 30 because I have several people with multiple degrees—some have both architecture and landscape architecture degrees, others have landscape architecture and urban design degrees, and some have architecture and urban planning degrees. I have a couple of people with graphic design degrees. It's a rich mix, but fundamentally, it is landscape architects and architects working in that crossover world between the two professions.

Who are some of the allied professionals you consult with?

❯ I have to give you two categories, as there is a distinction between diagnosing the problem and solving the problem. In the analysis and idea portion of the work, we generally work with attorneys and economists; currently, we're working with a philosopher, artists, teachers, and students. In terms of how things work technically, we often work with restoration ecologists, various kinds of scientists, or, very commonly, with people involved in water quality issues. On the implementation side, we are generally working with, again, restoration ecologists and attorneys, but also civil engineers, structural engineers, and so on.

How do you involve the community and/or end users in the design process?

❯ It is extremely important to get all points of view, and very often, because most of our work is national, we rarely know the community as well as the people who live there. The people are usually very passionate and very knowledgeable, so we can gain a great deal from them. On the other hand, those same people often have a narrowly focused idea of what their place is about and sometimes miss what the real possibilities are, and that's partly the role we play as a national design firm. We often come in and can see things other people aren't seeing, or we can help them prioritize things in a way they wouldn't be able to do by themselves.

Specifically, we have many strategies for involving the public and the community. For example, on a current inner-city park project, we have set up a technical committee of agency staff, a stakeholders' committee of people who have a direct stake in the outcome of the project, an arts and culture district committee, a citywide park and recreations advisory committee, and a multicultural committee. Every project has a different strategy, and every one is custom.

What tips can you provide about finding a professional direction?

❯ The best tip is, be yourself. When I was in undergraduate school, I set out to meet my heroes. I became friends with Grant Jones, Paul Friedberg, Larry Halprin, Pete Walker, Hideo Sasaki, and Ian McHarg. I did that because I wanted to know what made them so good. What I found is that each of those people simply lived through his own personality. They are authentic to themselves and unyielding in who they are going to be. That's what allows a professional to propel his or her career—just being who you are and being honest about that.

What role can landscape architects take in making our world better?

❯ Landscape architecture is not a knowledge-based profession, and I wish we had a better body of knowledge. But, in fact, because we are generalists and our stock-and-trade is synthetic thinking, we are able to see across those boundaries, and that's where the future of landscape architecture is. We need to focus on taking up leadership roles and moving into positions that allow us to exercise our synthetic intellect, to apply to intractable problems that others have difficulty solving.

Think Generationally, Act Urgently

ROY KRAYNYK

Executive Director

Allegheny Land Trust

Sewickley, Pennsylvania

Roy Kraynyk being interviewed as part of a documentary about abandoned-mine drainage. Photographer: Robert S. Purdy.

Why did you decide to pursue a career in landscape architecture?

❭ I thought it was an opportunity to marry my love for the land with my creative side. I pretty much knew I wanted to pursue landscape architecture, but I took a vocational aptitude test anyway. I came to school late; I was 25 when I started, so I wanted to be sure, and the test came back "landscape architecture."

Which aspect of your education has had the greatest impact on you?

❭ Learning the problem-solving process. Working through how to break things down, and to com-

partmentalize things into bite-sized challenges, is what is really paying off for me today. I feel this has had an influence on why I'm successful.

How did you get into the land trust side of landscape architecture?

❭ After graduation, my career went from one extreme to another. My first job experience was very frustrating because I was doing quite the opposite of what I thought I could be doing. This was due to the client base my employer had—very aggressive developers who wanted every square inch developed. It was such negative experience that I went out and created a land trust, the Hollow Oak Land Trust. I used to say I developed by day and conserved by night. The whole experience doing these massive subdivision projects was actually excellent training; it's like the analogy that the best policeman used to be a burglar.

How would you characterize the work of your organization?

❭ We provide a service to the community that the federal government recognizes as a charitable cause. Our charitable purpose is to protect land. Here in southwestern Pennsylvania, we are protecting land that helps address threats in this region. Those are landslides, water pollution from combined sewer overflows, a loss of biodiversity and scenic character, and flooding. What we do is large-scale planning. We're analyzing the landscape to identify the lands that are providing these ecological services.

Shouldn't municipal regulations play a role in protecting sensitive lands?

❭ In many cases, land use ordinances are outdated and are a blueprint for disaster. What we are trying

Part of the Ridge to River Continuum, land determined to be most vulnerable in Allegheny County, Pennsylvania. Courtesy of the Allegheny Land Trust.

to do is translate ecological services into economics. When we make the case to the municipal decision makers who write and enforce the codes, we say look at this on a scientific and an economic level, here's what's happening. For example, these woodlands are holding back XYZ gallons of water a year and preventing flooding in your community. If that gets developed, as your codes would allow, there is going to be increased flooding and this is not beneficial for your community. You have to understand how the politics work and get engaged in the negotiations and discussions.

What is your role in the organization?

❯ I'm the executive director, and I'm involved with everything. I negotiate with landowners to buy the land. I write grants to raise money to buy land. I'm the prime interface with local municipalities and other government officials on all of our work. I am the leader, and to me leadership is dancing on the edge of the scope of my authority. When I was hired, it was just me, and now there are four of us; we wouldn't be where we are now if I wasn't pushing that envelope and if my board didn't allow me to push that envelope.

What is the most exciting aspect of your work?

❯ It is exciting when the deal comes together and you raise the last grant to close the deal, because it takes years. You've got 90 percent of the money, and the closing date is around the corner; and if you don't make that last 10 percent, the deal falls through, and then all your work goes down the drain. It's probably like a ribbon-cutting for a big project. For us, the ribbon-cutting happens, too, but the land stays the same. That's what we celebrate. Also getting a handwritten letter from someone after you've protected a piece of property and they write and pour out their heart about what the land means to them, how conserving it is just the best thing that could have happened to them.

What role do new technologies play in your work?

❯ They play a big role. GIS, LIDAR, aerial photography, infrared photography, and Google Earth imagery are all really valuable. These tools are powerful in that they give us the opportunity to more quickly quantify things, and monitor and analyze change. Today it's a lot easier to quantify landscape attributes and their ecological functions and estimate impacts downstream.

What tips can you provide to someone regarding the job search process?

❯ Find the niche that really turns you on, and pursue it. Even if you can't find that early on, volunteer for it. Find an opportunity somewhere to follow that passion; don't forget it, keep it alive, and it will pay off. I volunteered for nine years doing what I am now doing professionally. Also remember that your first job is not your last job. Be willing to compromise, especially early on; the experience is invaluable.

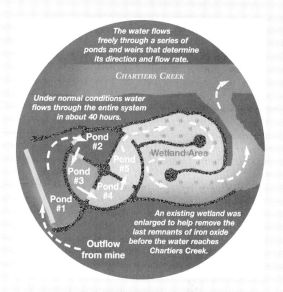

The water flows freely through a series of ponds and weirs that determine its direction and flow rate.

CHARTIERS CREEK

Under normal conditions water flows through the entire system in about 40 hours.

Pond #2
Pond #5
Wetland Area
Pond #3
Pond #4
Pond #1

An existing wetland was enlarged to help remove the last remnants of iron oxide before the water reaches Chartiers Creek.

Outflow from mine

Diagram of the Allegheny Land Trust's acid mine drainage treatment system. Courtesy of the Allegheny Land Trust

What role can landscape architects take in making our world better?

❯ Think generationally, act urgently. This applies to every design decision you could make. Everybody lives downstream or downwind. Think of the long-term impacts of a decision you make; that's why I'm saying think generationally, but act urgently in terms of making the right decisions today that will affect generations to come.

Project Profile

LOS ANGELES RIVER REVITALIZATION MASTER PLAN

A Multifirm Collaboration

Los Angeles River in concrete, channelized condition. © 2007, City of Los Angeles, Bureau of Engineering.

Sketch of proposed new environment for the Los Angeles River. © 2007, City of Los Angeles, Bureau of Engineering.

Proposal for curved weirs in the river and for providing access to the river's edge. © 2007, City of Los Angeles, Bureau of Engineering.

PROJECT OVERVIEW

Date: 2007

Type: Planning and Urban Design

Location: Los Angeles, California

Client: City of Los Angeles, Bureau of Engineering

Firms: Civitas, Wenk Associates, and Mia Lehrer + Associates

Awards: 2007 Waterfront Center Award, 2007 CCASLA President's Award of Excellence

Web link to project: www.civitasinc.com/

www.wenkla.com/portfolio/item/category/urbanWaterways/itemId/12/view/1/

www.mlagreen.com

*Overall the…[community]…reaction was positive, in that whether or not the
changes proposed aligned with an individual's views, the improvements will take
something that was largely ignored and feared and turn it into the centerpiece of a
revitalized community.*

—SCOTT JORDAN, Civitas[55]

Project Scope

The goal of the Los Angeles River Revitalization Master Plan (LARRMP) is to transform a 32-mile concrete, channelized urban river into a viable, green, public gathering place. The design is the result
of an 18-month study of the river and represents the ideas and strategies of three landscape architecture firms and the community at large. The key goals of the project are to regenerate a healthy
riparian ecosystem and to develop a series of green public parks in the neighborhoods along the
waterway. The regeneration of a riparian setting will alter the entire place by providing appropriate habitat for wildlife, improving water quality for the city, and ultimately, encouraging a closer
relationship between residents and their river. The design of a series of green parks will encourage socialization and activity along the river, as well as establish a linked network of green areas
throughout the city.

Given the size of the project, the design is proposed as a 20- to 50-year vision plan. The design
team recommended phasing strategy options, advice for short-term improvements, and several
small projects that could be implemented to enhance the neighborhood environment and improve
the residents' quality of life.

Importance of Collaboration

The LARRMP is an example of effective multilandscape architecture firm collaboration. The firms
include Civitas, Wenk Associates, and Mia Lehrer + Associates. Each office used its strengths in design to contribute to achieving the overall vision for the project.

Mia Lehrer + Associates, based in the Los Angeles area, contributed a solid grasp on the vernacular, social, and political forces in the community. Its local knowledge, familiarity with the primary
stakeholders, and regional insight enabled the trifirm team to better understand the site and context. Mia Lehrer + Associates was also able to help the team anticipate how the community might
respond to design proposals; and because of its location, was able to easily observe and survey the
site regularly.

Wenk Associates, based in Denver, is a firm widely recognized for its ability to integrate urban
environments and natural systems, as well as to create lively public spaces from derelict landscapes. For the LARRMP project, Wenk's staff used their understanding of river ecosystems and
stormwater strategies to develop design ideas that could manage the intricate environmental issues
the site posed.

Also based in Denver, Civitas' role in the design process was to formulate how to connect the open-space network with the land use network. The scale and importance of the project made it essential to have a grasp on the various land uses, as well as the politics of the area.

This process illustrates the beauty of successful collaboration, and also shows the breadth of the profession. A landscape architecture degree provides an individual with the opportunity to specialize, even within the setting of a landscape architecture firm. Moreover, these three firms all have unique skills and interests, even within the category of urban design and on the same project.

Community Involvement and Reaction

A project of this scale along a key urban waterway will undoubtedly affect the communities that border either side. In an effort to include the communities and hear their voices in the design process, the firms held 20 interactive public workshops in neighborhoods adjacent to the river. Several groups represented the ideas of the communities; they included: a city department task force (50 members), an advisory committee (40 members, composed of neighborhood and community leaders), a stakeholder committee (50 members), and a peer review committee (composed of experts on river revitalization). While the community representatives voiced concerns about gentrification, property values, and public reaction, the overall response was positive. Landscape architect Scott Jordan helped lead the project at Civitas. He shared this about the experience: "For me as an 'outsider,' non-Angelino, the thing I found most intriguing was the community's interest and overall desire to be involved in making the river better. Initially, I assumed that to a lot of people the River . . . [was just a] . . . concrete-lined channel . . . , but the hope and desire to make the change was visible in residents of all ages."[56]

The Human Factor: Society, End Users, and Allied Professionals

A landscape architect's design and planning process involves many other people at several levels and on a regular basis. One important group associated with a landscape architect's work is made up of allied professionals. Rarely is a project completed without the input and services of other professions. Landscape architects work regularly with architects, civil engineers, planners, soil scientists, arborists, and ecologists—though which will be required on a given project depends on the project type and any unique site issues. Other professionals that might be consulted include hydrologic engineers, transportation engineers, geologists, archeologists, sociologists, horticulturalists, lighting designers, and irrigation consultants. Some projects also require the services of real estate professionals, marketing experts, graphic designers, or artists. A landscape architecture project always benefits from the combined expertise of all the professionals involved.

Children playing with instructor in Wegerzyn Children's Discovery Garden. Landscape architects: Terra Design Studios. Photo Courtesy of Five Rivers MetroParks, Dayton, Ohio.

When preparing designs, human use and enjoyment are often important goals for a landscape architecture project. Understanding who those end users are is, therefore, a critical factor to the design process, as is involving users in the process. Inviting local citizens to attend a workshop during a park design process, or sending out surveys to the community to determine desired uses, are examples of approaches for soliciting input from the end users. In addition, local citizens are often very knowledgeable about the history of the project site and so should be encouraged to share their stories about the land. A richer foundation for the project will emerge by gaining the perspective of people familiar with the area and/or from those who will use the site most frequently. In public work, earning community support and buy-in is considered crucial to the ultimate success of a project.

Landscape architects also need to stay abreast of societal shifts in order to help advocate for or defend against changes that influence the quality of the built environment. If, for example, a proposed policy will encourage further suburban sprawl, landscape architects would be wise to get involved, offering their expertise and professional insight. The will of the people can be a pivotal factor in changes that can have positive consequences for both the environment and citizens. Landscape architects should become involved in such efforts, perhaps even taking on leadership roles.

Regeneration of the Landscape

JOSE ALMINANA, ASLA

Principal

Andropogon Associates, Ltd.

Philadelphia, Pennsylvania

Landscape architect Jose Alminana. Courtesy of Andropogon Associates, Ltd.

Why did you decide to pursue a career in landscape architecture?

❭ I went into landscape architecture to become a better architect. I had a degree in architecture and I figured if I was going to put a building in the ground, I better know how the ground is made and understand what the consequences of doing so are. In the current legal professional structure, it is very difficult to be an architect and a landscape architect at the same time. You are either one or the other. You can't be both.

How and why did you choose the school you attended to earn your degree?

❭ When I was in my second semester of architecture a studio professor said, "Here is the 'bible.' Read it." [The book] he gave me was a copy of [Ian McHarg's] *Design with Nature*. I had no idea what he was giving me to read. I finished my architecture studies and realized that McHarg was at Penn; I got my Master of Landscape Architecture at the University of Pennsylvania.

How would you characterize the work of your firm?

❭ Our work starts by looking at the environment as much as the client, the users. The firm takes its name from a grass that in many instances becomes the first intervention in disturbed land to pave the way back to ecosystem health. That regeneration aspect is what we do. We do it at all scales.

What is the size of your office and how is it structured?

❭ We have about 30 people. We have 5 principals and 24 landscape architects, altogether. We also have graphic designers and a person in charge of business development. We have people from mixed backgrounds professionally, such as soil science, environment studies, and architecture. I am one of the principals, and I do a little bit of everything. Our office is structured around a series of committees. Each committee deals with different aspects of the operation of the office. One deals with business development and marketing. Another deals with staff development, human resources, and continuing education. A third group deals with process. For example, quality control, scheduling, and ensuring the goals of a project stay intact.

Plaza at Thomas Jefferson University, Philadelphia, Pennsylvania, designed both to accommodate academic events and be inviting to the public. Courtesy of Andropogon Associates, Ltd.

sure it is coherent and has a subtle sculptural quality to it.

Then there is the whole component of ecosystems. We designed a system to capture the runoff from the roof and air conditioning and store it within the soil mantle, which supports the trees. It becomes a source of life for all the greenery in the space. This then makes a positive contribution to Philadelphia's water quality problem. A confluence of ideas have come together, which raises the bar for the next project.

Tell us about your role in ASLA's Sustainable Sites Initiative

❯ The Sustainable Sites Initiative is a coalition of stakeholder groups, of which ASLA is one, that seeks to educate the public on the role the landscape plays in making a project truly green and sustainable. Until now it has been seen mostly through the lens of the building, and site is nearly forgotten. This system, which will establish guidelines and performance benchmarks, will pay tremendous attention to the site and is going to put landscape architects on the map. I'm one of ASLA's members on the steering committee. The office is donating my time to this nonprofit effort for the profession.

What has been your most rewarding project to date?

❯ Our work for Thomas Jefferson University in downtown Philadelphia is a once-in-a-lifetime project. It pulls together many things, and in that sense it's very rewarding. It creates a very large open space, the size of a football field, in the city—that has not happened for years. We were challenged by taking advantage of that kind of openness while accommodating spaces for small and large groups of people, and making

You see a unique role for the contractor during the design process. Please explain.

❯ We look at the people who will be executing the design, the contractors, as part of the design team. You're not going be able to deliver a unique and different product with the same delivery system. You

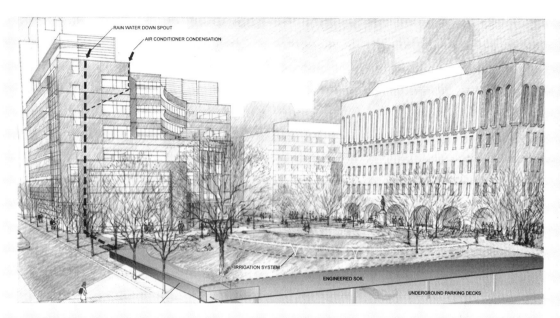

Diagram of site's permanent structural stormwater BMP, Thomas Jefferson University, Philadelphia, Pennsylvania. Courtesy of Andropogon Associates, Ltd.

have to bring that person in as part of the process. This is particularly true for projects that are going to obtain a high sustainability rating, because these are not projects that will be built the way projects have been built before. It is important to bring in those parties very early on complex projects; we try to bring them in at the schematic design phase. We are doing a project now where the construction manager is doing cost estimating and looking at the constructability of some of the ideas at the end of the master plan phase. We haven't even gone into the schematic design phase, and they are already bringing in their expertise and helping to make the project better.

What tips can you provide to someone regarding the job search process?

❯ The most important thing is to look really deep inside and figure out what is it you want to do to make a contribution. That will focus your search. If you want to be exposed to many aspects of the profession, then you probably want to go to a small firm where you can be aware of everything that is happening. However, smaller firms tend to be about an individual and that presents some limitations. Do some research and track down potential employers. Then meet with the staff and try to get an internship. That is a good way to determine if it is the place you want to be.

Storytelling to Connect Land and Culture

ROBIN LEE GYORGYFALVY, ASLA

Director of Interpretive Services & Scenic Byways

USDA Forest Service: Deschutes National Forest

Bend, Oregon

Robin Lee Gyorgyfalvy (left) with Terry Courtney, the last of the traditional River People from the Warm Springs Indian Reservation. Photographer: Marlene Ralph.

Why did you decide to pursue a career in landscape architecture?

❯ Growing up in Hawaii I developed a great reverence for and a fascination with native Hawaiian plants, especially because of the stories I heard about those plants and how they were used in early Hawaiian times. I went to Punahoa High School in Honolulu, Hawaii, where Barack Obama also went to school. The education I received there was quite unique because there's a focus on community service and values. I

grew up thinking that you always worked together to achieve a bigger goal. Those are some of the reasons why, for myself, landscape architecture combined the artistic skills I possess with the desire to make a better world and a stronger community.

How and why did you choose the school you attended to earn your degree?

❯ For my undergraduate degree I attended Mount Holyoke College in Massachusetts. It's a small liberal arts women's college, and I majored in sculpture and art. I felt having a liberal arts education is something of value and that I could specialize in graduate school later. I went back home to the University of Hawaii and enrolled in its architecture graduate program. I was exploring different professions and realized that landscape architecture is really where my interests are. I went to graduate school at the University of Oregon; I chose that school because of its excellent landscape architecture program.

One of your school projects resulted in you writing a book. How did that happen?

❯ At the University of Oregon I took a class called "Landscape Perceptions." That class seemed to jell for me all the different interests and directions I wanted to go. One of our assignments was a project to communicate an aspect of the landscape we felt was really important as a teaching tool. I did a poster on the legends of the Hawaiian forests and presented the aspect of storytelling in the landscape. My professor said, "Wow! It's great. What a wonderful teaching tool. You should turn this into a book." And I did. It became the book *Legends of the Hawaiian Forest,* for which I received an Award of Excellence from the American Society of Landscape Architects. The book is still used in the schools of Hawaii in their Hawaiian Culture Programs.

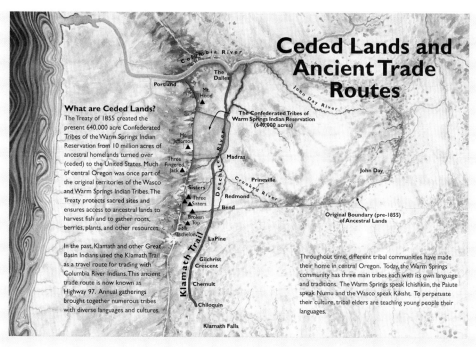

Ceded Lands and Ancient Trade Routes

What are Ceded Lands?
The Treaty of 1855 created the present 640,000 acre Confederated Tribes of the Warm Springs Indian Reservation from 10 million acres of ancestral homelands turned over (ceded) to the United States. Much of central Oregon was once part of the original territories of the Wasco and Warm Springs Indian Tribes. The Treaty protects sacred sites and ensures access to ancestral lands to harvest fish and to gather roots, berries, plants, and other resources.

In the past, Klamath and other Great Basin Indians used the Klamath Trail as a travel route for trading with Columbia River Indians. This ancient trade route is now known as Highway 97. Annual gatherings brought together numerous tribes with diverse languages and cultures.

Throughout time, different tribal communities have made their home in central Oregon. Today, the Warm Springs community has three main tribes each with its own language and traditions. The Warm Springs speak Ichishkiin, the Paiute speak Numu and the Wasco speak Kiksht. To perpetuate their culture, tribal elders are teaching young people their languages.

Interpretive sign panel designed in collaboration with the Warm Springs Indian Reservation's Tribal Committee on Culture and Heritage. Illustrator: Dennis McGregor.

How would you characterize the work of the U.S. Forest Service? What is your role?

❯ The U.S. Forest Service is a public agency. I work in the Bend Fort Rock District of the Deschutes National Forest in Bend, Oregon. We are a land management agency charged with stewardship of public lands. My work involves a lot of fieldwork. I manage the environmental design and scenic byways programs. I also manage conservation education programs. Conservation is one of the important missions of the Forest Service.

Since our national forests are multiuse, we have many different professions working here, from wildlife biologists, archaeologists, and foresters to engineers. Most people have no idea what it takes to manage these lands. As the only landscape architect, I'm pulled in on some of the projects for master plans, designing the aesthetics and trying to provide a bigger picture. I communicate with graphics, to illustrate how something will look, such as the visual impacts from thinning for fire safety, over 5, 10 years, or longer. I help the team see what their actions are going to do to the land.

Tell me more about the Scenic Byways program and your involvement.

❯ Scenic Byways is a national program. It is a highway, road, or a drive that has special values: cultural, environmental, natural, recreational, or scenic. We have three scenic byways that cross our forest. Cascade Lake Scenic Byway is the newest, and I worked hard to get this designation. It is a comprehensive approach to an entire visitor experience along the whole 66-mile drive. There's an orientation point at the beginning, and then there are different stops along the way. I'm responsible for writing grants and getting federal highway funding to install interpretive features, improve trailheads, and restore viewpoints that may have grown in. My work allows a visitor to have an environmental outdoor learning experience in a place that's well designed.

You work for the U.S. government. How are you able to do international work, too?

❯ Because of the Forest Service's expertise and reputation, we are invited to assist in other countries. I was involved in two really cool projects: one in Indonesia and one in China. In Indonesia we worked in Keli Mutu Volcanic National Park. It's a semiactive volcano, and there are issues with safety, as well as trying to provide storytelling to allow the visitor to experience the sacredness of the place. In China we worked through the Nature Conservancy on the Yunnan Great Rivers National Park. It was a conceptual plan I helped get off the ground. They had many traditional beliefs they wanted to communicate so visitors would understand why traditional plants were important—not just the economic value but the cultural values, too.

What is the most exciting aspect of your work?

❯ The most exciting aspect of my work is to make a difference in how people view the landscape, using

storytelling and cultural connections to get those points across. I get so excited because people visiting the Deschutes National Forest are learning some values that are important. The messages we teach are related to protecting wildlife or native plants, and having softer impacts on the environment.

About an hour from here is the Warm Springs Indian Reservation. They are the indigenous people of this area. I've worked hard to create a partnership with them so their stories of this landscape can be told. I think that brings more meaning to others and instills more of a conservation land ethic into people who want to do more or aren't aware that they could do more.

Which aptitudes, traits, and skills do you see in most landscape architects?

❯ Landscape architects seem to have cultural and social interests. They are big-picture thinkers. Often, they are visionaries. They are in tune with natural processes. They are also storytellers and artists, and have the ability to conceptualize ideas and articulate them into concrete living designs. An important part of that is listening to people and being able to reach consensus on all the different points of view out there.

Visitor reads gateway interpretive signs on the Cascade Lakes National Scenic Byway, Oregon. Photographer: Marlene Ralph.

Facilitating True Public Involvement

JIM SIPES, ASLA

Senior Associate, EDAW, Atlanta, Georgia

Landscape architect Jim Sipes. Courtesy of EDAW.

Why did you decide to pursue a career in landscape architecture?

❯ I was actually groomed to be the next great artist. My grandfather was an oil painter. I would get gifts of art supplies and started exhibiting art work when I was 10. Everybody assumed I would go into art, but it didn't seem quite real enough. So when I went to college I started in architecture because that seemed like a blend of my creative side, with something more tangible. It wasn't until I started that I even heard about landscape architecture. As soon as I found landscape architecture, it seemed to be a perfect fit. For me, growing up on a farm,

landscape architecture's land stewardship really set it apart from what I saw in the other professions.

How and why did you choose the school you attended to earn your degree?

❯ I grew up in Kentucky. The idea of going anywhere else but the University of Kentucky—I never even thought about it. I started in architecture and was very fortunate that there was a landscape architecture program there.

How would you characterize the work of your office?

❯ At EDAW we have a tendency to do an amazingly broad range of landscape architecture work. We often work on very big projects, and the reason is probably a combination of the size of the organization, the resources we have available, and our connections. Beyond those, our work ranges anywhere from land planning, to urban design, to resort planning, to small-scale site design—we cover the whole gamut of the profession.

What is the size of your office and what is your role?

❯ In our office here in Atlanta we have about 50 people, and maybe half of those are landscape architects. I'm a senior associate and project manager. Senior associates are expected to market and manage work; and, ultimately, our job is to keep clients happy. Part of my job is to make sure the project moves forward smoothly. It's a combination of doing the design work as well as figuring out how to build the right team. At the same time, I need to make sure the projects are done on budget and within the schedule. That's difficult to do; project management is an art form all its own.

What has been your most rewarding project to date?

❯ Sometimes the most rewarding projects are the ones you had to fight the hardest for. I worked on a 53-mile road project, U.S. 93 in Montana. We would have meetings, and there would be about 40 engineers and me. I felt as if I disagreed with them on every single thing they would say. This was a case where I had to stand up for what I thought was best. In the end we included more wildlife crossings than any other highway in North America. That was not easy. We battled very hard on that project in order for it to be successful.

How often do you involve the community and/or end users in the design process? In what way?

❯ Most of my work is with public clients, so community involvement in the design process is essential. The community is more interested than they have ever been. They feel they have a right to be involved and they want to know what's going on. I am talking about true public involvement where you get people involved in the process early on; you listen to their thoughts and they become part of that design process all the way through. Then, when you get to the end, everybody kind of nods their heads and says, "Yeah, that's what we thought; that's what we were expecting."

Who are some of the allied professionals you consult with? What role do they play in the design process?

❯ It's staggering the number of professions we work with: architects and engineers, horticulturalist, historians, ethnobotanists, biologists, wetland scientists, people involved with community participation, and politicians. Our projects are becoming more complex, therefore the number of allied professions is expanding. That's probably going to continue because the questions are becoming more complicated.

Lake Village Traditional Neighborhood Design (TND), Cherokee County, Georgia. Courtesy of EDAW.

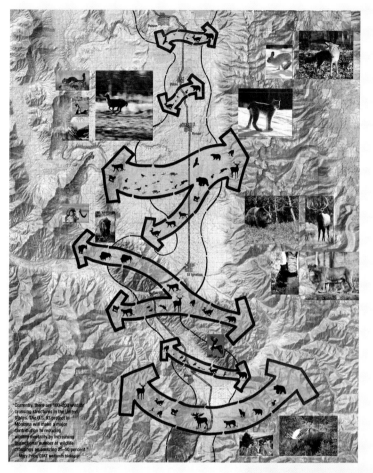

"Currently, there are 100–200 wildlife crossing structures in the United States. The U.S. 93 project in Montana will make a major contribution to reducing wildlife mortality by increasing the national number of wildlife crossings an amazing 25–50 percent."
—Mary Price/CSKT wetlands biologist

What role do new technologies play in your design process?

〉 In the past our response to questions was more of an intuitive sort of thing. Technologies now allow us to get beyond the guesses to building a strong foundation of information from which we can make really good decisions. Technology is also the foundation of our ability to ask new questions. So I think technology allows us to be more creative with what we want to do.

What tips can you provide to someone regarding the job search process?

〉 Before you start you need to learn who you are and what's important to you. Once you start, be prepared. It's surprising [how often people] don't do their homework; they don't really know the firm, and what we do. The other thing is to be politely aggressive. People want to know you're excited by this opportunity.

▲ The design of U.S. 93 used the "land comes first" approach. Wildlife habitat and travel corridors were well documented for discussion. Jones & Jones, Architects + Landscape Architects + and Planners.

▶ More than 40 wildlife crossings, such as this large culvert, give bear, elk, moose, and other mammals safe passage under U.S. 93, Montana. Jones & Jones, Architects + Landscape Architects + Planners.

Frankly, that's the kind of approach we take with marketing as well: We want a client to know that we are really interested.

What role can landscape architects take in making our world better?

❯ There are so many big environmental issues that are not really being addressed. The profession can really take the lead at a much broader level, mak-ing good decisions about the world we live in and the resources we have. I would like to see landscape architects getting into more advocate positions and more decision-making roles, whether that's running for public office or being a member of a city recreation board. I can't help but think what this country would be like if landscape architects made decisions about transportation and infrastructure, starting 50 years ago—it would be an entirely different place.

Incorporating Landscape Architectural Design Principles into Engineering Design Practices

KAREN COFFMAN, RLA

NPDES Program Coordinator

Maryland State Highway Administration

Highway Hydraulics Division

Baltimore, Maryland

Landscape architect Karen Coffman at her desk. Courtesy of Karen Coffman.

How and why did you choose the school you attended to earn your degree?

❯ I was attending the University of Maryland (UMD), in the prearchitecture program, and took an "Introduction to Landscape Architecture" course. The idea of making human-scale outdoor spaces and communities attracted me to the profession. The instructor said if I was interested in this as a career, to seek another school because it was not taught at UMD (at that time). I chose the five-year Bachelor of Landscape Architecture program at Virginia Tech because it was relatively close to home. While in school, I found that the site engineering courses had the greatest influence on me.

Which aptitudes, traits, and skills do you feel landscape architects should have?

❯ Continued development; know yourself, especially your shortcomings, and work to improve personally and professionally. Continue to learn and acquire new skills and seek new pathways. I find that simply reading gives me a tremendous boost in my abilities. Also, the ability to:

- Interact with and ask questions of people in other professions.
- Develop and use flexible approaches to problem solving.
- Anticipate and plan for problems and resistance, coupled with the ability to develop and implement effective strategies.

- Effectively communicate ideas verbally, in writing, visually, and graphically, and know which to use for a particular scenario.

For my particular professional track, an ability to understand hydraulic principles, and perform engineering calculations.

A working knowledge of psychological principles helps, too!

Legend
SHA Impervious Surface
BMP Drainage Area

Legend
SHA Impervious in BMP
NonSHA Impervious in BMP
BMP Drainage Area

SHA Impervious Acres by Structural BMP Treatment

Treated Impervious

Untreated Impervious

NPDES Phase I Counties

SHA
State Highway
Administration

How would you characterize the work of your organization?

❯ The Maryland State Highway Administration (SHA) has about 3,200 employees. About 750 people work in the headquarters office in Baltimore, Maryland. There are approximately 10 landscape architects, most of whom work in the Office of Environmental Design. I work in the Office of Highway Development (roadway design office) in the Highway Hydraulics Division. We are hydrologists responsible for the engineering design of hydraulic structures associated with roadways, park-and-ride lots, administration buildings, welcome centers, and rest areas—anything the SHA builds. This includes storm drain (closed systems), stormwater conveyance (open systems), erosion and sediment control and stormwater management design. Our office also designs stream restoration and stabilization projects.

Accounting for impervious surfaces and their impacts. Illustrator: Karen Coffman, Maryland SHA.

Wet Swale Design Options

Hankels Lane Wet Swale Retrofit

Traditional Wet Swale Design
A strongly linear alignment of swale centerline makes swale visually apparent.

MD 355 Wet Swale Retrofit

Meandering Wet Swale Design
A meandering centerline configuration has the affect of blending the swale into the surrounding site topography.

Display illustrating wet swale design options. Illustrator: Karen Coffman, Maryland SHA.

Because Maryland is within the Chesapeake Bay Watershed and the bay is quickly becoming a degraded natural resource, there is much concern for restoring it. This translates into many environmental laws and regulations targeting water quality. This, coupled with the Clean Water Act at the national level, creates a tough permitting environment for development. It falls to the Highway Hydraulics Division to coordinate permits for waterway work within drainage areas 1 acre or less.

What is your role in the office?

❯ I perform the role of NPDES coordinator for the SHA. NPDES is the National Pollutant Discharge Elimination System and is mandated by the Clean Water Act. Stormwater runoff is considered a point source pollutant, and the NPDES requires permits for municipal combined sewers and industrial activities. The storm drain systems on SHA facilities are regulated under the combined sewer requirements, while construction activities are regulated under the industrial requirements.

My role is to ensure the SHA is in compliance with these two sources of regulation and to maintain a watershed-based water-quality "bank" that allows us to trade water-quality credits on a project-by-project basis. I am also responsible for managing a team of engineers and a team of technicians and computer specialists. Because I am the sole landscape architect in an engineering office, I have developed guidelines to incorporate landscape architectural design principles into engineering design practices.

My role continues to evolve and change as the environmental sciences and technologies improve and as laws and regulations are written or revised. I will be working more on a watershed level in the future as the Environmental Protection Agency (EPA) and the green highways initiative implements more incentives for watershed-based stormwater management.

Who are some of the allied professionals you work with?

❭ Hydraulic engineers and other civil engineers, hydrologists, structural engineers, environmental engineers, environmental scientists, information technology specialists, GIS analysts, construction inspectors, college professors, and students. I wish I had more interaction with technical writers, biologists, and soils scientists.

I am a member of an American Association of State Highway Transportation Officials (AASHTO) technical committee on environmental design. In this capacity, I provide input on environmental design issues pertaining to water quality, stormwater management, and storm drain design. Participating in this national group is a particularly valuable experience and provides opportunities to meet and interact with professionals from across the country.

What is the most exciting aspect of your work?

❭ Although regulations and permits can be arduous to deal with, seeing our culture's values reflected in these laws is exciting. As compliance is enforced more, the values of the development and construction industries are beginning to change, and thinking is incorporated into design and construction that respects the environment, cultural heritage, people with disabilities, water quality, wildlife corridors, and so on. Innovation is increasing and development is moving beyond simply meeting the requirements and the letter of the law to embracing the intent.

Experiences of a Young Professional

NATHAN SCOTT

Landscape Designer

Mahan Rykiel Associates

Baltimore, Maryland

Why did you decide to pursue a career in landscape architecture?

❭ Mostly due to lack of exposure prior to college, I gave neither architecture nor landscape architecture much consideration when deciding what to study. However, I quickly found that my original major, engineering, did not provide the kind of creative outlet I needed. After some investigation and the positive experience I had in a landscape

Nathan Scott (left-center, with folded arms) participates in a charrette in Mississippi. Courtesy of Mahan Rykiel Associates.

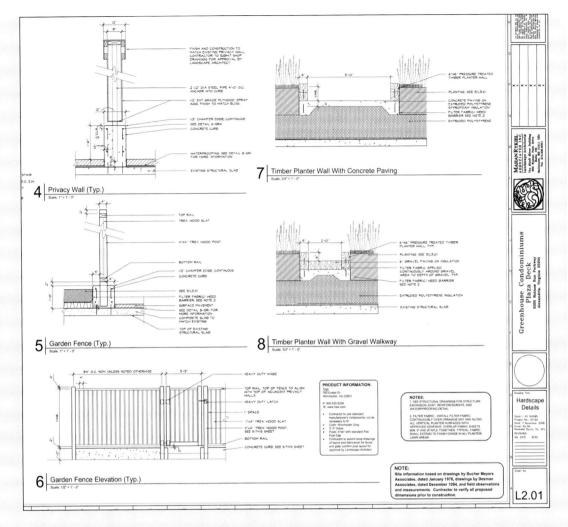

▲ Construction details for a roof deck. Courtesy of Mahan Rykiel Associates.

architecture history class I took as an elective, I decided to transfer to landscape architecture. I am extremely fortunate that the program I "fell into" at Penn State is one of the best in the country.

How has your educational background been helpful in your transition to the professional working world?

〉 I have found my educational background to be extremely helpful in transitioning to the professional world. This is mostly due to three things: an emphasis on the design process, the quality of the academic curriculum, and a focus on communication. When one has a good handle on looking for and revealing the main idea of a particular project, he or she has a framework in which to progress from the conceptual sketches at the project's genesis all the way through the completion of the construction document package.

I was also well prepared because of the breadth and depth of the curriculum at Penn State. In addition to understanding the more theoretical aspect of design, I was given practical skills and tools, which I could immediately use to help supplement work in the office. Also, and perhaps most importantly, my education afforded me the perspective to be an ongoing learner. I was challenged so much during my five years in college that I am now capable of confidently and positively reacting to new, unknown, and difficult situations.

Last, the ability to communicate is a life skill that my education helped to develop and reinforce. Working in groups, presenting ideas during critiques and final presentations, and even learning to interact with and listen to the needs of client groups, were all part of my college education. These all have direct parallels to the office environment. At nearly every stage of the design process, there is the need to discuss solutions, challenge ideas, ask for help, respond to instruction, and defend reasoning.

Perspective views show mid-term and long-term revitalization strategies for Salisbury, Maryland. Illustrators: Nathan Scott and Tom McGilloway. Courtesy of Mahan Rykiel Associates.

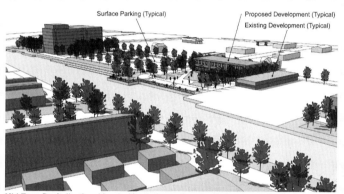

Mid-Term Revitalization: View looking to the southwest, with the proposed gathering area and hotel in the background.

Long-Term Revitalization: View looking to the southwest, with the proposed gathering area and hotel in the background.

Exhibit D7 - Perspective Views
North Prong Revitalization Plan
Salisbury, Maryland
Draft Strategic Revitalization Plan   31 August 2008

Mahan Rykiel Associates, Inc.
Arnett Muldrow & Associates
McCrone, Inc.
Murphy and Dittenhafer, Inc.

How would you characterize the work of your office?

❯ Mahan Rykiel Associates' practice is diverse. We engage work in the sectors of retail, hospitality/resort, garden design, green roof design, town planning, campus planning, and transportation, and do so in the Mid-Atlantic region of the United States and in countries around the world. However, regardless of the project type or location, the common goal is to develop places that are relevant and meaningful to people, places that reveal what the landscape stands for, and places that fulfill the needs of both clients and user groups.

As a young professional what are your primary responsibilities and duties?

❯ I've been involved for the most part in planning projects, but I also have helped complete several construction document sets for site-scale projects, and have been the staff landscape architect for a rooftop garden from schematic-level design through creation of the construction document package. In general, my primary responsibilities include completing tasks to move projects through the various phases of design, responding to and communicating ideas with clients, and contributing to the development of design ideas.

What has been your most rewarding project to date?

❯ A series of workshops for towns on the Mississippi Gulf Coast affected by Hurricane Katrina. The team was composed of architects, landscape architects, graphic designers, business developers, and local representatives. The client for the project was Mississippi Main Street, the state branch of the National Main Street Association. Our task for each of the workshops was to build upon previous planning efforts by providing tangible redevelopment ideas.

We spent time touring the towns and speaking with local residents in an attempt to quickly gain an understanding of the spirit of each place. What we saw and heard, as well as what we learned about the local history and economy, informed our visions for the towns. The late nights were well worth the smiles and comments of gratitude bestowed on us by local citizens at the conclusion of our final presentations. I felt as though we empowered them to improve the quality of their hometowns.

What do you hope to be doing in 5 to 10 years in terms of your career?

❯ I want to participate in projects that are concept-driven and people-centered. I want to feel like I'm contributing to the greater social and environmental good of my city and region, and I want to be working in an office that fosters a studio environment through collaborative design and healthy, authentic relationships. I am currently working to become a LEED AP and I hope that in 5 to 10 years I am also a registered landscape architect. At this point, I honestly do not think much about pay and advancement. My belief is that if I am doing the things I enjoy and consistently work hard with the tasks before me, those things will follow.

Project Profile

CEDAR RIVER WATERSHED EDUCATION CENTER

Understanding an Ecosystem and Engaging a Community

▲ Natural ground cover from the surrounding landscape is incorporated on-site and on living-roof-covered walkways that connect the buildings. Courtesy of Stuart P. Echols and Eliza Pennypacker, Penn State University.

▼ Roof water gathers in a stone basin then flows in a curved runnel before cascading over the courtyard wall. Courtesy of Stuart P. Echols and Eliza Pennypacker, Penn State University.

▶ Rain drums enliven the Education Center with different tones during a rain event. Courtesy of Stuart P. Echols and Eliza Pennypacker, Penn State University.

PROJECT OVERVIEW

Date: 2001

Type: Ecological Design

Location: Cedar Falls, Washington

Client: Seattle Public Utilities

Firm: Jones + Jones, Seattle, Washington

Awards: 2004 ASLA Professional Design Award of Merit

Web link to project: www.jonesandjones.com/JJ/livingplaces/cedar/cedar1.htm

We really didn't want to hit people over the head with interpretation. We were more trying to show what makes a good watershed, to give a sense of what the pristine Cedar River watershed is all about.

—NANCY ROTTLE, Jones + Jones[57]

The Site

The city of Seattle and the surrounding suburban region receives 60 to 70 percent of its drinking water from the Cedar River. The river itself, some 35 miles outside the city, is surrounded by a 91,000-acre watershed. The land is owned by the Seattle Public Utilities (SPU), and due to the pristine quality of the landscape, there are numerous restrictions on use and access. In an effort to educate the public about their watershed and provide some exposure to an incredibly rich and diverse environment, the SPU worked with the firm Jones + Jones, architects and landscape architects, to develop a watershed education center. The project site includes five buildings: a library, two learning laboratories, an education center, and restrooms. The buildings merge into the surrounding scenery through the creative use of green roofs and wood siding. The site's landscape design includes an entry pool, various water features, and place-specific vegetation, which give visitors a further sense of immersion with nature.[58]

The Role of Environmental Stewardship

Prior to developing the Education Center, the site was a run-down railroad station suffocated by a host of invasive plant species. It has since been environmentally transformed into a nexus of biodiversity, in both plant species and wildlife. A large portion of the 3,000 native plants on the site help to conserve water, and in certain cases, such as the wetland bioswales, collect water for filtration and future use. Some of the plants are seed products of the surrounding plant communities; others were selected based on compatibility with the watershed ecosystem, soils, and elevation.[59]

Jones + Jones pushed this project beyond the requirements of a typical landscape by placing a strong emphasis on environmental stewardship. Through educational signage, the landscape elements, and their details, the firm created an opportunity to showcase how ecological systems function, individually and holistically, at the site scale and regionally. Thanks to the designers' approach, visitors can easily understand how they can help to promote healthy environments in the core of the watershed as well as at their own homes.

Materials Selection

Because of the strong environmental nature of the project, recycled and recyclable materials are integral to the design. The predominant materials are wood and stone, both capable of reuse. Moreover, of the wood used in the project, 98 percent was salvaged or a product of "well-managed" Forest Stewardship Council (FSC) forests. While not all materials in the project are recyclable, Jones + Jones pushed for some component of reuse in all materials; for instance, fly-ash concrete was used, which is a more sustainable alternative for traditional concrete. Additionally, all site lighting is focused toward the ground and at a low level to avoid light pollution, thereby preserving the remote area's dark night sky.[60]

Experiential Value

The project sits in the heart of the Cedar River Watershed, and visitors are encouraged to learn not only about the significance of this watershed, but to understand how to promote a healthy ecosystem while accommodating development. From site details to larger systematic ideas, the center's landscape educates visitors in various ways. For example, a building downspout collects water from the roof, which is made visible by flowing into a small, ground-level basin. Once in the basin, the water continues to be visible to visitors through a courtyard runnel. The runnel animates the flow of water as it heads to a bioretention area for filtration. Often this process is hidden in pipes; however, here, while the process is happening within a developed condition, it is designed to mimic nature. There are larger concepts that emerge as well, such as the idea of enhancing regional biodiversity through the generous use of native plants and their design placement. Even cultural and artistic details, such as the rain drums, are intended to play off the regional character. Dan Corson, the rain drum artist, worked with the landscape architects to create the 21 drums on-site. He describes them as "[having the ability to] conjure the underground world that allows trees to absorb water through the gnarled masses of a tree root system."[61] Visitors leave the Education Center with a greater understanding of healthy watershed, along with appropriate building and development options to consider for a more ecologically healthy future.[62]

Project Profile

GORILLA FOREST

Telling a Story of the Gorilla Lifestyle

Kids get an up-close view of a gorilla in a natural setting. Courtesy of CLRdesign. © 2005, Robb Helfrick.

Carefully placed signs tell the story of the impact of logging on gorilla habitats. Courtesy of CLRdesign. © 2005, Robb Helfrick.

Chainsaw artifact in the landscape helps immerse visitors in the story of the impact of logging on animal habitats. Photograph: CLRdesign.

PROJECT OVERVIEW

Date: 2003

Type: Zoological Exhibit Design

Location: Louisville, Kentucky

Client: Louisville Zoo

Firm: CLRdesign, Philadelphia, Pennsylvania

Awards: 2003 AZA Exhibit Award

Web link to project: http://clrdesign.com

The essence of the Gorilla Forest is an appreciation for the intricacies of our ecosystem and the necessity of its preservation. The remarkable work of Dian Fossey is highlighted throughout the exhibit.

—JANE BALLENTINE[63]

Zoological Design

Imagine designing a space where the primary user group is a family of gorillas. In traditional landscape architecture practice, there are guidelines such as the Americans with Disabilities Act (ADA) that provide details and quantities for universal design and access. But when it comes to animals and the landscape, how does one understand what the animals need or want?

CLRdesign is a unique landscape architecture firm. Its design practice is primarily focused on zoological exhibit design. Jeff Sawyer, a landscape architecture associate with CLR, explained the firm's outlook as designing for three clients—the animals, the zoo staff, and the visitors—rather than just one. Each client group influences the design with their specific needs and wants. This provides the opportunity to develop creative strategies for dealing with each issue from three angles.[64]

CLR staff aim for innovation in their designs, resulting in both a safe and natural-looking environment. They have developed a reputation for designing zoo exhibits that innovatively re-create an animal's natural habitat, which promotes an optimum lifestyle for the animals, and makes zoo visitors feel as if they are there, immersed in the space, rather than standing outside as an observer. To achieve this, CLR puts a great amount of energy into research and conceptual design, relying heavily on in-house libraries and databases. Additionally, the firm's project managers and principals bring inspiration into the office through their travels to destinations across the world, studying the native ecosystems of wildlife habitats.

The Storyline

The driving force behind the design of Gorilla Forest is telling the story of the gorilla lifestyle and enlightening visitors to the plight of wildlife. The site design allows visitors to step inside the shoes of a field researcher or explorer in the forests of Africa. Several spaces engage visitors in a role-playing adventure. One space is arranged as a field research station facility. Visitors make their way into a large dayroom and peer through the glass to view the gorilla habitat. A second space is a mesh-enclosed wooden structure that overlooks the habitat. Inside, visitors encounter props used by scientists, such as binoculars and notebooks. Interpretive signs and graphics further illustrate significant processes the scientists use. Another space is designed to be totally different: it takes the form of a typical African village. Thatched-roof structures and open space provide a place for school groups or families to meet and discuss the exhibit. Finally, a discovery trail winds through the hillside, to give visitors a fully immersive forestlike experience. The edges of the trail are packed with dense vegetation. At select points there are unpaved trails that appear as if they were created by wildlife; there are also special spots to discover a unique glimpse of the wildlife.

Primarily, however, the exhibit is a story of the gorilla lifestyle, so it also highlights current issues that challenge their survival today. An old logging truck is on display as a reminder of the continual effects of logging on gorilla habitats.

Collaboration Is Key

The design of zoos is quite complex. Although CLR is a landscape architecture, architecture, and exhibit design studio, its work is also informed by others. In most cases, projects begin by gathering basic materials and testing initial concepts. This is followed by a kickoff workshop that may include animal managers, head curators, keepers, horticulturists, and the zoo's educational staff. Including clients and specialists in the design process results in a richer understanding of the project and a more successful design. During the design process, in-house horticulturists often help the designers with plant selection. The goal is to use plants suitable for the zoo's local geography and climate, but that mimic the animals' native setting, while also being appropriate to the needs of the animal species.

Also informing the process is information from the Association of Zoos and Aquariums (AZA), an organization with well-documented advice for wildlife. Its information is based on studies from zoos across the country, and is thus seen as recommendations, which by necessity vary based on the zoo and client. With this detailed zoological information and participation by the zoos, CLR then creates a zoo-campus vision plan for 30 to 100 acres and/or sometimes a site-specific exhibit design.[65]

Communication: Sketching, Multimedia, Written, Visual, and Oral Presentations

Not everyone learns effectively in the same way. Some people process information more easily when it is delivered orally, through a well-crafted presentation, for example. Those who are more visually oriented find they gain a clearer understanding of an idea or concept when they are shown

Melinda Stockmann, landscape architecture graduate student, presenting her work. Photographer: Christopher R. McCarthy.

information represented graphically. Others learn best by reading. The point is, landscape architects must be able to communicate their ideas to people in a variety of forms, whether it be to the client, public officials, or the public at large. It is, therefore, imperative that landscape architects be adept at all forms of communication.

Landscape architecture students learn early that they will be expected to present their work in a portfolio, which might lead to the conclusion that visual communication is paramount in the profession. Certainly, being able to showcase your grasp of the design process in a graphic portfolio is important, but it's just as important to also have solid oral and written communication skills; in fact, the latter are increasingly being recognized as essential to success in the profession.

Landscape architecture students are sometimes surprised at how often they are required to stand up in front of an audience to present their work. In professional practice that is the common forum in which projects are discussed and reviewed with clients and the public. Consequently, developing public speaking skills through continual practice during college is essential.

Professional landscape architects also recognize writing as an important part of their daily work. They are expected, for example, to produce written proposals and reports on a regular basis, as well as, on occasion, articles for media publication, in which they explain design ideas and

Laser-cut model of Greenacre Park, New York, by first-year Penn State landscape architecture students Adrienne Angelucci, Erin Gross, Suzanna Mayer, and Kaylynn Primerano. Photographer: Peter Aeschbacher.

concepts to the public. Our profession may never have advanced if it had not been for the prolific published output of early landscape architects such as Frederick Law Olmsted and Charles Eliot. It is no different today; writing remains an effective vehicle for helping to advance the profession.

Having a facility in graphic communication is a more obvious skill landscape architects must include in their skill sets. They may be called on to produce on-the-fly sketches for a client, or to create dynamic 3D computer models of proposed designs. They must, in short, become adept at many forms of graphic representation to convey design ideas and spatial relationships in the landscape. Each year there are new and exciting advances being made in computer technologies. These enable more detailed explorations of design alternatives as well as enabling them to be generated more quickly. Computer programs such as geographic information systems (GIS) also make possible a more refined and detailed understanding of resources and how they interact on a site or in a region. The result is a richer, more comprehensive realization of the factors that influence plans, as well as more realistic depictions of design ideas; the latter helps the lay public to more fully comprehend landscape architecture proposals.

Similarly, 3D computer modeling and computer-controlled laser cutters are changing the way physical models are produced. A computer-aided drafting (CAD) plan can be translated into a 3D computer model in SketchUp, which can then be exported for laser cutting into a physical model.

Exciting as these new technologies are, there's still a place in the profession for well-developed hand-drawing, especially when it comes to transferring an idea that's so clear in your mind's eye to a piece of paper. Fortunately, the profession embraces and values all these forms of communication.

A Sculptural Approach to Landscape

THOMAS OSLUND, FASLA, FAAR

Principal

oslund.and.assoc.

Minneapolis, Minnesota

Landscape architect Tom Oslund. Courtesy of oslund.and. assoc.

Why did you decide to pursue a career in landscape architecture?

〉 I was a prearchitecture student as an undergraduate. I heard landscape architect Dan Kiley give a lecture, and I changed my major the next day. I was struck by the work Dan was showing, with projects like the St. Louis Arch, which was a collaborative competition piece, where the site condition was just as important as the arch itself. I was struck by how he was manipulating the horizontal plane, and he just seemed to be having a lot more fun than the architects I'd heard lecture.

Which schools did you attend to earn your degrees, and which aspect of your education has had the greatest influence on you?

〉 I have an undergraduate degree from the University of Minnesota. I went through the Institute of Technology and got a degree in landscape architecture and in environmental design. I have a graduate degree from Harvard Graduate School of Design (GSD). I worked for about five years before going back. I wanted to come into graduate school with more of a working knowledge of the profession, and what the liabilities are. There were strong influences as an undergraduate, but my years in graduate school were the most significant. It was an amazing time at the GSD; there were several noted designers teaching, such as Pete Walker and Frank Gehry. There was a lot of intellectual rigor that has really shaped the way I think about my work.

How would you characterize the work of your office?

〉 The work of our office is inspired by more of a sculptural approach to the landscape than it is any other approach. We have a very interactive work environment, which has a direct influence on the kind of work we do. Most of our work has been in the private realm, and that's a conscious decision. Our approach seems to resonate better in the private realm than in the public realm. Saying that, however, right now we are working on two very large public projects. One is an infrastructure project. You probably remember the bridge collapse over the Mississippi River in August 2007? We were asked to work as a design consultant with the bridge designers, which has been really fascinating.

Minnesota Twins
baseball stadium.
Courtesy of oslund.
and.assoc.

What is the size of your office and what is your role in it?

> We have 12 people in two offices, one in Minneapolis and one in Chicago. Of those 12, 10 are landscape architects. I set up the office with a business partner who is actually a businessperson, not a designer. He went to business school and understands how to run a business. He takes on the roles for that work. My role in the office is to set the design intent for all the projects.

What is the most exciting aspect of your work?

> For me it has always been creatively solving issues or problems that seem complex, in the simplest way possible.

Who are some of the allied professionals you consult with? What role do they play in the design process?

> We love the collaborative process and we like getting everybody involved as early as possible. We work with a lot of artists and architects. On larger, more complex projects we might also work with agronomists, civil engineers, and lighting designers. We have a civil engineer who we really enjoy working with. We have a tendency to do a lot of the early technical stuff then get her involved soon after.

What role do new technologies play in your design process?

> It evolves every year, from materials to abilities to communicate ideas through computer animation and so on. Lately, one of the things that has been really interesting is how the role of the triad—our understanding of the client, the designer, and the contractor—is changing because of these computer programs. They really ensure that things are built the way they are intended, and that is very positive. It has been fascinating because we can do these full-scale mockups and lay them out in our office and look at them off of a computer-plotted sheet, and it's very convincing.

When hiring a student for an internship, which aspects of their education do you find to be most important?

❯ It is their attitude—a can-do attitude. They may be chasing down materials; they may be building mockups. It's about being willing to put the energy into it and being able to ask questions if you don't know. It is more interesting and fun for us if we can challenge these interns to go beyond their current abilities or their current thinking about the profession.

What role can landscape architects take in making our world better?

❯ This whole sustainability thing is funny because now everybody thinks of it as a new thing, and we've been doing it for 25 years. Hence, I think the landscape architecture profession as a whole is about making the world a better place. Because of the interest in sustainability, we are in a position to really be the leaders in this effort. We are going to be surpassing the architects as a valued role in the world.

The focal point of Gold Medal Park in Minneapolis' Mill District is a 32-foot-high sculptural observation mound. Illustrator: Michael Mingo. Courtesy of oslund.and.assoc.

Sketch of river overlook as part of public space below St. Anthony Falls Bridge, I-35 W. Illustrator: Jerry Ohm. Courtesy of oslund.and.assoc.

Shaping the Future through Writing

FREDERICK R. STEINER, PHD, FASLA

Dean

School of Architecture

University of Texas

Austin, Texas

Frederick "Fritz" Steiner (second from left) participates in the Venice Biennale Project. Photographer: Christina Murrey, UT-Austin Office of Public Affairs.

Why did you decide to pursue a career in landscape architecture?

❯ I was a design student at the University of Cincinnati organizing the first Earth Day in 1970 and part of my job was to do a book fair. There were several books on the environment and only one was written by a designer; it was *Design with Nature*. I read it and decided I would study with Ian McHarg.

Why did you go into the academic realm of landscape architecture?

❯ I have several degrees in planning. During the 1970s the economy was bad, so I kept going to school and ended up with a PhD from the University of Pennsylvania. I pursued becoming a landscape architecture educator, as a result of Ian McHarg's influence. Over the course of those experiences I found that by being an academic I could choose the projects I wanted to work on. The other plus is that I was always a writer—by being an academic I got rewarded for writing.

Describe your research focus and why it is important for the landscape architecture profession?

❯ My work has been derived from real projects, and most is collaborative work that involves landscape

architects, architects, planners, ecologists, hydrologists, and soil scientists. If there has been a focus, it has been on how to do land suitability analysis for community regional plans. I work reasonably hard to help develop a research agenda within landscape architecture, both by promoting others' work as well as my own. I think it's very important for the future of the profession to have a strong research base.

You have authored a number of books. What has that meant for your career?

❯ Publishing is an important way to work out ideas—it has a reflective aspect. For example, Frederick Law Olmsted was a writer before becoming a landscape architect, and he wrote prolifically. And certainly McHarg was an incredibly influential writer. I wrote *The Living Landscape* for an American audience, so it was very unexpected that its translation into Italian and Chinese would do so well. Italy and China are two of the oldest cultures in the world, and the fact that I found an audience there has been very rewarding.

What has been your most rewarding project to date?

❯ The Flight 93 Memorial competition. We didn't win but we were finalists. It was great to work with our team; it was cross-generational: two in their 20s, I in my 50s, and another in his 70s. We all contributed different things from our understanding. Also, my brother was an FBI agent and he was one of the chief investigators. I remember after 9/11 what he went through, and so it was also personally gratifying because of his involvement.

What role do new technologies play in your work?

❯ The Internet and computers, from laser cutters to GIS to Photoshop to SketchUp, are really transforming how we can represent the world. One of the challenging things about landscape architecture is, how do you represent landscapes? A wonderful thing about the overlay process is that you can see different layers of information simultaneously, which GIS technology certainly allows you to do. All these technologies are quite literally changing the way we view the world.

You have been a member of numerous boards and commissions. What has that involvement meant for your career?

❯ It is one thing to study the planning process; it's another thing to serve on a planning and zoning board where you come to grips with the reality of politics and decision making. Right now I am involved on a board planning the expansion of rapid transit in the metropolitan area. I can look back to past involvement and see tangible results that come out of those kinds of work. It has been very important in giving me a too real understanding of how the built environment is really shaped.

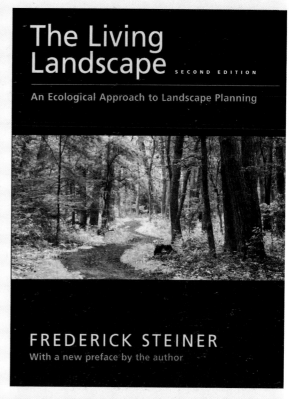

Cover of *The Living Landscape: An Ecological Approach to Landscape Planning* (paperback) by Frederick Steiner. ©2008 Frederick Steiner. Reproduced by permission of Island Press, Washington, DC.

What is your primary responsibility as the dean of a design school?

❯ I see my primary responsibility as being able to help shape the future of the professions in our school—landscape architecture, architecture, planning, and historic preservation—and moving toward a more sustainable approach in each. I am proud of my role in contributing to the establishment of several landscape architecture programs at different universities. Therefore, as part of a larger mission for the school, bringing landscape architecture into a university of this caliber has been a very important part of my responsibility.

SACRED GROUND
AND THE FAMILY CHAPEL

The family of Flight 93 walk along a more intimate trail directing them to the Family Chapel, a place for contemplation and meditation, nestled in a quiet grove of hemlock.

Chapel for Family Members, part of finalist design for the Flight 93 National Memorial. Illustrators: Jason Kentner, Karen Lewis, Lynn Miller, and Frederick Steiner (2005).

Describe your fellowship with the American Academy in Rome.

❭ Every landscape architect should do it! There are two endowed positions for landscape architects each year. The American Academy is a tremendous institution. It is often said there are very few glamorous fellowships for landscape architects; well, it doesn't get more glamorous than this. Half of the academy are artists, architects, and landscape architects, people engaged in designing and making, and the other half are scholars who are involved in reflecting about things that have been created. You are encouraged to pursue whatever you want and you have frequent interactions with this group of very interesting people. It's really a great experience.

Reflecting on Two Years of Practice

DEVIN HEFFERON

Landscape Designer

Michael Van Valkenburgh Associates, Inc.

Cambridge, Massachusetts

Devin Hefferon selecting trees in central Ohio nursery for Blossom Music Center. Courtesy of Michael Van Valkenburg Associates, Inc.

Why did you decide to pursue a career in landscape architecture?

❯ My summer jobs were doing landscaping. It was something I enjoyed, I had an uncle who was a landscape contractor. So I knew there was a field where people made a living doing this, but I didn't know there was a professional design field. I started my college education in wildlife biology;

however, the more classes I took, the more I felt like it wasn't fulfilling my creative interests. I was going to school at Colorado State and it has a landscape architecture program. At that point I became aware of the profession and decided to transfer into landscape architecture.

How and why did you choose the school you attended to earn your degree?

❯ Because I was at Colorado State I initially started landscape architecture there, as a sophomore. As I learned more about the profession, I started to look more closely at schools and remembered SUNY–ESF from when I was looking at wildlife biology. I decided to switch to the State University of New York School of Environmental Sciences and Forestry, SUNY–ESF, because it had brand-new computer labs, I liked the types of electives that were offered, and I felt the student-to-teacher ratio for studios was better.

How has your educational background been helpful in your transition to the professional working world?

❯ ESF really focuses on practical knowledge. As a student, it's important that you are creative, but it is also important to stay grounded. I learned you have to be realistic about design. That is really helpful for me now in my construction administration. I have a much better base understanding of how things are built.

My understanding of computer programs was really important. When you come into an office, your knowledge of computer programs is one of your greatest assets, because while you are new to everything else in the office, you know these and they can be your specialty. If the firm decides to

Before-and-after perspectives using Photoshop and SketchUp for the University of Virginia, Whitehead Road Project. Illustrator: Devin Hefferon. Courtesy of Michael Van Valkenburg Associates, Inc.

purchase new software, you can be the person who trains everyone. This is a really fun and exciting thing to do as a new hire, to have senior associates sitting in front of you, and you are teaching them.

How would you characterize the work of your office?

❯ I have heard Michael [Van Valkenburgh] use the term "naturalism," and I think that speaks to the type of work we do. It's what I would call a soft touch on the landscape. We're not interested in going in and putting a stamp on it that says it's recognizable as an

MVVA design. In fact, I don't think we're looking for people to really know they're in a designed landscape. We pride ourselves on having a true understanding of landscape and landscape processes, and we spend an incredible amount of time understanding the types of people who might use that place. The scale of our work runs the gamut from small residential sites up 20- to 30-acre parks. We also do a fair bit of work with universities and corporations.

Michael Van Valkenburgh Associates has two offices, one in Cambridge and one in New York. We are all landscape architects and landscape designers, with about 15 in Cambridge, and about 30 designers in New York. Both offices have about 5 support staff.

As a young professional, what are your primary responsibilities and duties?

〉 I'm not sure my responsibilities are typical. Because it's a small office, everyone is relied on to pitch in. I do a fair bit of CAD work for construction documents and a good amount of graphics work, such as using Illustrator, Photoshop, or hand drawings for plans, sections, and perspectives. I also do some management of my own projects. I do the project schedule, and coordinate with clients and subconsultants and contractors. I keep track of project budgets and am in charge of all of our fees and expenses. I'm basically the head of design development for my projects, with input from the principal and from Michael. Then eventually on to construction administration, which involves travel to project sites, tagging trees, and working with the contractor and the client.

What has been your greatest challenge as a young professional?

〉 Because of the amount of exposure I've been given, I have found it to be difficult to get respect from people when I'm the youngest one in the room. This is especially true for contractors. But I have to say, it's important that when you're put in the position of working with people outside the firm, you need to assert yourself in those situations. If you're there and there's something you're either recommending or defending, you need to speak up. At the same time, you need to make sure you don't come off as sounding pompous or arrogant. When it comes down to it, you're probably the only landscape architect in the room, which means your opinion really does count.

I want to share an important piece of advice I was given: You should never fudge an answer or make up something on the spot. If someone asks a question and you don't know the answer, just say, "I'm

Early concept sketch and model of proposed terrace at Blossom Music Center. Terrace is designed to take advantage of spectacular views of Cuyahoga Valley National Park, the concert stage, and the Blossom Pavilion. Illustrator: Devin Hefferon. Courtesy of Michael Van Valkenburg Associates, Inc.

going to have to check and get back to you." At first it's a little tough to do because you want to sound like you know what you're talking about. But it is important. The longer you're in an office, the more you see that everyone, associates and the senior associates, have to do this occasionally.

What do you hope to be doing in 5 to 10 years in terms of your career?

❯ I always thought when I started my career that I would move around and try out different firms,

expose myself to different types of work. But since I started working here, the types of work I have been exposed to leads me to think I'll be here for a while. It's not very often you get to work on projects such as the London Olympics, or the University of Virginia, or the restoration of the historic Miller Garden in Columbus, Indiana. My biggest hope is that I don't stagnate; I don't want to end up falling into a rut. Part of what's exciting about my work is the opportunity to travel. It's exciting to be able to keep doing projects that are not just local.

How would you describe the diversity of landscape architectural professional work as currently practiced?

❯ A degree in landscape architecture can lead to a wide variety of career paths, from work for governmental agencies or public institutions to the private sector; from the development industry to nongovernmental special-interest organizations. Our practice alone has an interesting mix of work, from urban planning and redevelopment to cultural and campus planning to ecotourism.

Douglas C. Smith, ASLA
Chief Operating Officer, EDSA

❯ It is extremely diverse. There are a lot of opportunities, and landscape architects are leading a lot of interesting and complex projects right now because of the nature of combining planning and architecture, and site and landscape engineering. All those things together means that landscape architects are the logical leaders of the team, to hold together complex projects.

Jim Burnett, FASLA
President, The Office of James Burnett

❯ Landscape architecture can focus on any of many areas. Some of these are ecological restoration, environmental mitigation, urban renewal, residential/ corporate/commercial development, parks and recreation, planting design, environmental policy and law, stormwater management, research and development, and planning.

Karen Coffman, RLA, SHA
NPDES Coordinator, Highway Hydraulics Division, Maryland
State Highway Administration

❯ There is a world of difference between broad categories. First is work done in the public sector, such as the Forest Service and the National Park Service; state park agencies and preservation agencies employ quite a few landscape architects. Then there is work done by large firms, which are major contributors to land planning as well as urban design. Many call themselves planners and urban designers, but if you look at their training, it is dominated by landscape architects.

Then there are boutique firms, which do edgy, beautiful, and inventive things. Last, there are small firms that do more localized, mostly residential, work.

Frederick R. Steiner, PhD, FASLA
Dean, School of Architecture, University of Texas

❯In my 30 years of practice I have been exposed to a great variety of project challenges. A decade ago I was working simultaneously on the vastness of the Isthmus of Panama and the integration of the canal to its adjacent metropolitan regions; and on the design of news racks, which involved mediating between its potential for clutter and its constitutional use for free speech.

Ignacio Bunster-Ossa, ASLA, LEED AP
Principal, Wallace Roberts & Todd, LLC

❯The practice is extremely diverse. I would like to see more landscape architects in the public sector and in nonprofit organizations. We need to have champions—landscape architects—infiltrated in all different parts of the decision-making process to promote change. Their skills in synthesis and integration can lead organizations and make a huge impact on the quality of the environment.

Barbara Deutsch, ASLA, ISA
Associate Director, BioRegional North America

❯Diversity measured by scale suggests practices focused on the residence to those focused on the city. Many practices work across all of these scales. But diversity of professional work can also be understood by mode of practice. CLEAR is a small research-based practice, and some of our products are books. So a product can be a book, a drawing, or a built work. They all contribute to the field.

Julia Czerniak
Principal, CLEAR

❯What we do is increasingly integrated into a broader spectrum of day-to-day elements; not only are we working at the homeowner scale, but we're working at a global scale on climate change. We're working in natural forests on reforestation projects. We're working with hospitals to help those who are elderly or sick have a higher level of sensory perception. We have blossomed into all kinds of things.

Juanita D. Shearer–Swink, FASLA
Project Manager, Triangle Transit Authority

❯There has been a big change from when I entered the market 20 years ago. Professionals have the ability to push a button and send drawings around the world in seconds, which changes how you do work and where you do work. That has really opened up new avenues or new territories for the profession.

Robert B. Tilson, FASLA
President, Tilson Group

❯The boundaries on what a landscape architect is become more blurred all the time. There is also diversity in terms of the regions that people work in. My idea of what a landscape architect is here in Indiana is somewhat different from the West Coast. The profession is not standardized, and I think that's nice.

Dawn Kroh, RLA
President, Green 3, LLC

❯The diversity of the profession is great. There are different kinds of foci. Some firms specialize in, for example, public participation or historic preservation. There is also diversity in the different practice types, between public, private, and design/build. So there is a very great range.

Nancy D. Rottle, RLA, ASLA
Associate Professor, Department of Landscape Architecture, University of Washington

How would you describe the diversity of landscape architectural professional work as currently practiced? (Continued)

❭I will take the risk of characterizing landscape architecture at three scales. The largest is the scale at which landscape architects' work systemically affects the management of resources and people. For example, EDAW is currently doing a national plan for the African country of Rwanda, and trying to figure out all of the land use, education, and economic issues that go into stabilizing and growing a country in a more healthy way. The second is interventions in cities. Today, the most fruitful market for landscape architecture is repairing landscape systems that were eradicated or highly damaged. The third is the small, site-specific design scale where the imperatives might be fairly minimal. These three scales range from the detailed expression of place at the small scale up to the conceptual strategies for changing whole societies at the large scale.

Mark Johnson, FASLA
Founding Principal and President, Civitas, Inc.

❭For the first time in the ASLA's surveys of the profession, single practitioners are no longer the most common form of practice. That speaks both to the growing sophistication of the profession and the demand of practice. These statistics suggest that many practices are highly focused at a particular scale or type of work.

Kurt Culbertson, FASLA
Chairman of the Board, Design Workshop

❭The diversity is growing, and with climate change and trying to make our cities more walkable or livable, there will continue to be more opportunities. Landscape architects are also involved in large transportation projects, where we're often the facilitators on these massive projects, such as new light rail systems.

John Koepke, Associate Professor
Department of Landscape Architecture, University of Minnesota

❭We have a really broad diversity nationwide. Landscape architects are involved in stormwater management, green roofs, low-impact design, visual impact analysis, and transportation design—the list is endless. In our local market it's a lot of parks and recreational planning, downtown redevelopment, and site plans for office parks and housing developments. I know a landscape architect who has incorporated maintenance as a part of his practice, which is an up-and-coming necessity. This is our design, this is what it costs to build it, this is what it takes to maintain it.

Gary Scott, FASLA, Director
West Des Moines Parks & Recreation Department

❭ I see the diversity of the profession continuing to increase, and I think the idea of a more diverse profession constrained by the current definition simply doesn't make sense. There are a lot of opportunities where the profession could really step up and take a major role; so, in 20 years, I would like to see the profession doing things we can't even imagine right now.

Jim Sipes, ASLA
Senior Associate, EDAW, Atlanta

What are the core values that guide your work?

❯ One of our core values is integrity. Also key to our business is taking a project from A to Z, meaning from design to implementation to marketing. We want to ensure it does not lose its authenticity. Also, our clients' needs come first: Does our proposal accomplish their goals and objectives? We try to come out with greener solutions by collaborating with our clients.

Eddie George, ASLA
Founding Principal, The Edge Group

❯ Advancing design and raising disciplinary questions of design as they relate to contemporary culture are big interests and values of mine.

Julia Czerniak
Principal, CLEAR

❯ Honesty: It's always number one. Also important is a commitment to respect the users of the site. I don't necessarily believe in design by committee, but I believe you have to listen to everybody to try to understand what their expectations are. In terms of the values we look for in design, this sounds very simplistic, but we focus on safety, functionality, and aesthetics, pretty much in that order. Those things in a park system, in a public environment, are very important.

Gary Scott, FASLA
Director, West Des Moines Parks & Recreation Department

❯ The design process is a mutual educational process. It is about making sure all parties have access to all the knowledge everyone else has. I also believe passionately in the idea of environmental stewardship. You can have a great design without sacrificing the ecological function or the cultural integrity of a site.

Kofi Boone, ASLA
Assistant Professor, Department of Landscape Architecture, North Carolina State University

❯ My core value is that, ultimately, I am doing things to make my city a better place to live, and our world a healthier place, and that we can really help mitigate some of these environmental problems through the landscape.

Meredith Upchurch, ASLA
Green Infrastructure Designer, Casey Trees Endowment Fund

❯ Core values, for me, started with growing up on the farm. It is understanding that we are part of that larger process. In the universe there's kind of a rhythm and a beat; the more you understand it, from the design standpoint, the more creative we can be and the more enduring our designs will be.

Jim Sipes, ASLA
Senior Associate, EDAW, Atlanta

❯ My core values are related to my spirituality and religion, which are linked but not necessarily the same thing. I have a strong empathy and relationship with Native American people, so I place a value on working with them. You might call it a social justice issue. I try to provide services in a way that is culturally responsible. I strive to make the world a better place, improving the environment in terms of livability for humans, but also for the other beings on the planet.

John Koepke
Associate Professor, Department of Landscape Architecture, University of Minnesota

❯ We have a three-part value statement. The first is that the answer is always in the problem. The second is that our work must express a genuine sense of place that's authentic to that place. And, the third part is that we work for the benefit of people. We don't work to promote ourselves.

Mark Johnson, FASLA
Founding Principal and President, Civitas, Inc.

What are the core values that guide your work? (Continued)

❯ A basic core value is to focus on the quality of the final product. Doing everything to ensure that the built element is the best quality means we must make extra efforts to keep business processes and funding restrictions from getting in the way of achieving the goal. Defining the "best quality" means looking at all aspects of the environment and cultural resources and working for the best fit.

Karen Coffman, RLA
NPDES Coordinator, Highway Hydraulics Division, Maryland State Highway Administration

❯ Strong conceptual thinking, process-driven design, healthy debate, and environmental stewardship.

Gerdo Aquino, ASLA
Managing Principal, SWA Group

❯ The core values of my work are listening, respecting other points of view, and working toward consensus building. Establishing partnerships and collaboration is also valuable. There is a trend in our country whereby people are losing their connection to the outdoors. Making connections through traditional storytelling are values we bring into our work, to bridge generations and to help make better connections to nature.

Robin Lee Gyorgyfalvy, ASLA
Director of Interpretive Services & Scenic Byways, USDA Forest Service: Deschutes National Forest

❯ One of the core values we founded our firm on is that landscape architects have something to contribute. Ours is an equal profession to architecture and other allied professions, and we should be justly compensated for our work and our creativity. This mind-set has helped us become an equal player with other firms. We have done that by applying other core values: We listen; we want to be collaborative; and we seek projects where we can collaborate. We strive to provide appropriate design solutions to build functional, meaningful, and artful landscapes that endure.

Frederick R. Bonci, RLA, ASLA
Founding Principal, LaQuatra Bonci Associates

❯ We have a tagline at our office that it's fun, innovative, and smart. If you don't enjoy what you're doing, you're not going to do a good job. Being innovative, especially for a small firm—and ours is a very small firm—is your leg up on the competition. And last, just being smart about what you do. If you are really smart and strategic about what you're doing, it saves you money and time—and again, gives you a leg up on your competition.

Dawn Kroh, RLA
President, Green 3, LLC

❯ We focus on open-ended strategies. For example, if it's a small playground, people are still given a lot of choice about how they want to engage or discover a place. We're not building typical structures that are "single-minded"—here you climb, here you slide, and so on. We're much more interested in offering free play opportunities where people make up their own games. Take that to a larger scale, we're interested in how landscape systems can begin to engage a project and change over time.

Chris Reed
Founding Principal, StoSS

❯ My core values are more urban in nature: To work on projects that allow people to come back into the city and understand that the city is something to be cherished. Something I learned early on, which is a guiding principle of proper community design, was to live close to where you work. I've kept that idea with me. I have never owned a car; I walk or bike to work, or I take public transportation. I think it's important to show people it is easy, and that you practice what you preach.

Todd Kohli, RLA, ASLA
Co–Managing Director, Senior Director, EDAW San Francisco

❯A passion and respect for life, this planet, and the urgency to help "turn the ship around." By that I mean all the impacts from climate change, from global warming, and the core value of having a responsibility to take care of life on this planet and sustain it.

Barbara Deutsch, ASLA, ISA
Associate Director, BioRegional North America

❯I place core values in two categories. One set comprises values that guide the practice. We have evolved a company culture centered around four main strategies: content, people, business, and leadership. Members of the executive team provide leadership in each of these areas.

The other set is composed of values that guide the work itself. The two overlap in many ways. The firm is called Design Workshop because the founders wanted to create a firm that emphasized a spirit of collaboration. There are no "names on the door," so people can come and go over time and the firm can endure. This spirit of collaboration drives the role of a studio environment in which each person's contribution is valued.

Kurt Culbertson, FASLA
Chairman of the Board, Design Workshop

❯Simplicity and artful results, and the rigor of building beautiful landscapes.

Thomas Oslund, FASLA, FAAR
Principal, oslund.and.assoc.

❯For me, it is design with nature. We have the freedom to do what we want; but what is the responsibility that goes with that freedom? A key is being mutually supportive, interdependent. If we consider that we are interdependent with nature, then we will be able to design with nature better.

Tom Liptan, ASLA
Sustainable Stormwater Management Program, Portland Bureau of Environmental Services

❯One is a land ethic, and that's quite essential to the work we do on big pieces of land. The question we ask is: Is what we are doing right for the land? We've actually come up a series of ecological metrics. The second part is craftsmanship. We try to be as detailed as possible and spend a lot of time thinking about the details.

Kevin Campion, ASLA
Senior Associate, Graham Landscape Architecture

❯Providing exceptional professional service to our clients. Being leaders in creative problem-solving. Enhancing community livability while conserving natural resources. Providing a workplace where people can grow personally and professionally.

Mike Faha, ASLA, LEED AP
Principal, GreenWorks, PC

❯My core values are probably rooted in something I learned in the Girl Guides: "Always leave camp cleaner than when you found it." This means that our footprint is very light on the natural systems. Another core value has to do with understanding long-term impacts. This means looking to the past and to the future to ensure decisions we make have a long-term value, as opposed to short-term benefit. Which is why I'm interested in transit, and not highways.

Juanita D. Shearer–Swink, FASLA
Project Manager, Triangle Transit Authority

❯We value places of heritage, where there are multiple tangible and intangible values. The values we apply are respect for the place and its vibrancy, meaning, ecological health, and sustainability. We are interested in managing as well as intervening in evolution for the betterment of the place.

Patricia O'Donnell, FASLA, AICP
Principal, Heritage Landscapes, Preservation Landscape Architects & Planners

What are the core values that guide your work? (Continued)

❯It is refreshing to experience sustainability becoming more mainstream, as EDSA has incorporated these concepts for decades. It is now easier to convince clients that this is the way to proceed, and that the conservation of resources generates value in the marketplace. Along with this core value, practicing with a high level of ethics is important to me.

Douglas C. Smith, ASLA
Chief Operating Officer, EDSA

❯The re-creation of cities as sane environments—that is, as places that can sustain human life while mitigating their effect on the biomes they occupy.

Ignacio Bunster–Ossa, ASLA, LEED AP
Principal, Wallace Roberts & Todd, LLC

❯The National Park Service's core values: Shared stewardship: We share a commitment to resource stewardship with the global preservation community. Excellence: We strive continually to learn and improve so that we may achieve the highest ideals of public service. Integrity: We deal honestly and fairly with the public and one another. Tradition: We are proud of it, we learn from it, we are not bound by it. Respect: We embrace each other's differences so that we may enrich the well-being of everyone.

Joanne Cody, ASLA
Landscape Architect Technical Specialist, National Park Service

❯We strive to do work that doesn't look like it is of an era; rather, we create designs that appreciate over time. We also focus on smart systems, and challenge ourselves: Is this the right thing to do for the environment? We continue to take a closer look at sustainable landscapes.

Jim Burnett, FASLA
President, The Office of James Burnett

❯Respect for place; and places are both social and natural phenomena. It is sensitivity to both people and nature. I find it odd that those get separated.

Frederick R. Steiner, PhD, FASLA
Dean, School of Architecture, University of Texas

❯Part of the reason I have become a public landscape architect is that I want what I do to be sustainable; it should be the right solution. I'm in the Hollywood area, where everyone has to make their mark; but that type of work did not satisfy me. The kind of relationship I have developed with the community is the reason this is the right place for me.

Stephanie Landregan, ASLA
Chief of Landscape Architecture, Mountains Recreation & Conservation Authority

❯The most important core value I operate under is that there is a clear and distinct order to this planet—order to the way the ecosystems operate. It's a strong land ethic that the ecosystem services have value. It's wrong for us to impact these without understanding the consequences, without weighing those, and saying, okay, this is of value.

Jacob Blue, MS, RLA, ASLA
Landscape Architect/Ecological Designer, Applied Ecological Services, Inc.

❯To provide outstanding design and services to a select group of clients. To apply the art and craft of landscape architecture to each project that I do.

Ruben L. Valenzuela, RLA
Principal, Terrano

❯I care most about ecological integrity and biodiversity; in other words, the long-term survival of species as humans impact the world. A second core value is conserving the cultural, educational, and aesthetic heritage that landscapes have, and the potential of those landscapes to help people learn. Landscapes have this great capacity to teach, to create a human response that is aesthetic and causes delight.

Nancy D. Rottle, RLA, ASLA
Associate Professor, Department of Landscape Architecture, University of Washington

❯Integrity cannot be overstated. Professionalism, competence, and giving more than you promised. What guides the appropriateness of the solution? That's a really hard question. You deal with it on a case-by-case basis. Whether it's a physical, political, or a budget impediment, the solutions can be very different.

Roy Kraynyk
Executive Director, Allegheny Land Trust

❯Every place has a DNA—something is unique about it. We understand there are human, economic, and environmental circumstances that make an opportunity special. We develop solutions that are about that, which results in designed responses that are different all the time. I don't believe in a style, but I do believe there is an economy of intervention: How do I get the biggest return for the smallest investment?

Jose Alminana, ASLA
Principal, Andropogon Associates, Ltd.

3 Practice Opportunities

A UNIQUE ASPECT OF THE PROFESSION is the wide variety of places landscape architects can be employed to pursue their occupation. They may decide to work in a private firm, of any size, or find they prefer a public agency or a nonprofit group. Common to all these practice types, however, are abundant opportunities to work outside the office; it is, after all, largely an "outdoor" profession. Whether it is to perform a site analysis, visit precedent design examples, or do construction observation, landscape architects will spend considerable time out of doors; travel is also an essential component of the work.

If you, as a landscape architect, choose the private sector, you may work in an office ranging from a one-person shop, to an office with hundreds of professionals representing several disciplines. If you choose the public arena, you'll find myriad opportunities in government, from a local parks department to the U.S. Forest Service. Nonprofit organizations and nongovernment organizations (NGOs) provide another specialized realm in which landscape architects' skills and expertise are in great demand. Hundreds of landscape architects also have made successful careers as academics, teaching the next generation of landscape architects, or advancing the profession through research and innovative design and planning.

The purpose of this chapter is to provide an overview of these employment options and to discuss various vital aspects of professional practice, such as marketing and finding a job. You'll also read summaries here, describing who is practicing what, and where. Finally, you'll find information about professional associations that represent landscape architects and related professionals.

Pool, deck, and planting at residence in New York. Courtesy of Oehme van Sweden and Associates.

Private Practice Business

The majority of landscape architects practicing in the United States do so in a private office setting; approximately 80 percent identify themselves as being employed in the for-profit, private sector. Of those, nearly 20 percent have their own businesses, meaning they are co-owners or the sole owners of their firms.[1] Within the private landscape architecture sector are numerous business types and approaches. Factors that influence the type of projects a firm targets include geographic location, client base, and/or the firm's mission or philosophy. Most private firms create and follow a strategic plan that outlines their goals for sustaining and growing the business.

As a landscape architect in private practice, you might work in a firm, of any size, comprised solely of landscape architects and landscape designers—a "pure" landscape architecture business. It's just as likely, however, that you'll find yourself in a multidisciplinary office, where your colleagues might include architects, planners, engineers, or scientists, such as ecologists and soil scientists. Depending on the firm's core goals and the type of projects they do, any number of professional combinations is possible. There are also private design offices that specialize in a one kind of work, such as golf course design, therapeutic design, or historic preservation.

▲ Gateway interpretive site
on the Cascade Lakes National
Scenic Byway, designed by U.S.
Forest Service landscape architect,
Robin Gyorgyfalvy. Photographer:
Marlene Ralph.

▶ Landscape architecture offices
and studio space. Courtesy of
Oehme, van Sweden & Assoc.

Another important private business employer is the design/build sector. Traditionally, design/ build firms have focused almost exclusively on residential work, but that is changing. There are several larger design/build firms today that do both corporate and commercial design. Public projects are just starting to reexamine their request for proposal (RFP) processes to consider including the design and construction components from the onset of design. This, too, will provide more opportunities for design/build firms.

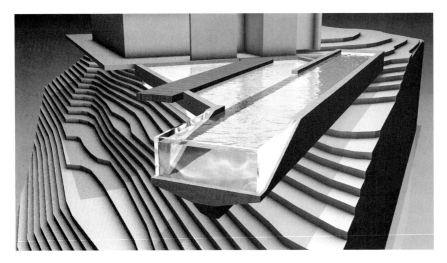

▲ Digital model of custom-designed cantilevered lap pool. Illustrator: Ben Dozier. Courtesy of Root Design.

▶ Two-inch thick acrylic panels being installed to complete lap pool, an example of a design/ build office's work. Photographer: Ben Dozier. Courtesy of Root Design.

Pursuing the Legacy of Urban Design

FREDERICK R. BONCI, RLA, ASLA

Founding Principal

LaQuatra Bonci Associates

Pittsburgh, Pennsylvania

Fred Bonci (left) and Jack LaQuatra at their office. Photographer: Michael Haritan.

Why did you decide to pursue a career in landscape architecture?

❯ My uncle was a builder and I wanted to be an architect. But then I wasn't sure, so I took a year to "find myself." Luckily I worked a summer job with a young man who was in landscape architecture at Penn State, and we carpooled together. In his back seat were books on design and the environment. He let me borrow them and I became highly interested the profession. I met with Penn State's department head and spent four hours with him. We walked around campus, he observed certain things with me and asked me questions, and at the end he told me I would be a perfect fit. So I found it totally by accident and fell in love with it.

What ideas do you have about educating today's landscape architects?

❯ Students need to make themselves well-rounded. Take electives in other allied arts. Take a speech class. Learn how to communicate. But more importantly, learn how to draw. Hand drawing is still critical, because when you hand-draw you actually figure things out. If you take the tack that you are never done learning, you'll eventually get to be a pretty good, well-rounded landscape architect.

How would you characterize the work of your office?

❯ The work in our office is quite diverse. We do everything from a single-family residence up to neighborhood design, town planning, and master planning design. We think that diversity is critical, because if you do not know how to design a space meaningful to an individual, you are never going to be a good urban designer. We focus primarily on urban design. It is a field landscape architecture does not focus on enough. A lot of our professional roots were in urban design and we've sort of pursued the profession's historic legacy in that area.

What is the most exciting aspect of your work?

❯ The thing I love, particularly at this stage of my professional life, is to start a new project, meet a new client, and be able to help define what the issues are. It is that first rush of the development of the project, sharing of ideas, and the design of the project at a conceptual design that sets all the frameworks for the future work. We really try to concentrate on that in our office because we feel the up-front design is critical.

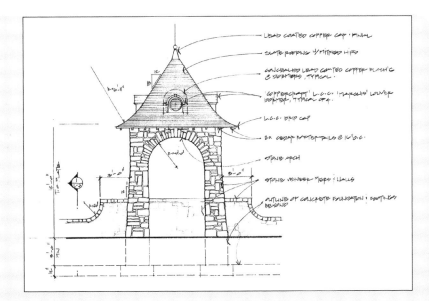

Sketch of stone pavilion at Summerset at Frick Park, Pittsburgh, Pennsylvania. Illustration: LaQuatra Bonci Associates, Inc.

What has been your most rewarding project to date?

❯ If you take a project as a whole, I would have to say it is Park DuValle in Louisville, Kentucky. It was such a tremendous transformation from a public-housing, derelict neighborhood. This was one of the first Hope VI projects that we worked on. Hope VI was a HUD initiative to tear down public housing and put people back into mixed-use urban neighborhoods that blur the lines between public housing and market-rate housing. The housing was torn down. It is now a traditional urban neighborhood. It has parks and great streets. It is a tremendous transformation, and it works. It has been built for about 10 years now.

Another thing I enjoyed about that project was that it was on the edge of the Algonquin Parkway, which is one of Olmsted's historic parkways in Louisville. I was able to work with the Olmsted Park Commission and the Olmsted Conservancy in Louisville on the creation of two new parkways that bisected the site. So they wound up with this classic landscape architecture story: a town built on a park

framework that had great urban components to it; and it was a great collaboration between residents, the architects, the urban designers, us as landscape architects, and all the social service people.

What role do new technologies play in your design process?

❯ We use all the current technologies to make hand drawings into state-of-the-art computer drawings. Our office lays over the CAD work with other graphic design products to produce more beautiful presentations, because we think CAD drawings really do not convey the warmth of spaces. We also use SketchUp, which is a wonderful tool, to give people an idea of massing of buildings and a sense of scale of the space. Then we use an illustrator to hand-draw over those and make a "warm and fuzzy" sketch of the hard-line computer drawings. We are now starting to do 3D animation. There are a lot of wonderful programs that turn those into movies so people can simulate driving down the street and get a sense of what it will be like to be in a public space or walk through a plaza.

What tips can you provide to someone regarding the job search process?

❭ Even if you are coming in to work as an intern, you need to present yourself professionally. It means being able to communicate, being courteous, being able to present your work with confidence and pride. One of the things we like is when people send us samples of their work as a preliminary look. That helps us be prepared to interview them and ask questions. During the interview we spend much more time having a dialogue and talking to them about their goals, their ambitions, where they want to be in the profession, and why they want to work here versus somewhere else.

Residents enjoying the new Park DuValle neighborhood, Louisville, Kentucky. Photographer: Paul Rocheleau.

What role can landscape architects take in making our world better?

❭ Early in my career I worked for Ed Stone at one of the largest landscape architecture firms in the country. He let us know that our job is to always give the client an alternative if we don't like his ideas. Keep teaching the client how it can be done better because you'll eventually win. But when you give up, you lose. He said never forget the educational aspects of the profession.

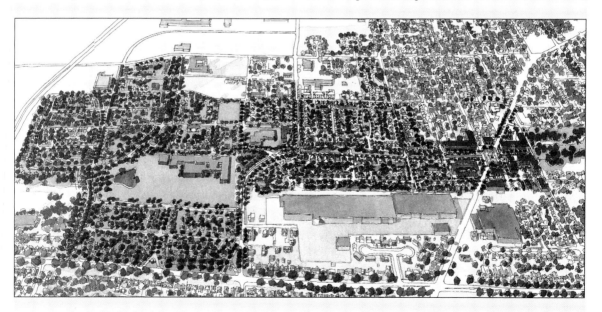

Aerial view sketch of Park DuValle community design, Louisville, Kentucky. Illustration: Urban Design Associates, LLC.

Design/Build with a Twist

ROBERT B. TILSON, FASLA

President

Tilson Group

Vienna, Virginia

Robert Tilson in his office. Photographer: Clark E. Tilson.

Why did you decide to pursue a career in landscape architecture?

❯ A neighbor owned a nursery, so I asked if I could have a summer job. That first summer was just basic work around the nursery, but the next summer I was on a work detail crew building retaining walls and planting plants. The following summer I went to work for a design/build landscape architect who was trained in the CCC, the Civilian Conservation Corps. Sometimes he would show me the park designs that he'd done back then. That's where I was introduced to landscape architecture, and I said, "Well, I've got to go do this."

How and why did you choose the school you attended to earn your degree?

❯ My high school guidance counselor sent for information (back then it had to be mailed to you) and I had about 20 brochures to review. I looked at Illinois, Wisconsin, Iowa State, and Purdue. I thought a Bachelor of Science degree would be a better fit for me. Purdue had a co-op program where you work off-campus in an office for a year. I really liked the idea of that, so I chose Purdue based on the co-op program.

What part of your education had the greatest influence on you?

❯ The relationships I developed with my professors were very profound. The one thing I really like about landscape architecture is that the faculty-student ratio is very low; you really get a lot of one-on-one with faculty. My friends in other majors were always surprised that I knew my professors. Over the past 20 years, there are still three or four professors I keep in contact with.

How would you characterize the work of your office?

❯ My firm is defined as a design/build company, but we're more than design/build. We are construction managers and landscape architects within the landscape industry. We don't have a shovel or a truck, yet we build million-dollar properties based on our aptitude as landscape architects and our ability to run construction practices. We use the design side of the business to drive the construction side. Once a project enters our door from a design standpoint, we tend to carry that all the way through completion, through construction. Our goal is not just to design it, but to build it, too.

Pool and arbor at residence in McLean, Virginia. Photographer: Robert B. Tilson.

Stone wall and bubble fountain at residence in McLean, Virginia. Photographer: Robert B. Tilson.

What is the size of your office and what is your role?

❯ There are two people in our office. I am the landscape architect and my wife is the CFO. She does all the billing. My role is everything, from design work to managing construction projects to doing the marketing. We outsource all the detailed design work. I do the conceptual design and then I scan that and e-mail it to a firm in Iowa and they further develop it and put it into CAD drawings.

For the construction part, we subcontract everything. I work with a landscape contractor, a lighting contractor, an irrigation contractor, a concrete contractor, a carpenter, a fountain specialist, and a swimming pool installer. I've got three or four subs I can turn to for each of those different pieces.

How did you come up with your unique approach to a design/build business?

❭ I wanted to see the things I designed get built, so I went to work for a large landscape contracting company. That's where I learned the sales side of the construction business. I saw that my sales represented a large percentage of the company's total sales, so I had to be making them a lot of money. I like to be in control of the design and the construction process. At that company, the construction really drove the design. I started thinking, how do I create a company that's going to allow me to do design to complement the construction? The construction business is very highly capitalized and I didn't want to have all the trucks and headaches. That's why I came up with this concept to focus on sales, project management, and design, and that's basically what my company does.

What has been your most rewarding project to date?

❭ The Korean ambassador's residence in Washington, DC. Turns out, the site was on a former World War I ammunitions testing facility. When we began to build the garden, we hit a toxic chemical dumping pit. I had to work with the Army Corps of Engineers, the government of South Korea, and then the landscape architect, so I basically had three different clients on that project. It was interesting because I had to sit down with State Department people, with embassy people, the ambassador himself, so it was very challenging but very rewarding. In the end, we put together a world-class garden that won several national awards for design, as well as national awards for contracting.

You said the sales process is an exciting aspect of your work. What does that involve?

❭ I was taught the design process, which is a step-by-step process to get a client to understand how we're going to solve their problem. But there is also a sales process for getting the client to sign on the dotted line, that says you will do X amount of work for this fee. It is a multistep process to get a client to do that. I've taken several classes and read many books on how to make a sale, and there is an art to it. I like seeing the client's face once I've come up with a design idea that they're really happy with, and I also like the process of leading them up to signing a contract.

When hiring a student for an internship or entry-level job, which aspects of their education do you find to be most important?

❭ I look for someone who has a good grasp of the core competencies—the design and construction processes—and that they can show me these in their portfolio. So including design work is important, and then having a good understanding of the technical side of the business, creating dimension plans, and construction details.

What role can landscape architects take in making our world better?

❭ Our role is to use sustainability as the core value in building new communities. We can be players in that environment worldwide as we see other countries grow and help them avoid the mistakes that we made here, in terms of the degradation of our resources.

Bringing Value to a Project

EDDIE GEORGE, ASLA

Founding Principal

The Edge Group

Columbus, Ohio, and Nashville, Tennessee

Eddie George reviewing office projects. Courtesy of The Edge Group.

Why did you decide to pursue a career in landscape architecture?

❭ When I first got to Ohio State, I wanted to look at architecture, but going that route wouldn't allow me the flexibility to be an athlete. I discovered that landscape architecture would allow a little more flexibility. I remember

The central square at Greene Town Center, Dayton, Ohio. Courtesy of The Edge Group.

my freshman year I had an introductory course where I did several models. I came up with design concepts and used 3D modeling to move through it—I loved it. I became enamored with landscape architecture, so I stuck with it. I learned about the history of the profession, and took design and construction classes. It was very difficult to juggle that workload along with the responsibilities of an athlete, especially at a school such as Ohio State.

What is the most exciting aspect of your work?

❭ The most exciting aspect is definitely the relationships. In this business, it's not just based on what you know, or what your expertise is; it is really based on your relationships with people. We take great pride in having a diverse group of people we work with, from developers to governments to universities, and high schools. We feel very proud of our network and how we are expanding our

Site design rendering of St. John Arena, Jesse Owens Plaza, Columbus, Ohio. Courtesy of The Edge Group.

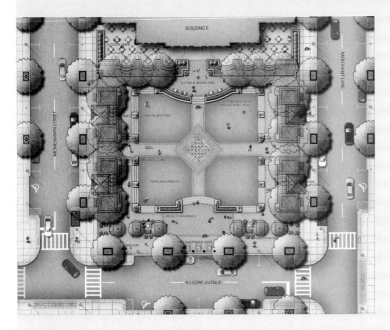

Rendering of the town square at Peninsula Town Center, Hampton, Virginia. Courtesy of The Edge Group.

network by thinking outside of the box. So it is always exciting because of this diversity of people and projects.

What has been your most rewarding project to date?

❭ My most rewarding is the first project, which we did for Ohio State. We did a corridor study for the gateway area around the university's athletic venues. We prepared a master plan and re-development vision, and did the design work for the Jesse Owens Plaza. It was especially rewarding given that I played for Ohio State right at that stadium, and that I then had an opportunity to give back to the school where I gained my education. It was rewarding to return and make it beautiful.

Which aptitudes, traits, and skills do you see in most landscape architects?

❭ You have to have a passion for design and a desire to want to find and create solutions. It is important to be open to ideas that are innovative, which will give you the ability to think outside of the box. Landscape architects are also curious about the layers of the land, have an understanding of how people move within space, and they also have a love of the arts.

What role can landscape architects take in making our world better?

❭ With the interest in green products and concerns about global warming, landscape architects have the opportunity to do creative design solutions with a green thumbprint. As developers are moving toward building greener, we're showing them how our work brings value to their project: coming up with sustainable solutions, or how we can use less of certain materials, and so on. I think it's our duty as landscape architects to build responsibly. Our motto is we work with the land, not against it.

Conducting a Seamless Collaboration

IGNACIO BUNSTER–OSSA, ASLA, LEED AP

Principal

Wallace Roberts & Todd, LLC

Philadelphia, Pennsylvania

Ignacio Bunster–Ossa in his office. Photographer: Dave Moser. © 2006, www.davemoser.com.

Why did you decide to pursue a career in landscape architecture?

❭ By accident. After graduating as an architect the only job available at the time was as a designer in a two-person landscape architecture office, and they, well, embraced me. I never looked back.

How and why did you choose which school to attend for your degree?

❭ I was directed to the MLA program at the University of Pennsylvania by my first employer, who was an alumnus of the program. The key to that program, and that which influenced me the most, was the diversity of lecturers, led by Ian L. McHarg, who collectively placed men and women in a very large and complex social, cultural, and natural milieu.

How would you characterize the work of your office?

❭ As a multidisciplinary group of creative individuals seeking to make the world a better place, one collaboration at a time. Wallace, Roberts, and Todd consists of about 50 landscape architects embedded in a 200-person firm that also includes architects and planners. My role is design principal and co-manager of the firm's headquarters in Philadelphia.

What has been your most rewarding project to date?

❭ The design of the Santa Monica Palisades Park and Beach Boardwalk, part of a comprehensive effort to revitalize a cherished oceanfront. The project required a seamless collaboration between the landscape architect and an artist, Jody Pinto. The success of the project was underscored when, after the final design presentation, a member of the city's public art board frustratingly inquired, "Where's the art?"

How often do you involve the community and/or end users in the design process? In what way?

❭ Much of my work involves public resources. Public involvement is central to what I do, from canvassing community leaders and stakeholders to making public presentations.

What role do new technologies play in your design process?

❭ There has been tremendous advancement in sustainable technologies, from recycled materials to bioengineering and green energy systems. Knowing these technologies will continue to be essential tools in helping us lead projects and exceed our clients' goals and expectations.

Who are some of the allied professionals you work/consult with? What role do they play in the design process?

❭ I work with architects, planners, artists, engineers, economists, ecologists, archeologists, and many other specialists. Everyone has a vital voice. I often play the role of "conductor," guiding everyone toward something that in the end can be greater than the individual notes.

Which aptitudes, traits, and skills do you see in most landscape architects?

❭ Aptitude: Creative thinking; not being satisfied with the ways things are.

Traits: Curiosity for the human needs of, and behavior in, outdoor environments.

Santa Monica beachfront renovation from the pier to Bay Street, California. © 2001, David Zaitz Photography.

Aerial view of Beach Improvement Group (B.I.G.) Project, Santa Monica, California. Photographer: Tim Street–Porter.

Palisades Park historic renovation, Santa Monica, California. Courtesy of WRT.

Skills: Design and communication; ability to lead, interact, and collaborate with multiple allied disciplines.

What tips can you provide to someone regarding the job search process?

❯ Review the firm's Web site, then visit them to get a feel for what they do and how they manage the design process. Find the right fit, regardless of reputation. Rather than trying to contact busy principals, go through the human resources department. Also, apply for internships—it's a sure way to get a relationship going in preparation for a postgraduation position.

What role can landscape architects take in making our world better?

❯ We do already: leading comprehensive teams of consultants in the design of better cities.

Global Opportunities to Connect Sustainable and Economic Design

TODD KOHLI, RLA, ASLA

Co-Managing Director, Senior Director

EDAW

San Francisco, California

Todd Kohli, senior director of EDAW's San Francisco office. © 2006, Andreas Vogel.

Why did you decide to pursue a career in landscape architecture?

⟩ In tenth grade we had a project that started with an aptitude test on career potential. Mine came back biologist, landscape architect, and math. I had been thinking about architecture. Since math and biology were inherent within landscape architecture, I chose that one because it had the word "architecture" in it. For that project we researched the profession, and

I realized as a landscape architect you would have a bigger impact than with one piece of architecture.

How and why did you choose the school you attended to earn your degree?

⟩ Due to my research in tenth grade, I picked Penn State. I also looked at Virginia Tech, but decided on Penn State because it had lower tuition and was closer to the home. I was also very interested in the option to go to Rome and study for a semester.

How would you characterize the work of your office?

⟩ EDAW prides itself on a platform called DEEP, with each letter standing for an aspect of our work: design, economics, environment, and planning. Within our design studio we work on small to medium-sized projects from 1 acre to up to 100 acres. Typically, we push the design process all the way through construction documentation and follow through to the project opening. We are focused on built work, whereas our planning and urban design studios work on projects from 100 acres all the way up to 2 million acres. No matter the studio, we're all striving to find the thread that weaves the best way to socially, economically, and sustainably formulate a design for a client.

What is size of your office and what is your role?

⟩ EDAW is headquartered in San Francisco, which is also the office I direct, and it has 110 professionals. However, worldwide EDAW has

34 offices and roughly 1,800 employees. I am one of 30 landscape designers in the design studio in San Francisco. Since joining EDAW, I have gained more responsibility each year, from design and production to marketing and managing people. EDAW has been around since 1939, and recently there has been a paradigm shift: to foster and mentor younger leaders sooner, and that's part of my new role.

What has been your most rewarding project to date?

❯ Tokyo Midtown, for a client who is the second largest developer in Japan. From the beginning this was to be a project "on the green." It ended up that almost half of the 25-acre site is open space—which is a huge change from typical Tokyo developments. Its

▲ Central Plaza, Tokyo Midtown project. © 2007, EDAW. Photographer: David Lloyd.

▶ SketchUp model for bamboo planters at Tokyo Midtown. © 2004, EDAW.

success helps people, and developers especially, understand that open space is a vital portion of a project. It is what helps to attract visitors and buyers to the retail areas and why people want to work and live close to it.

This was a regeneration project for the district of Roppongi, which used to be very unsafe in the evening. When Tokyo Midtown opened, it had an immediate impact. The design allowed people to come outside and recreate in their own community. It's just amazing to see how a park, an urban plaza, and a streetscape have provided so much enjoyment and interest, not only locally, but also with other developers and other cities within Asia.

I was able to travel to Japan more than 20 times for this project. I immersed myself to understand the culture as much as I could; and it has been really rewarding.

What is the most exciting aspect of your work?

❯ I love my job. I get to draw for a living, explain the drawings, watch them become reality, and then see people actually use and enjoy the space. I get to tell people about my profession, and get them excited about the creativity, the importance of how ideas are translated into built form, and about its positive impact on society.

Perspective of Grand Boulevard, Jumeira Gardens, Dubai, United Arab Emirates. © 2008, EDAW, Shawn Jackson, Jeremy Siew.

Who are some of the allied professionals you consult with? What role do they play in the design process?

❭ We work with civil engineers, structural engineers, architects, graphic designers, sign designers, and lighting designers—everyone. We also work with environmental lawyers, for example, in figuring out best practices for a community. On mixed-use projects, we work with retail consultants. The goal is that the outcome will be seamless, and it truly looks like each complements the other in the built form.

What role do new technologies play in your design process?

❭ The newest technologies we are working with include several 3D modeling programs that enable us to build a space, move it, shift it, change the proportionality of items, and immediately have what we call creative reviews—in-house critiques. The great thing about these 3D programs is that you're able to put yourself at eye level in that plaza, and see different views, or pretend that you are in a helicopter and have an aerial view.

When hiring students for internships or entry-level jobs, which aspects of their education do you find to be most important?

❭ Field trips and studying abroad are invaluable to understanding space and the proportions of places. Sitting in places that are unfamiliar are good to challenge peoples' perspectives and to understand new cultures. In the end, we are designing public rooms; so visiting places throughout the world can help designers relate their current project to the precedents they've experienced.

What role can landscape architects take in making our world better?

❭ Our profession is a blending of different professions into one because we think about civil engineering, about sculpture, about biology, about water, and how people will use the space. We blend all of these things into one seamless integrated system of public space. All of these add up to a sustainable approach to design that will ultimately help make the world's ecosystems much better.

Project Profile

THE VILLAGE OF WASHINGTON'S LANDING

Bringing a Neighborhood to Life on a Former Brownfield Site

▲ The community of Washington's Landing on an island near Pittsburgh, Pennsylvania. Courtesy of LaQuatra Bonci Associates, Inc. Photographer: Michael Haritan.

▲ Riverwalk overlook with views to downtown Pittsburgh skyline. Courtesy of LaQuatra Bonci Associates, Inc. Photographer: Michael Haritan.

▶ Pavement detailing and arbor at a seating area along the riverwalk. Courtesy of LaQuatra Bonci Associates, Inc. Photographer: Michael Haritan.

PROJECT OVERVIEW

Date: 1997

Type: Brownfield/Community Design

Location: Pittsburgh, Pennsylvania

Client: The Rubinoff Company and the Urban Redevelopment Authority of Pittsburgh

Firm: LaQuatra Bonci Associates, Pittsburgh, Pennsylvania

Award: 2001 Pittsburgh Chapter of the AIA—Washington's Landing Overlooks and Arbors—Landscape Architectural Details Award

Web link to project: www.laquatrabonci.com/portfolio/portfolio_main.php?view=project&id=7&folder=2

This once blighted island was transformed into a high-quality, multiuse development, including market-rate housing, office/research and development, and light industrial uses. It also features a marina, a rowing center, and a public park.

—URBAN REDEVELOPMENT AUTHORITY OF PITTSBURGH[2]

History of the Island

Washington's Landing is a 42-acre island in the middle of the Allegheny River, a mere 2 miles north of Pittsburgh's Point. The island's early development was farming; however, with Pittsburgh's exponential industrial growth in the mid- to late 1800s, the island became a rest stop for transportation operations carrying livestock. With the regular inflow of livestock, the island began to cater to the meatpacking industry. Before long, Washington's Landing, then called Herr's Island, was renowned throughout the city for its foul odor.

As the transportation industry evolved, Herr's Island was no longer needed as a stopping point for livestock. By the late 1960s the City of Pittsburgh began to consider future uses for the deserted island, which, along with the meatpacking industry, had also hosted stockyards, garbage collection, railroad operations, sawmills, and various scrapyards.

Given the island's unique location yet undesirable abandoned condition, eventually the City's Urban Redevelopment Authority (URA) took over the island in the hopes of transforming the brownfield into a flourishing community. It is purported that George Washington spent a night on the island in the mid-1700s when his raft capsized. Because of Herr's Island's notorious reputation, it was renamed Washington's Landing in the late 1980s.[3]

Brownfield Redevelopment

Brownfield sites are places whose past uses resulted in the ground and subsoils becoming polluted. Problematic uses typically associated with brownfields are garbage landfills, industrial disposal sites, petroleum processing plants, and the like. In recent years, with land becoming more limited in urban centers, the redevelopment of former industrial and brownfield sites is emerging as an important trend in many cities. With guidance from agencies like the U.S. Environmental Protection Agency (EPA) and environmental consultants, landscape architects are among the professionals called upon to assist in creating visions for the reuse of these contaminated brownfield sites.[4] This, however, is no simple task. Several rounds of environmental assessment are required to determine how best to mitigate and clean up the site. In the example of Washington's Landing, the cleanup and overall redevelopment took some 20 years and cost millions of dollars. In addition to environmental concerns, the landscape architects had to consider what new infrastructure would be necessary, the best placement for various types of development, and how new development would alter traffic patterns.

A New Community

LaQuatra Bonci Associates, a Pittsburgh-based landscape architecture firm, was hired by the Rubinoff Company and the URA of Pittsburgh to develop a master planning strategy for the entire island. Over the course of the project, the landscape architects also provided services for design development and construction documentation. LaQuatra Bonci is a firm known for creating neighborhoods that integrate natural systems and public open space. The landscape architects' community design for the Village of Washington's Landing included a network of shared green spaces and townhouse groupings that front on traditional neighborhood streetscapes. The backs of the units face the river and an adjacent riverside trail. The river trail provides an important pedestrian circulation route, and has been called a "visual masterpiece" due to plantings, wildflowers, and the placement of several scenic overlooks.[5] At the westernmost point of the trail, there is an overlook pavilion that provides excellent views of the downtown skyline. While the western portion of the island is occupied by this new neighborhood, the eastern segment is host to a marina and corporate office buildings.[6] Currently, the Three Rivers Rowing Association and the Western Pennsylvania Conservancy have located their headquarters on the island.[7]

Private Practice: Size and Configuration

As noted earlier in the chapter, private landscape architecture offices can vary greatly in size. The smallest is the sole proprietor—the owner is the only employee and is, therefore, responsible for all aspects of the business. Firms with up to about 25 employees are considered "small businesses" within the landscape architecture profession. Working in these smaller firms typically provides employees with broad exposure to the various phases and details of the firm's projects.

Offices that employ between 30 to 70 people are deemed to be medium-sized firms; and those with more than 75 people are considered large. Larger firms tend to have more than one owner or principal; a rough estimate is 1 principal to 10 design staff. Medium and larger offices also typically have a staff person or a department devoted to marketing, to assist in generating work for the firm.

The largest landscape architecture firms are usually also global in reach. Only a handful of firms fall into this category. There are numerous global multidisciplinary offices, with architects, planners, and/or engineers, along with landscape architects, on staff. Global-reach practices are typically headquartered in the United States, with branch offices located in other countries. Landscape architects from the offices in the United States often have the opportunity to work in the branch offices on a temporary basis, from a few weeks to several months or more.

The San Francisco offices of EDAW. © 2008, EDAW. Photographer: Christine Bolghand.

Small = Efficient

RUBEN L. VALENZUELA, RLA

Principal

Terrano

Tempe, Arizona

Ruben Valenzuela at his office. Courtesy of Terrano.

Why did you decide to pursue a career in landscape architecture?

⟩ I began my design studies at Arizona State University with the goal of studying architecture. But during my second year I took an elective class, "Introduction to Landscape Architecture," which I found to be incredibly interesting, and I realized that was the field I wanted to pursue.

How and why did you choose the school you attended to earn your degree?

⟩ I chose the university that is, in essence, in my backyard. The architecture school has been highly regarded for a long time. In-state tuition is always helpful.

How would you characterize the work of your office?

⟩ I am definitely a small office. Since opening my practice, I have never had more than two other

Saguaro Branch Library, City of Phoenix libraries, Arizona. Courtesy of Terrano.

▲ Kensington Grove Park, a 5-acre park in northeast Mesa, Arizona. Courtesy of Terrano.

employees. That was by design. I wanted to keep things simple, lean, and efficient. Fortunately for landscape architects, landscape design projects are not as personnel-intensive as architecture or engineering projects. I am currently a one-person shop, so I do everything.

What is the most exciting aspect of your work?

❯ For me, it is the design process. Starting with, essentially, a blank canvas and creating an environment that people can enjoy and that benefits the environment.

▲ Salt River Project Information Services Building, part of a 40-acre project consisting of plazas and open space in Phoenix, Arizona. Courtesy of Terrano.

How often do you involve the community and/or end users in the design process? In what way?

❭ I have done numerous public projects, and governing agencies usually require public meetings to gather data from the end users. The design process is often initiated by a public meeting. The purpose of the meeting is to determine concerns and the desired improvements for the project. I have developed a system whereby I post large boards with prompting questions on them. Examples are: Add ramadas? Add skateboard facilities? Remove soccer field? Blank spaces are left at the bottom of each board for attendees to fill with their own concerns or desires, if they wish to do so. The attendees are then asked to place a small "agree" or "disagree" sticker next to the prompting questions. The goal is to generate consensus on each question. Participants are also given comment sheets on which to identify issues, offer potential solutions, and prioritize the issues. This approach to data collection provides a means for all attendees, including children, to give input in a casual, no-pressure way. It also avoids the typical public meeting scene, where attendees are asked verbally for their input and where only a few of the more vocal attendees typically dominate the proceedings.

Who are some of the allied professionals you work/consult with? What role do they play in the design process?

❭ I work most often with architects and civil engineers. The role these allied disciplines play in the design of a project depends on the architect or engineer. Some architects or engineers (especially architects) may take a greater role in the design process. It's my opinion, however, that the best-designed projects result from a collaborative, inclusive effort from all the disciplines on a project.

Which aptitudes, traits, and skills do you see in most landscape architects?

❭ Design skills, sensitivity to the environment, a love of nature, people skills, patience (it takes time for plants to reach maturity, thus the full measure of a landscape design may take years to be realized), understanding of demographics, and an understanding of how people move in space.

What role can landscape architects take in making our world better?

❭ Designing quality exterior environments. Also important is to participate on citizen boards and commissions, or seek an elected office, and use our skills to influence how our cities, towns, open spaces, and wilderness areas look and are managed.

Celebrating Place

JEFFREY K. CARBO, FASLA

Principal

Jeffrey Carbo Landscape Architects

Alexandria, Louisiana

Landscape architect Jeffrey Carbo.

Why did you decide to pursue a career in landscape architecture?

❯ When I enrolled at Louisiana State University (LSU), I was in general studies. I didn't know anything about landscape architecture. I discovered it through a seminar class. A couple of landscape architecture professors came to the class and explained what they do. Soon after I made an appointment to meet with them. Learning more about the curriculum and the overall profession, it all seemed extremely interesting, and at that point I knew what I was going to do.

How would you characterize the work of your office?

❯ We attempt to celebrate what is significant around us. The best design work is that which is at

least somewhat contextual—there is a derivative extracted from something, either subtle or significant, in the places where we work. As young designers, we all have a tendency to want to do everything we've ever learned, and the composition becomes overloaded. One thing that we've begun to cultivate over the last 10 years is telling clients it is often more about what you don't do, than what you do. It is this idea of being restrained and thoughtful. In initial design sessions, we put everything on the table, and then begin to extract what is significant and meaningful. I'm convinced this process makes projects better in the sense of their enduring qualities, their longevity, and their timelessness.

What is the size of your office and what is your role?

❯ Our staff varies from 10 to 12 people; typically, 8 or 9 are landscape architects, and some are associates. I am the owner and the principal of the firm. Beyond running a business, my main strength and influence is overall design direction. I like to touch every project in the office. This is becoming a little more difficult as our firm grows. However, we want everyone to be involved in every aspect of a project. We think the final product ends up being better if you have lots of eyes on it.

What has been your most rewarding project to date?

❯ A botanical garden and environmental education center that we just completed in east Texas, which has been in our office for seven years. Two components make it very meaningful. First, it was one of the best examples of a healthy collaboration among a multitude of disciplines. It was a very complex commission. Second, as we were getting ready to break ground to build it, the unthinkable happened.

Cypress Gate and boardwalk crafted from recycled cypress trees felled by Hurricane Rita. Shangri La Botanical Garden and Nature Center, Orange, Texas. © 2008, Marc Cramer.

The site was devastated by Hurricane Rita. When the client called us to inspect the site after the storm, we thought it was over. The meeting was quite the contrary. They said we need this project now more than ever; show us what you can do now with what you see out there. Although we lost a lot of trees, the end product ended up being better because of what happened. We used a lot of the downed materials in ways that acknowledge nature's cycles. When you think about it in that way, instead of the catastrophic implications—that it's nature and it's part of what could happen—and this is how the site was impacted, the project becomes more interesting.

Who are some of the allied professionals you consult with? What role do they play in the design process?

❭ During the last five years, it has really changed because our work has evolved. From the beginning,

we've always worked with architects. The working relationship is dictated by whether or not the people you are working for know what a successful collaboration looks like. Everyone has their primary interests, but the most successful collaborations are where they let us be landscape architects. Beyond that, recently and with greater frequency, we've worked with interior designers, graphic designers, and interpretive exhibit designers.

On a recent botanical garden project, we came up with some concepts for sculptural elements, so we conducted a national search for an artist to collaborate with us. We had 40 submissions and selected one. It was wonderful to work with this artist because she bought into the overall concept, but then tweaked it with her ideas. Design collaboration is like a symphony, and every instrument has its part in the final composition. In that regard, this botanical garden project was a lot of fun because everyone knew their role, played their part, but there was some flexibility for input from each of the disciplines, and because of this, it made the project better.

Which aptitudes, skills, and traits do you see in most landscape architects?

❯ It's either one of two things, or a hybrid of both. It's either an inclination to be interested in art and/ or a little bit of science, or an inclination to be interested in the outdoors and nature. For me, it was initially the art component. Then, after discovering more about the profession, it became more about nature and learning to recognize the beauty in things you took for granted.

What tips can you provide to someone regarding the job search process?

❯ Find out more about the places you would like to work. I understand that salary is important. But what's more important when you are young, and there is so much to learn, is to go to a place where you are likely to learn the facets of the profession that most interest you. That is how you are going to cultivate value in your abilities.

What role can landscape architects take in making our world better?

❯ We're going to find that landscape architects will be sought out for what they know and what they do in a much greater way than they have in the past. With the impact of humans on our environment, and the consequences of things that have been done in the past, which no one has recognized much until recently—then think about how long it is going to take to remediate those things. How do we begin to change how people think about those issues? Landscape architects are poised to be on the forefront of this education.

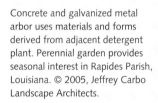
Concrete and galvanized metal arbor uses materials and forms derived from adjacent detergent plant. Perennial garden provides seasonal interest in Rapides Parish, Louisiana. © 2005, Jeffrey Carbo Landscape Architects.

Cultural Expertise in Public Sector Work

ELIZABETH KENNEDY, ASLA

Principal

EKLA Studio

Brooklyn, New York

Landscape architect Elizabeth Kennedy. Photographer: Jason Berger.

Why did you decide to pursue a career in landscape architecture?

❯ I come from an architectural family; my father and uncle were architects. He had model-making materials in the house, so I was always around this. I would design houses, too, but mine always had streams running through them. When I learned people actually designed landscapes, I was really taken by that idea. I went to school in the West Indies where you choose your career path early. I had a lot of support and tracked this profession from an early age.

How and why did you choose the school you attended to earn your degree?

❯ I made a decision not to study landscape architecture as an undergraduate. I got my undergraduate degree in environmental psychology at Cornell University. I decided to stay at Cornell for my graduate degree. I felt it provided a lot of opportunities and I was comfortable there. Also, I had been a scholarship student my entire academic career and Cornell was generous with funding to stay on for graduate school. I attended Cornell's MLA program for three years; however, I did not complete my thesis. The State of New York allows candidates to also get a license through working under a landscape architect for 12 years, which means I took the long road to becoming a registered landscape architect.

How would you characterize the work of your office?

❯ We are a small office. We have been as large as 14 and now have 2 landscape architects and 1 support staff. This is a minority, woman-owned firm and we do mostly public sector work. We have developed an expertise in cultural and historical restoration work. We balance that with infrastructure work. One hundred percent of our work gets built. We are known for having construction documents that are tight and very credible. We detail more than most, often to the level of shop drawings.

What has been your most rewarding project to date?

❯ The Weeksville Heritage Center has been a series of projects. The center is the reconstruction of a historic nineteenth-century African

Photorealistic rendering of the Weeksville Heritage Center interpretive site, new education center, and the historic Hunterfly Road Houses, Brooklyn, New York. Illustrator: Elizabeth Kennedy Landscape Architect.

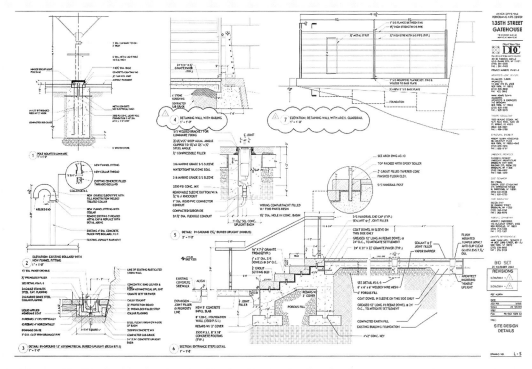

Construction drawing details for Harlem Stage Gatehouse Theatre. Courtesy of Elizabeth Kennedy Landscape Architect.

American community. The first project was the restoration of the domestic landscape around the Hunterfly Road Houses, which are on the National Register of Historic Places. Then came the large interpretive site, which is almost an acre of land that leads from a new education center to the houses. It was rewarding because our work ranged from historic restoration to interpretive planning, programming, and narrative development.

Detail of custom-designed handrail. Photographer: Sigal Ben Shmuel.

You often work on teams; who are some of the allied professionals you work with?

❭ Because we are a minority, woman-owned business, we are usually part of teams. Generally, we work with architects and engineers. We've had situations where we took the lead in terms of the site development. This needs to happen more often. We find that if the civil engineer is leading the site design work, in our opinion, there are opportunities that are lost.

We have worked on archaeologically sensitive sites, and I have worked with anthropologists and archaeologists. Usually, the client has retained them and we incorporate their research findings as part of our analysis and design for the project.

What tips can you provide to someone regarding the job search process?

❭ Show me how you think. Where you really see this is in sketching, especially process sketching. I would like to see a strong grasp of the fundamentals of design, such as the rules of composition. I am looking to see that there is a strong connection between the concept and its constructability. The portfolio should synthesize all of these things.

What are your feelings about the profession becoming a necessity?

❭ I remember a professor excitedly saying that the profession is growing. He said we need to have more landscape architects in order to become more integrated in society in the way that doctors and lawyers are, for example. We can only thrive if the profession is seen as a necessity, and not a luxury. Because of our training, most landscape architects believe we are a necessity. One of the ways to inculcate that message is to have more landscape architects who are more visible and doing more things; then the diversity of the profession will be understood by the public.

What role can landscape architects take in making our world better?

❭ Landscape architects have to integrate themselves, meaningfully, in green technology development. From what I understand, renewable energy development, such as windmill and solar farms, require large tracts of land. There is an impact on the land and a need for the management of resources. This includes the visual aspect, as well as the natural and human habitats. Landscape architects need to be part of the professional support services for these developments. I believe this is a huge opportunity.

Mexico-based Landscape and Urbanism Practice

MARIO SCHJETNAN, FASLA

Founding Partner

Grupo de Diseno Urbano

Colonia Condesa, México

Landscape architect Marion Schjetnan. Photographer: Francisco Gomez Sosa.

Why did you decide to pursue a career in landscape architecture?

❯ Being an architecture student, I wanted to expand my notion of design into the world of open space and the city.

Where did you obtain your degree(s)?

❯ I studied architecture at the National University of México, UNAM (1968).

I obtained a master's degree in landscape architecture with an emphasis in urban design at the University of California, Berkeley in 1970. In 1985, I was appointed a Loeb Fellow in Advanced Environmental Studies by the Graduate School of Design (GSD) at Harvard University.

What are the core values that guide your work?

❯ Our design philosophy is based on the conviction that environmental design, either rural or urban, must be transformed through a creative process

Grand promenade connects Museum of Anthropology to Tamayo Museum at Chapultepec Park, Mexico City. Photographer: Francisco Gomez Sosa.

Thematic Cornerstone Garden, Sonoma, California, pays tribute to immigrant farm workers. Photographer: Richard Barnes.

in balance with nature and observing local culture and environment, while involving the client or community in the process. Our objective is to produce creative and contemporary solutions to our design proposals. These proposals must be implementable, efficient, sustainable, and aesthetic.

What has been your most rewarding project to date?

❯ We have many rewarding projects at many different scales. Some are valuable in their social and community appreciation; others for their ecological and/or historical relevance; and, finally, others for their aesthetic or artistic reward.

Which aptitudes, traits, and skills do you see in most landscape architects?

❯ In addition to loving nature and the city, a good landscape architect must be skilled in design, and the capacity to work for people, communities, or individual clients. They must also be able to work in teams. He or she must be an expert in the notion and recognition of place, to be interested in the history as well as the physiographic and natural condition of place. Finally, he or she must be a person interested in the arts and culture.

What role can landscape architects take in making our world better?

❯ We believe strongly that landscape architecture can improve the quality of life and people in many ways. It is a profession ideally related to communities and people at large. The excitement of our profession comes when a specific project is finished and it is being used and enjoyed by people.

Customized Resorts in a Global Practice

DOUGLAS C. SMITH, ASLA

Chief Operating Officer

EDSA

Fort Lauderdale, Florida

Doug Smith (right) and colleagues conducting site analysis in the Dominican Republic. Courtesy of EDSA.

Why did you decide to pursue a career in landscape architecture?

〉 I started college in general education courses, and then decided to pursue a business degree. But the coursework did not excite me so I re-evaluated my options. Knowing I had displayed artistic abilities as a child, my parents steered me in the direction of a design-related degree. It was then that I discovered landscape architecture. I made the switch and never looked back. I chose Iowa State University because it was close to my hometown.

Much of your work focuses on resorts and recreation; why have you chosen that as a career direction?

〉 About 60 percent of my work is heavily resort influenced. I say that because many of our resort assignments involve not only typical "high design" resort elements, but also incorporate the best of community planning and urban design. Upon graduation from college, I accepted an offer from EDSA. As it happens, EDSA has long been recognized as leaders in resort design; therefore, my career has also taken that path.

What is the size of your office and what is your role?

〉 EDSA has five offices, four in the United States and one in China. We have 240 on our staff, and about 180 of those are landscape architects. We are a diverse group, with employees representing 32 different countries. I am the head of a landscape architecture "studio," which is a team that works together on a variety of planning and design projects. My studio role is to generate new business; oversee design, contracts, and billing; ensure quality control; and mentor members of the studio. In addition, I am the chief operating officer for EDSA. This role involves assisting the managing principal and overseeing many facets of the administration of the firm.

What has been your most rewarding project to date?

〉 The project is the Florida Nature and Culture Center, a 120-acre religious retreat campus in south Florida. It was memorable because it was the first time I was exposed to all the intricacies of implementing a design plan, from interface with the client and the consultant team to working with the contractor through all of the site issues that invariably arise during construction. At completion, the client was very pleased, and with that comes a tremendous sense of accomplishment.

What is the most exciting aspect of your work?

〉 Having a team of people come together to see an assignment through from initial concept to completion. Every team member contributes something unique and everyone learns about process and teamwork. If we have done our jobs well collectively, we have created a successful design. Our profession generally creates a final product that can be physically experienced. With that experience comes gratification and an enormous sense of pride.

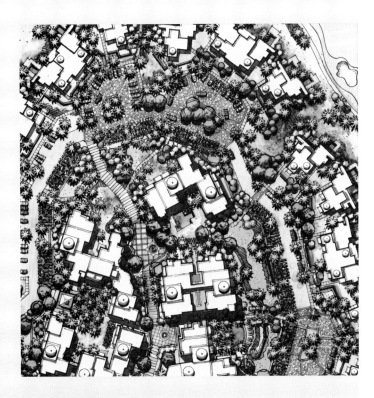

▲ Illustrative site plan for the hilltop village at Ancient Sands Golf Resort, Egypt. Courtesy of EDSA.

◀ Interior plaza at the Florida Nature and Culture Center campus in Weston, Florida. Courtesy of EDSA.

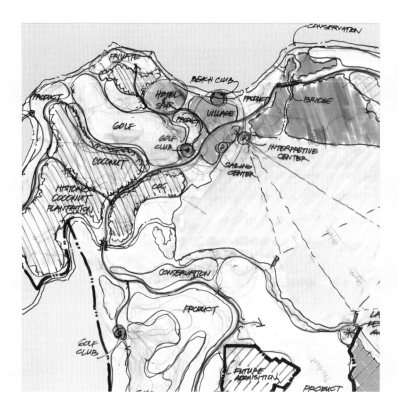

Conceptual sketch for a 3,000-acre resort and residential development in the Dominican Republic. Courtesy of EDSA.

Who are some of the allied professionals you consult with? What role do they play in the design process?

❭ We espouse to our clients the importance of assembling the best possible team, and then we work hard at team collaboration. There is no doubt the best results come when all team members work together to generate a solution. Respect for each team member's role and expertise is crucial. We routinely collaborate with engineers of all varieties, architects, interior designers, economists, contractors, and other design professionals to produce successful and exciting places.

When hiring students for an internship or entry-level job, which aspects of their education do you find to be most important?

❭ We seek out well-rounded individuals who have demonstrated a passion for the profession, but also those who have been active or involved in more than just their landscape architecture curriculum during school. We find that those who branch out into community service or leadership positions in allied professional organizations ultimately become the strongest leaders within our firm.

What role can landscape architects take in making our world better?

❭ Our profession inherently plays a role in the responsible development of our built environment. No matter what experience or expertise we as landscape architects have, we have a responsibility to practice our craft at the highest level possible, as most everything we do impacts both the created and protected places that people love to experience.

Project Profile

EL CONQUISTADOR

Revamping a Resort

The main pool at El Conquistador Resort, enhanced with sculpture and plantings. Courtesy of EDSA.

El Conquistador's golf course traverses major elevation changes and has dramatic views of the rainforest and the sea. Courtesy of EDSA.

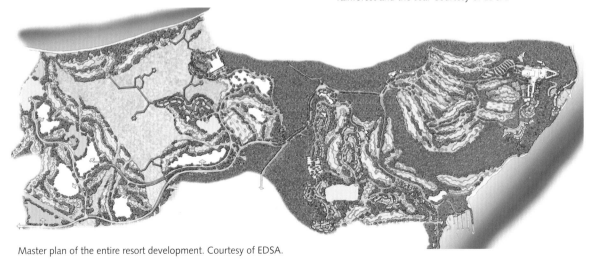

Master plan of the entire resort development. Courtesy of EDSA.

PROJECT OVERVIEW

Date: 1993

Type: Resort Design

Location: Fajardo, Puerto Rico

Firm: EDSA, Fort Lauderdale, Florida

Web link to project: www.edsaplan.com

El Conquistador's $250-million rehabilitation is a story of optimism, high finance, global economics, clever management, and a keen awareness of the differences between designing for the sunseeker of the 1960s and the sophisticated traveler of the 1990s.

—VERNON MAYS[8]

History

In the 1960s, El Conquistador was a beach-set vacationer's dream. Designed by renowned architect Morris Lapidus, the 400-room resort was a greatly admired destination tucked in the scenic beachside cliffs of Fajardo, Puerto Rico. After some 20 years of business, the resort closed its doors. In the late 1980s, when EDSA's Joseph Lalli visited the derelict resort, he noticed a significant amount of overgrown vegetation but also the potential for something tremendous. After the effects of Hurricane Hugo in 1989, the resort and landscape were in dire need of a revival effort.

Leadership Role

EDSA was hired as the prime consultant on the project, responsible for the redesign of this once shining resort. The first move for project manager and the current president and CEO of EDSA, Joseph Lalli, was to bridge connections and form a team. With $250 million invested in the project, and the opportunity to dramatically boost tourism for Puerto Rico, this was no small task.

EDSA considered location, trust, experience, and working relationships when selecting their team. Jorge Rossello & Associates, out of Condado, Puerto Rico, was selected as the interior designer. Edward Durell Stone Associates from New York was selected as the primary architect because of their previous work experience with EDSA. Due to the location, EDSA chose Ray Melendez & Associates, located in San Juan, Puerto Rico, as the architects of record.

The landscape architects' leadership role also meant they were responsible for arranging meetings and directing the entire design and redevelopment operation. This proved beneficial in many respects because the vision for revitalization was predominately landscape-driven.

Renewal

Under the leadership of EDSA, El Conquistador evolved from a 400-room hotel into a 924-room resort, attractive to the twenty-first century Caribbean vacationer. The renewal efforts included the development of a convention center, health spa/golf club, and tennis club. Existing landscape elements were considered as well, and in most cases were altered or redesigned. Existing tennis courts were repositioned away from their previous location at the cliff's edge, where they had been impacted by high winds. An existing 18-hole golf course was redesigned by golf course designer Arthur Hills. Additionally, trellises, columns, fountains, and gardens were built into the existing pool areas to add aesthetic value day and night.

The renewal concepts and the need to boost tourism in Puerto Rico gave rise to the resort's new vacation ownership and hotel suite clusters, called Las Casitas village. The village is a 200-unit condominium complex, infused with pedestrian streets and courtyards that mimic southern Europe's charming hillside towns. EDSA drew their inspiration for Las Casitas from another project in their office at the time, in the south of France. This is a familiar scenario in design firms, because there are multiple projects underway in the office at the same time, research and information about one project may also provide precedents and ideas for another.

Resort Environments

Some people may question the ethics of resort design in the field of landscape architecture. Is it environmentally sensitive design or large-scale dramatic development in the midst of pristine forest or beach? This question is a common one within the profession, and puts further pressure on firms that specialize in resort design to consider the details and project impacts when accepting and designing projects.

EDSA, a thriving company for 50 years, has created some of the most appreciated and popular resort destinations in the world. Given their experience and passion for resort design, it is no surprise that El Conquistador is in many ways an environmentally sensitive design. Early in the process the firm arranged for a temporary nursery on-site for salvaged trees. Additionally, salt-tolerant plant species were densely planted on the cliffs and hillsides to mitigate erosion. Beyond these gestures, it is the concept of reusing an existing derelict site as a canvas for redevelopment that provides the most merit. By investing in existing planning and infrastructure, EDSA was able to recycle an environment, revive a major resort destination, and bring tourism back into Fajardo.[9]

Public Agencies

Much of North America's cherished open spaces and parks are in the care of public agencies. Many important facilities, such as roads and waterways, also fall under the jurisdiction of government offices. It is, therefore, logical that landscape architects would find meaningful employment in public sector jobs. State and local governments employ approximately 6 percent of all landscape archi-

Extensive trail and greenway system in Minneapolis, Minnesota.

tects.[10] The public sector also includes employment opportunities for landscape architects at the national level, in federal agencies. Landscape architects work in public jobs at local levels, too, in such venues as a town's parks and recreation department, a city's environmental services division, or a county's planning agency. Along with carrying out design and planning work for their communities, landscape architects in public jobs are well positioned as advocates for quality-built environments, open spaces, and recreation facilities.

Landscape architects also serve at a multijurisdictional level, such as regional parks or transportation agencies. At the state level, landscape architects might find employment in any of a number of different departments—among them, planning and economic development, historic and museum commissions, state parks and greenways, or a state highway department. In most of these situations, landscape architects work in cooperation with other professions, providing their design expertise in support of the mission of the agency. Diverse opportunities also abound for landscape architects at the federal government level. In the United States, some of the agencies that employ landscape architects are the U.S. Fish and Wildlife Service, the U.S. Forest Service, the National Park Service, and the U.S. Army Corp of Engineers, to name a few. No matter the level of government, a hallmark of public sector work is service to both citizens and to the resources within the agency's purview.

Creating a Park System Legacy

GARY SCOTT, FASLA

2010 President of ASLA

Director

West Des Moines Parks & Recreation Department

West Des Moines, Iowa

Landscape architect Gary Scott. Photographer: Todd Seaman.

Why did you decide to pursue a career in landscape architecture?

❯ I started college at the University of Illinois in engineering and then tried three other majors before dropping out. After working in a factory for awhile, I realized I needed to go back to college. I was getting interested in environmental design, but didn't really know what that meant. I had the opportunity to visit a friend in Boston and that is where I learned about landscape architecture. I was unemployed and had no money, so everyday I would walk through the Emerald Necklace [a string of linked parks] to downtown or the art museum. I had never seen a park system quite like this. My friend, who was an architect, told me about landscape architecture. I went to the Boston Public Library and read [John Ormsbee] Simon's book about landscape architecture [*Landscape Architecture*, 4th edition, 1961], and I was hooked.

How would you characterize the work of your organization?

❯ We are a department of parks and recreation for a city government. We have four landscape architects in a variety of roles. My superintendent of parks is a landscape architect, and we have two others. The core of what we do is plan, acquire, design, build, and manage the park system. We have a historic downtown, so we also deal with municipal building sites, cemeteries, natural areas, and streets.

What was you role in revitalizing the historic downtown?

❯ When I began here, I was working as a planner, and the downtown was in need of improvements to attract more people. We developed a plan and it took four years to implement it. The plan focused on enhancing the streets, sidewalks, and lighting, as well as recommended improvements to the architecture. When we were done, that investment let building owners know the city was committed. By improving the look of the downtown, it made it more attractive both for the consumers and for the businesses.

What has been your most rewarding project to date?

❯ Raccoon River Park. It was a 700-acre sand pit that the city wanted to make into a park. I naively thought, we'll get this done in a couple of years. It

Raccoon River Park

WEST DES MOINES PARKS & RECREATION

Legend

EXISTING FEATURES

1. Biddle Shelter
2. Nature Lodge
3. Beach
4. Playground & Sprayground
5. Restrooms
6. Coneflower Shelters
7. Softball Playground
8. Softball Restrooms
9. Softball Concessions
10. Paved Trail
11. Dog Park
12. Gravel Trail
13. Main Entrance
14. Accessible Fishing Pier
15. Boat Ramp
16. Soccer Restrooms
17. Soccer Fields
18. Mown Trail
19. Portable Restroom

E. Emergency Phone

FUTURE FEATURES

A. Gravel Trail
B. Shelter
C. Parking Lot
D. Playground
E. Inline Skating/Ice Hockey*
F. Sand Volleyball*
G. Concessions/Restrooms
H. Basketball Courts*
I. Beach House
J. Paved Trail
K. Nature Lodge Terrace
L. Boat Rental/Storage
M. Council Ring
N. Soccer Concessions

*Indicates Lighted Areas

CITY OF
West Des Moines

FOR MORE INFORMATION:
West Des Moines Parks & Recreation
4200 Mills Civic Parkway
West Des Moines, IA 50265

515.222.3444

or visit us on the web at:
www.wdm-ia.com

Blue Heron Lake

Browns Woods Park

Walnut Woods State Park

Future connection to Jordan Creek Trail

Existing paved levee trail

Gas Motors Prohibited in This Area

Future connection to Walnut Woods State Park & Hidden Valley Soccer

Raccoon River Park master plan. Courtesy of West Des Moines Parks & Recreation Department.

took 10 years before the first phase of construction occurred. There was a lot of work involved in the planning and financing. We have developed the park in phases over 15 years. So it took a couple of decades, but we have created a jewel in our park system. It includes a 250-acre lake and a beach, as well as several native areas; we also have athletic complexes. I am very proud of that mix; people love it and that's what gives me joy.

What is your role in securing land for future parks?

❯ I have bought every piece of land the city has acquired in the last 25 years. This is a fast-growing community so being ahead of the land speculators is important. I like looking at what would be the best plan. We do the classic suitability analysis—look at the soils, the topography, the character of land for the use. I like searching records, and calling people and saying, we are trying to find 80 acres in an area that the city is going to grow into within 10 or 20 years. I try to find a willing seller—someone who would like to eventually see their land as a park instead of a development. The last park I bought took four years and eight people before I found a willing seller. It took a lot of work but I was very pleased that I got it done because the next year land that was adjacent became the largest commercial development in our town. We wouldn't have been able to afford it. I like enabling the public to be happy.

▲ Aerial view of the beach at Raccoon River Park. Photographer: Todd Seaman.

▶ Entry arch is part of streetscape improvements for Valley Junction commercial area, a revitalized part of the historic downtown. Photographer: Gary Scott.

How often do you involve the community and/or end users in the design process? In what way?

❭ We do it for every initial master plan for neighborhood parks, or when we are building new parks. We involve them it at the beginning, as part of the information-gathering process. We come to the public again in the middle to let them see what alternatives are proposed. Then at the end, we show them what we are going to recommend and ask for their input. We believe we get better product; and if

there's controversy, we always work it out before the end. We give people opportunities to tell us what they want, because we serve the community.

What tips can you provide to someone regarding the job search process?

❭ Make personal contacts. This will expand your network and allow you to tap into theirs. Keep an open mind and take less than glamorous work to get the experience. My first four years were spent in a planning and engineering firm, and the experience was invaluable. Get as much exposure to different things, because everything about the design and construction process is valuable.

What role can landscape architects take in making our world better?

❯ We create value in the world. If you look at the history of landscape architecture, the early parks and park systems created a huge value in those cities. Landscape architects should volunteer outside the profession to raise the visibility of the profession, but also to show that landscape architects are connected to their communities. We need to be a stronger voice in holding officials accountable for actions on planning boards and city councils. Landscape architects need to step up and speak out for our values and advocate for our beliefs.

Serving the Public and the Community

STEPHEN CARTER, ASLA

BRAC NEPA Support Team

U.S. Army Corps of Engineers

Mobile, Alabama

Why did you decide to pursue a career in landscape architecture?

❯ I was at a crossroads and trying to determine something else I wanted to do with my life. I had a bachelor's degree in American History and had worked as a schoolteacher in Memphis, but I didn't want to go back into that. I was in the military at the time, and was the head of a graphic art shop at Fort Bragg in North Carolina. A young man working with me saw my artwork and told me, "You ought to look at becoming a landscape architect." He was a landscape architect and architect. He gave me information, and I liked what I saw.

Stephen Carter, named landscape architect of the year in 1995. Courtesy of Stephen Carter.

How and why did you choose the school you attended to earn your degree?

❯ I applied to the University of Illinois and spoke with Al Rutledge; he seemed quite interested in my coming to get my master's degree there. I had applied to a couple of other schools, but I had a brother in the area at the time, and my wife found a good job as chief of physical therapy at the hospital there, so it worked out for us in that regard.

You had a unique graduate thesis. Tell us about that.

❯ I had the opportunity to design a playground for an apartment complex, and I was going to

utilize young teenagers as the labor force. The site was near the recreation building, but it had graffiti on the walls and was poorly maintained. One of the first things I did was meet the neighborhood kids, and I hired about 20 guys to work with me. We met and discussed what they wanted in a playground, as well as what their younger siblings would like. So they were involved in the generation of ideas, which I then drew up. Since they were involved in the construction, I had to teach them to safely use the power equipment. These were all poor kids, and very excited about this project. We painted over the graffiti wall; we got a young artist in the community to paint a beautiful picture of Martin Luther King, Jr. It is now the wall of respect, and nobody touches it. The bottom line is, when kids get involved, it becomes theirs; they have ownership. They respect and watch over that playground.

How would you characterize the work of your organization?

❯ I work as a project manager with the U.S. Corps of Engineers. I am on the BRAC team, which stands for military base realignment and closure. I am on the NEPA support team [National Environmental Policy Act]. Our charge is to coordinate all work for environmental assessments and environmental impact studies. The fact that the work entails environmental impact and assessments means it is a good fit for me. I travel to the sites to review the schedule and scope of work. I also travel to review milestones in the course of a project. Prior to 1997, I did quite a bit of design work, but now the design work is contracted out.

◀ Children enjoying playground that neighborhood youth helped construct. Photographer: Stephen Carter.

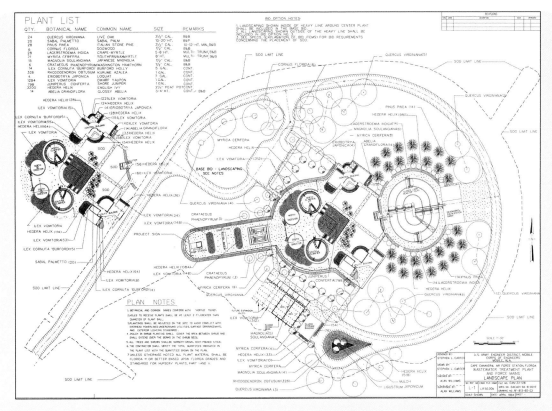

Construction plans of planting design for wastewater treatment plant, Cape Canaveral Air Force Station, Florida. Courtesy of Stephen Carter.

Why did you decide to go into public practice with the Army Corps of Engineers?

❯ I had friends who were working for the Corps and I knew they were making a good salary. Initially, I thought I would only do a three to four year stint with the Corps. I selected Mobile, Alabama, because of the project: Tennessee–Tombigbee Waterway Corridor. I was one of four staff coordinators for a 200-plus mile corridor between two rivers that, when completed, made a navigable connection from the Gulf of Mexico all the way up to the northern states. After that aggressive four-year schedule, I realized I was making investments in Mobile, and my wife had a good job. Seeing some of the design work opportunities I could do, I decided to stay in the Corps.

What has been your most rewarding project at the Corps to date?

❯ What really made us like it—not only me, but the architects and engineers, was our customer— he was an Air Force colonel who talked tough but knew what he wanted. "I want this project to be an award-winning project. Period." We thought, an award for a wastewater treatment plant? He did not want to see utilitarian-type things sticking out of the ground. He wanted everything designed in such a way that it would be hidden. He wanted a thing of beauty. That was really a challenge but we met his expectations. And guess what? It is an award-winning project. I give credit to the customer for the positive outcome.

You have been quite active in ASLA. Why did you decide to get involved in this professional organization, and what were your greatest accomplishments?

❯ You're going to get the most out of your career by joining the professional organization that speaks to your needs and concerns. That's the reason I first got involved, and because I wanted to network with other professionals. Once I became a member, I saw how few were African American. I became active and gathered information to move forward. ASLA headquarters saw my interest and we started the Committee on Blacks in Landscape Architecture. Through organizing and word of mouth, we put together the first directory of blacks in the profession. Then I pursued getting a policy on blacks in landscape architecture. This provided recognition and gave us some standing. I have also served on the Accreditation Committee, which visits schools going through the accreditation process. Then, in 2000, I was elected to a major leadership position as vice-president of membership, which is a two-year term.

Planning for the Future

JUANITA D. SHEARER–SWINK, FASLA

Project Manager

Triangle Transit

Research Triangle Park, North Carolina

Landscape architect Juanita Shearer–Swink reviewing plans at a construction site. Courtesy of Triangle Transit.

Why did you decide to pursue a career in landscape architecture?

❯ I was born in New York, but I grew up in Jamaica, so I was always interested in nature. I was also interested in art and design. While we were having our house designed, I was able to do some work for that architect. While getting exposure to that aspect of design, I met a landscape architect. I became fascinated with the kinds of things he was doing. I liked the integration—it gave me the art and architecture and natural systems balance I enjoy.

How and why did you choose the school you attended to earn your degree?

❯ I found the University of Florida attractive because of the geographical context. Living in a tropical country, I wanted some overall context to the way the landscape might look—or at least I thought so before I got there and discovered how flat it was.

Which aspect of your education has had the greatest influence on you?

❯ The most important thing was learning that design, and policy development, is a process; it's not a product. It is a process of integrating elements and ideas and working together until you reach a point where they coalesce into something that works.

How would you characterize the work of your organization?

❯ I work for an agency, Triangle Transit, whose responsibility is to develop and supply regional public transportation or transit, in a large three-county area. It is a region predominantly characterized by auto-oriented development, so it was created by the State of North Carolina in 1989 to develop a different balance; different opportunities for travel throughout the region without a car.

What is your role at the agency?

❯ My responsibility has evolved over time. The first few years, I worked with the community to develop a vision for what people would like to see in the next 25 to 30 years. We did a current trends analysis projection of what it would be like if we kept building highways and sprawling all over the landscape. I then moved into determining where we might have future rail systems. So my role moved from working to build a vision to looking at the right places for transit stations to be developed. The next step in the process was to move into the design phase of the rail system, and then I became the project manager for the stations. My role was to work with consultants to devel-

Phase 1
REGIONAL RAIL SYSTEM
Durham to Raleigh to North Raleigh

The Big Picture

In 1989, the Triangle Transit Authority (TTA) was created by the NC General Assembly, Durham, Orange and Wake Counties and Durham, Cary, Chapel Hill and Raleigh, to develop **long-term regional public transportation**. Through the Triangle Fixed Guideway Study, the TTA, representatives from federal, state and local governments, major employers, universities, business and community groups and the general public developed **the Regional Transit Plan.** The Plan includes **rail service and expanded bus service, shuttles, park and ride, and enhanced pedestrian and bicycle access.**

In Ph. I a 35-mile Regional Rail System connecting Durham, RTP, Morrisville, Cary, downtown Raleigh and North Raleigh, with shuttles to RDU Airport, will be developed. **Service will run 18 hours per day, 7 days per week,** with trains in both directions arriving at stations every **15 minutes during AM and PM peak** hours and every **30 minutes non-peak** and weekends.

As a result of additional technical studies combined with ongoing community participation and support, the Federal Transit Administration has **authorized TTA to develop Preliminary Engineering (PE) and an Environmental Impact Statement (EIS)** for Ph. I Regional Rail Service. The PE/EIS study, which is currently underway, **will include the evaluation of the environmental, social and economic impacts of the Ph. I Service.** Sites for the Ph. I stations and the Yard and Shop Facility will also be selected.

The **PE/EIS should be complete by Fall 1999.** Final Design, Right-of-Way Acquisition and Construction will follow. Ph. I Regional Rail Service, supported by shuttle, feeder and local buses should begin operating by 2004.

Whats Inside...
❯ What to expect in a station
❯ Station evaluation criteria
❯ Maps and descriptions of the station sites
❯ Sketches and photos of station issues
❯ The station planning schedule
❯ How to get more involved

Triangle Transit Authority, November 1998

STATION PLANNING WORKBOOK

Screening . . .The First Step

This Station Planning Workbook is designed to **help you evaluate the different sites** that have been identified for each of the **Regional Rail Stations.** It includes some technical requirements for regional rail stations and information about the roles that different stations will need to fulfill as part of the overall transit system. **Maps for each station** will help you to locate each of the potential sites. The **initial environmental evaluation** or **screening summaries** will give you an overview of opportunities and constraints. **Tell us what you think** about each site. **Fill out a comment card** and help us track the issues that are important to you.

Preparing the **EIS** for the Ph. I Regional Rail System includes the **evaluation of alternative locations** for the 16 Ph. I Regional Rail Stations. Working with representatives from Durham, Cary, Morrisville, Raleigh, Wake and Durham Counties, as well as Major Employers, Organizations and Institutions, a variety of sites for the 16 stations have been identified. More input will be gathered through meetings with elected and appointed officials and the public as well as through TTA's web page. As a result of this information gathering process and further engineering and design the **most reasonable and feasible sites will be selected for analysis** through the EIS process. *Keep reading to find out more.*

second track
lighting shelter   platform   diesel multiple unit (DMU) train

barrier

platform   ramp   *Regional Rail Station in Australia*

▲ Cover of public outreach publication outlining regional rail station planning. Courtesy of Triangle Transit.

op station design standards. The work I do is applied design, design policy, and integrating community ideas to build a future people want to live in.

What is the most exciting aspect of your work?

❯ To do something that people far in the future will be able to enjoy or appreciate. I have the potential to make peoples' lives better for a long time—

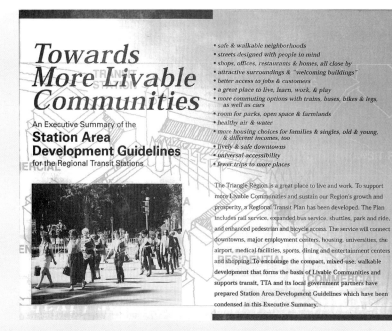

Towards More Livable Communities

An Executive Summary of the
Station Area Development Guidelines
for the Regional Transit Stations

- *safe & walkable neighborhoods*
- *streets designed with people in mind*
- *shops, offices, restaurants & homes, all close by*
- *attractive surroundings & "welcoming buildings"*
- *better access to jobs & customers*
- *a great place to live, learn, work, & play*
- *more commuting options with trains, buses, bikes & legs, as well as cars*
- *room for parks, open space & farmlands*
- *healthy air & water*
- *more housing choices for families & singles, old & young, & different incomes, too*
- *lively & safe downtowns*
- *universal accessibility*
- *fewer trips to more places*

The Triangle Region is a great place to live and work. To support more Livable Communities and sustain our Region's growth and prosperity, a Regional Transit Plan has been developed. The Plan includes rail service, expanded bus service, shuttles, park and ride, and enhanced pedestrian and bicycle access. The service will connect downtowns, major employment centers, housing, universities, the airport, medical facilities, sports, dining and entertainment centers and shopping. To encourage the compact, mixed-use, walkable development that forms the basis of Livable Communities and supports transit, TTA and its local government partners have prepared Station Area Development Guidelines which have been condensed in this Executive Summary.

Cover of executive summary report about regional rail station development guidelines. Courtesy of Triangle Transit.

"better" means they will have a life that is more reasonable and balanced—and to ensure the animals who live around them do, as well.

Who are some of the allied professionals you work/consult with? What role do they play in the design process?

⟩ I have always worked with multidisciplinary design teams. Some of those professionals include architects, engineers and other landscape architects, accountants and financial advisers, graphic artists and communications specialists. You get the best of everyone's skills because they're all willing to be at the table working for a common purpose.

What tips can you provide to someone regarding the job search process?

⟩ It's important to talk to a lot of different landscape architects while you are still in school. And talk to people you might not believe you are interested in, because you never know what's going to happen in the next year or so. There could be wonderful

opportunities you previously thought would have been something you didn't want to do. Another key aspect is to be an intern at a firm—whether it's for two weeks, the whole summer, or over spring break. The opportunity to shadow someone and to develop mentors is going to help tremendously in understanding the opportunities the profession affords.

What role can landscape architects take in making our world better?

⟩ We need to take leadership roles in the public. We have to be willing to serve on more public boards, to volunteer, and we have to be willing to work with politicians and help them understand the good things that we, the profession of landscape architecture, can do; or we have to become elected officials ourselves. Landscape architects need to be involved in the broadest levels of decision making, in policymaking, because we have the holistic tools that can help to make things better for our streets, our neighborhoods, and the world.

Protecting and Preserving National Treasures

JOANNE CODY, ASLA

Senior Landscape Architect

National Park Service

Denver Service Center

Lakewood, Colorado

Joanne Cody at her National Park Service office. Courtesy of the National Park Service.

Why did you decide to pursue a career in landscape architecture?

❭ I always loved designing—towns and road networks in the dirt for our matchbox cars when I was young. Later, I always had to doodle in my notebooks to pay attention in school. This love for drawing and love of nature made an easy choice of landscape architecture for me. Most important, my father, Willis Hartman, is a landscape architect; learning about the profession early made it easier to take the best prep classes in high school.

How would you characterize the work of your agency?

❭ The Denver Service Center (DSC), the centralized planning, design, and construction project management office for the National Park Service, provides environmentally responsible and fiscally sound products jointly with private industry. Landscape architects have many, varied roles in the National Park Service. At the DSC, landscape architects are on planning teams, and they are project managers and project specialists for design and construction projects. The Denver Service Center employs approximately 240 people, with about 45 landscape architects.

What is your role in the office?

❭ As the senior landscape architect for the Denver Service Center, I work with project teams on design solutions, review projects to assure they meet the National Park Service (NPS) design ethic, work on special projects for parks, and develop design guidelines for the NPS. I provide guidance to project teams on landscape architecture, universal design and accessibility, contextual design, and sustainability.

What has been your most rewarding project to date?

❭ My most rewarding project, known as "The Restoration of Giant Forest" in Sequoia National Park, took more than 20 years to complete. I worked on the project from 1989, as a campground designer, through 2005, as project team captain and manager for the final component to remove roads and parking near the world's largest tree: the General Sherman. The goal of this project was to remove development from the

Aerial view of recently restored Saugas Iron Works National Historic Site, Saugas, Massachusetts. Courtesy of the National Park Service.

Tactile three-dimensional map aids all visitors, including the visually impaired, in understanding the Saugas Iron Works site. Courtesy of the National Park Service.

sequoia grove, replace this development with new visitor use areas in the park (outside the grove), and provide appropriate, environmentally responsible visitor access to the Giant Forest.

The demolition work was phased over five major projects. More than 250 buildings and 1 million square feet of asphalt were removed. Following demolition in each area, sites were restored to natural grade. A shuttle system provides transportation for visitors so they can park once, hike or shuttle to different areas of the forest, and shuttle back to their vehicles, thereby reducing the impacts of vehicles in the park. Standing in the restored grove that was once a parking area has to be one of the greatest experiences in my life.

What is the most exciting aspect of your work?

❯ The most exciting aspect of working for the NPS is having a role in protecting, preserving, and providing access to many of our national treasures. Day-to-day governmental process can get frustrating, but as a whole, all park service employees are proud of the work they are accomplishing. My work in accessibility and universal design has been very exciting as well. By providing tactile exhibits and assistive listening devices, we are making the parks' stories available to all visitors.

Who are some of the allied professionals you work/consult with? What role do they play in the design process?

❯ Among others, we work with architects, engineers, cost estimators, compliance professionals (for compliance with environmental and historic preservation laws), contracting officers, and park staff. Parks typically have expertise on staff with knowledge of native plant materials, site history, archeology, maintenance requirements, and general park information that is invaluable to designers. This broad team is important to developing sites that fit park needs without impairing natural or historic resources.

Which aptitudes, traits, and skills do you see in most landscape architects?

❯ Creativity, commitment, and enthusiasm are the key traits landscape architects need. Skill in art, math, and computer graphics and design are important, but can be learned. Landscape architects have an ability to see and think three-dimensionally, and are adept at building consensus. A good sense of humor is a must, as well.

Which aspect of your education has had the greatest influence on you?

❯ Learning how important the construction classes and civil engineering classes are to our profession. I came into college thinking I was a designer, that I could sketch out a design and someone else would implement it. Thankfully, my construction professor at Penn State, Don Leslie, made it clear that if I could not translate my design into buildable construction documents, it was very unlikely my vision would be realized. Learning to combine the art and the science of landscape architecture was the best lesson I learned in college.

What tips can you provide to someone regarding the job search process?

❯ One of the best ways to get a job with the National Park Service is through the student intern program and summer employment listings. It is invaluable

to have work experience in a park, even as a volunteer. Utilize the www.studentjobs.gov during college years for summer and internship employment; and the www.usajobs.gov Web site for employment information. If working for the NPS sounds like an interesting career, it would be good to focus on detailed design skills, along with the broad landscape architecture classes in school, such as transportation design, stormwater design, and sustainability.

Giant Forest Museum before and after. Meadow is quickly regenerating after pavement was eliminated. Courtesy of ASLA. Photography: The National Park Service.

Project Profile

THE RESTORATION OF GIANT FOREST

Large-Scale Ecosystem Preservation

Round Meadow, once lined with buildings, is now circled by an accessible trail. Courtesy of ASLA. Photography: The National Park Service.

An overlook on the trail to the General Sherman tree includes the exact footprint of the tree in granite paving. Courtesy of ASLA. Photography: The National Park Service.

The Giant Forest before and after. Restoration involved restoring natural grade, and planting with native species. Courtesy of ASLA. Photography: The National Park Service.

PROJECT OVERVIEW

Date: 2006

Type: Preservation

Location: Sequoia National Park, California

Client: Sequoia National Park

Firm: National Park Service

Awards: 2007 ASLA Professional General Design Honor Award

This shows true leadership, sustained vision, and solid commitment. It's done with great subtlety. They should be applauded for sticking with it for so many years.

—ASLA 2007 PROFESSIONAL AWARDS JURY[11]

Project Scale

Arguably one of the best aspects of landscape architecture is the flexibility to work on a variety of projects at different scales. The restoration of Giant Forest showcases a large-scale project that involves thinking expanded to the realm of land planning, and collaboration with hundreds of designers and scientists, to achieve a long-term vision. The project included the removal of over a million square feet of asphalt and 282 buildings. These removals provided more space for forest growth to occur and established a more organized and aesthetic experience for visitors.[12]

A Need for Restoration

Giant Forest Grove, the site, is one of 75 existing old-growth forest groves left in the Northwest. While the creation of Sequoia National Park (over 100 years ago) preserved the forest, development and management since has led to degradation of the forest. Due to the scarcity and value of these forests, the National Park Service has devoted a great amount of time and funding to restoration efforts.[13]

Project Phasing

All landscape architecture projects involve phasing, to some degree. With larger projects, phasing is usually an integral part of the design development. Giant Forest is an excellent example of this because of the clear sequence and strategy of phasing. The process began with the relocation of services, campgrounds, and lodging to a less environmentally rich area in the park. Those areas of demolition then had to be regenerated to healthy conditions that would have existed prior to development. Following the design and planting for regeneration of the forest, the final phase included designing circulation routes and destinations for pedestrians and vehicles and the creation of an interpretive museum. While the lifetime of a typical landscape architecture project can range from three to five years, larger projects such as the restoration of Giant Forest, with an in-depth phasing strategy, can last 20 to 50 years.

Design

The redesign of Giant Forest focused on preserving the ecosystem and making it more enjoyable and equally accessible for all visitors. This was achieved through the relocation of overnight facilities to an area outside of the forest, the restoration of viewsheds and placing an emphasis on pedestrian rather than vehicular experiences. Therefore, the design required the removal of buildings, a decrease in the amount of on-site parking and an increased attention to walkways and pedestrian zones. Considering the amount of development that previously existed on site, several environmental design strategies were also necessary. Invasive species were removed from the forest and native plant species were reintroduced. The soil composition and topography were restored to a healthy state, and erosion control and irrigation strategies were put into place.

Preservation

This project demonstrates an interesting aspect of landscape architecture: the flexibility to work with a federal agency, like the National Park Service, on the preservation of place. With many large-scale land planning and landscape architecture projects, preservation can be significant, but often it comes second to development strategies that put financial gain for clients ahead of preservation. Unlike a typical firm, the National Park Service is one entity, which means the design firm and client are in the same organization. This creates a unique and somewhat refreshing work environment and relationship, resulting in exceptional projects like the restoration of Giant Forest. The care and concern with the precious environment of the Giant Forest, combined with the interest of visitors, is visible in every aspect of this comprehensive effort of preservation.

Nonprofit Organizations and Educational Institutions

A growing area of practice for landscape architects is in nonprofit organizations and educational institutions. One of the first land trusts in the United States was formed by Boston landscape architect Charles Eliot in the late 1800s. A key component of the Trustees of Reservations structure was acquiring land that would be open to the public but exempt from taxes. This became a role model for future nonprofit organizations.[14] Most nonprofit organizations do not sell services, as a for-profit business does; rather, they seek to provide some broad benefit through helping disseminate information and/or protecting resources, depending on their mission. If the nonprofit is a federally designated charity, its mission must be directed at providing a public benefit.

Some types of nonprofit organizations—also called nongovernmental organizations (NGOs)—that employ landscape architects include land trusts or conservancies, green building councils, low-impact development centers, or community design centers. There are a few well-known international NGOs where landscape architects might work, such as the World Wildlife Fund and Conservation International. A landscape architect's training in holistic thinking and creative problem solving are attractive skills to nonprofit organizations such as these.

Many landscape architects enjoy satisfying careers in academia, due to the mix of teaching, research, and service afforded them in this arena. Landscape architecture professors appreciate the creative energy of their students and the excitement of helping them discover the variety of choices available in the field. The notion of service learning, whereby students work with an actual community on a project, is beneficial to the students, the citizens, and to the professors, who help facilitate the process. The other important aspect of a job in academia is research, or research-based practice. Professors report they enjoy the freedom to devise a research agenda based on their own interests. As one professor put it, being employed at the university is like having several small businesses of your own—"your teaching business, your publication business, your scholarship business and your consulting business."[15] As the profession continues to grow, there will be an increasing need for landscape architects to go into the academic side of practice.

Promoting Green Infrastructure in the City

MEREDITH UPCHURCH, ASLA

Green Infrastructure Designer

Casey Trees Endowment Fund

Washington, DC

Why did you decide to pursue a career in landscape architecture?

❯ I have my bachelor's degree in engineering and I practiced in the aerospace engineering field for 11 years. I was becoming more aware of environmental issues and I also loved to garden. I realized I could combine these interests in the field of landscape architecture. I came to it later in my professional life and started to study first on a part-time basis and then full-time to get a master's degree.

Meredith Upchurch (right) promotes community greening at a neighborhood fair. Photographer: Dan Smith. © 2008 Casey Trees.

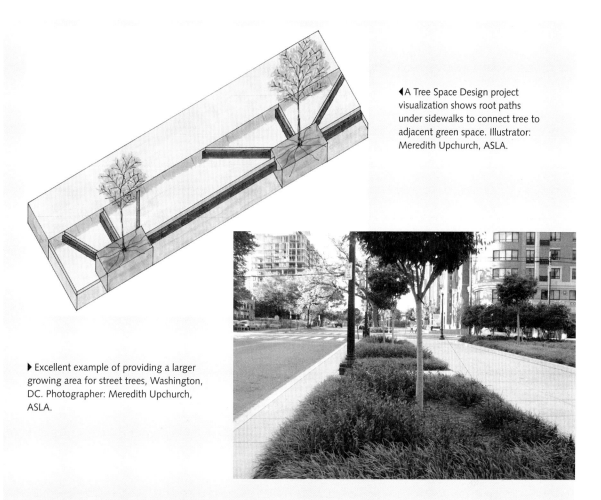

◀A Tree Space Design project visualization shows root paths under sidewalks to connect tree to adjacent green space. Illustrator: Meredith Upchurch, ASLA.

▶ Excellent example of providing a larger growing area for street trees, Washington, DC. Photographer: Meredith Upchurch, ASLA.

How and why did you choose the school you attended to earn your degree?

❯ I chose the school that was a few miles down the road so that I didn't have to move. I consider myself extremely lucky that I could do that. Virginia Tech had just started an MLA program at a satellite campus in Alexandria, Virginia.

How would you characterize the work of your organization?

❯ My organization, Casey Trees, is a nonprofit, funded through an endowment. That might make us unique from other nonprofits in that we don't have to worry about raising money. Our primary mission is to restore, protect, and enhance the tree canopy of Washington, DC. We do that through community building, which is going out into the community and educating people about the importance of trees and green infrastructure, and the role it plays in the environment. We do a lot of advocacy to the public, to private organizations, and to developers, and emphasize why they should place the landscape at a higher importance.

What is your role in the office?

❯ We have four main program areas within our organization and I'm in the planning and design program. There are three of us in that group; two are landscape architects. My official title is green infrastructure designer. Our program looks at the policies in the District of Columbia and how they can be updated to promote more trees and green infrastructure. There was not really anyone within the city government working on promoting landscape issues. That was why my organization started in 2001. We were funded by a private donor to help get the city's trees back on track. In these last seven years the city now has a fully functioning Urban Forestry Organization, and that group is doing very well. We ask, "Where do you need support?" and then we help push to enhance what they do.

The main project I've been working on for the past couple of years is called "Street Tree Space Design—growing the tree out of the box." We have an advisory group of landscape architects, arborists, and government people to help determine how we can create better growing environments for street trees. We will produce policy recommendations and develop construction drawings. We're trying to reach out to those who don't know what to do and give them solid direction. This has been an exciting way to work with the larger landscape architecture community within Washington, DC. This is something that no single private firm could do on its own, bringing together all these different people from within private industry and the public sector to come to this conclusion and get everyone's support.

What is the most exciting aspect of your work?

❯ What I find really exciting about my job is working with all the different organizations, different non-

profits, and various government agencies and other designers. To think there are so many different people who are interested in making landscape an important part of the city, by adding more green spaces or developing policies to encourage that; I find that exciting.

What has been your most rewarding project to date?

❯ A recent rewarding project, that's still in the works, is a citywide task force looking at stormwater. It is a part of the DC Department of Environment, but they've invited representatives from nonprofit organizations and various private design firms. We've been looking at stormwater regulation and how to levy a fee, but also how to include discounts for green infrastructure. There's so much support behind this now that it's really exciting to be able to work with a diverse group of people toward this common goal of cleaning up our rivers and making our city a better place.

What role do new technologies play in your design process?

❯ The technologies are advantageous in that we can show a more accurate and vivid representation of what places could look like in 20 years. For example, 3D views can show how trees enhance a site and really add value to it. It gives people that ah-ha moment of how things may look in the future, and provides incentive to do it.

When hiring students for an internship or entry-level job, which aspects of their education do you find to be most important?

❯ I look for a strong plants knowledge and computer skills because that's really what's going to differentiate them from somebody who's not a landscape architect in my organization. Being able to work with design software and do graphic representations and know how to put the right plants in the landscape, especially in dealing with sustainable landscapes where we want to do more natural and native plantings.

What role can landscape architects take in making our world better?

❯ Landscape architects have such a great holistic view of how the land fits into our lives and into our communities. We are learning how a good-quality landscape can improve children's ability to learn and people's ability to heal, and reduce stress levels. As we become a more urban society, there is so much opportunity, and a need to have quality landscapes in our cities to improve our quality of life. I think that's where landscape architects can really have a great role.

New Public Parks for the Urban Core

STEPHANIE LANDREGAN, ASLA

Chief of Landscape Architecture

Mountains Recreation & Conservation Authority

Los Angeles, California

Why did you decide to pursue a career in landscape architecture?

❯ I have an art background but learned about landscape architecture while working as an aerial photographer. I was in New Mexico and was flying the Rio Grande Valley while I worked with landscape architects on the Rio Grande Recreation Master

Stephanie Landregan speaking at the groundbreaking for the Augustus F. Hawkins Park, Los Angeles, California. Debris pile (left) was crushed to make the base for hills in the park. Photographer: Deborah Deets, MRCA.

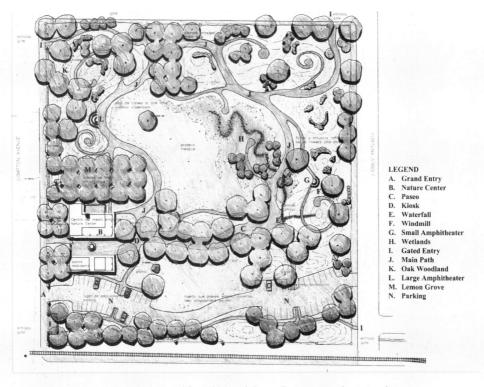

Natural Park illustrated concept plan used for public workshops. Illustrator: Stephanie Landregan.

LEGEND

A. Grand Entry
B. Nature Center
C. Paseo
D. Kiosk
E. Waterfall
F. Windmill
G. Small Amphitheater
H. Wetlands
I. Gated Entry
J. Main Path
K. Oak Woodland
L. Large Amphitheater
M. Lemon Grove
N. Parking

Plan. Working with them, I realized, here is a profession that uses every single thing I know how to do. After relocating to California, a friend suggested I check out a landscape architecture program where you can go to school in the evening. This allowed me to finally act on the epiphany I had years ago. I enrolled in the extension program at UCLA. I was able to keep working full-time at the Santa Monica City Planning Department. UCLA does not have a degree program, but rather a certificate program. It is recognized by the state, and I did get my landscape architect's license.

A waterfall fountain is a central feature of the Augustus F. Hawkins Natural Park. Photographer: Stephanie Landregan.

How would you characterize the work of your organization?

〉 We're a small local government agency funded through grants. We're very lean and mean, and we think like we are a 501C3 charity, but we have a little more authority. We have 70 employees, including park rangers, operations and maintenance, and a construction division. Our landscape architecture group is part of the planning division. Two landscape architects and a landscape architectural intern work with me. We design our own work, we oversee other designers, and we bid our work according to state contracting codes. We also do collaborative work with other agencies because we tend to be less encumbered by governmental bureaucracy. We hire other designers for larger projects that are too big for us internally.

Can you clarify the relationship between recreation and conservation in your mission?

〉 Our agency locates properties and willing sellers, and puts together funding to purchase the property. I'm not involved with the acquisition, although I do go look at the property and make sure, if we're going to take it on, that it would be appropriate. We buy property so that it can be opened to the public and shared. We are creating usable open space and recreation in downtown Los Angeles, but we're also trying to reinsert nature into the urban core, which is pretty darn exciting.

How do you involve the community and/or end users in the park design and construction process?

〉 The public is very involved, including hiring people from the neighborhood to help build it. We require our contractors to hire a certain number of people from the neighborhood. If it's a community at risk, it's not just the youth that need to be hired;

East 57th Street entrance to Augustus F. Hawkins Natural Park with stone pillars and metal gate. Photographer: Stephanie Landregan.

some of the parents too. We also hire community artists and ask them to hire local children. By engaging all members of the community, including sometimes even gang members, you are projecting the community into the park, and it becomes owned instead of something that has to be "taken over." We have the lowest incidence of graffiti of any of the parks in Los Angeles County. We have a very good success rate because they are not just stakeholders; I call them "stockholders," since they have really invested in their park.

What has been your most rewarding project to date?

〉 An 8-acre park called Augustus F. Hawkins Natural Park in South Los Angeles. It had been a pipe yard, and we reused some of the piping in the fountain design. The joy for me was how excited the community was about this park. I worked with the community throughout and told them, "I am your landscape architect." Many people from the community were working with me, and the contractor, to help build it. I think they were quite surprised when I got very angry with the contractor one day. The contractor had put in something and it was wrong. He said, "It's only South Central, who cares? This is what you get." I was so mad. I said, "You're going to build it according to plan. I don't care where we're building this. This is what you bid on." These young men and women who were putting in the trees… well, I don't think they had ever seen anybody tear something out because it was not good enough. It's a beautiful park. The community loves it, and they really respect it. If you do something of value for communities, they value it.

What is the most exciting aspect of your work?

〉 We're making something that should last for generations to come. Whether it's purchasing a piece of land that is going to be a park for generations or it's designing an element that is going to be appreciated by future generations—to me, that is very exciting. For example, when Olmsted designed Central Park, the original drainage system he designed is still in there 100 years later.

Which aptitudes, traits, and skills do you see in most landscape architects?

〉 We have an aptitude to listen. The biggest success of landscape architects is we become key collaborators. We take the different disciplines and different needs and we put them together. We provide the sky behind the stars. We're problem solvers, we're listeners.

What role can landscape architects take in making our world better?

〉 Landscape architecture is a kinetic state. It's a potential. The skills we have touch social justice, environmental justice, economic justice. What we do changes the way of life for people regardless of their economic status. We are making the world better, but more of us need to become leaders and push sustainable agendas and best management practices.

Engaging with Environmental Justice

KOFI BOONE, ASLA

Assistant Professor

Department of Landscape Architecture

North Carolina State University

Raleigh, North Carolina

Landscape architecture professor Kofi Boone.

Why did you decide to pursue a career in landscape architecture?

❯ I went to a performance arts high school; I wanted to be a performing musician, but my parents made me continue to take science and math. I had one more science class to take so I took ecology and I got turned on by all the environmental stuff. Thanks to high math SAT scores, I received an invitation to the University of Michigan for a free visit. While there I told a counselor I am interested in the environment, and I like to draw, and I would like to go into something that lets me do both. He

said you need to talk to the chair of the Landscape Architecture Department. I met Ken Polakowski and he offered me a job that summer doing research—behavioral mapping—at the Detroit Zoo. Once a week I'd sit with Ken and he would ask me to tell him what I saw, and he'd be sneaking his landscape architecture into those conversations. He told me, "You could do whatever you want, but I think you'd make a great landscape architect, so you should consider it." Michigan doesn't have an undergraduate program, but I could take a higher credit load and graduate with my undergraduate degree in three years and start the MLA program as a senior; then I'd only have to do two years of graduate school. He had this whole thing mapped out—six years of my life. Basically, he snatched me. He was a really strong mentor who got me to look at landscape architecture.

How did you get interested in environmental justice?

❯ When I was at Michigan, several faculty were playing some role in the emerging environmental justice movement, and I took many classes related to that. I was also involved in extracurricular activities; a lot of community activism. I guess you could say I had an imperative, which was enabled through being a college student there at that time. I didn't really think about it or realize the impact until after I had decided on an academic direction for my career.

My research is about the overlap between environmental justice and landscape architecture. Environmental justice is articulating the environmental perspective of marginalized people, and it had its formal origins in North Carolina after a big protest to block a PCB landfill in 1982. Landscape architecture hasn't been formally engaged with that

Conceptual vision plan for renovation of the W.E.B. DuBois Center campus, Wake Forest, North Carolina, including restoration of historic structures. Courtesy of North Carolina State Department of Landscape Architecture.

movement, but we do things that are similar to its principles and goals. For example, we focus on participatory design and how we engage people in terms of community design. I am filtering through how landscape architects have dealt with people who have low access to power. I have been measuring and comparing that to the environmental justice literature, and am looking at how to modify our approach to landscape architecture to be more inclusive.

What is the most exciting aspect of your work?

❯ Being at a university, it's really about the students and my peers. It is great seeing that light come on with a student. It is exciting to see the design engine turning on and them being critical and diligent, as well as being humble and responsible. In regards to my colleagues, they are always doing interesting work. You go to conferences and work together on projects and papers—it's very stimulating intellectually.

How often do you involve the community and/or end users in your work? In what way?

❯ With community design it's hard to define what you mean by community. The first step is developing a profile to figure out the components: Who are the stakeholders that represent these different interests and how can I pull them in at the beginning? With community design it also is important to engage them in defining the problem. Often the problem you're given is, for example, "build a plaza; that's what people want." But is that really the problem? Next is engaging them in the analysis and programming of the site. The community can provide a background and richness that leads to a different reading of the site.

What role do new technologies play in your process?

❯ As a professor, I am working with students and communities to use media early as part of the process, instead of waiting until the end to use digital media to make it beautiful. Three-dimensional modeling in a computer is huge because it allows you to integrate a lot of rich information in a way that people understand better. With an aerial photograph, you extrude buildings up, you create some flythroughs and walkthroughs—you can simulate your ideas pretty quickly. I feel that 3D visualization and simulation is pretty important.

What tips can you provide to someone regarding the job search process?

❯ Present yourself honestly about what your strengths are and what you are interested in. In your portfolio, don't feel you have to show that you can do everything really well. The problem is people are trying to convey themselves as being equal in everything, and that sends a misperception. It leads to disappointment. If you are just graduating, it's going to be an extended internship. People hire you fully expecting you're going to need more training; they want to see how you can contribute now. You need to be clear what you are passionate about, and then supplement that with evidence you can do other things, too.

What role can landscape architects take in making our world better?

❯ People recognize that change happens in the environment around them, but don't know why and don't know how the consequences of change will affect them. The world is so complex, and there are only a few professions comfortable with that level of complexity. Landscape architecture is in that realm. We have to make really complex things more understandable and show that what you experience in your own individual life is connected to a bigger whole.

Asanteman Park, Kumasi, Ghana; in collaboration with KNUST in Kumasi. North Carolina State faculty and students lead a park design workshop with neighborhood children. Photographer: Kofi Boone.

Efficiencies through Technology

SCOTT S. WEINBERG, FASLA

Associate Dean and Professor

College of Environment and Design

University of Georgia

Athens, Georgia

Professor Scott Weinberg in his office.

Why did you decide to pursue a career in landscape architecture?

❯ I grew up in New York City, and when you're in junior high, you pick a high school. I went to a high school that specialized in horticulture. Ever since I was a little kid, I would be in charge of planting our small front yard in the summertime. When I was about 14 I was reading a nurseryman's magazine from the library and it had something about landscape architects. I showed my mother the article and she said, "Doesn't that sound better than nurseryman, landscape architect?"

How and why did you choose the schools you attended to earn your degrees?

❯ I ended up getting both my undergraduate and graduate degrees at Iowa State. Since I lived in New York, I was looking to get off the East Coast. I applied to schools in California and Arizona, too. But once I saw Iowa State's central campus, I fell in love with it. At the time I did not know this, but Olmsted did the initial design for the Iowa State campus. Seven years later, after practicing and becoming a licensed landscape architect, I went back to Iowa State for my master's degree. I could be a teaching assistant and teach part-time. Because I was licensed in Iowa, going to school there also allowed me to do a little bit of practice on the side to help pay the bills.

Why did you decide to go into the academic realm of landscape architecture?

❯ I always wanted to be a teacher; however, I worked first before getting into the academic side of practice. I owned a company in St. Louis for seven years. We did design/build. At one point, we had an office crisis, so I decided it was time for a change. I sold my company and went back to graduate school. I wanted to teach for a number of reasons. I was inspired by both good and bad professors I had had, and I wanted to see how well I could do. I am now an associate dean, but I still teach. I love teaching. I won't give that up.

What is your research focus and why is it important for the landscape architecture profession?

❯ My research over the last 20-plus years has been in the use of technology. My focus is trying to get people to be more efficient and enable them to do things faster. By working more quickly you can explore many different alternatives and come up with either a combination of two or an entirely new idea that works better. I think this helps to advance design.

What role do new technologies play in our profession?

❯ New technologies are extremely important. They allow you to do things quicker and to explore more possibilities. The other thing is, they allow you to communicate better with your client. You can take a CAD drawing and put it out in 3D and do a quick perspective, print it out, and add some color. This enhanced communication means you'll have a better idea about what you are proposing. It's also nice that you can show a client what the design is going to look like the day it's installed; then you can also show them what it will look like 10 or 15 years later after things mature.

Which aspects of a student's education do you feel are most important?

❯ You can't travel enough. While you travel, you need to look at things. I take a camera, not because I like to take pictures, but it makes me focus on things. I take a

During study abroad students flee an area at Villa Lante when "water tricks" turn on. Photographer: Scott Weinberg.

Student design for a fountain at a mental health garden located in Washington, DC. Model completed in SketchUp. Illustrator: Elizabeth Brunelli.

The image created as part of a "walkthrough" using the computer program Realtime. Illustrator: Scott Weinberg.

lot of pictures of good design; and it's also good to critique bad design.

What tips can you provide to someone regarding the job search process?

❯ Take the first job you're offered, if you can live with the salary. Don't worry about the job. By that I mean, during your first job you're going to learn things wherever you work. It's always easier to get a job if you have a job. Then wait at least six months to figure out if you're happy there, and if not, start looking for something else. You will also have a better idea about what you want in an office environment and then can make your next search focus on firms that do that.

Working from a Native American Perspective

JOHN KOEPKE

Associate Professor

Department of Landscape Architecture

University of Minnesota

Minneapolis, Minnesota

Professor John Koepke (right) with colleague M. Christine Carlson, senior research fellow, Department of Landscape Architecture, University of Minnesota. Photographer: Warren Bruland.

Why did you decide to pursue a career in landscape architecture?

❯ Family friends owned a nursery, so ever since I was a kid I "worked" around plants. They knew a landscape designer and suggested I do something like that because I liked plants so much. The other thing that made me pursue landscape architecture is my Native American cultural background. I spent a lot of time in the natural environment, berry picking and fishing and hunting. I grew up with a general respect for the earth, so I wanted to do something related to that.

How and why did you choose the schools you attended to earn your degrees?

❯ My sisters and I were the first in our family to go to college. I grew up 10 miles from the University of Minnesota, so I chose based on location and finances. Luckily, they happened to have a landscape architecture program, and it was a fantastic experience. When I went to graduate school, I almost got a fine arts degree, but as I evaluated my life, I couldn't find anything I liked better than landscape architecture. I was living and working in Seattle and had taught part-time at the University of Washington. They had a solid program and really good faculty. It was also affordable, because after my first semester I got a teaching assistantship. Since I already had a professional degree, I was given flexibility to take some different, nondesign courses.

Which aspects of your graduate education have had the greatest influence on you?

❯ In my undergraduate education there was a focus on creative thinking and process. When I went to graduate school, it was about research process: how to use primary sources, how to formulate questions and organize your thinking to get involved in research on a particular subject. One of the greatest influences was a pair of environmental science courses that were taught concurrently. We had a series of wonderful speakers, such as the head of the National Park Service, and a lawyer who had argued at the Supreme Court about an environmental case; and we read a number of environmentally oriented books. Several scientists talked about how their data was used or misused. I learned a great deal about politics, policy, and science, and then how that could be used in landscape architecture.

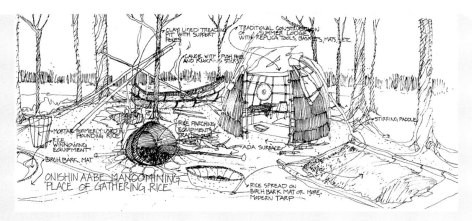

▲ Sketch of interpretive "stopping place," which teaches about Ojibwe life. Part of Battle Point Historic Site at Leech Lake Reservation, Minnesota. Illustrator: John Koepke.

◀ Tribal center campus master plan developed by graduate students at the University of Washington in consultation with the Port Gamble S'Kallam Tribe in Washington State.

Why did you decide to go into the academic realm of landscape architecture?

❭ While working at Jones & Jones in Seattle, I was asked to teach drawing at the University of Washington. I found that I really liked teaching. I decided to get a graduate degree because I thought it would make me a better writer and therefore a better professional. Once I got into it, I decided teaching was more fulfilling in terms of helping other people—I got a bigger thrill helping students. Then I found, if you get into academia, it's kind of like having your own business. You have your teaching business, your publication business, your scholarship business and your consulting business. There is a lot of autonomy, which I found was really great.

Describe your research focus on Native Americans and why it is important for the landscape architecture profession.

❭ I have a couple of research foci related to Native Americans. I started out looking at ancient Native American sites. There is something for us to learn, as landscape architects working on this continent, from Native Americans and how they originally arranged, managed, and organized their spaces and worked with indigenous materials. Recently, I have been looking at more contemporary examples of tribes—their cultural centers and museums—and understanding how the landscape is used as a vehicle for cultural interpretation. I then try to understand the culture of the tribes in order to see what the relationships are between people and the environment and how those can be manifested in the design of landscape. It is interesting, because you deal with cultural symbolism, appropriateness, and how much you can convey based on what people want to reveal or not.

What has been your most rewarding project?

❭ I did a project with the Leech Lake Band of Ojibwe. That is the tribe I belong to, so I knew what I was working with, and it was wonderful to be able to give back to them. It was a cultural center museum. I worked with an architect friend of mine, Janis LaDouceur, and another Native American landscape architect, Ron Melchert. It was great because we worked quite closely with the community members, and the design included really strong cultural symbolism. It is completely funded but has not been built yet.

Which aptitudes, traits, and skills do you see in most landscape architects?

❭ Landscape architects are pretty creative folks; often they are environmentally oriented, socially responsible, and possess a general curiosity about the issues. We have a graduate program where I teach, and we have students who come with backgrounds in writing, psychology, biology, ecology, art, and accounting—they come from all walks. So I don't know if there is a typical set.

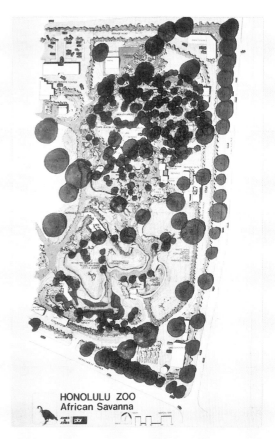

Honolulu Zoo African savanna master plan. John Koepke was the lead landscape architect for design and construction, working closely with several Jones & Jones staff and principals. Illustrator: Joan Gray, Jones & Jones.

What role can landscape architects take in making our world better?

❭ There is no bigger issue facing humans and the rest of the world than climate change. Landscape architects play a huge role in trying to mitigate and make adaptations to climate change, based on how we impact people's movement, and depending on how we do design and planning. In the northern latitudes, we actually see the climate changing in Minnesota because it is so pronounced. It's critical that landscape architects take up a strong role of environmental advocacy.

Project Profile

THE HILLS PROJECT

Learning through Service

Stakeholder participation: a variety of activities and formats. Courtesy of ASLA. Illustration: University of Kentucky Department of Landscape Architecture.

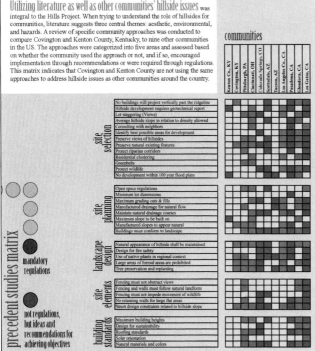

Precedent studies: Students conduct research to learn from others' experiences. Courtesy of ASLA. Illustration: University of Kentucky Department of Landscape Architecture.

The Hills Project

6 Areas of Interest
LEED and Sprawl Evaluations

Stakeholder input was an essential element of the six areas of interest exercise. However, a more complete evaluation of potential development was gained through the incorporation of additional evaluation frameworks. This included the U.S. Green Building Council's Leadership in Energy and Environmental Design (LEED) for Neighborhood Development evaluation and the Hasse (2004) evaluation. LEED evaluates developments based on smart growth, urbanism, and green building by the acquisition of credit points for meeting standards based on these principles. For the LEED evaluations, all green practices were assumed during the pre-construction phase. Hasse evaluates development on a continuum from urban sprawl to smart growth with negative numbers indicating sprawl and positive numbers indicating smart growth.

Utilizing the data gathered from the initial stakeholder input session and the results from the two evaluation frameworks to generate final designs, the concepts were reintroduced in Meeting 3. The designs were displayed using three-dimensional photo-realistic models, with buildings color-coded according to the Kenton County zoning map index for their associated land uses. The respective LEED and Hasse evaluation rankings were displayed, and stakeholders rated the designs on a scale from 1 (like) to 7 (dislike).

higher density model

LEED: 24 Hasse: 45

lower density model

LEED: 8 Hasse: 17

preservation model

LEED: 55 Hasse: 34

LEED model

LEED: 69 Hasse: 23

Three-dimensional photorealistic models were evaluated based on two different methodologies. Courtesy of ASLA. Illustration: University of Kentucky Department of Landscape Architecture.

PROJECT OVERVIEW

Date: 2008

Type: Undergraduate Course/Community Design Studio

Location: Northern Kentucky

Client: Northern Kentucky Area Planning Commission

University: University of Kentucky

Project Manager: Dr. Brian Lee, Assistant Professor of Landscape Architecture, University of Kentucky

Awards: 2008 Student ASLA Community Service Honor Award

This is a very professional project. The modeling of the building scenario was very clear and accessible. It was a process and not just an event.

—2008 STUDENT AWARD JURY COMMENTS[16]

A Semester-Long Assignment

In the spring semester of 2008, 14 fifth-year students and their landscape architecture professor, Dr. Brian Lee, began work with the Northern Kentucky Area Planning Commission on the Hills Project. The project goal was to analyze both preservation and development scenarios for the hillsides of northern Kentucky and propose alternatives to the community.[17]

The debate over hillside development in northern Kentucky has been in the media for several years. Additionally, many areas in the surrounding region also deal with this topic, both in the past and today.[18] These issues, combined with the current pressures of population growth, created an interesting basis for a class assignment. The students spent the entire semester investigating the issues, formulating their opinions on the subject, and creating their proposals for consideration.[19]

The Process and Evaluation Framework

The students' process relied heavily on research, analysis, and stakeholder participation. The term "stakeholder" refers to all who have an interest in the subject, such as local citizens, elected officials, and business owners. The students organized and led three public meetings. They devised surveys and participation strategies to gain a better understanding of the study area and the stakeholders' ideas about the area. During the meetings, attendees participated in informal discussions, focus groups, visual preference surveys, landscape value surveys, and landscape typology surveys.[20] In the first meeting, students discussed their inventory and analysis of northern Kentucky, such as history, demographics, hillside issues, context and key locations, physical identity, precedents, and land use planning. At the second meeting, the landscape architecture students revealed their conceptual designs; and in the final meeting, the students presented their refined ideas. The three meetings over the course of the semester gave students and stakeholders a chance to learn from each other and build upon ideas.[21] Dennis Andrew Gordon, the executive director of the Northern Kentucky Area Planning Commission and fellow of the American Institute of Certified Planners said, "We were pleased to have the students join our effort…. They brought a tremendous level of enthusiasm to our process and helped the stakeholders focus on the issues that will ultimately be the basis for new public policy."[22]

Based on their inventory, analysis, and initial concepts, the students produced build-out scenarios for six sites. Participating stakeholders selected the demonstration sites for the students to study, which ranged from rural to urban, and were approximately 100 acres in size. Four site designs were developed for each of the six sites: a higher-density model, a lower-density model, a LEED model, and a preservation model. The four site plans were analyzed under the criteria recommended by the U.S. Green Building Council's LEED for Neighborhood Development, as well as a framework for urban sprawl and smart growth published in the *Landscape Journal*.[23] Students used computer programs such as ArcGIS 9.2, AutoCAD, and Vue 6 Infinite to create models.[24]

The Outcome

After a semester's worth of hard work, the students were able to give back to the stakeholders and the community that had helped them along the way. The students produced a series of brochures for distribution, in an effort to build upon and perhaps implement the proposed ideas. Additionally, the team produced a lengthy report documenting their process and suggestions for the community.[25]

However, the student's work reaches beyond the final products of the semester. Their presence in the community and their professional-caliber work helped get the word out about landscape architecture. This type of landscape architecture studio, often called "service learning," helps communities gain a richer understanding about the possibilities inherent in the land, given careful analysis and study. Moreover, the students initiated and helped facilitate a dialogue in the community, among all stakeholders, about the future of that place, which will certainly benefit the environment and the local population.[26]

Marketing: Getting Work

Marketing one's professional work is very different from the process used to market a product. Landscape architecture, like many professions, is considered a service-based business—we sell our knowledge, expertise, and skills. A landscape architect's work is not tangible, is not a "product," until it has been completed. Therefore, unlike buying, say, an article of clothing, which can be touched and tried on before deciding to purchase it, landscape architectural design cannot be evaluated in that very hands-on way and so necessitates a different approach to marketing it.

When thinking about marketing, it is instructive to consider the differences between product- and service-based businesses. There are four key distinctions:

1. Service businesses sell expertise and knowledge; therefore, an office's primary asset is its employees' talent and skills.
2. Because knowledge is the "product," and it is never the same, there are unique opportunities for service choices, as well as different approaches to pricing and fees.
3. Except for custom-made products, service businesses typically have greater contact with and involvement by the client.
4. Because a consumer cannot evaluate the quality of the service before buying, most service-based and public-interest professions are subject to ethical codes of conduct and regulations regarding their work. This is one of the many reasons landscape architects must be registered to practice professionally.

The first point regarding human resources being a primary asset highlights one of the key aspects of marketing a professional service: human relations. Developing solid relationships with clients is

The Civitas office, Denver, Colorado, with group meeting space visible on left. Courtesy of Civitas, Inc.

very important. Related to this is the notion of trust. To feel secure in hiring your firm, a client has to trust you, and trust that your office can perform the needed design services to meet or exceed their objectives. Other critical factors in marketing service-based businesses include reputation and perception, both of which relate back to relationships—your firm will not go far if previous clients are not happy with your work. A good reputation takes hard work to achieve and must be safeguarded carefully in all activities of the office and its employees. Another factor in marketing a design firm is creating distinction. What is your specialty? How are you different from the competition? What new skills, services, or staff expertise can you offer? While firms who have been in business for some time say they do not market very often, all offices are in fact doing marketing every time they do quality work. Without a body of exemplary work and satisfied clients, there will be no future work.

How does your firm approach marketing?

❯ That's a complicated topic. In a design profession, not just landscape architecture, but all design professions, our products are intangible. You hire me to do something and you don't know what I'm going to do; and neither do I. That means our reputation is our primary asset, and our people are our secondary asset, and finding a way of aligning our reputation and our people is critical. Marketing begins by knowing who you are internally. The next step is making sure people in the outside world know who you are and what you stand for. That's called positioning. We have two full-time people who do our marketing. We are, on a daily basis, looking for leads, maintaining our network and alliances, investigating opportunities we've heard about, and responding to requests for proposals.

Mark Johnson, FASLA
Founding Principal and President, Civitas, Inc.

❯ At least half of our work comes to us from referrals, from our clients, so we don't have to do nearly as much marketing as we used to. They find us. We also respond to RFPs (requests for proposals). Those are usually sent to us directly, or we're contacted by an allied professional who thinks we would be a good fit and wants to team with us.

Dawn Kroh, RLA
President, Green 3, LLC

❯ This piece of what we do is undervalued, or it's only taken in a "I'm doing marketing to get us more work with this type of client" approach. You can market a city and a project at the same time that you're marketing a firm. The public relations piece is as critical to the project as the technical detail of how the boardwalk interfaces with the river's edge.

Chris Reed
Founding Principal, StoSS

❯ We do that in a variety of ways. We started by pursuing work through competitions because we didn't have connections. We also look at RFPs and RFQs that are sent to us. These [requests for proposals or qualifications] tell what the project is about, what the budget is, what the schedule is, who the client is, and what the goals are for the project. We're at the point now where we have established relationships with architects, engineers, and clients, and they have asked us to participate with them on multiple projects. This is wonderful because it sure makes marketing easy.

Jennifer Guthrie, RLA, ASLA
Director, Gustafson Guthrie Nichol Ltd.

How does your firm approach marketing? (Continued)

❯ Marketing professional services is primarily a process of cultivating relationships. To borrow from John Guare's play, "Six Degrees of Separation," one's goal is to reduce the distance to potential clients down to one or two steps. That means building a strong network of contacts. A young practitioner who assumes that "the principals" will bring in the work is making a grave mistake. Continually maintain your relationships from university, prior work experiences, or other activities, and they will pay dividends professionally in the long run. Advertising, awards, publications, speaking engagements, and similar activities all have a role but they are no substitute for long-term personal relationships, and satisfied clients.

Kurt Culbertson, FASLA
Chairman of the Board, Design Workshop

❯ From the academic side, we're trying to position our department to have a legacy in community design. We are working with communities in North Carolina to help them solve their problems. We position ourselves when we go for grants to be able to say we have a track record with these approaches, and have the research to back it up, and that makes us unique.

Kofi Boone, ASLA
Assistant Professor, Department of Landscape Architecture,
North Carolina State University

❯ I get referrals from engineers, architects, and clients, or someone who is a friend of a friend or someone who visited the work we have done. Whenever I get the chance to write, I do that. Locally, I try to stay involved in the community and get to know the reporters and publishers in newspapers and the local magazines, so when they are looking for an expert opinion on something, you get those calls. That is a community service, but it's also marketing.

Edward L. Blake, Jr.
Founding Principal, The Landscape Studio

❯ Writing is a very important way of getting your ideas out and helping to define what the profession is. Look at contemporary practice, from Martha Schwartz and Michael Van Valkenburgh and George Hargreaves to younger landscape urbanists like James Corner and Chris Reed—we know them mainly because they write.

Frederick R. Steiner, PhD, FASLA
Dean, School of Architecture , University of Texas

❯ Public agencies don't really market to get work, but we have to sell ourselves in other ways. Because we are a public service, we make sure people have a clear understanding of what we're able to accomplish, why we're there, and what our mission is. It's really about making sure people understand the value you bring; the good things that will come from working with you.

Juanita D. Shearer-Swink, FASLA
Project Manager, Triangle Transit Authority

❯ Most of our clients, 85 percent, are repeat, long-time clients. But we are now finding we need to do more marketing as the profession diversifies, with the green movement and the issues of global warming. We see a real opportunity to grow, so our marketing now is to present what it means to have a full comprehensive landscape architectural project—everything from research through design to built environment that uses state-of-the-art technology. We are trying to present process, and how our process gets to the heart of solving their design problems in a unique way.

Frederick R. Bonci, RLA, ASLA
Founding Principal, LaQuatra Bonci Associates

❯ My approach to get funding is all the grant writing I do. To do it well involves developing partnerships in the community, and networking. I also write articles for professional publications to get support for different ideas. All organizations have conferences, Web sites, and newsletters, so being able to present at their conferences or write articles for their publications can provide visibility for our agency and our work. For landscape architects, having skills in writing, speaking, and communicating is a plus because you can really promote your work better.

Robin Lee Gyorgyfalvy, ASLA
Director of Interpretive Services & Scenic Byways, USDA
Forest Service: Deschutes National Forest

❭ Being a charitable organization, providing a public benefit, it's common that we get solicited from community groups or municipalities to help protect land. We look at our criteria and decide what we'll take on. The land is the connection between the organization and the community. If the community doesn't benefit, then we won't do that project.

Roy Kraynyk
Executive Director, Allegheny Land Trust

❭ For marketing, we're always widely published. I am working on my fifth book. We also have a consultant who comes in once a month to steer us in the right direction from the marketing standpoint. She encourages the younger partners to get out there and do the social part—go to parties, give speeches, and get their name out there.

The other thing is, clients can simply check out the Web site, so they know what we do before they call us. We have 15,000 hits a month from all over the world—Saudi Arabia, Korea, you name it. But you have to keep it up to date, as the part of the Web site that gets the most hits is new projects.

James van Sweden, FASLA
Founding Principal, Oehme, van Sweden & Associates, Inc.

❭ There are issues pertaining to building relationships; you need to stay on people's radar and build credibility. You also need to capitalize on opportunities; for example, we are figuring out how to effectively market that we won four awards last year. We are a minority, woman-owned firm, so in the New York market that provides an opportunity in public sector work.

Elizabeth Kennedy, ASLA
Principal, EKLA Studio

❭ We're big enough so that our reputation gets our foot in the door, but that's not what wins a project. What wins a project is, fundamentally, do they have confidence in you, and that really happens at the personal level. Some may think "that's not fair; EDAW has such an advantage" (due to our size), but we'll go in and do an interview for a project and somebody will say, "Are you too big for us? We're not sure we're going to be that important to you." We have to be careful to find a balance; we want to let people know about our tradition, our history, and our resources, but we also have to make that one-on-one personal connection, too.

Jim Sipes, ASLA
Senior Associate, EDAW, Atlanta

❭ We market to consumers who use our services. We have flyers and brochures; and through public meetings, we try to create relationships with a neighborhood. We want them to understand we are looking out for their interests, so we market by doing the right things. Since I have been here, we went from no trails to 46 miles of trails, and people love trails here. We do market studies to determine what people want and why. We have a number ways we get what would qualify as market information to and from our customers.

Gary Scott, FASLA
Director, West Des Moines Parks & Recreation Department

❭ You can be a great designer, but if you can't market yourself, you are not going to make any money. It used to be all word of mouth, and I still like that form of marketing; but about three years ago I hired a director of marketing. His full-time job is to put our best foot forward and make people aware of what we do. I find it's good for business, but it's also good for the staff because they like to see their projects in print and get recognized.

Douglas Hoerr, FASLA
Partner, Hoerr Schaudt Landscape Architects

How does your firm approach marketing? (Continued)

❯ It is not quite marketing in the conventional sense of a private office, but we are somewhat of a firm within the city. We do a lot of what might be called research-type work or demonstration projects. We actually market ourselves to other city agencies: "You know we can do this for that project," or "Wouldn't you like to try this?" For example, with the Headwaters Project, we worked with the Transportation Department to take out a street and put in a creek.

Tom Liptan, ASLA
Sustainable Stormwater Management Program, Portland Bureau of Environmental Services

Marketing Yourself: Finding a Job

Few people find job hunting an easy process; certainly, it makes most of us uncomfortable to think we are marketing ourselves, but that is, in fact, what we are doing: We're putting our best professional selves forward so that this firm or that agency will "buy" what we have to offer—our knowledge, skills, capabilities, and/or experience. To do that, to get the job, we must "package" ourselves as effectively as possible. Here, the term "package" refers to your resume, cover letter, and portfolio, and it's critically important that you assemble these components so that you "market" yourself in the best light.

Think about it: When you are considering the purchase of something, what influences your decision? Quality? Value? Whether it meets your needs? Whether it has unique qualities or special features? Reliability? Now combine those ideas with what is expected of you as a young professional: What specialized skills and knowledge do you have? What underlying principles guide you? Are you passionate about what you do, and about learning more? What are your goals for advancement? All these point out how important and challenging assembling your package will be. Each person entering the field is unique, therefore you have to determine how best to convey your unique "selling features," using the accepted "marketing tools" of the profession.

YOUR RESUME

You only get one chance to make a first impression. Often your resume and cover letter comprise that first impression. When you realize that, you will begin to understand how important it is to use these tools to present a solid, positive portrayal of yourself and your capabilities. It takes hard work to do this well. You must consider carefully how to describe all your qualifications in a succinct and well-written presentation—one that fits on a single page, if you're seeking an entry-level position. (Those with more experience, or who have worked in another career before entering landscape architecture, may use two pages.)

If a firm, agency, or organization is hiring, chances are it means the staff are busy; it also means the potential employer won't have more than a couple of minutes to read your cover letter and scan your resume. How can you set your two documents apart from all the others they will be reviewing? The goal is to distinguish yourself while tailoring the letter and resume to meet that firm's needs and interests. To that end, there are four key objectives to meet when crafting your resume:

- Consider aesthetics—visual appeal.
- Be concise—be brief and use high-quality, effective writing.
- Be pertinent—include only information that contributes to a positive portrayal of you and your assets.
- Be organized—make it easy for employers to find the information they're looking for.

Consider Aesthetic Appeal

Landscape architecture is a profession rooted in creativity and design, so it will come as no surprise that employers will expect your resume to be visually strong. In short, looks matter. Before potential employers even begin to read your resume, they will make a quick, automatic judgment based on how it is designed and formatted.[27] Fortunately, our profession allows for greater creativity in resume formatting than in, for example, the corporate business world; that's not to say, however, that bizarre or wildly unusual resumes will be welcomed. Never forgo basic design principles: balance of positive and negative space, establish a hierarchy, strive for legible page composition, and so on. Also, use easy-to-read font styles (not too many!), and high-quality paper, if you will be sending hard-copy versions of your resumes.

Be Concise

Your resume will be both more visually appealing and easier to read if you err on the side of brevity—be concise. Keep your sentences short, or use bulleted phrases. Streamline your thoughts; avoid losing important information in a lengthy block of text. And be sure to choose logical and meaningful headings and subheadings to group your qualifications into distinct categories. Select precise, descriptive words, and use action verbs to describe what you have done, such as "achieved," "produced," "initiated"; and pick positive modifiers, such as "actively," "effectively," "accurately," and so on, to spotlight your accomplishments.

RESUME CATEGORIES AND HEADINGS

This list is not meant to imply that only one heading per category is appropriate. For example, under "Work/Jobs," both "Employment" and "Research Experience" might work best to highlight and explain your background. Very likely two or more headings will be used from the "Other" category. The list here is not exhaustive; it is intended only to illustrate possibilities and get you thinking.

SCHOOLING

Education; Academe

Possible subheadings

Study Focus; Related Coursework; Coursework Emphasis; Study Abroad; Thesis Title

HONORS/AWARDS

Honors; Academic Honors; Professional Achievements and Awards; Honors and Assistantships; Special Awards

WORK/JOBS

Employment; Professional Office Experience; Work Experience; Teaching and Related Experience; Teaching Responsibilities; Research Experience

PROFESSIONAL RELATIONS

Professional Activities; Professional Status and Awards; Professional Affiliation (or Societies); Registration (or Licenses)

OTHER

Personal Attributes; Key Accomplishments; Capabilities; Computer Proficiencies; Interests; Personal Interests; Language Skills; Research and Creative Projects; Manuscripts; Published Articles and Professional Papers

EXTRACURRICULAR ACTIVITIES

Travel; Independent Travel; Activities/Organizations; Volunteer Work; Service; Organizational Memberships

Be Pertinent

How do you decide what to include on a document that has to be so short? The first guideline is to make good use of every word; choose each one carefully to achieve your goal—helping a potential employer to understand who you are. Ask: Does what I've written here emphasize my strengths? Does it provide insight into my interests? Does it show I am willing to take responsibility and/or initiative? Does it portray my skills and abilities in the best light?

Don't forget to leave room to list your outside interests and activities, too. Firms are looking to hire a real person, not just a drafting drone, so they will want to gain a fuller understanding of who you are when you're not being a landscape architect. This is not to suggest you list every hobby; feature only those most important to you, or that might have relevance to your professional direction.

Be Organized

Once you have figured out all the wonderful things you want to say about yourself, you then have to determine how to lay it out to its best effect. One of the first rules in resume organization is to use reverse chronology—that is, list the most current information first. For example, let's say that under the "Employment" heading, you want to list three summer internships; in this case, you would list the most recent one first. This practice also makes it easy to update your resume in the future; you simply drop the older items off the bottom the list when they are no longer relevant. For instance, when I was looking for my first job, my resume included my dining hall work experience, which I included to demonstrate I could juggle the responsibilities of a job with my college studies. Needless to say, after I had my first full-time professional job, I took that dining hall job off my resume.

The second organizational guideline is to arrange your resume categories so they have the greatest impact. Standard practice is to list your educational background first. From there, you need to determine in what order to best feature your experience and skills. A good way to determine this is to review carefully how the job description is worded—see what it lists as most important—then tailor your resume accordingly.

YOUR COVER LETTER

Your cover letter is the second part of the important dynamic duo that comprises a first impression you want to make with a potential employer. You have spent some time crafting a solid resume, now you must also work to create an effective introduction to that resume. Remember that this set must project confidence in yourself and your abilities.

A cover letter is just that—a one page, well-written piece that will set the stage for your resume. This is the place where you can elaborate a bit more about key items on your resume as well as specifics about your interest in the job opening. There are three key aspects to a good cover letter:

- Format
- Content
- Writing style and grammar

Format

Your cover letter and resume will arrive together, therefore they should look like they belong together—they form a set. These two documents should be both visually and graphically similar. At the least, they should be printed on the same paper. Also consider that both have the same or a similar graphic style—same font, margins, and the like. It might also be desirable to use the same moniker or graphic "emblem" or heading—almost like a letterhead that a company might use. Though, as cautioned above, the use of something like this should not be overly stylized or ornate. It should project professionalism and your sense of design.

Content

First and foremost, do your homework. This means getting an actual name to whom you will address the letter as well as researching the office's work. Below, in the interview discussion, the importance of this is reinforced, but in order to write a nongeneric cover letter, which should be your goal, you must know something about that office. Next, realize that there is an expected structure in regard to what you should include in a cover letter. This includes proper, professional salutations (both at the beginning and closing), an introductory paragraph, the body, which is one to two paragraphs in length, and a closing paragraph.

This first paragraph is quite important—it needs to grab the addressee's attention. Therefore, if you have a name the addressee might know or recognize, mention that within the first two sentences—who you know and/or how you found out about the job is important. If done well, this is not "name dropping," rather your first foray into using your network to make professional connections. Your letter will already carry a bit more weight than another letter that does not have that connection.

As this first paragraph is your introduction, you must quickly explain who you are and why you are interested in this particular job opening or internship (or why you are inquiring about an office visit, if there are no job openings at the time and you want to introduce yourself). It is very important, however, to make sure you do not tell them what they already know; instead work to phrase it so it reads that YOU know what they do, or how you might fit into their office setting or design approach. For example, do not say: "XYZ Firm is known for their range of designs, from wetland rehabilitation to corporate office parks." A better way to illustrate your understanding about them is: "Through reading about your office, I am impressed with XYZ Firm's range of designs, from wetland rehabilitation to corporate office parks." This is a subtle but important distinction.

The body of the letter is where you develop interest and refer the reader to your resume. For example, you can mention something you've been involved in or something you have accomplished that relates to the position or type of work anticipated in the job. This is also where you expand on a key item or two from your resume that demonstrates your capabilities for this job. Here is where you will highlight your skills and qualifications—in short, this is the toot-your-own-horn paragraph (or two at the most). The trick is to do this professionally and not sound boastful.

In the closing paragraph you must be proactive—ask for the interview. Reinforce your interest in the position. Suggest when you will be in the area and/or how soon you could be available to meet. Too often students don't "close the deal" and come out and ask for an interview or office visit. Close your letter with a positive note about looking forward to meeting that person and their staff or to introducing yourself to their office.

Writing Style and Grammar

It cannot be stressed enough how important good writing skills are for landscape architects. And here is the first writing sample an office will see; therefore, it simply must be an exceptionally well-written letter, period. Keep in mind that offices will get many cover letters, so the smallest thing can get your letter tossed on the "not impressive" pile.

It is suggested you consider these couple of key points about your writing style and quality:

- Have a trusted friend read and/or edit it—another set of eyes will be valuable.
- Use your own voice/style, but ensure that it is also professional.
- Employ excellent grammar.
- Ensure there are no spelling errors and typos.

The bottom line is that this letter and the resume it refers to are about YOU. Make sure the best about you and your understanding of the profession comes through very well and demonstrates your readiness to enter the professional world.

YOUR PORTFOLIO

The definition of "portfolio" has evolved over the years. It originally referred to the actual case that was used to carry loose sheets of paper on which were displayed examples of one's work, commonly artwork.[28] Today, a portfolio is more often thought of as an entire package, the contents as well as the carrying case—which in this digital age might be a "virtual" one, viewable on-screen or online. Whatever form it takes, however, you will invariably be asked to show a portfolio containing representative examples of your work when seeking an internship or a full-time job. Three aspects of a portfolio require your careful attention: what to include, how to organize it, and how best to package it.

What to Show

It is always fun to see how students who have all gone through the same curriculum and completed the same series of assignments come up with totally unique and different approaches to the portfolios they produce. Deciding what to include in your portfolio is always challenging, but it is these choices that will set your portfolio apart. The decisions you make here also begin to say something about your understanding of the landscape architecture profession and your design sense.

Like your resume, your portfolio must illustrate your strengths; at the same time, you are expected to demonstrate awareness of all stages of a project, which means you must include examples of everything from quick concept diagrams from your sketchbook to construction drawings and detailing. Therefore, even if for example landform grading design is not one of your great strengths, you must include a representation of that skill. Probably you won't "feature" it, by showing a close-up of spot elevations or by providing several different examples. In general, however, include work you are most confident about. Sometimes students will go back and rerender or rework a project after receiving final reviews from their professors. This is fine, especially if it means you will feel better about showing it. Featuring group work is also acceptable, and valuable, in your portfolio. Just be sure to acknowledge it as teamwork, and specify your role on it. Often, group work results in a report or publication, in which case you might want to include a page or two that you wrote or contributed to. You might also consider bringing a copy of the full publication to pass around during the interview.

It is never too early to start an archive of your work; the more you have to choose from, the easier it will be later on to produce an impressive and comprehensive representation of your work. To ensure that you have a broad scope of your work to select from, it's a good idea to scan or photograph early concept sketches made on trace paper, as those are the kinds of things that get lost and you'll wish you had when it comes time to assemble a portfolio.

Obviously, digitally produced projects are easier to archive. Digital cameras make it nearly effortless to photograph physical models. You can also ask friends to photograph you making a presentation, especially if it is in a public venue. To be on the safe side, archive at a higher resolution than you might ultimately need. For example, you may determine it is best to include only a portion of a larger plan; but if the resolution is too low, that zoom-in could be too grainy to be usable.

How to Organize

Organization is not necessarily the "next" task in assembling your portfolio, as all aspects of this process work together in concert. That said, you do need to craft a structure, sequence, or "flow" to your portfolio. Here are some approaches to consider:

- Group by design phase or skill (e.g., analysis; computer graphics; construction details; etc.).
- Show projects individually.
- Present work chronologically.
- Use a combination of the preceding.

An important piece of information to know when organizing your portfolio is that many professionals say they like to see at least one representative example of how you followed a project through the entire design process. This helps them to understand your thought process, and how you resolved it in the final design. Therefore, a common way to organize a portfolio is to group several examples of specific skills, such as hand sketching or computer drafting, coupled with showing all parts or phases of a complete project or two.

Another factor in organization is labeling. It is advisable that you include on each page of your portfolio a series of statements and/or labels, organized appropriately, that provide a brief description of what you're showing. A word of caution in this regard: As in the resume discussion, refrain from inserting large blocks of explanatory text. (Note: This does not refer to any text that is part of project sheets/boards included as examples.) Follow a consistent layout on each page (or for each project), identified by brief headings or statements about project type, site size/location, project goals, date or class, media used, and so on. This results in a solid overall structure to your portfolio.

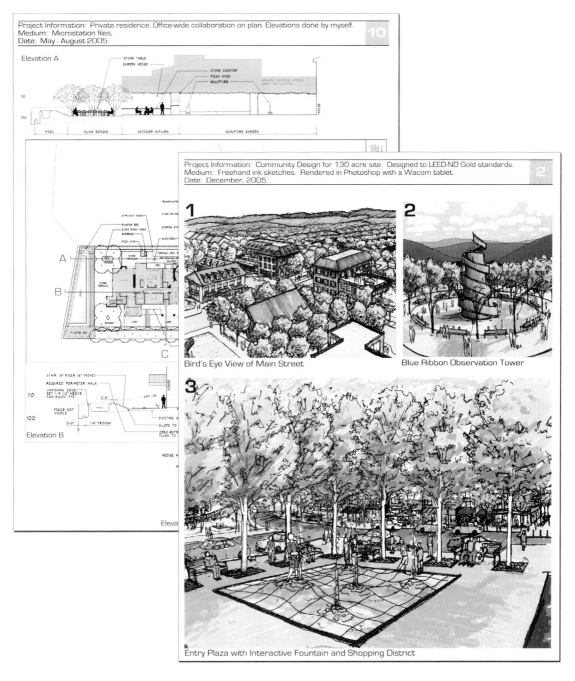

Project Information: Private residence. Office-wide collaboration on plan. Elevations done by myself.
Medium: Microstation files.
Date: May - August 2005.

Elevation A

Elevation B

Project Information: Community Design for 130 acre site. Designed to LEED-ND Gold standards.
Medium: Freehand ink sketches. Rendered in Photoshop with a Wacom tablet.
Date: December, 2005.

1   Bird's Eye View of Main Street

2   Blue Ribbon Observation Tower

3   Entry Plaza with Interactive Fountain and Shopping District

Two pages from an undergraduate landscape architecture student portfolio. Courtesy of Bill Staley and Arentz Landscape Architects.

Packaging Options

How you will "package" your work is the final decision you will make in producing your portfolio. There are two main choices: paper/printed and digital/online. If you choose the latter, you should, nevertheless, also create a paper version of your work to bring with you to discuss during an interview. Although some firms now accommodate digital displays of portfolios for interview purposes, it is still the exception.

DIGITAL PORTFOLIOS

Preparing a digital portfolio can be quite exciting. Online services are now available to help make this easier. Commercial ventures are certainly out there for hire, and some schools and universities offer e-portfolio options for their students. A major advantage of this approach is that it is very easy to send a Web link to your digital portfolio to potential employers. Depending on the online service you use, you may even be able to set up several different versions and select the most applicable to send to each particular firm.

But before you opt to "go digital," keep in mind that not all employers may be as computer-oriented as you are (especially if they were schooled and trained in the precomputer era) and will prefer to view your portfolio in the traditional paper fashion. It is important to find out a firm's preference. Of course, you will need to ensure that the online format you select will be visually appealing and easy to read on all the major browser programs.

PAPER PORTFOLIOS

There are several options for producing a paper portfolio:

- *Spiral bound*: You can achieve a more customized look with a spiral bound copy, and it keeps your work very secure. The disadvantage is that you cannot easily change/update its contents.
- *Leather or vinyl folios*: These typically come with clear, plastic sleeves in which to insert your work. They, too, keep the work secure, and the pages can be swapped to change the sequence or focus of your presentation.
- *A folder or small box*: This choice makes it possible to leave sheets loose, and so is very easy to update. The downside is that the contents can more easily get out of order.

Other creative ways to raise the professional level of your portfolio are to: add tabs, to identify the various sections of your portfolio (like chapters in a book); use a consistent graphic theme throughout, which could even tie into the design of your resume; introduce themed colors, screened background images, borders, or frames.

To select the portfolio packaging choice that's right for you, weigh the pros and cons, as well as differences in costs associated with each approach. Whichever option you chose, keep in mind it must have strong visual appeal and be in an imageable graphic format.

INTERVIEWING

The interview is an essential step in winning a job as a landscape architect. It is a valuable opportunity for you and the potential employer to get to know one another. Many students believe that interviewing is a singular event; in fact, it is a process, typically composed of three steps: (1) preparation for the interview, (2) the interaction during the interview, and (3) follow-up afterwards. As you embark on this process, keep in mind these important points as they relate to the landscape architecture profession:

- As described at the beginning of this chapter, landscape architecture is a service-based profession, meaning that employees are a firm's key assets. Therefore, your abilities, personality, interests, and more, will be evaluated carefully to determine your "fit" in a firm. Employers will want to find out that you can think creatively, take responsibility, and stand on your own two feet.

- Rarely does anyone work entirely on his or her own in landscape architecture; therefore, during an interview, employers will be looking for clear indicators that you are a team player; that you understand how to work effectively with others.

- Any interview is a two-way street: As you are being interviewed, you, too, should be "interviewing" the firm, to determine whether you think you would be happy working there. You should ask questions, such as, what your role would be, what are the chances for advancement, and the like.

Preparing for an Interview

Rehearsing is critical to the success of any performance, and you can think of an interview as a performance, albeit one tailored to a very particular, and usually very small, audience. With that in mind, one of the first things you must do is conduct due diligence about that "audience"—the landscape architecture firm where you will be interviewing for a job. Fortunately, information gathering of this sort is now easier than ever, thanks to the Web. Most firms today have Web sites, and that is a good place to start. But don't stop there. Find out if anyone in the firm has published any articles or books; or, conversely, if any articles have been written about the firm principals or their work. Have they won awards? Does staff do pro bono or volunteer work? You also want to learn whether there are any skills or specific project experience they are looking for in a new hire. Sometimes the job announcement will highlight these; if not, when scheduling your interview, ask if there is anything they are particularly interested in seeing.

Insights you gain from your research about the firm will help with the next preparation goal: deciding what you want to emphasize about yourself and in your portfolio. Many students report being surprised at how quickly interviewers flipped though their portfolios. You can slow them down by identifying beforehand where you want to stop to point out something—and you must not be afraid to do this. Flag a few key (not too many) projects or skills you want to be sure get noticed. From the interviewer's perspective, when you do this, you are demonstrating leadership qualities and taking initiative. At the same time, you must be prepared to discuss *anything* in your portfolio, as you never know what might catch an interviewer's eye. This is why you need to formulate a positive, succinct statement about the contents of each page in your portfolio.

There's no doubt about it, interviews can be nerve-racking, but you can alleviate some of your nervousness by anticipating questions that are likely to be asked of you, and formulating answers to them prior to the interview. In addition to giving you more confidence going into the meeting, it will also lower the chances that you will be caught off-guard, causing you to fumble for the right words and seem unsure of yourself. The following are some typical interview questions for which you should prepare responses, so that you can appear composed and self-assured about yourself and your goals:

- Why did you apply for this job? Or, why are you interested in this job?
- How do you think you can contribute to the firm?
- What are your professional goals? What do you want to be doing in three to five years?
- What would your colleagues/peers say about you as a team member?
- What has been your most gratifying and challenging (not necessarily successful) project to date, and why? What was the least, and why?
- What are your salary requirements?
- When are you available?
- [If you are looking to change jobs.] Why are you looking for another job? (Mention advancement, better opportunity, etc.; never complain about your current job!)

Don't forget, no interview is just about you. You are also interviewing the firm. You need a good understanding about the place if you are to make the right decision about working there. Moreover, your inquiries about the firm will spark important dialogue that will benefit the interview process. In this regard, here are some questions you might want to pose, if they are not addressed during the interview:

- What is the organizational structure of the office?
- Do you work with outside consultants? What types? How often?
- What percentage of your design projects get built?
- How often is travel required?
- To what degree does the office use digital media (CAD, multimedia, 3D visualizations, etc.)? In what capacity? At what stages of the design process?
- Do you typically conduct field/construction observations?
- How does the office support registration exam candidates?
- What do you find to be the most rewarding aspect of your work?
- Describe the position: What would be my responsibilities?
- When will a hiring decision be made?

The final preparation step is deciding what to wear to the interview. To continue with the performance metaphor, you need to think about your "costume." To prepare for your "role" as a professional landscape architect, you want to dress as the others in that office do. So, as part of your research, try to find out how casual or corporate the office is, and then dress to that level. If you can't find this out, it is better to err on the side of formal/conservative. Today, however, it's fairly safe to assume that most design offices do not have overly corporate dress codes—for example, men rarely wear three-piece suits. Aim to dress appropriately, yet comfortably, and be yourself.

During the Interview

On the day of the interview, plan to arrive a little early—though don't go in way ahead of your scheduled time. You will be more relaxed if you arrive 15 to 20 minutes early than if you are racing to get there on time. This assures you will be able to absorb unexpected delays in travel. You can spend any extra time at a nearby coffee shop, or in the car, reviewing your notes and portfolio and gathering your thoughts. You will then appear for your interview composed and ready to "perform."

Greet your interviewer(s) with a firm handshake and a smile. A solid handshake is a good way to start to exhibit your professional confidence. During the introductions, it might be a good idea to ask how much time the interviewer can spend with you. This will enable you to better gauge what the pace of the interview might be. The interviewer will, of course, set the pace. But, as mentioned previously, don't hesitate to interject comments or questions, if you feel things are moving too fast, and especially if you see opportunities to highlight your skills slipping by.

Throughout the interview, be positive and upbeat about your work and your abilities. Be succinct; if your comments or explanations drag on, you will lose the interviewer's attention. He or she can ask follow-up questions if more information is desired. It is a good idea, and a good way to demonstrate a level of professionalism, to have a small notepad or sketchbook on hand to jot down a few notes. You can also use the notepad to refer to the questions you want to ask.

Don't forget to show interest in the firm or agency. Ask for a tour of the office. If the interviewer does not have time for this, ask if another staff can escort you around. It is important to at least get a glimpse of the work environment and to observe the employees—do they look content, excited, harried? How do they interact? What is the workspace like? Many design offices pride themselves in having a work environment that fosters creativity. The more offices you can observe, the better idea you will have about the kind of place you will feel most comfortable working.

Interview Follow-up

As soon as possible following the interview, review your notes and make additional notes. Write down the names of the people you met; the projects you saw, and what you liked, or didn't like, about them; and other key observations. These will be valuable for comparison purposes with other offices you visit, as well as for use in your follow-up correspondence. File these notes for future job search reference, too. You might not get a job at this place this time around, but you might have another opportunity, so keep this information available. You never know when it will come in handy.

A courtesy that has, unfortunately, become all too rare in business is to send a thank-you note to the person or persons who interviewed you. You would be well advised to add this professional courtesy as the final step in your interview procedure. It takes only a few minutes to write and send out a note of thanks as soon as possible following an interview. In it, if you are still interested in the job, reiterate this, and say why. Personalize the note by mentioning the names of people you met, stating what you liked about projects you saw, and so forth. Although correspondence these days tends to be mailed electronically, you have the opportunity to stand out from the crowd by "snail-mailing" a handwritten note or hand-delivering it, if convenient. Many professionals say they appreciate the sincerity and effort behind a handwritten note.

If you are fortunate to be offered the job, make sure to request that the details of the arrangement be outlined in writing. This, too, is a highly professional tack to take. This will ensure you understood all the details of the offer, and it makes official what may have only been verbalized in person or over the phone. Having offers in writing also makes it easier to compare with other offers you may receive.

Once you have the offer in writing, take the time to make sure you understand salary separate from benefits. Remember, healthcare benefits and retirement savings options can add significantly to the total value of the offer, so don't focus too much on just the salary.

Finally, realize you have been offered the job because they believe you will be a valuable member of the team. This means you need to be satisfied with the offer, and therefore should feel free to negotiate its terms. For example, if you were hoping for a higher salary, ask if it can be raised, or if the office would agree to reevaluate the amount at a three- or six-month employment evaluation. Another negotiation tactic is to ask for assistance in moving expenses (if applicable), or for the office to pay your professional licensing exam expenses in two years—which, if paid out of pocket, can be considerable.

> ## What do you see as the greatest business challenge for landscape architecture firms?

> The biggest business crisis is going to be if we don't market ourselves, and our rightful place, to ensure we are a part of the early team on a project, and not the late team. We have to get in early and help create the right response, and do it in a business-savvy way.

Douglas Hoerr, FASLA
Partner, Hoerr Schaudt Landscape Architects

> Being diverse to avoid peaks and troughs; we'll take on projects of varying sizes, shapes, and objectives. So even though from the outside we might look like a niche firm, within our niche we are very diverse.

Patricia O'Donnell, FASLA, AICP
Principal, Heritage Landscapes, Preservation Landscape Architects & Planners

> To be able to do the research and the thinking you want, to take time for innovation and still

make a profit, still make your fee structure work—this I consider to be very challenging. You want to constantly be advancing new things while still making your fee structure work.

Julia Czerniak
Principal, CLEAR

> We are at a critical point. As small firms get gobbled up by multidisciplinary firms, and everybody says they can do everything, the profession needs to work very hard to retain its identity. People are eating away at our profession's margins. We have to cement a foundation to become a very strong profession.

Gary Scott, FASLA
Director, West Des Moines Parks & Recreation Department

> Landscape architecture firms (even the largest in the field) tend to be rather small economic enterprises compared to other industries; therefore,

the institutional knowledge about how to grow and build successful practices is limited. For the good of the profession, we need to find a way to record and disseminate this knowledge. The CEO Roundtable has awakened to some of this with their annual salary survey, but there is much more to be done.

Kurt Culbertson, FASLA
Chairman of the Board, Design Workshop

❭ Leadership. Landscape architects are qualified to lead complex projects and teams. Confidence building needs to happen in the public and private sectors, to where that can be the expectation.

Kofi Boone, ASLA
Assistant Professor, Department of Landscape Architecture,
North Carolina State University

❭ How do you grow a firm without losing the subtleties and things that influence the end product, because your workload is greater than it used to be? The ability to maintain the integrity of your strengths all while running a business is tough. The business part for me is the least interesting, but it's a necessary evil.

Jeffrey K. Carbo, FASLA
Principal, Jeffrey Carbo Landscape Architects and Site
Planners

❭ Historically, if the budget for a project goes over, landscape is the item that has costs cut. What we've been doing to solve that is at the beginning of every project to pull the budget for the landscape out as a separate item. For example, the landscape on a project may be $5 million, we will design diligently to that and ensure that when bidding happens, the bids come back specifically targeted toward that landscape budget. It is much less likely to get cut out; this has been one of the smartest things we've done.

Jennifer Guthrie, RLA, ASLA
Director, Gustafson Guthrie Nichol Ltd.

❭ Attracting the kind of work that allows you to build or sustain your capacity. Some landscape architects do whatever comes across their table; if it were medicine, you'd call it a general practice. Whether or not you specialize or you are general, attracting work has to do with marketing, with visibility, and with credibility—it has to do with all these things coming together.

Elizabeth Kennedy, ASLA
Principal, EKLA Studio

❭ Landscape architectural firms have to stay at the edge, at the cutting edge, of progress on sustainability. In other words, they can't be in the past. Something worked before, but is it appropriate for the future? The business challenge is staying out there, always striving to understand what's up, what's coming, and how does an office get into that?

Tom Liptan, ASLA
Sustainable Stormwater Management Program, Portland
Bureau of Environmental Services

❭ People really value the end, and they don't realize it takes a process, and that takes time and, therefore, costs money to get to that end. Bringing what it takes to get a great project in line with what someone is willing to pay for it is the greatest business challenge.

Nancy D. Rottle, RLA, ASLA
Associate Professor, Department of Landscape Architecture,
University of Washington

❭ Staying within the budget allowances while maintaining the integrity of the design work. Saying no to projects when they are not the right fit for the kind of work we do.

Mikyoung Kim
Principal, mikyoung kim design

❭ It is a challenge to position yourself well. There are many other firms that can do this kind of work, so how do you differentiate your firm in the marketplace? This is why marketing is so important.

Eddie George, ASLA
Founding Principal, The Edge Group

What do you see as the greatest business challenge for landscape architecture firms? (Continued)

〉 The greatest business challenge is to help the general public understand that we provide an intellectual service. Our profession has been hampered by the HGTV sort of industry, where the public perception is that someone can scrape in a bed line and then the crew shows up and starts popping plants in place. Those programs provide no insight as to how a landscape architect works. Our greatest challenge is getting the public to understand we provide a service, not a product. We might give you a plan, but the plan is just capturing what is in our head.

Jacob Blue, MS, RLA, ASLA
Landscape Architect/Ecological Designer, Applied Ecological Services, Inc.

〉 Get to know those who are the businesspeople in the community—our bankers, our realtors, and all those folks. I have learned that a banker is really my best friend. They want to see you succeed. I always looked at a bank as like going to a parent and asking for an allowance; but now I understand they know what it takes to run a business. You can visit them and have honest discussions about where you'd like to be down the road and let them be a part of helping you figure out how to get there.

Edward L. Blake, Jr.
Founding Principal, The Landscape Studio

〉 How do we present ourselves globally? The engineers and architects have a foothold in the markets internationally because of their name and the type of work they've done previously. We have to continue to battle internationally for the profession.

Robert B. Tilson, FASLA
President, Tilson Group

〉 A great challenge is how landscape architecture firms show their value to the client—differentiating their skills from architecture and civil engineering firms. In a lot of projects I see those firms doing work that should be done by landscape architecture firms. I see architecture firms billing themselves as urban design, but they don't have any landscape experience. So the role for landscape architects is there, but somehow they're not always included when they should be.

Meredith Upchurch, ASLA
Green Infrastructure Designer, Casey Trees Endowment Fund

〉 Landscape architecture hasn't always been as aggressive at pursuing new opportunities as we need to be. One of the business challenges is not just maintaining what the profession is, but letting people know we have the ability to do more, and then being able to market that, pursue that, and make it pay.

Jim Sipes, ASLA
Senior Associate, EDAW, Atlanta

Overview of the Profession: By the Numbers

According the Bureau of Labor Statistics, U.S. Department of Labor, there were nearly 28,000 landscape architects practicing in the United States in 2006, the most recent year for which statistics are available.[29] The bureau projects growth for the profession to be just over 16 percent through 2016. This rate of expansion is considered to be faster than the average for all other occupations.[30] The reasons for this anticipated growth are discussed in greater detail in Chapter 4, but in general it can be attributed to a growing interest in green and sustainable design, more people living in urban areas, the need to respond to climate change, and an increasing recognition of the environment's role in human health and well-being. Add to that, more jobs will open up as older landscape architects begin to retire from the workforce.[31]

For nearly 10 years now, reports have raised concerns that the profession will fall short in meeting its projected growth. The number of students graduating with landscape architecture degrees has increased only slightly in the past decade or so, averaging about 2.5 percent more each year. In 2004, just fewer than 1,500 students graduated with landscape architecture degrees.[32] It is estimated that the number of graduates needs to grow by 6 percent per year to replace retiring landscape architects and to keep pace with the growing demand. This nearly 4 percent gap highlights the fact that there will be ample opportunities for young people launching their careers in landscape architecture.

A 2008 Graduating Students Survey found that landscape architecture students had an average of three job interviews during their final semester, and resulted in an average of two job offers. The starting salary for undergraduates was just under $41,000; for those with graduate degrees, it was about $44,000.[33] Again according to the Bureau of Labor Statistics, the 2006 median annual earnings for landscape architects were $55,140. The middle 50 percent earned between $24,720 and $73,240. The highest 10 percent earned over $95,420.[34] Salaries for landscape architects have increased annually at an average of 7.4 percent since 1998.[35]

In all but one of the American states and two Canadian provinces, a person may not legally practice as a landscape architect unless he or she holds and maintains a license. (A detailed discussion about the process and requirements for licensure and registration is included in Chapter 5.) Because registration occurs at the state and provincial levels, the total number of registered landscape architects is not known, but it is estimated to be between 17,000 and 18,000 in the United States.[36]

An important issue the profession must continue to address is the diversity of the individuals who practice landscape architecture. For many years the profession has had a fairly good track record on gender diversity. The Graduating Student Surveys of 2007 and 2008 showed that approximately half of the students were female (55 percent in 2007; 45 percent in 2008).[37] The same cannot be said for ethnic diversity. In the Graduating Students Survey of 2008 and the 2008 ASLA National Salary Survey, African Americans represented only 2.0 percent and 1.5 percent, respectively. The Graduating Students Survey was more encouraging than the National Salary Survey regarding Asian or Pacific Islanders and Hispanics. The Graduating Students Survey showed 8 percent Asian or Pacific Islanders and 5 percent Hispanics, while the National Salary Survey showed 2.9 percent and 1.8 percent, respectively. As these recent surveys seem to indicate, ethnic diversity in the landscape architecture profession may be changing, but only very slowly. In the National Salary Survey of current practitioners, 92 percent identified themselves as Caucasian,[38] but in the Graduating Students Survey only 81 percent did so.[39] As new graduates begin to enter the profession, the diversity of the ethnic makeup of practitioners will begin to be affected. While this seems to indicate a trend in the right direction toward diversifying the profession, these numbers also tell us there is still much room for improvement.

Professional Associations

The American Society of Landscape Architects (ASLA), founded in 1899, is the primary professional organization representing the interests of landscape architects in the United States. The counterpart in Canada, the Canadian Society of Landscape Architects (CSLA), was established in 1934. The number of members in the ASLA is approximately 18,000,[40] and more than 1,300 in the CSLA.[41] Along with their national organization and structure, both of these societies also include chapters to represent their members at the state, provincial, or territory level. As with most such organizations, their main goals are to advocate for the needs of the professionals, work to increase public awareness about the profession, assist in organizing and providing development opportunities, and aid in the advancement and growth of the profession through support for education and research. Both organizations also participate in the dialogue between the accrediting bodies (LAAB [Landscape Architecture Accreditation Board] in the United States and LAAC [Landscape Architecture Accreditation Council] in Canada) and the colleges and universities that offer landscape architecture degrees.

The ASLA has eight categories of membership, from student to corporate.[42] The CSLA has two categories, regular and life members.[43] Both organizations also bestow honorary memberships on individuals who have performed meritorious service to the profession. In ASLA, an individual becomes a member of the national organization and then selects a desired affiliate chapter. In Canada, it is the reverse; professionals join as members at the appropriate provincial component and then become national CSLA members. Both ASLA and CSLA require that their members abide by the Society's by-laws and a professional code of ethics.

ETHICAL STANDARDS

In the personal sense, ethics pertain to one's moral duties and obligations; in the professional sense, ethics have more to do with the principles and rules of conduct governing a profession. Establishing a set of ethical standards is a way for a profession to formalize what actions are considered right or wrong in the performance of one's professional work.

The American Society of Landscape Architects has both a Code of Professional Ethics and a Code of Environmental Ethics. The Code of Professional Ethics is applicable to all those with professional-level memberships (i.e., not students). It establishes important principles related to a member's duties to clients, employers, employees, and other members of the society. The code is arranged into two canons—Professional Responsibility and Member Responsibility. Each has a series of ethical standards, which are goals members should strive to meet. Some of these standards also have a subset of rules. A violation of rules could subject the member to complaint.[44] ASLA's Code of Environmental Ethics also contains Ethical Standards.

ALLIED PROFESSIONS

The increasing complexity of the sites and projects on which landscape architects provide their services necessitates collaboration and consultation with allied professionals. Landscape architects are knowledgeable about a wide range of topics related to design, construction, and conservation, but there are, nevertheless, many projects on which additional expertise is needed to complement their skills and knowledge base. Other professionals most likely to work with landscape architects on design and planning-related issues are architects, planners, engineers, and geographic information specialists.

In the structure of a project team, one professional is usually designated as the lead consultant. Depending on the project type and focus, it might be the architect, the engineer or, increasingly, landscape architects. The most successful collaborations seek and respect the input from all team members, no matter who is serving as the lead. The site, the client, and the community all benefit when allied design professionals work closely together, each sharing his or her area of expertise for the betterment of the final outcome.

On environmentally related issues, the allied professionals landscape architects might consult with include ecologists, foresters, wetland scientists, fisheries specialists, soil scientists, hydraulic engineers, and arborists. Experts in the construction industry are increasingly involved in both the design and the implementation phases. Those professions include landscape contractors, nursery specialists, fountain and pool designers, irrigation experts, and professional cost estimators.

Depending on a project's location and scope, there are several other professionals who may be brought in to provide consultation and expert opinion. Some of these include: attorneys, in environmental, land use, and/or contract law; real estate appraisers and realtors; retail consultants and marketing experts; business and finance professionals; transportation engineers; sociologists; healthcare professionals; artists; and graphic designers.

These are not meant to be exhaustive lists. The inherent diversity of projects on which landscape architects are involved means there is an equally wide variety of professionals they must consult with in order to enhance knowledge and understanding about the tasks and challenges at hand. A list of allied professional organizations is included in Appendix A: Resources.

4 The Future of Landscape Architecture

The landscape is constantly changing, and here the agents of change are not only biological or chemical, but also increasingly social. Shifting economic balances, changes in community structures, strengthening or weakening political power are all reflected in the works of landscape architecture, and indeed, landscape architecture influences these shifts…by inclusion or exclusion. Not all of these changes may be comfortable, for future landscape change can and will move in many directions.

—D. M. JOHNSTON AND J. L. WESCOAT, JR., *Political Economies of Landscape Change*[1]

Trends and Opportunities

There are a number of trends today, nationally and internationally, that have the potential to provide unparalleled opportunities to the landscape architecture profession. These are trends rooted in demographic shifts, the consequences of several decades of lifestyles changes, growing awareness of environmental issues, and societal preferences. Many of these trends are connected to human beings and how we interact with the environment, meaning they create circumstances that hold great promise for the future of landscape architecture. This chapter briefly discusses some of these trends and the opportunities they present to landscape architects.

Kids cool off beneath an interactive waterfall at the Children's Healthcare of Atlanta Children's Garden, at the Atlanta Botanical Gardens, Georgia. Photographer: Geoffrey L. Rausch.

BEING "GREEN"

To paraphrase the recent advertising slogan of Cotton Incorporated, "Cotton: Green before it was even in style,"[2] landscape architecture was a green profession long before it became popular. Some would go so far as to say that landscape architecture is the original green design profession. Given the growing interest in the so-called green movement, landscape architecture's track record and expertise mean that landscape architects are well positioned to become leaders in this evolving movement.

Both individuals and corporations are demanding products and services that are energy-efficient and good for people and the environment. Today, being green means being innovative, as well as practical. Landscape architects are skilled at designing communities and spaces that not only

The James Clarkson Environmental Discovery Center, White Lake Township, Michigan. Design integrates wholly with the Kettle Lake. Freshwater marsh and Council Ring in foreground. Landscape architects: MSI Design. Courtesy of ASLA. Photographer: Justin Maconochie.

respect the natural environment but often improve it. Landscape architects demonstrate time and again that green can have many benefits; besides being beautiful, it respects diversity, is better for the local ecology, and sometimes costs less because the design works in concert with the environment, instead of fighting it.

One evolving approach to being green is the use of green roofs. Landscape architects work with horticulturists and engineers to design energy-efficient and beautiful rooftops. These planted roofs lower mechanical cooling needs in a building and absorb rainwater, thereby reducing stormwater runoff.

URBANIZATION

Recently, the Landscape Architecture Foundation organized a series of symposia, entitled "Landscape Futures," to analyze the processes that influence landscape transformation and how those will affect people and culture, the environment, and the design professions. Several key fac-tors driving landscape change were identified, the first of which is urbanization.[3]

For the first time in the history of the world, more people are living in urban areas than outside of them. In 1999 the United Nations predicted that by 2030 over 60 percent of the global popula-tion would be living in cities.[4] How can cities with rising populations be shaped to ensure that hu-man health and well-being *and* the environment are not compromised? Landscape architects are already being called upon to help rejuvenate previous industrial sites, called brownfields, in order to make them safe and usable again. The need for this will continue as the locations for industry, and the types of industry, change.

Landscape architects will also play a key role in "greening" cities, such as designing meaning-ful and valuable open space systems. As cities become more dense and complex, there will be an increased need for places that inspire people, protect nonhuman biodiversity, cleanse stormwater and wastewater, as well as places for parks and recreation corridors. All of these must be appropri-ately designed for their context and diverse user groups. Also important is the need to ensure that growth and changes in a city respect and restore natural as well as cultural and historic resources. Crafting designs that provide a strong sense of rootedness in place is an approach at which land-scape architects excel.

CLIMATE CHANGE

There is mounting evidence that the earth's climate is changing. It is generally agreed that the world will be facing more powerful storms, rising sea levels, and changes in regional weather patterns, with some places experiencing hotter temperatures. Changes in snowpack will affect stream flows and flooding. Rising temperatures will mean that plant and animal communities will be impacted. With more than half the population of the United States living along a coast, focusing on how to deal with larger numbers of stronger storms and hurricanes and rising sea levels is paramount.[5] Working with allied professionals such as engineers, planners, and ecologists, landscape architects have the training and expertise that enables them to be key members of teams that are analyzing and addressing these important issues.

One of the suspected causes of global warming is the emission of greenhouse gases, of which carbon dioxide is a main contributor.[6] Because of this, there is a growing interest in carbon seques-tration. To sequester carbon, carbon dioxide (CO_2) must be placed into a repository in a manner that results in permanent storage. There are only two ways to accomplish this: deposition into appropriate geologic formations or through terrestrial means.[7] Certain plants and soils are recognized as carbon "sinks," meaning that carbon can be stored in roots and the soil. The use of natural processes to re-move CO_2 from the atmosphere is thought to be one of the most cost-effective means to reduce green-house gases.[8] Because of the potential for trees and ecosystems, such as forests and wetlands, to play a significant role in carbon sequestration, landscape architects will increasingly be called upon to help in these endeavors through environmental stewardship, restoration, and preservation.

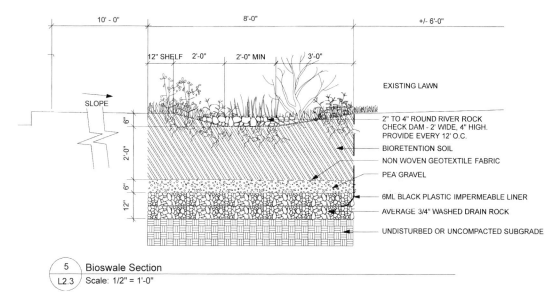

10' - 0"   8'-0"   +/- 6'-0"

12" SHELF   2'-0"   2'-0" MIN   3'-0"

EXISTING LAWN

SLOPE

6"   2'-0"   6"   12"

2" TO 4" ROUND RIVER ROCK
CHECK DAM - 2' WIDE, 4" HIGH.
PROVIDE EVERY 12' O.C.

BIORETENTION SOIL

NON WOVEN GEOTEXTILE FABRIC

PEA GRAVEL

6ML BLACK PLASTIC IMPERMEABLE LINER

AVERAGE 3/4" WASHED DRAIN ROCK

UNDISTURBED OR UNCOMPACTED SUBGRADE

5   Bioswale Section
L2.3   Scale: 1/2" = 1'-0"

Construction detail section of a bioswale. Courtesy of Lager Raabe Skafte Landscape Architects.

HUMAN HEALTH

The ability of outdoor environments to have a positive influence on human health and well-being is at the core of why the profession of landscape architecture was founded in the United States 150 years ago. Today there is mounting research that outlines a variety of ways in which human well-being is enhanced by contact with nature. As recognition of this research and its importance gains more attention, landscape architects will become the professionals at the forefront of creating environments that improve human health and well-being.

As an example, consider studies that show that time spent experiencing nature improves a child's academic performance. Children who spend time outside are healthier than their counterparts, who spend an average of six hours a day watching television or sitting in front of a computer.[9] Concerns about these statistics led to the coining of the term "nature deficit disorder." It encapsulates the growing problems associated with human alienation from the outdoors, among them, attention difficulties, diminished sense of wonder and curiosity, childhood obesity, and mental and emotional illnesses.[10]

Other research emphasizes how exposure to natural environments, and even natural views, improve the ability of our bodies to heal (or hasten the healing process when we are sick).[11] It is widely recognized that even moderate physical activity and recreation reduces stress levels, and that people enjoy restorative benefits from a walk in the woods or a glimpse of wildlife in a natural setting.[12] The presence of vegetation in a neighborhood has also been shown to reduce crime, produce stronger ties among residents, and foster a greater feeling of safety.[13]

Many landscape architects have developed specialized practices designing children's recreation areas or healing gardens. In fact, landscape architects have continually been at the forefront of designing healthy communities, whether through creating desirable, walkable neighborhoods or through the preservation or re-creation of nature in close proximity to places where people live and work. These areas of practice and evolving new approaches to enhancing human health will continue to grow in the future.

LAND USE PATTERNS AND ENERGY

Society is rapidly recognizing that western civilization's lifestyles of the last few decades will not provide a sustainable future. As the cost for energy and gasoline fluctuates, but trends upward, there is growing interest in more energy-efficient homes, businesses, and communities. The type of development that predominated at the end of the last century, commonly referred to as "sprawl," is auto-oriented, with single uses segregated from each other, requiring one to drive to go just about anywhere. This type of development does not respond well to a region's or a site's environmental resources; it does not provide adequate open space, and precludes the use of transportation alternatives for residents. It also segregates people and results in fewer residential living choices.[14] Landscape architects have been and will continue to be leaders in designing sustainable communities.

To be considered green or sustainable, community design must:

- Encourage walking and biking,
- Enable and promote the use of public transportation,
- Provide for a mix of uses and residential housing choices,
- Make use of green infrastructure for enhanced stormwater management, and
- Provide suitable natural, inspirational, and/or recreational areas.

As the need expands to retrofit existing places to be more energy efficient, and to build in new ways that reduce energy use, landscape architects will head teams of designers, planners and engineers in these endeavors.

THE VALUE OF NATURE

Natural systems, if left alone or restored, provide countless benefits to our world: trees and vegetation clean the air by ridding it of pollution; vegetation, soils, and the underlying geology clean and purify water; wetlands mitigate floods; plants help modify temperatures and humidity; as mentioned previously, plants' roots and soil store carbon—to name just a few. These benefits are called *ecosystem services*.[15] Take the services provided by just one tree as an example: In 50 years it generates $30,000 in oxygen, recycles $35,000 of water, and removes $60,000 of air pollution.[16] Lacking a formal "market," the value of these services often go unrecognized and are not accounted for until they are gone; for example, flooding increases because wetlands have been removed.

Hogan Butte Nature Park, Gresham, Oregon. Photorealistic visualization: GreenWorks, PC.

Increasingly, designers, developers, planners, and all levels of government are looking to the environment—its ecosystem services—instead of mechanized, technology-based or hardscaped solutions. Landscape architects are trained to be keenly aware of the value of natural systems and have always advocated for the use of more biological and environmental processes. As understanding about the role and value of ecosystem services grows, landscape architects, in concert with scientists, will lead the way toward ecosystem respect and restoration.

The ASLA's Sustainable Sites Initiative is developing new guidelines that will establish a rating system and framework that is intended to assist designers and developers in incorporating natural systems into the design process. This is meant to be complementary to, and eventually incorporated into, the U.S. Green Building Council's Leadership in Energy and Environmental Design (LEED) system for green buildings and neighborhoods.[17]

THE CONCEPTUAL, OR INNOVATION, AGE

Many agree that the information age is on the wane. The end of the dominance of a more left-brain, deductive, and logic-based approach to life and work is a good sign for all creativity-driven professions. The advent of a new age—referred to as "conceptual" by Daniel Pink in his 2005 book *A Whole New Mind*—is based on changes in the complexity of the world and a forecast that the future economy will be fueled by those with "inventive, emphatic, and big-picture capabilities."[18] This paradigm shift has prompted others to call it the "innovation age."[19] Whichever term catches on, it seems clear we are entering a time when a strong design sense, emotional intelligence—the ability to see issues from many perspectives—and proficiency at synthesizing information into a broad vision will be the skills needed for success. Landscape architects typically possess many of these skills, and their training enhances these capabilities.

In his book, Pink goes on to say that the answers to three questions determine how well one will survive in this new age:

1. Can someone overseas do it cheaper?
2. Can a computer do it faster?
3. Am I offering something that satisfies the nonmaterial, transcendent desires of an abundant age?[20]

Fortunately for landscape architecture, the answers are no, no, and yes. Landscape architects solve unique problems, which are different for every location, and for which there are no routine solutions. Landscape architects create places that are not merely just functional, but also beautiful, meaningful and oftentimes inspirational or emotionally engaging. If Pink's projections are true, the future for landscape architecture will be very exciting, indeed.

PROJECTED GROWTH OF THE PROFESSION

Based on the trends just outlined, it is no surprise that several surveys and career rankings over the past several years reveal an exciting trajectory for the landscape architecture profession. It is consistently listed as a top 10[21] or top 30[22] career choice for the new millennium. *U.S. News and World Report* assesses five factors to determine its career rankings: (1) job satisfaction—the amount of time that work activities are considered rewarding or pleasant; (2) training difficulty—the length of training needed, as well the amount of math and/or science involved; (3) prestige—from the perspective of college-educated adults; (4) job market outlook—analysis of U.S. Labor Department data and susceptibility to overseas outsourced; and (5) pay—including employee compensation profiles.[23]

The U.S. Department of Labor projects growth for landscape architecture over the next decade to be very solid—16 percent—which is faster than average among all occupations.[24] Add to this statistic the fact that many landscape architects practicing today are nearing retirement age and the opportunities for those embarking on a landscape architecture career are likely even more optimistic than the Labor Department's forecast. At present, however, there is concern within the profession that too few students are entering the field to meet the growing demand.[25] Even in the face of an economic recession, the profession seems destined to experience some growth thanks to the increasing demand for the types of services and work that landscape architects perform.

Challenging the Conventional

CHRIS REED

Principal

StoSS

Boston, Massachusetts

Chris Reed on a site visit. Courtesy of StoSS.

Why did you decide to pursue a career in landscape architecture?

〉 In college, as an undergraduate in urban studies at Harvard, I became interested in how cities develop, and became fascinated by the work of Frederick Law Olmsted. I was interested in his city-building efforts and the way that his landscapes functioned as social and urban infrastructure. It is the multiplicity within which these systems function that began to really raise my interest.

How did you decide that you wanted to get a master's degree in landscape architecture?

〉 After receiving my undergraduate degree I worked for a year at Michael Van Valkenburgh's firm to get

to know an office situation. Michael gave me a great opportunity. It was a very formative experience and absolutely convinced me I wanted to go into this profession. I then did my graduate work at the University of Pennsylvania, under James Corner. That is where I started developing the core of how I think and work.

How valuable was your first professional work experience?

〉 I worked at Hargreaves Associates, in its Cambridge office, for six years. George Hargreaves gave me enormous opportunities to learn not just how to be a designer but how to get projects built, and organize and run teams to be able to execute more complex work. I learned about contracts and project management. I learned how to deal with subconsultants, clients, and the public. He gave me a lot of opportunity and responsibility that really allowed me to grow.

How did you get your practice started?

〉 I decided there were some issues that I wanted to address, so I left Hargreaves and started my firm. I've always been the sole principal, but began with a young man who had just graduated, and he helped me start the firm. We decided to look beyond our immediate region for the type of work we wanted to do. We looked for opportunities on limited design competitions where they paid a little bit of money.

I supplement the work with teaching, which is part of the research I do. I've also been trying to write and give talks in different places. It allows for dialogue and criticism about the work and helps to push my own thinking. Speaking is also a vehicle for getting our work out there. That combination approach, after eight years, is starting to gain some momentum.

Rendering of Green Bay, Wisconsin, waterfront in winter at night. Courtesy of StoSS.

Children playing at "Safe Zone," StoSS' Grand–Métis garden festival entry. Photographer: Louise Tanguey. Courtesy of StoSS.

How would you characterize the work of your office?

❯ It's a smaller practice; we number from 4 to 10 at any one time. Our work tends to challenge convention in its approach to the urban environment and to landscape issues and processes. We look at a brief on a project and help the client to reformulate and expand it. We are focused on the public realm

and are starting to diversify our practice. And are working internationally—in Dubai and Israel and Toronto—and throughout the United States.

What has been one of your most rewarding projects to date?

❯ It is a small play garden for Grand–Métis Quebec, an international garden festival that invites designers

Riverfront boardwalk "folds" three-dimensionally to create overlooks, an urban beach, and a series of hybrid benches and chaise longues for people to occupy in various ways. Courtesy of StoSS.

to do a temporary installation. We were interested in the notion of free play and testing ideas that our public clients would be too reluctant to do because it had not been done before. A product that has always intrigued us is the squishy rubber surface material used on playgrounds, but you never find the stuff in situations other than a playground or on flat or gently sloped surfaces. We thought, there is a potential here; a material that already exists and wasn't being exploited. So we created undulating topography with rubber on it. It was quite dramatic, because it was black and yellow in a clearing in a wood. Visitors were in a natural environment, with gardens, and suddenly encountered this thing, made entirely of safety product. It was very rewarding for us to see all the ways that people would interact with this.

What is the most exciting aspect of your work?

⟩ Working with the public can be quite rewarding and challenging at times, but there's a payoff: being able to transform places in ways that benefit people, benefit environmental systems, benefit cities, and benefit economic development. The other nice part about the type of work we do is we get to go to a number of different places. We can be in Green Bay, Wisconsin, one day, and in Dubai a couple days later. You start to understand different environments and different people, and worlds other than your own. That is quite rewarding.

How often do you involve the community and/or end users in the design process? In what way?

⟩ We work in public environments all the time—public presentations, workshops, interviews, focus groups, and so on. The public is one of the most creative consultants we can have. They have a kind of energy and enthusiasm and caring about their environment. It's important to both the immediate and long-lasting success of the projects we execute that people have a forum and be taken seriously.

What tips can you provide to someone regarding the job search process?

> You've got to think strategically and represent yourself honestly. You want to give people enough of a sense about you in a way that makes a key impression. The best way for somebody to make a splash with me is to send an email and write three or four sentences that explain you're looking for a job, you're at this university or this firm, and then tell me something interesting about yourself. It's not a four-paragraph letter, because I don't have time to read that. It's just a couple of quick things; and then attach your resume and a couple of design sheets to show your range of interests and skills. It's very focused and efficient.

Transdisciplinary Practice

JULIA CZERNIAK

Principal

CLEAR, Syracuse

New York

Director

UPSTATE: A Center for Design, Research, and Real Estate

Associate Professor of Architecture

Syracuse University

Professor Julia Czerniak providing desk critiques to her students.

Why did you decide to pursue a career in landscape architecture?

> I didn't go to college knowing I wanted to be a landscape architect. I remember having lunch with a friend and he was telling me he was in landscape architecture. He described it as a discipline that encompassed many different scales of exterior work. It really appealed to me because of my love for both landscape, in general, and design culture.

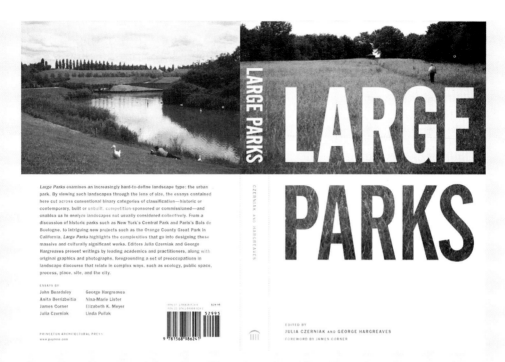

Jacket cover for *Large Parks,* edited by Julia Czerniak and George Hargreaves. Reprinted by permission of Princeton Architectural Press.

Which schools did you attend for your landscape architecture and architecture degrees?

❯ I was already a student at Penn State when I discovered landscape architecture. I have a Research Master of Architecture from the Glasgow School of Art in Scotland and a Master of Architecture from Princeton. I think of myself more as a landscape architect, because that's the field I'm working in. My undergraduate education provided me with a solid foundation in soils, plants, and geology, and I learned to think both regionally and at a small scale. My architecture degree at Princeton brought a different set of skills, which were critical theory and history. Bringing the critical thinking lens I got from architecture to my landscape work has created my identity, so the order in which I studied these disciplines was important.

Your professional life has several facets. What are your various roles?

❯ I built my career as an academic through teaching, research, writing, and lecturing. My private practice then grew out of that. At the Syracuse University School of Architecture I am the director of a think tank called UPSTATE. My private design work is a small academic practice with two principals, myself and my husband and partner Mark Linder, who is also an academic and chair of the graduate program in the School of Architecture. My role in the office is, well, I sort of do everything—I'm founder, principal, designer, and accountant.

How would you characterize the work of your office?

❯ CLEAR officially started in 2005 when we were short-listed for the Toledo ArtsNET competition,

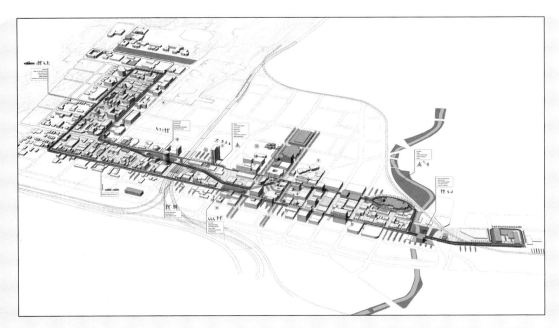

Axonometric of the Syracuse "L" as a transit loop and urban redevelopment figure. Project Team: Field Operations and CLEAR. Illustration: Field Operations and CLEAR.

which came with a honorarium to do the work. There are two things that characterize our work. The first is research on large urban landscapes, which manifests itself in books and publications like *CASE: Downsview Park Toronto*, and *Large Parks*, the most recent book that I did with George Hargreaves. The second is urban design work in what is called the "Rust Belt City." We've done projects and won competitions in Toledo, Pittsburgh, and Syracuse. Our work addresses how we can rethink, through design strategies, and reinscribe vibrant urban life into these decaying downtown cores.

You've written two books about parks. Explain your belief about the value of public space.

❯ It's about valuing life outside the private realm— outside of your computer, or your TV, or even your backyard. It's based on believing people still want to be in the world interacting with others.

The question then is how public parks can provide things missing from contemporary life. The roles parks play now are very different from those they played in the nineteenth century. For example, now they help create density, not provide relief from it.

What has been your most rewarding project to date?

❯ My published works. *CASE: Downsview Park* has been sold out for some time, and *Large Parks* was in its second printing a few months after it came out. It seems that people are eager to learn about what appears to be a kind of normative typology—a park—through the lens of some disciplinary speculation. Whether that is the role creative ecological thinking has on their design and maintenance, or whether it is about the challenge of public space in contemporary culture, which are both chapters in *Large Parks*, I think it is rewarding that people are interested in reading about this.

The Pittsburgh Rectangle, view of the North Avenue Strips' interactive surface. Illustration: CLEAR.

What is the most exciting aspect of your work?

❯ I am making a living doing something I love. I am able to hybridize my interest in landscape, architecture, cities, and design culture. That's very exciting.

How often do you involve the community and/or end users in the design process? In what way?

❯ Because of the scale and nature of our work, community interface is often built into the design process. We involve the community in two different ways. One is more advisory, and the second is more educational. In the first, an advisory group of local professionals is formed. At the end of each project phase, we present to them and receive feedback. In other projects, a more traditional community public meeting approach is used. We present to neighborhood groups to get feedback from them, but it has more of an educational component to it, so the public knows what is going on.

What role do new technologies play in your design process?

❯ Two roles. The first is material and system research. A new kind of permeable recycled material, or a new synthetic, may offer ways to do more design with fewer resources. And every one of our urban projects deals with the use of green infrastructure systems and strategies, the technology of which is quickly improving. We also are rethinking workflow, or how we work between the various roles digital technology plays in our work.

Who are some of the allied professionals you consult with?

❯ Ecologists, real estate developers, and lighting and graphic designers. The real estate component is important when working in decaying urban areas. We need to understand vacant and tax-delinquent land, or how we can acquire property or use tax credits. Our strategies are closely related to the economic and political feasibility of playing them out.

Which aptitudes, traits, and skills do you see in most landscape architects?

❯ Strong analytic skills, good organization, leadership, and creativity; and most landscape architects tend to have a passion for the environment, both the natural and the built.

Applying Research for New Solutions

NANCY D. ROTTLE, RLA, ASLA

Associate Professor

Department of Landscape Architecture

Director

Green Futures Research and Design Lab

University of Washington

Seattle, Washington

Why did you decide to pursue a career in landscape architecture?

❯ I was a teacher at the time and I was taking kids to places like zoos and aquaria, and I saw the real value that these educational landscapes had. I became aware of the work landscape architects were doing, such as river conservation work at the large scale, as well as the design of educational landscapes. That inspired me to pursue landscape architecture as a profession.

How and why did you choose the school you attended to earn your degree?

❯ My husband was going to school at the University of Oregon when I was ready to switch careers, so it was just natural that I went there. It is known as a design school, very strong in design thinking, perception, and history, and it also has a very strong plants program, so that grounded me in the science quite a bit.

How would you characterize the work of your former office, Jones and Jones?

❯ The work focused on a three-pronged approach that Grant Jones identified. The first is about understanding places very fully, and the second is about making stronger connections to places, so a design would make a place more of what it was or what it was meant to be. It would strengthen its biological or ecological integrity, or strengthen its cultural communication. The third part, related to

Professor Nancy Rottle in Copenhagen, leading a two-week tour with students studying that region's sustainable landscapes. Photographer: Liz Stenning.

Landscape architecture student Rochelle Hohlfeld surveys pedestrians in Seattle's Olympic Sculpture Park, as part of the Green Futures Lab work on "Public Spaces Public Life" with Gehl Architects. Photographer: Nancy Rottle.

As an academic, we do teaching, research, and provide service. I teach theory, as well as the professional courses. The studios I teach are often at a planning infrastructural level.

I direct a research and design lab that is focused on green infrastructure. The Green Futures Lab uses design as a method to research potential practices for a greener future.[26] We have projects, and I hire graduate students to work on those. Sometimes the projects are integrated with the studio work we are already doing. It was established in response to Seattle 2100, a community plan involving local professionals to create a 100-year vision plan for Seattle's green infrastructure.

What has been your most rewarding project to date?

> The Cedar River Watershed Education Center. It was a very long project from the planning, design,

Students and design professionals work together on Seattle's open space network, looking 100 years into the future. Students helped lead the 23 teams working on different parts of the city. Photographer: Nancy Rottle.

that, is that the design would more strongly connect people to landscapes. That was the overall focus, whether it was for native tribes or for public agencies, or even private clients.

Can you talk about your experience as an academic and your role at the university?

> We use the classic design educational methods to help students become better professionals. Starting from the very beginning, understanding what design is about, and skill building, such as graphics, on to more advanced studios where we are working closely with communities and we are applying research to come up with new solutions.

Seattle 2100 student proposal for treating neighborhood sewage in a living machine, then using the cleaned water to irrigate agriculture in the street. Illustration: Vanessa Lee.

through construction phases, and I was able to follow through with all of that. We had a great client who wanted the same things we wanted. After I began teaching, I was able to do what we call postoccupancy evaluations where I conducted interviews with people. We received very positive responses about people understanding the messages. They appreciated what we had done. All of those things made it a very rewarding project (see profile, page 131).

What is the most exciting aspect of your work?

❭ The most exciting aspect of landscape architecture is the diversity of the work—it's always fresh, it's always new. You're always sort of a detective, only it's not just problem solving; it's about how to create something new and wonderful. It's about putting all the pieces together, and that to me is really exciting. I think that is why I find teaching so exciting—seeing students get turned on and realize their own capabilities and the opportunities.

The classes you teach often involve the community. Explain why and how.

❭ It's a value in our department that community participation be a part of every project, at least in advanced studios. By the second year, almost every studio has a community aspect to it. There are often many surprises. You assume what the end users will want, then learn that isn't necessarily what they want. Also, sometimes you have to think about others in the community, and beyond the immediate community, and bring them to the table. Those users may also be future generations; and sometimes there are the silent users. Grant Jones used to say the land is our client and we need to speak for the land.

What tips can you provide to someone regarding the job search process?

First tip is to be aware of the different places you might want to look for a job, whether it's in the private sector or the public sector, or design/build—in general, look at what the profession is about. If you can articulate your own interests, then you can target firms for a better match. And last but not least, have a strong portfolio. You want to make sure you've got a good diversity of work, that you can show some technical skills like CAD, and that you know how to put together a construction document set. Also letting them know you are a really good team player is important because that is the nature of the profession.

What role can landscape architects take in making our world better?

Creating a vision; enabling people to see what kind of future we can have is a huge role. Then landscape architects can shepherd those visions through, to help them be realized. More at the design level is being able to translate and apply state-of-the art science and knowledge to create new approaches to design, new approaches to how we shape our world toward better local environmental integrity. We have to be able to come up with new solutions, and that demands understanding all sides of the problem.

What do you see as the future for the landscape architecture profession?

❯ Landscape architecture is essentially the profession of the future because it deals with the key issues of the twenty-first century: resources, urbanity, social justice, and quality of life.

Mario Schjetnan, FASLA
Founding Partner, Grupo de Diseno Urbano

❯ I see the future of landscape architecture as increasingly relevant and necessary to sustain and enhance the quality of our communities. Landscape architects understand the city, the public park, and the residential neighborhood, for example, as the summation of myriad factors. They understand that while the natural environment is important, it is the relationship that it shares with people and the built environment that, in many cases, makes it most relevant. To what degree landscape architects take seriously this knowledge and share it with other professionals, clients, and

the public will determine the profession's prominence and relevance over time.

Nathan Scott
Landscape Designer, Mahan Rykiel Associates

❯ This profession will continue on a definite upswing in the future. Recognition of our role in shaping the face of land use, conservation practices, and site design is growing steadily. This is evidenced by the growth in numbers of practitioners and the relative affluence of our profession.

Douglas C. Smith, ASLA
Chief Operating Officer, EDSA

❯ The sky is the limit, especially with the whole greening movement—it's pretty hard to be green without including landscape architects. Salaries have gone up. We want to attract the finest and brightest kids into our schools. I am very bullish on the long-term profession.

Douglas Hoerr, FASLA
Partner, Hoerr Schaudt Landscape Architects

What do you see as the future for the landscape architecture profession? (Continued)

❯The opportunities in the profession continue to expand as the need for green integration with architecture and urban planning becomes integral to the planning of our built environment.

Mikyoung Kim, Principal
mikyoung kim design

❯ I would say accountability is the future. There are many examples of professions or industries where the conservation model didn't support the economic model, so it got laid aside. In the future, that can't be the case, and we need to find ways to make conservation profitable. Landscape architecture is a profession where this could work—where the conservation model can support the economic model.

Kevin Campion, ASLA
Associate, Graham Landscape Architecture

❯ The future of landscape architecture will be blending a sustainable approach to design and materials with a social and economic responsibility. Those three elements blended together are the practice of the future.

Todd Kohli, RLA, ASLA
Co–Managing Director, Senior Associate, EDAW San Francisco

❯ It's the profession of today; it will be the profession of the future. Little else is or will continue to be as vital as making places for human habitation that help conserve planetary resources.

Ignacio Bunster–Ossa, ASLA, LEED AP
Principal, Wallace Roberts & Todd, LLC

❯ The diversity of the profession will be even greater than it is now. Those who are in a position to influence the profession need to embrace this diversity, instead of looking at it as divisive. Not all landscape architects are good at every facet. I believe in the future you are going to see more landscape architects aligning with other landscape architects. As projects become increasingly complex, you are going to see professionals collaborating as a team of landscape architects.

Jeffrey K. Carbo, FASLA
Principal, Jeffrey Carbo Landscape Architects and Site Planners

❯ I think landscape architecture is going to split. You will have ecological designers and you will have more conventional landscape architecture. I think you will even end up with a specialized licensing process for ecological restoration design.

Jacob Blue, MS, RLA, ASLA
Landscape Architect/Ecological Designer, Applied Ecological Services, Inc.

❯ It's going to be like law. You've got litigators, the people battling it out in the courtroom; then you've got lawyers who just do briefs and write stuff. But most lawyers don't practice law; they are in government, they are taking that legal training and applying it to whatever they do. Landscape architects won't have to practice landscape architecture in order to impact the world; just how they view the world will permeate other professions, and that will be great. The dominant one is going to be the globalization of the profession, both in the context of where people work and where people are getting educated about landscape architecture. The tipping point is coming, where there are going to be more people learning and practicing landscape architecture outside the western world than within it. The globalization of the profession is a huge future.

Kofi Boone, ASLA
Assistant Professor, Department of Landscape Architecture, North Carolina State University

❯ The future will be great if the profession can teach a combination of skills and ideas—teach people to understand the need for knowledge, and the need for craft, and the need for ideas.

Mark Johnson, FASLA
Founding Principal and the President, Civitas, Inc.

〉 It has a strong future as long as landscape architects can show their value to the public. We have to become more assertive in dealing with environmental issues by showing the interrelationship of our design and aesthetic skills, and science and ecosystem know-how, and how landscape architects have those combinations of skills that other professionals don't have. If we do that, we can ensure that strong future.

Meredith Upchurch, ASLA
Green Infrastructure Designer, Casey Trees Endowment Fund

〉 The true potential of the profession will come when we have found our voice in broader society. We have much to teach the world. We listen well. We need to find the confidence and maturity to speak out on issues of importance.

Kurt Culbertson, FASLA
Chairman of the Board, Design Workshop

〉 Books have come out, such as *Silent Spring* and *Sand County Almanac,* that really had a big impact. It would be interesting to write a book that would have as big an impact at those, and really look at making the world a better place. Changing the public conscience about what the major issues are, I think that's really important.

Jim Sipes, ASLA
Senior Associate, EDAW, Atlanta

〉 We have to become lobbyists; we have to publish and make our views known and try to impact legislation. I think this is going to be a very important task in the future.

James van Sweden, FASLA
Founding Principal, Oehme, van Sweden & Associates, Inc.

〉 Our future is strong and vibrant, but we have to firmly establish our unique abilities, and our leadership, because other professions are seeing what we do and they want to be part of that. They are either saying they can do it too or they are "buying us." Our profession as a business is being absorbed into a larger multidisciplinary octopus. I think we need to retain our specific identity and not just be auxiliary to the design of the landscape.

Gary Scott, FASLA
Director, West Des Moines Parks & Recreation Department

〉 The challenges are going to be increasingly urban. In the twenty-first century, the first urban century where half the world's population lives in urban regions, landscape architecture is really going to have to get engaged in urban environments.

Frederick R. Steiner, PhD, FASLA
Dean, School of Architecture, University of Texas

〉 We will continue to research and develop coherent strategies that integrate environmental stewardship and urban systems with placemaking.

Gerdo Aquino, ASLA
Managing Principal, SWA Group

〉 We really need to take the lead in this green movement. Landscape architects need to become urbanists. We need to talk about landscape preservation and sprawl by understanding what urbanism means. If we learn how to do urbanism very well we are going to preserve landscapes for both agriculture and natural systems. We are going to hit head-on, by good design, how to address global warming and other related issues.

Frederick R. Bonci, RLA, ASLA
Founding Principal, LaQuatra Bonci Associates

〉 The park movement has seen an incredible jump that probably hasn't happened since the turn of the last century. Parks and large open spaces are being designed all over the world—it's great. It's a really interesting time for landscape architects. It's now more about the world than it is about the United States or a region. We are finding ourselves doing work in Vietnam, Korea, and China—to me, that's pretty amazing.

Thomas Oslund, FASLA, FAAR
Principal, oslund.and.assoc.

What do you see as the future for the landscape architecture profession? (Continued)

❯ Landscape architects will continue to have a strong role in sustainable site design and site planning. Globally, we will work with other countries to establish and manage natural and historic national parks.

Joanne Cody, ASLA
Landscape Architect Technical Specialist, National Park Service

❯ I see good things. I think we're rising globally. I know at the International Federation of Landscape Architects (IFLA) there is a big initiative to bring the profession into Africa and help found new programs there.

Patricia O'Donnell, FASLA, AICP
Principal, Heritage Landscapes, Preservation Landscape Architect & Planners

❯ It's about social-cultural issues and engaging politics at a very broad scale, and thinking through the economics of a project, start to finish. It's about being a cheerleader, a political stage setter, and building constituencies for a project. It is taking a lot of personal initiative and expanding the role from the absolute first conception of the project through the construction to long-term maintenance issues. I think that's where the greatest potential is for the profession.

Chris Reed
Founding Principal, StoSS

❯ The role of the landscape architect as consultant should be supplanted by the landscape architect as prime, so that landscape architects are leaders of interdisciplinary teams, not just team members. The landscape architect's skills and abilities, and what is at stake with the need to bring biodiversity into the city—put them in the role of being prime on these projects.

Julia Czerniak
Principal, CLEAR

❯ The field is going to continue to grow. There is this shift in society in thinking toward green: That is going to translate into more work for landscape architects. This shift is already happening—we're the prime on projects; we hire architects, we hire civil engineers, and we're basically in charge of running projects.

Devin Hefferon
Landscape Designer, Michael Van Valkenburgh Associates, Inc.

❯ Focus on creating legacy projects—projects that people want to come back to time after time. We can't design places just to look good; they also have to be memorable, bring healing, or bring an incredible experience to the people using the space.

Eddie George, ASLA
Founding Principal, The Edge Group

❯ I see it getting a lot greener. I think it's necessary for some profession to step up, and we're the people to do it. It's not the engineers and it's not the architects. We're the folks who have a more holistic view of the environment. It's already happening—we have surpassed architecture in terms of students going out and getting their first jobs, so I think people are recognizing the abilities we have.

Scott S. Weinberg, FASLA
Associate Dean and Professor, School of Environmental Design, University of Georgia

❯ With ever diminishing developable land and resources, it will be as critical as ever to include landscape architects in the design of the exterior environment and decision-making process as to how these limited resources will be used.

Ruben L. Valenzuela, RLA
Principal, Terrano

❯ There are four areas that we can work with as a profession that would have a huge impact: carbon sequestration, stormwater management, reducing energy use in the way we plan and organize our communities, and the ecological footprint of the projects we design. We have to work with the scientists to understand what's possible, but I'm actually really excited about that.

John Koepke
Associate Professor, Department of Landscape Architecture, University of Minnesota

❯ Landscape architects have to learn to be more territorial. People shouldn't think that they can do what we do. Our expertise should make our involvement critical.

Elizabeth Kennedy, RLA
Principal, EKLA Studio

❯ Our profession has a great and critically important future to the health of our citizens and our country, and even our world. We will need to return to sustainable practices (agriculture, soil conservation, water quality and conservation, limit development in water-starved regions, etc.), and we as a profession are poised and trained to help with that transition.

Cindy Tyler
Principal, Terra Design Studios

❯ Landscape architecture will become much more focused on nature and the natural processes conducive to sustainable design. Less emphasis will be placed on architectural elements, and the most celebrated landscapes will be the ones that appear not to have been designed by people but by nature itself.

Emmanuel Thingue, RLA
Senior Landscape Architect, New York City Parks Department

❯ The future is very solid and strong. I am hoping there will be greater diversity in terms of types of people we attract into the profession. Landscape architects are well equipped to address more complex global issues, such as climate change.

Robin Lee Gyorgyfalvy, ASLA
Director of Interpretive Services & Scenic Byways, USDA Forest Service: Deschutes National Forest

❯ It's bright. Go out and take advantage of it! Make it happen. It is one of the fastest-growing professions because of what's needed out there.

Barbara Deutsch, ASLA, ISA
Associate Director, BioRegional North America

5 Design Education

In North America, most states and provinces (49 American states, two Canadian provinces, and one U.S. territory) require a license to practice landscape architecture, or to use the title "landscape architect." [1] This puts the profession on par with the allied building and design professions of engineering and architecture. Except in rare cases, a person can become a licensed landscape architect only after having earned a degree from an accredited university program. A formalized education is, therefore, an essential step on the path to becoming a landscape architect. Another important step, discussed in this chapter, is to take—and pass—the Landscape Architects Registration Exam (LARE). This chapter also reviews the need to advance as a professional through continuing education, and offers insights into the educational experience from the perspective of several landscape architecture students.

Site hydrology diagram of River East Center, Portland, Oregon. Project Team: GreenWorks, PC, with Group McKenzie.

What advice would you give to someone who is considering becoming a landscape architect?

❯ Find your true self. What is it about the profession that really motivates you to become a landscape architect? Then pursue a school, a graduate school, and offices that resonate with that passion. I think that's the key to success. In the next couple of decades opportunities are going to be expanding exponentially around the world. It's going to be a really exciting time for landscape architects.

Thomas Oslund, FASLA, FAAR
Principal, oslund.and.assoc.

❯ This is the best job I've ever had. It's a wonderful profession. We actively change the world for the better. If you enjoy working with people and enjoy working with the outdoors and want to make this world a better place, then landscape architecture would be a good profession for you.

Stephanie Landregan, ASLA
Chief of Landscape Architecture, Mountains Recreation & Conservation Authority

❯ Visit projects and sites of important landscape architects of the nineteenth, twentieth and twenty-first centuries, and visit historical world sites of perpetual transcendence.

Mario Schjetnan, FASLA
Founding Partner, Grupo de Diseno Urbano

❯ Read—reading opened up the world for me. If someone is thinking about becoming a landscape architect, they should read to further their understanding about the field.

Julia Czerniak
Principal, CLEAR, Associate Professor of Architecture, Syracuse University

❯ It's a fantastic field and it can be something that opens doors to lifelong learning and a wealth of experiences. If you have the choice of going into the business world, I think landscape architecture has some of those aspects in it; but at the end of the day, at the end of the year, you will feel like you did something—you can make a contribution through this profession.

Patricia O'Donnell, FASLA, AICP
Principal, Heritage Landscapes, Preservation Landscape Architect & Planners

❯ I have an engineering background and I'm really good at math and science, but I'm not good at drawing and artistic representation. So don't get discouraged if that's not your strongest skill, as there are other skills that are valuable. If building things interests you, figure out the details of how to build things and that can be your area of expertise. Be open to a variety of career paths. Figure out what your best skills are and find the path that suits you best.

Meredith Upchurch, ASLA
Green Infrastructure Designer, Casey Trees Endowment Fund

❯ Go to as many great outdoor spaces as you can in this country and Europe. Learn from the masters. An art teacher taught me a saying I will never forget: "Look to see to remember." So pay attention to spatial dimensions, hardscape detailing, great plant combinations and the great fragrances that go with them—it's an endless list.

Cindy Tyler
Principal, Terra Design Studios

❯ It's important to gain a wealth of experience and knowledge to be able to draw upon. So besides some key classes in high school like biology and drafting, figure out outlets for creativity, whether it's learning another language, taking classes on another county's history, taking sculpture classes, or figure drawing, or watercolor, or perhaps photography to document spaces. All of that will help give you a broader base to draw upon as a designer.

Todd Kohli, RLA, ASLA
Co–Managing Director, Senior Director, EDAW San Francisco

❯ Keep and use a sketchbook. Digital graphic communication tools are not a replacement for the observation and creative skills that are developed from drawing with your hand.

Mike Faha, ASLA, LEED AP
Principal, GreenWorks, PC

❯ A lot of people think, "If I become a landscape architect, I'll have to learn these certain skills." But I'd like someone to think more about what he or she, as a unique individual, brings to the profession. What unique way of thinking do you have, and different point of view do you have, and passions do you have that can add to the profession of landscape architecture?

Robin Lee Gyorgyfalvy, ASLA
Director of Interpretive Services & Scenic Byways, USDA Forest Service: Deschutes National Forest

❯ Do it strictly for the love of it.

Ignacio Bunster–Ossa, ASLA, LEED AP
Principal, Wallace Roberts & Todd, LLC

❯ I don't think it's a good 8-to-5 job, because it is always there, and there's always something to learn. Being a landscape architect has very little to do with whether you are licensed or how long you practice; it's how you look at the world. You're on vacation and you walk through a spot and think, "Oh, that's so cool; I like how this works, or I like how that works as a landmark."

Jim Sipes, ASLA
Senior Associate, EDAW, Atlanta

What advice would you give to someone who is considering becoming a landscape architect?(Continued)

❯ Open your mind and your heart to all the possibilities within the profession. If you think of a wild, crazy design concept, or a different form of expression on a project, don't be afraid to go there and seek it out—you will be surprised what comes out of you. Trust the fact that you chose this because something in you vibes with the profession and that the work is already inside of you; so allow that work to come out. I also want to say that landscape architects are cool.

Eddie George, ASLA
Founding Principal, The Edge Group

❯ If you are doing it to become rich, find a field that is more lucrative. However, if you consider that we spend one-third of the day working, spend it doing something you love to do. I love going to work because I love what I do; making a decent living for it is a good fringe benefit. I feel I'm doing something worthwhile with my life.

Emmanuel Thingue, RLA
Senior Landscape Architect, New York City Parks Department

❯ The profession allows individuals to stake out unique territories in various environmental scales and client groups. It's important that individuals entering this profession define for themselves what their vision is within this profession and make it a lifetime endeavor.

Mikyoung Kim
Principal, mikyoung kim design

❯ The profession can be very rewarding, but it is not an easy profession. You are selling something that is very complex and changing and dynamic.

You need to understand that you have to be able to take all of these different knowledge sets and put them together into a design that is comprehensive. That is not easy, but it's very rewarding.

Kevin Campion, ASLA
Senior Associate, Graham Landscape Architecture

❯ Be a sponge. Learn as much as you can about art, science, nature, music. All those things have a tremendous influence on your ability to be a good landscape architect.

Jeffrey K. Carbo, FASLA
Principal, Jeffrey Carbo Landscape Architects and Site Planners

❯ Explore what this profession is about and find out as much as possible: study ASLA's Web site; look at different firms and see the kind of work they do; read *Landscape Architecture Magazine* and maybe read some of the academic publications, such as *Landscape Journal*. A second thing is to learn how to draw. I always tell people to take drawing classes to exercise their creativity.

Nancy D. Rottle, RLA, ASLA
Associate Professor, Department of Landscape Architecture, University of Washington

❯ You can't be overly interested in money—it is not like the dot-com world—but you will make a comfortable living. It's a labor of love but you're going to have an awful lot of fun doing it. You'll be so satisfied because of the creativity of this profession. What could be better than going back and seeing places you designed, like the World War II Memorial, which is always filled with people.

James van Sweden, FASLA
Founding Principal, Oehme, van Sweden & Associates, Inc.

College Preparation

HIGH SCHOOL COURSEWORK

A typical college preparatory curriculum in high school should be sufficient for preparation to study landscape architecture in college, particularly if you have an interest and some background in art or natural sciences. However, if you discover landscape architecture in time, take some targeted classes and create a high school plan; doing so will be very beneficial as you enter college. If you have not already done so, speak with a high school counselor for assistance in crafting an approach to taking electives and arranging certain classes.

A number of high school courses have been identified as helpful in forming the foundation for a student who is planning to enroll as a landscape architecture major in college. In the sciences, biology, ecology, chemistry, and environmental sciences are deemed valuable. In math, useful courses are algebra, geometry, and trigonometry. For gaining a wider worldview, social studies, humanities, and art history, as well as foreign language study, would all be beneficial. To assist with the development of your visualization skills, art classes in drawing, painting, and sculpture are highly recommended. Classes in computer-assisted graphic arts or drafting might also be good, though most university programs will teach these computer software programs. While an interest in design may be sparked by an architectural drafting class, typically a sound development of visual aptitude and arts-related skills will be more beneficial than technical proficiency in computer-aided software programs.

Involvement in extracurricular activities such as theater or the debate club may also be worthwhile, as landscape architecture students give many presentations of their design work initially to peers, and eventually to invited jurors and community members.

EXPLORATION

A student can go down several avenues to explore the possibilities that a career in landscape architecture might offer. These range from involvement with the Boy or Girl Scouts to career discovery camps to visits with landscape architecture design offices.

Both the Boy Scouts and Girl Scouts of America offer badges and programs related to landscape architecture. For example, earning the Boy Scouts' Landscape Architecture Merit Badge involves researching the differences between landscape architects and related careers, such as an urban planner and civil engineer, as well as either visiting a professional office or a built project designed by a landscape architect, among other options and requirements.[2] The Girl Scouts of America presents an Interest Project Award called Architecture and Environmental Design. The Girls Scouts also have formed a cooperative relationship with federal natural resource agencies for a program called Linking Girls to the Land. One of the goals of this program is to encourage Girl Scouts to investigate careers in environmental, outdoor, and science-related fields.[3]

A few universities offer career awareness programs such as design camps and career discovery workshops for students interested in learning more about the field of landscape architecture. The duration of these programs ranges from a couple of days to a week to several weeks long. They often include guest speakers who are practicing professionals, field trips to visit design offices and built-project sites, as well as a hands-on experience in the design studio working on a project. Harvard offers a well-known intensive six-week summer program. During the winter, the University of Washington presents a series of evening lectures, called "Career Discovery Week." Auburn, North Carolina State, Penn State, and Texas A&M each offer weeklong summer design camps that feature landscape architecture, along with other design and/or arts fields. These are just a few of the opportunities that are available.

Visiting several different types of design offices is another really wonderful way to explore the landscape architecture profession. Landscape architects are listed in the telephone book; the American Society of Landscape Architects (ASLA) lists landscape architecture firms in the Firm Finder section of its Web site; and universities are usually more than willing to connect students with their alumni. Most offices also are happy to host prospective landscape architecture students for a tour. It would be wise to visit offices of varying sizes, and consider including public practice landscape architects, at city, state, or federal agencies, to get a well-rounded overview.

Landscape Architecture Programs

A key theme throughout this book is the inherent diversity of landscape architecture; therefore, it is probably not surprising that schools offering degrees in landscape architecture are equally diverse. Because the profession is rooted in both art and natural sciences, landscape architecture programs are typically housed in colleges that are either more arts-related or more natural sciences-related. If the program is an accredited degree, then the coursework between the various schools should not be markedly different; however, the type of research that faculty and graduate students undertake could be distinctly different, depending on both the focus of the home college and the geographic location.

Because landscape architecture is considered a public-interest profession, the degree that most students receive is a "professional" degree. This means that the curriculum leading to that degree meets specific standards and is accredited by a special authority. Each school undergoes an intensive review every five years to be reaccredited. In the United States, schools are accredited by the Landscape Architecture Accreditation Board (LAAB). In Canada, the accrediting body is called the Landscape Architecture Accreditation Council (LAAC). An important reciprocal arrangement ensures that those getting degrees at a LAAB- or LAAC-accredited school are all eligible to become licensed in any state or province that has professional licensure for landscape architects. (A more detailed discussion about professional licensure is given later in this chapter.)

Academic studio setting
at Kansas State University.
Photographer: Ian Scherling.

The accredited degree is often referred to as a *first-professional degree*. There are three main types of first-professional degrees: a Bachelor of Landscape Architecture (BLA), a Bachelor of Science in Landscape Architecture (BSLA), and a Master of Landscape Architecture (MLA); the latter is for students who have an undergraduate degree in another field. Due to the need to satisfy accrediting standards, there is not much distinction between the undergraduate degrees. The difference in nomenclature seems to be partly a factor of an institution's degree-naming preference. A list of accredited schools in the United States and Canada is included at the end of this chapter. The American Society of Landscape Architects maintains an up-to-date list of schools on its Web site.

Additional advanced degrees are available in landscape architecture; however, these will not enable the graduate to pursue professional licensure. These types of masters and doctoral degrees are typically sought by those who already have a first-professional accredited degree, or who want to do further research on a topic, and/or who plan to teach at the college level and feel they won't need a professional license. These degrees are a Master of Landscape Architecture (MLA), a Master of Science in Landscape Architecture (MSLA), or a PhD—a Doctor of Philosophy in Landscape Architecture.

FIRST-PROFESSIONAL DEGREES

The undergraduate first-professional degrees in landscape architecture (BLA and BSLA) are either four-year or five-year programs. The five-year programs typically require a minimum one-semester of study aboard or other off-campus experience. The graduate-level first-professional degree (MLA) is almost always a three-year course of study. Generally, in the first year and a half, graduate stu-

Second-year landscape architecture studio in Penn State's Stuckeman Family Building.

dents take similar courses to those pursuing the undergraduate degree. These courses cover core visual communication and construction-related technical skills, as well as the foundational design studios. The biggest difference between an undergraduate and graduate first-professional degree is that the MLA student concludes by preparing a thesis or a focused project that combines research and design.

The term "studio" is used frequently when referring to the education of a landscape architect. Anyone who has taken art classes in high school will be familiar with a studio learning environment. A studio setting typically involves working at a larger desk, due to drawing sizes and building models, and entails a considerable amount of one-on-one interaction between a professor and the student. It is also a more collaborative setting where sharing of ideas between students is encouraged; there are rarely precisely right or wrong answers, and this sharing enhances students' growth and understanding. Students often form strong friendships with those in their studio and frequently refer to the setting as an almost familylike atmosphere due to the close-knit relationships that result. This is a totally different experience from the classic college classroom where students sit in a sea of seats in a large lecture room. In a studio, faculty and students get to know each other quite well thanks to regular close interactions and the sole-searching nature of the design work.

Most first-professional undergraduate curriculums are pretty tightly arranged to ensure that all the required skills are acquired in a comprehensive sequence. Students would be wise, therefore, to target the few electives available to courses that will enhance an area of interest or to explore related topics. A sampling of electives that students often find valuable includes drawing, painting, or sculpture classes, art or architectural history, cultural or physical geography, horticulture, and ecology. If you think you might be interested in starting your own firm in the future, consider taking some business and marketing courses, as well.

Students in the graduate first-professional degree programs (MLA) often have a bit more flexibility in their curriculum. These students can seek electives that will further their area of interest, or courses that may provide support for the intended research direction. Faculty advisors are readily available to review course offering options and recommend a program of study tailored to your educational goals.

North Carolina State landscape architecture graduate and undergraduate students lead participatory design workshops for comprehensive renovation of WEB DuBois Center, Wake Forest, North Carolina. Photographer: Kofi Boone.

POSTPROFESSIONAL AND RESEARCH-RELATED DEGREES

Many universities offer advanced study in landscape architecture as nonaccredited, research or focused-inquiry degrees. Individuals who already hold a professionally accredited degree, or those who do not intend to formally practice landscape architecture and therefore will not need an accredited degree, are well suited for these programs of study. These advanced degrees, both the master's and the doctoral degrees, enable a person to further their understanding or expertise. People frequently use an advanced degree to boost their professional credentials or to pursue a new direction within the field. The coursework for the nonaccredited degrees varies greatly from school to school due to faculty research interests and established areas of expertise at different universities. Students considering an advanced degree typically investigate program offerings carefully to ensure a good match between their desired study emphasis and a school's expertise in that area.

In schools that also offer undergraduate degrees, graduate teaching assistantships are often available to students who possess an accredited undergraduate degree. That background is desirable to a university and could also result in a research assistantship or fellowship. Assistantships and fellowships, which typically include a tuition waiver, a stipend, and coverage of some healthcare costs, can help to make one's graduate education more affordable.

Chapter 4 outlined the predicted growth of the landscape architecture profession. One of the key issues associated with accommodating that desired growth is having enough new professors to teach this increase in student numbers. Professors do not necessarily have to become licensed professionals to maintain their positions. Individuals who only intend to teach are good candidates for nonaccredited research-focused degrees. Gaining skills in research methods via graduate work will serve them well as they move into a tenure-track position at a university.

Gaining Experience Working with Real Communities

MALLORY RICHARDSON

Undergraduate Candidate

Department of Planning and Landscape Architecture

Clemson University

Clemson, South Carolina

▲ Mallory Richardson sketching on site. Photographer: Patrice Powell.

▶ Landform model based on "Anxiety" for first-year design studio. Constructed out of cardboard. Photographer: Mallory Richardson.

Why did you decide to pursue a career in landscape architecture?

❯ When I went to orientation before my freshman year and learned more about my major, I realized it wasn't right for me. My parents and I then spent an entire day trying to figure out other majors. Upon reading about landscape architecture, my dad suggested I try it. After talking with the department chair of landscape architecture, I took a strong interest in that as career choice. I chose to attend Clemson because it was close to home and I have family who are students at the university.

What has been the most satisfying part of your education?

❯ Learning how much landscape architecture has shaped our history has been very exciting. The most satisfying part by far, however, has been my success in this major. I've always had fears of not being able to succeed in college, but I've come very far and I'm very proud of my accomplishments.

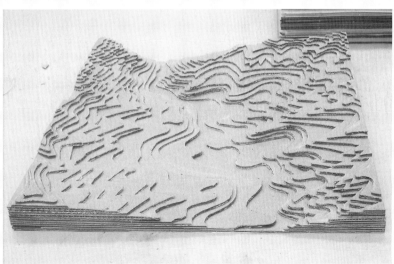

Plan of outdoor dining hall proposal for Furman University. Second-year design studio project. Illustration: Mallory Richardson, Kyle Goebel, and Patrice Powell.

What has been your greatest challenge as a landscape architecture student?

❭ Time management. Landscape architecture students spend a great amount of our time in the studio, which is where we complete our work—although, currently, my favorite place is the GIS lab, which is where we use computer programs to map and design regions. I spend a great deal of time here, and when I'm also involved in other activities, sometimes it can be very hard to manage it all. Fortunately, I'm managing pretty well this semester.

As an undergraduate student, what are some of your courses and key tasks?

❭ First we learn the basics. This includes drafting, which, simply put, is learning how to draw proper, professional-looking plans. We also learn how to show views of a site from different vantage points, such as perspectives, and sections, which show "slices" of the site and how the site changes in elevation.

We then learn how to render. Rendering is another term for coloring and adding shading or shadows. Another basic skill that goes hand in hand with drafting and rendering is learning how to create a composition with our design. It is through the design courses that we learn about composition. In those courses we learn the value and symbology of different patterns, and the use of themes in our designs, and also the role of emotion. A design should create a flow, where all parts fit together and make sense.

We also learn how to build models, both by hand and using computer programs, such as AutoCAD and SketchUp. Additionally, we learn about grading the site, which means changing the elevations to fit the design to the site, and explaining how water will drain. We also cover key subjects such as the history of landscape architecture, landscape architecture theory, plant identification, and plant function. It seems like a lot, but it really does fly by very quickly.

Have you had the opportunity for any off-campus experiences? If so, how have these been valuable to your education?

❯ Most of the projects I've been assigned have been real projects where we interact with people in a community and get their input on what they would like to see in the design. I'm currently taking a regional design class. We've been assigned a project that spans two counties in Virginia. We spent five days attending community meetings, doing site analysis, and researching cultural aspects of the area. We worked hard to involve community members, and to try to understand what they feel the area needs to help boost recognition and the economy. It's challenging, but also very interesting, and is extremely valuable. After college, we'll be dealing with real people living in actual communities.

What do you hope to be doing 5 to 10 years after graduation in terms of your career?

❯ I see myself practicing landscape architecture, perhaps in historic preservation, which is an aspect of the profession that has been a growing interest of mine. Maybe I'll be an accomplished landscape architect by then, living in Charleston, South Carolina, and changing the nation, one landscape at a time.

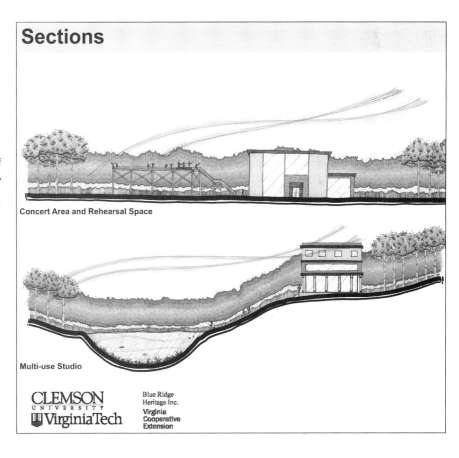

Site sections for design of Floyd and Patrick County, Virginia, Artisan Center. Illustrations: Kyle Goebel, Mallory Richardson, Zac Wigington, Mike Leckie, and Taylor Critcher.

Sections

Concert Area and Rehearsal Space

Multi-use Studio

CLEMSON UNIVERSITY
VirginiaTech

Blue Ridge Heritage Inc.
Virginia Cooperative Extension

Enjoying the Interrelationship of Required Skills

NICK MELDRUM

Undergraduate Candidate

Department of Landscape Architecture and Environmental Planning

Utah State University

Logan, Utah

Nick Meldrum at his studio desk at Utah State.

Why did you decide to pursue a career in landscape architecture?

❯ I enjoy the interrelationship of the skills required—problem solving, creativity, graphic ability, communication, and so on. I also appreciate the broad range of possibilities that I will be able to pursue as a professional.

How and why did you choose the school you're attending to earn your landscape architecture degree?

❯ To be completely honest, the school I am attending is the only program in my home state and I wanted to avoid out-of-state tuition. Luckily, the program is well respected and I am very pleased with how things have turned out. The studio atmosphere provides one-on-one interaction and a more personalized experience with professors than in traditional lecture courses.

What are your primary tasks when working on a design?

❯ The tasks related to a project usually begin with a site visit to conduct an analysis to assess opportunities and constraints. Next comes sketching out preliminary ideas and brainstorming in a sketchbook. I then develop a conceptual plan that relates to the goals and objectives of the project, as well as addressing the needs of the users. All of that is then refined and synthesized into a more detailed master plan, detailed drawings and other graphics to better convey the design.

What has been the most satisfying part of your education?

❯ I am a nontraditional student (28 years old, married with two kids). When I decided to pursue a degree in landscape architecture many people told me I should consider an alternative because of the demanding nature of the program. The most satisfying part has been accomplishing all that I have in such a difficult program.

Proposal for alley as part of master plan for a resort community in southern Utah. Illustration: Nick Meldrum.

Have you had the opportunity for any off-campus experiences? If so, how have these been valuable to your education?

❯ The landscape architecture department hosts an annual weeklong design charrette, selecting a different city each year. These experiences have been helpful in understanding the diversity of needs and desires of real people, and learning how to approach addressing the challenges posed by their aspirations and needs. One specific example involved helping a community that was experiencing a deteriorating downtown and had major vehicular circulation problems. We had meetings with many local government leaders and citizens to get their input and insights. Through those meetings we gained a wide perspective on the problems. A charrette is an intensive design session— working very quickly in a short period of time. When we finished, we presented the

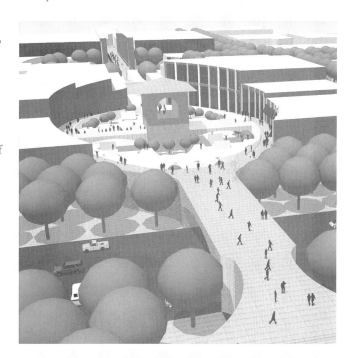

Redevelopment of two city blocks in Sugarhouse, Utah, for urban design class. Illustration: Nick Meldrum.

ideas at a public meeting. The government officials and citizens all expressed their appreciation and seemed pleased with the results.

What role have internships played in your educational experience?

❭ I was lucky to land an internship with a respected firm in Salt Lake City. The experience allowed me to better understand my posteducational goals. It was also very helpful in increasing my knowledge, skills, and abilities while gaining a wider perspective about the profession. Specifically, I was able to take the reins on one complicated aspect of a very big project. I worked closely with consultants and the firm's principal. It was a rewarding experience in that I was able to feel engaged and valuable.

What do you hope to be doing 5 to 10 years after graduation in terms of your career?

❭ I hope to be a licensed landscape architect working toward owning my own firm, or perhaps already running my own firm. I would like to get my first job with a small to medium-sized firm. I am interested in finding a firm that does a variety of projects, such as urban design, community planning, and parks. I feel exposure to a diversity of project experiences will serve me well in preparation for starting my own firm.

Many Professional Aspects to Explore

BRITTANY BOURGAULT

Undergraduate Candidate

Department of Landscape Architecture

University of Florida

Gainesville, Florida

Why did you decide to pursue a career in landscape architecture?

❭ I have always had an interest in architecture and design. The idea of creating outdoor spaces that are both functional and aesthetic appealed to me a great deal. I love designing outdoor spaces that users will enjoy.

Brittany Bourgault with community members from the village of Pemuteran, Bali. Photographer: Kevin Thompson.

Fourth-year Urban Design Studio, St. Augustine, Florida. Second home ecoclusters, incorporating extensive boardwalk trail system. Illustration: Brittany Bougault.

As an undergraduate student, what are some of your courses?

❭ The College of Design, Construction, and Planning offers students a diverse studio setting with many opportunities to grow with respect to design. The landscape architecture program consists of design courses ranging from urban design, environmental planning, and site planning to construction. Students work individually as well as in groups. Some of the work involved in the courses includes developing your design concepts, creating master plans, working out the details of how to build something, and producing renderings to graphically communicate your ideas. One of the most satisfying parts of my education is the close relationships I have formed with fellow students and professors.

What has been your greatest challenge as a landscape architecture student?

❭ Finding a creative and unique way to take my thoughts and ideas and bring them forward into a design, and then how best to graphically represent that so others will understand my ideas.

Elaborate fountain design created during extended internship. Illustration: Brittany Bougault.

Summer-abroad program in Indonesia. Group at ancient Buddhist temple, Borobudur, on the Island of Java. Illustration: Brittany Bougault.

You have had a unique international study opportunity. How was this experience valuable to your growth as a designer?

❯ I had a great opportunity to travel to Indonesia for a month. We worked with a university in Java on a community planning project. It was great to work with students studying landscape architecture on the other side of the world. It was rewarding to learn about another country's culture, and how its historical values have such an impact on how landscapes are designed.

What role, if any, have internships played in your educational experience?

❯ I was fortunate to have two summer internships in very different firms. In my first internship I worked for a firm that specialized in working with private clients, creating high-end residential designs. I was able to satisfy my creative side and experiment with ideas. I had a lot of fun working closely with our cli-ents. My second internship was valuable from a technical standpoint. I got to work on a large-scale city project and I was able to work closely with engineers. I learned a great deal about the kinds of work I can do as a landscape architect in regard to engineering. I highly recommend students to get as much professional experience as possible before entering the field as a young graduate. Internships have provided me with valuable tools to bring back to the classroom, as well as valuable tools that I will be able to use in my future career.

What do you hope to be doing 5 to 10 years after graduation in terms of your career?

❯ I have a goal to start my own company. There are so many different aspects of the field that I want to explore, such as design for commercial settings, urban development, and preservation. I want to have a positive impact on the profession and the community through my design work.

Learning the Vocabulary of a Landscape Architect

IAN SCHERLING

Non-Baccalaureate Undergraduate MLA Candidate*

Department of Landscape Architecture/ Regional and Community Planning

Kansas State University, Manhattan, Kansas

Why did you decide to pursue a career in landscape architecture?

〉 I went to college to pursue my dream of being an architect. As a kid, I loved building things and I loved to draw. I was also influenced by growing up in rural Kansas and spending much of my time outside. I enjoyed helping my grandfather, who was a tremendous farmer and outdoorsman. It wasn't until college that I heard about landscape architecture.

In the architecture curriculum at Kansas State University, all first-year students work on the same projects. The projects that dealt with outdoor spaces intrigued me the most and were the ones at which I excelled. After learning about career options in landscape architecture through other classes and touring a few local landscape architecture firms, I knew that was where my heart and abilities were leading me.

*This is a new degree: The 11-semester Non-Baccalaureate MLA Degree Program for undergraduate students begins in the freshman year. Students apply to the university's graduate school for entry into the MLA program during the sixth semester of study and, if accepted, complete an accredited MLA degree.

Ian Scherling discussing a design.

Who or what experience has been a major influence on your landscape architecture education?

〉 If I pick just one experience, it is my internship in Philadelphia. No other occasion has shown me the value of hard work, logical thinking, and the pursuit of good design. As an intern I was able to work on a number of different projects and a variety of project phases, and travel to new places. One example of a project I enjoyed was at Duke University. It involved working with architects and other consultants on a new school of the environment. Much research was conducted on designs of sustainable systems that could be included in the project. I learned about North Carolina, its ecosystems, universities and people, and I learned how to integrate a new building on a historic campus.

▶ Chipboard model of the Taos Institute of Arts and Crafts, New Mexico. Illustrator: Ian Scherling.

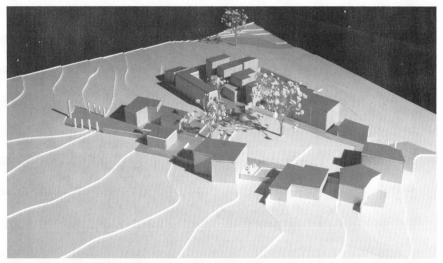

▼ Conceptual hand sketches of a business incubator in Greensburg, Kansas. Illustrator: Ian Scherling.

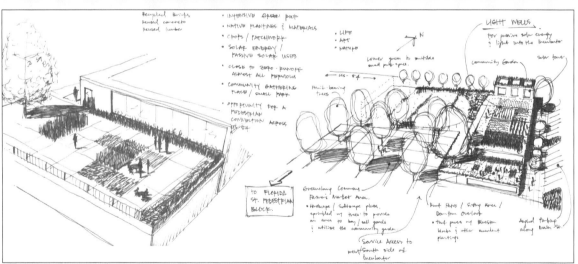

As a design student, what are your primary tasks?

❯ The most important task as an undergraduate is learning time management. From day one, professors ask much of their students, and each professor expects a certain quality of work. All of the other major tasks in school involve learning, whether it's learning the vocabulary of a landscape architect, building models, studying hard, or meeting with professors. One has to understand that his or her role in college, along with having an enjoyable time, is to prepare for life after college, and the more you learn, the better off you will be.

Section showing existing site conditions at the University of Pennsylvania's Palestra Green. Illustrator: Ian Scherling.

What has been your greatest challenge as a landscape architecture student?

> It seems like frustration builds as I discover that previous ideas about a project's design were not going to work. It is during those times that I questioned my love for landscape architecture and the pursuit of my dream. But I have no doubt these times made me understand, all the more, that a landscape architect is what I want to be. It makes sense now that nothing comes easy, and that to succeed one must be tested in more ways than imaginable.

What do you hope to be doing 5 to 10 years after graduation in terms of your career?

> I hope to be building a strong reputation in the design world. I also hope to be publishing essays and other written works regarding landscape architecture and the theories and philosophies that shape my view of the profession. I thought I'd stay in the United States throughout my career, but I find myself wanting to travel and experience the world, not only to learn new cultures and customs, but to try to help people understand their role as it relates to the landscape. Social and mission work appeals to me, so in 10 years you might find my family and me working in a village in South America, trying to solve landscape and social issues.

Using Talents for a Socially Just Cause

TABITHA HARKIN

Candidate

Master of Landscape Architecture

College of Environmental Design

California State Polytechnic University

Pomona, California

Tabitha Harkin (right), during summer internship, with Katherine Beauchamp, from the Association to Preserve Cape Cod (APCC).

Why did you decide to pursue a career in landscape architecture?

❯ I was working in a field that I was passionate about, in housing advocacy, but it was outside my original career goals. I hold a dual BFA in Painting and Visual Communication Design from Hartford Art School. I wanted to go back to school to pursue something that used my talents toward a socially just cause. After some research, I felt a career in landscape architecture could be a great fit for me, and it has been.

How and why did you choose the school you're attending to earn your Master in Landscape Architecture degree?

❯ I made the choice to return to school and make a large change in my life by moving to California from Connecticut. I applied to UC Berkeley and CalPoly Pomona for Landscape Architecture, and USC (University of Southern California) for planning. I got into all three, but chose CalPoly for its remarkably affordable price, as well as its "studio" learning environment, which reminded me of my undergraduate experience.

As a graduate student in landscape architecture, what are your primary tasks?

❯ You are exposed to all sorts of tasks, from site visits and fun bonding trips with classmates to calculating stream flow velocity, sketching renderings, CAD (computer-aided design) plans, and building models. The most important rule for me has been organizing these tasks, allotting bits of time for each. I tend to break down projects into manageable pieces, put a few hours in each evening and use the day wisely. For example, I find I write better in the morning and can draw at night.

What has been your greatest challenge as a master's degree candidate?

❯ As far as the curriculum, I suppose I could say grading and drainage is difficult, but that's what studying is for. Most things are less difficult than

Drainage to Cisterns for Stormwater capture

Stormwater Planters & Permeable Paving

Greenroof Stormwater capture

they are time-consuming. The software you need to know is extensive, but not too difficult, although GIS takes time to learn. Plant identification requires a lot of memorization, so I made good cue cards and studied often.

What role have internships played in your educational experience?

⟩ Internships played a huge role for me. I had the fabulous chance to work for the Association to Preserve Cape Cod (APCC) in Massachusetts last summer, and am currently working in the Parks and Natural Resources Department for the City of Pasadena, California. At APCC, I worked with Cape Cod villages to develop conceptual renderings for smart growth zoning, something I'm passionate about. I also got to do some great hands-on work

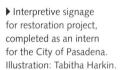

▲ Conceptual rendering for second-year design studio project: Building a Resilient Los Angeles. Illustration: Tabitha Harkin.

▶ Interpretive signage for restoration project, completed as an intern for the City of Pasadena. Illustration: Tabitha Harkin.

by monitoring the salt marsh with staff biologists. This gave me a new appreciation for coastal ecology.

At the City of Pasadena, I get to work on a broad spectrum of projects, from construction drawings to interpretive signs and maps, and the work is much larger in scale. It's great to be able to ask questions of engineers, landscape architects, and others. It is very hands-on and I learn so much that way.

Have you had the opportunity for any off-campus experiences? If so, how have these experiences enriched your education?

⟩ At both of my internships I have had the chance to attend community meetings and

design charettes. I also took a class at CalPoly where we were required to attend and mingle at community meetings. This, along with my background in policy work as an advocate, has raised my interest in public discourse, and inspired me to pursue a thesis topic that includes participatory planning.

What do you hope to be doing 5 to 10 years after graduation in terms of your career?

⟩ I hope to be involved in socially and ecologically just urban design work at a firm in New England, producing conceptual artwork and plans for smart growth, pedestrian-friendly environments.

Gaining Knowledge to Help Improve Environmental Conditions

STEPHANIE BAILEY

Candidate

Master of Landscape Architecture

Department of Landscape Architecture

University of Oregon

Eugene, Oregon

Why did you decide to pursue a career in landscape architecture?

⟩ I have a Bachelor of Arts degree in psychology. I have always been interested in the environment and its relationship to human well-being. I chose to pursue a career in landscape architecture because of its traditional tenets: meeting societal health and well-being through sustainable planning and urban design. I applied to graduate school with the intention of gaining knowledge to help improve en-

Stephanie Bailey during summer internship with the National Park Service. Photographer: Saylor Moss.

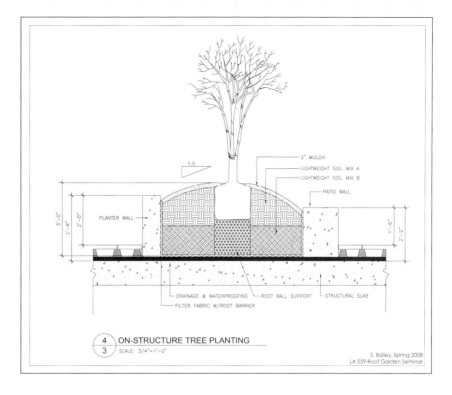

Detail drawn in AutoCAD for Roof Gardens seminar, second year of graduate program.

vironmental conditions. I believe my undergraduate degree is a good foundation for my career as a landscape architect. It affords me depth of insight into the linkage between the environment and societal health.

How and why did you choose the school you're attending to earn your Master of Landscape Architecture degree?

❯ A mentor, who is an architect, went to the University of Oregon and informed me about their landscape architecture master's program. I also consulted the Landscape Architecture Foundation's Web site. I was interested in a program with a commitment to sustainability and environmental education. I felt the University of Oregon's first-professional master's program was the best fit for me.

What are your thoughts about assistantships or fellowships for graduate students in landscape architecture?

❯ In most landscape architecture departments there are different types of assistantships and fellowships that allow students to gain teaching and research experience. At the University of Oregon, students may apply for a teaching or a research fellowship. An additional advantage, beyond the experience gained from the fellowship, is tuition remission and health insurance for the term. Prospective graduate students should consider which area of the profession they would like to work in after graduation, whether in practice or academia, and try to gain as much experience as necessary to confirm if that is a good choice for their interests.

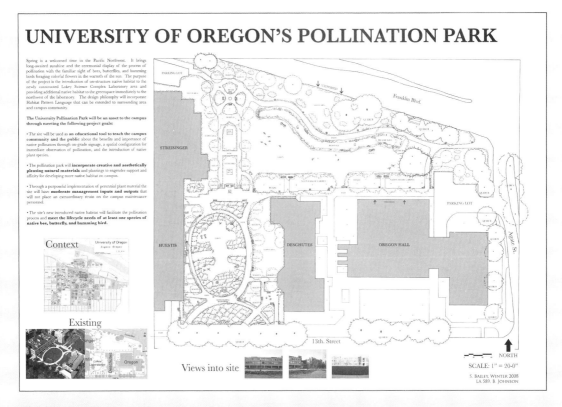

UNIVERSITY OF OREGON'S POLLINATION PARK

Spring is a welcomed time in the Pacific Northwest. It brings long-awaited sunshine and the ceremonial display of the process of pollination with the familiar sight of bees, butterflies, and humming birds foraging colorful flowers in the warmth of the sun. The purpose of the project is the introduction of on-structure native habitat to the newly constructed Lokey Science Complex Laboratory area and providing additional native habitat to the greenspace immediately to the northwest of the laboratory. The design philosophy will incorporate Habitat Pattern Language that can be extended to surrounding area and campus community.

The University Pollination Park will be an asset to the campus through meeting the following project goals:

• The site will be used as an educational tool to teach the campus community and the public about the benefits and importance of native pollinators through on-grade signage, a spatial configuration for immediate observation of pollination, and the introduction of native plant species.

• The pollination park will incorporate creative and aesthetically pleasing natural materials and plantings to engender support and affinity for developing more native habitat on campus.

• Through a purposeful implementation of perennial plant material the site will have moderate management inputs and outputs that will not place an extraordinary strain on the campus maintenance personnel.

• The site's new introduced native habitat will facilitate the pollination process and meet the lifecycle needs of at least one species of native bee, butterfly, and humming bird.

Context

Existing

Views into site

SCALE: 1" = 20'-0"

S. BAILEY, WINTER 2008
LA 589, B. JOHNSON

Plan of proposed University of Oregon Pollination Park. Illustrator: Stephanie Bailey.

What experience has been a major influence on your graduate school education?

❭ A major influence was the second-year curriculum: there were several classes that involved ecology and landscape planning. The course material introduced me to many new concepts about ecosystems and healthy landscape functioning. Throughout my second year, I was encouraged to become knowledgeable and think critically about criteria for evaluating the intricacies of landscapes and ecosystem functions. This has become ingrained in my worldview and has made a significant impression upon the way I will practice landscape architecture in the future.

What has been your greatest challenge as a master's degree candidate?

❭ Maintaining a balanced life. Graduate school can become an all-consuming force, if you allow it. There is always something else you may want to read, do, or complete perfectly. You have to be purposeful in your time management in order to maintain your health and significant relationships, while actively directing your desired future career path.

What has been the most satisfying part of your graduate school education?

❭ I have developed a greater confidence in my ability to integrate the skills I have gained in graduate school to effectively analyze and interpret a landscape, and subsequently, to prescribe viable and effective landscape solutions.

You are an Olmsted Scholar. What was the process for that distinction and what has it meant to your career?

〉 Being chosen as the 2008 Olmsted Scholar Runner-up is a great honor and unique experience. The application process enabled me to succinctly define the heart of who I am and the landscape architect I aspire to be. The process was initiated by a nomination from my department faculty, submission of an application package, and then review by a Landscape Architecture Foundation jury. This distinction has significantly affected my career because it has given me exposure to the greater landscape architecture community earlier than most students. Since the Landscape Architecture Foundation's Olmsted Program has distinguished me as a student leader and promising future landscape architect, my opportunity for gaining employment in my area of interest is greatly enhanced.

What role have internships played in your educational experience?

〉 Having a nine-week summer internship working with the National Park Service's Cultural Landscape Program in Washington, DC, was a privilege. Through their professionalism, openness to my many questions, and agreement with my desire to experience as much as possible, I gained valuable research skills and personal experiences. Even though I do not plan to develop a career in historic preservation, the internship changed my view—the horizon of what I thought I could do as a landscape architect was extended.

What do you hope to be doing 5 to 10 years after graduation in terms of your career?

〉 I would love to work in a multidisciplinary firm that specializes in sustainable and low-impact urban design to support my interests in urban natural systems. In 10 years, I anticipate being a leader in sustainable landscape architecture. I also anticipate contributing to professional advocacy for environmental justice issues. I will also avail myself of opportunities to invest in the viability of the profession, and encourage emerging landscape architecture professionals to practice in a way that is grounded in the roots of the profession, meeting societal health and well-being through sustainable planning and urban design.

Realizing the Synergy between Economic, Community, and Ecological Health

MELINDA ALICE STOCKMANN

Candidate

Master of Landscape Architecture

Department of Landscape Architecture

SUNY College of Environmental Science and Forestry (ESF)

Syracuse, New York

Melinda Stockmann working at a light table. Photographer: Christopher R. McCarthy.

Why did you decide to pursue a career in landscape architecture?

❯ I have a Bachelor of Arts in biology from Colby, a liberal arts college in Maine. After college, I pursued three unusual and significant work experiences. I conducted sea turtle research in Costa Rica. I worked with underserved urban youth at a

nonprofit in Boston. And I supported college students at a semester abroad program in Namibia as they studied nation building, globalization, and the HIV crisis. Each of these experiences built on the one before and I began to realize how many people fail to see the links between economic, social, and environmental problems. Pursuing solutions that addressed all three seemed like a good idea.

The fact that the MLA degree is a professional degree that prepares students for licensure was appealing to me. It affirmed my interest in becoming proficient in specific skills that could be applied to myriad opportunities having to do with ecological rehabilitation, green infrastructure, and community revitalization.

How and why did you choose the school you're attending to earn your Master of Landscape Architecture degree?

❯ When deciding on a graduate program, I considered the following criteria: academic reputation; cost and financial support; location; faculty; program strengths or emphases, and interdisciplinary opportunities. I applied to five MLA programs and was accepted by four. I received offers of merit-based scholarships from two of the four programs. When I weighed all of the variables above, SUNY–ESF (State of New York College of Environmental Science and Forestry) came out on top.

I initiated early communications with faculty at all of the universities I was considering. This helped bring the programs to life for me. Faculty members also put me in contact with current students and alumni, who shared the inside scoop and further shaped my impressions of the programs. The size and diversity of faculty at ESF was a real draw for me. I got a sense that faculty members were very accessible.

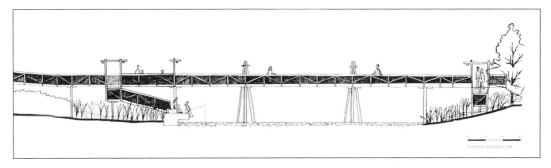

Community design studio: pedestrian/fishing bridge connects community to resources to the north in Coeymans Landing, New York. Illustrator: Melinda Alice Stockmann.

What has been the most satisfying part of your graduate school education?

⟩ Some of the most satisfying moments are the breakthroughs—a feeling of fulfillment when a lightbulb goes on and I understand how a concept is applied. Other moments are the high I feel after completing a project or critique successfully; working with other students as a teaching assistant, helping them figure out how to read topography and provide for positive drainage around a house, and therein reinforcing those skills for myself; understanding how things work together and appreciating just how much I have learned.

Have you had the opportunity for any off-campus experiences? If so, how have these experiences been valuable to your education?

⟩ One of the reasons I chose ESF was the opportunity for off-campus experiences. Facilitating workshops and doing video documentary work for ESF's Center for Community Design Research (CCDR) has allowed me to continue working in partnership with people to help effect change in their communities. Last semester, my design studio focused on creating green infrastructure in a low-income neighborhood. One of the most fulfilling moments was hearing people from the neighborhood respond positively to my design ideas and realize the synergy between economic, community, and ecological health.

Who or what experience has been an important influence on your graduate school education?

⟩ Two of my professors, George Curry and Cheryl Doble, have inspired me through their dedication to teaching, as well as their outstanding accomplishments in community visioning and revitalization.

I have worked with urban foresters, arborists, and landscape maintenance supervisors who interact professionally with landscape architects on a regular basis. They have helped me to understand how important it is for landscape architects to have horticultural knowledge as well as a collaborative spirit. The perspective they have shared has motivated me to thrive in these areas.

One of the benefits of pursuing landscape architecture as a first professional graduate degree is that students have a wealth of academic as well as work-based knowledge. I have spent countless hours with the 11 other people in my graduate class. My classmates have consistently provided me with constructive, friendly, and genuine support. I am still struck by a feeling of profound appreciation when I think about how many exhausting and overwhelming experiences have managed to be enjoyable.

Proposed Alternatives for Residential and Right-of-Way Landscaping

at least two new shade trees
meet 50% canopy cover goal

understory shrubs (silky dogwood)
add visual interest, wildlife habitat

vines on fence (virginia creeper) improve air quality,
provide for wildlife, soften property edge

Existing   Proposed

stop mowing streetside turf to
increase rainwater infiltration

formalize streetside planting,
design rain garden

replace driveway with pervious paving,
include unmowed strip to increase rainwater infiltration

Green infrastructure studio: image simulations show greener public housing in Syracuse, New York. Illustrator: Melinda Alice Stockmann.

What do you hope to be doing 5 to 10 years after graduation in terms of your career?

> I hope to be a licensed landscape architect. I would like to be working in some capacity to inspire and empower underrepresented young people (particularly people of color and people from urban areas) to fill the growing need for innovative design. I am excited about using design as a vehicle to help people gain a greater appreciation for natural processes. I can't wait to be playing a part in rehabilitating landscapes and to be creating inspiring spaces that bring people into closer harmony with the natural areas they inhabit.

Pursuing a Second Degree in Landscape Architecture

TIM JOICE

Candidate

Master of Landscape Architecture

Department Landscape Architecture

Penn State University

University Park, Pennsylvania

Tim Joice during final presentation to Maryland Transit Authority officials.

Why did you decide to pursue a career in landscape architecture?

❯ Initially, I thought engineering was a fit, given my abilities in math, but I had an immediate revelation that I needed to go in a more creative and visionary direction. I felt landscape architecture presented the best opportunity to connect to nature, the built environment, and society. Progressing through undergraduate studies, it evolved into a decision to imagine a better urban and rural continuum, where a greater balance existed between man and nature.

How and why did you choose the schools to attend for your landscape architecture degrees?

❯ For my undergraduate degree, I stayed in my hometown and attended the University of Kentucky. I chose Kentucky to pursue engineering. After deciding that path was not for me, I realized a connection with Department of Landscape Architecture and decided to stay. For graduate school, the Penn State Department of Landscape Architecture provided the most natural fit and opportunity to pursue individual interests, which had been brewing since my junior year at Kentucky.

Why did you decide to pursue a second degree in landscape architecture?

❯ My decision is closely tied to my undergraduate experience. An undergraduate degree in landscape architecture provides exposure to many different aspects of the profession, which ultimately form the foundations for economic, societal, and environmental functions. In my opinion, it is one of the best undergraduate educations one can receive. At the same time, it can be a hindrance. In my junior year I had a desire to learn much more about ecological functions; however, due to the prescribed, holistic curriculum, I was restrained from going further with those studies. Thus, my reason to pursue a master's in landscape architecture was rooted in a desire to more specifically define a landscape architect's role in designing the built environment, and better incorporating ecological functions, particularly hydrologic functions.

How does being a graduate student differ from being an undergraduate student?

❯ As a graduate student, greater freedom exists for developing a curriculum that is more closely

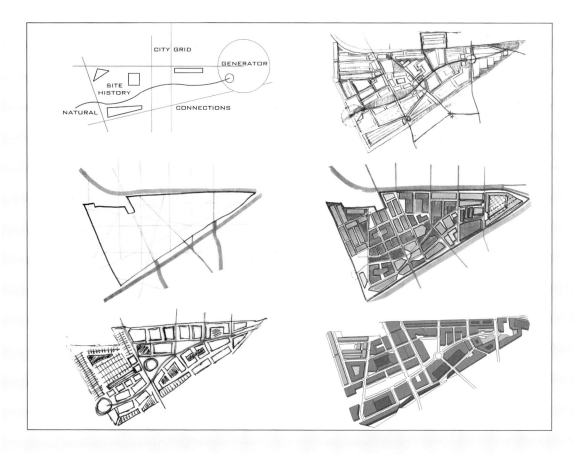

aligned with one's interests. More is expected of graduate students, as it should be, and graduate students should expect more of themselves. Particularly in landscape architecture, graduate education has a much stronger focus on reading and critiquing research, whereas undergraduate landscape architecture is organized around gaining a holistic understanding of the social, natural, and economic aspects of landscapes, and learning about and developing a design process.

What has been the most interesting part of your graduate school education?

〉 Thus far, one of the most interesting aspects is the diversity of backgrounds of the faculty. At

⬆. Evolution of design process from analysis through concept to several design refinements. Illustrator: Tim Joice and Danielle Hammond.

Kentucky, every faculty member had landscape architecture degrees, whereas at Penn State, faculty bring expertise from anthropology, geography, architecture, ecology, planning, and other fields inherent in the broader profession of landscape architecture.

What role have internships played in your educational experience?

〉 During my undergraduate education, I spent the summers after my third, fourth, and fifth years as an intern in various office environments, from

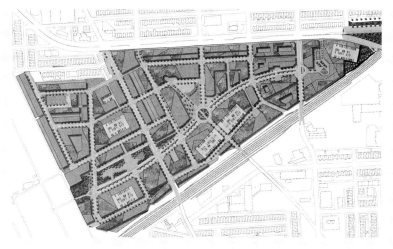

◀ Sustainable community design emphasizes urban hydrologic cycles and green infrastructure networks— here, in West Baltimore, Maryland. Illustrator: Tim Joice.

▼ Three-dimensional model illustrates spatial conditions and the mix of uses in the community design. Illustrator: Tim Joice and Danielle Hammond.

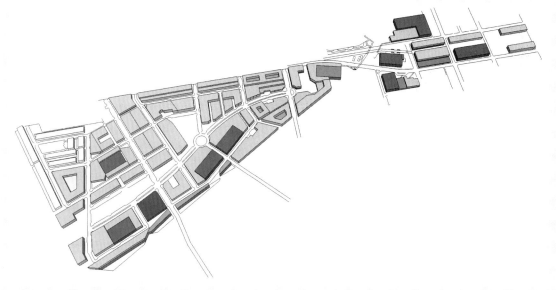

a multidisciplinary medium-size firm to smaller engineering-based firms. These internships provided valuable knowledge of regulatory systems, hands-on learning from current professionals, and an overall better understanding of the profession. More importantly though, it made me realize what the professional environment is lacking, and needs to improve upon, such as moving toward more interdisciplinary work.

What do you hope to be doing 5 to 10 years after graduation in terms of your career?

❯ In five years, I hope to have returned close to home in Kentucky, with a high likelihood of working in government or in the nonprofit sector, such as for a watershed planning organization. Over the course of the next 5 to 10 years, I will push for a new direction in the built environment, toward a more economically, environmentally, and socially sustainable future.

The Importance of Internships

Internships provide the opportunity for students to take what they have learned at school and apply that in a professional setting, while continuing to learn and grow. The benefits of internships are widely recognized in the landscape architecture community. Sometimes after the second year, and certainly after the third year of undergraduate study, students have acquired sufficient skills and knowledge to be of value to an office in an internship arrangement, which typically occurs during the summer. Students pursuing an MLA can usually acquire an internship after their first year of study. A few firms offer longer half-year or full-year internships. Those are valuable experiences, but must be weighed against the additional time that will be needed to complete a degree.

Depending on the firm or organization offering the internship, and the state of the economy, students may be paid for their internship work; and some internships that do not pay may offer to cover living expenses for the summer. Internship opportunities are as wide and varied as the profession itself. Part of your decision to apply for and accept an internship will depend on location and

Graduate student Stephanie Bailey using GPS equipment during a summer internship with the National Park Service. Photographer: Saylor Moss.

One of the studio spaces at Michael Van Valkenburg Associates, Cambridge Massachusetts. Image courtesy of Michael Van Valkenburgh Associates, Inc

your upcoming financial needs. There may be opportunities very near your home, or you may have to travel or relocate for the summer to do an internship. When you are a first-year or second-year student, it would be wise to talk to those in the classes ahead of you to learn about their internship experiences—where did they go, what was it like, how did they get the internship, and so forth.

A large number of internships are widely advertised at all schools, particularly internships available through the larger design firms. Some of these firms run competitive but highly esteemed internships. The American Society of Landscape Architects (ASLA) has an Internship category on the Job Link portion of its Web site. Also, most chapters of the ASLA (typically by state, but larger states have multiple chapters) include job and internship listings on their Web sites. You might also consider initiating conversations with local firms or nearby city or state agencies, possibly over the winter break before the summer when you would like to work. This will let them know you are in the area, what your skills and background are, and how you could contribute. Refer to Chapter 3 to learn about assembling a portfolio and preparing to interview for an internship position.

There is a misperception among students that they must have an internship in a design office before they graduate. Certainly that would be helpful, but there are also many other jobs and experiences that can be as valuable to your future career, such as working in the landscape contracting industry, traveling, or working at a public agency or nonprofit organization.

What role did internships play in your educational experience?

❯ I did internships but I did not work in a design firm. I went for a design/build firm. We did all kinds of landscapes. But more importantly, I was out in the field learning whether we could build it or not, and it was a great experience. Internships are very important. It would be ideal to do one in an office and then one where you are in a design/build situation, where you actually learn craft.

Frederick R. Bonci, RLA, ASLA
Founding Principal, LaQuatra Bonci Associates

❯ My summer internships made me realize I would need to chart my own path. They made me question whether or not working in an office for someone else was how I wanted to spend my professional life. This didn't mean that I would abandon the field; it meant I realized I wanted to expand what I would do professionally.

Julia Czerniak
Principal, CLEAR, Associate Professor of Architecture, Syracuse University

❯ I worked for two summers in an office that was more focused on planning. That work helped broaden my focus in terms of thinking about the bigger picture. I learned a lot and got my start working with Native American communities. We had a project working with the Prairie Island Band of Dakota on an archeological site. It was a great introduction and a very formative experience.

John Koepke
Associate Professor, Department of Landscape Architecture, University of Minnesota

❯ I was required to have an internship. I worked at a local civil engineering/landscape architecture firm. This was a tremendous learning experience. Since the firm did civil engineering work, I learned quite a bit about that discipline. Nothing beats hands-on experience.

Ruben L. Valenzuela, RLA
Principal, Terrano

❯ I interned at Yellowstone National Park. Having this opportunity to see the diversity of work there made it clear to me this was the career I wanted. As an intern, I designed site plans for new and existing buildings, conducted visitor use studies at Old Faithful, and went into the back country to climb peaks to photograph and inventory vistas.

Joanne Cody, ASLA
Landscape Architect Technical Specialist, National Park Service

❯ [Internships] played a huge part. I recommend [students] do them as early as possible—even if all [they're] doing is stacking paper or organizing pencils. The amount of information [they] will absorb is irreplaceable.

Gerdo Aquino, ASLA
Managing Principal, SWA Group

❯ I just had an internship this summer, and it was a lot more than I expected. There is so much work that goes on behind the scenes. Although I worked harder than ever before, my internship was a good experience. It showed me how much dedication it takes. It also taught me, at least from my perspective right now, that I do not want to own my own firm.

Mallory Richardson
Undergraduate Candidate, Department of Planning and Landscape Architecture, Clemson University

❯ My first summer internship was with a firm in Tempe, Arizona. To be in a professional office setting for the first time was a thrilling experience and confirmed my decision to follow a career in landscape architecture. During that summer, I was mentored by one landscape architect in particular who really took time to teach me what he knew.

Douglas C. Smith, ASLA
Chief Operating Officer, EDSA

❯ I got to travel to California on an SWA internship, and that was an eye-opener. It was a professional experience but it was also very open, very experimental, and allowed me a lot of freedom.

And, I appreciate this more now than I did as a 22-year-old, they showed us how they got work. They showed us their marketing and presentation materials. I would kill for that stuff now.

Elizabeth Kennedy, ASLA
Principal, EKLA Studio

〉 Internships played a huge role. I worked for two summers at Campbell Miller's office. I got to meet a lot of folks who were at the height of their careers, people like Eckbo. Going back into the curriculum again, I could see the direct relevance from what I was learning to what I would be doing later on, and it just sped up what I was able to pull out of my education.

Edward L. Blake, Jr.
Founding Principal, The Landscape Studio

〉 I did do an internship, and it was not my best experience. However, internships are key. I wish that everyone would get some kind of experience in a construction firm, too, whether that's design/build or purely building, to truly understand the other side of design.

Jennifer Guthrie, RLA, ASLA
Director, Gustafson Guthrie Nichol Ltd.

〉 Purdue's co-op program was a big influence. In that program you take a year off from school and work in an office. I chose Charlotte, North Carolina. I loved it and came back a much better and more focused student. It really allowed me to know what I liked and what I didn't like.

Robert B. Tilson, FASLA
President, Tilson Group

〉 I had an internship at Alexander & Baldwin, a sugar corporation in Hawaii. It was very important because I was able to work on community planning projects in a variety of rural agricultural communities. It was my first time learning to collaborate with communities and to speak in public and try to communicate what the plans were, while also trying to build consensus. That has followed me through to what I'm doing now—I've come full circle.

Robin Lee Gyorgyfalvy, ASLA
Director of Interpretive Services & Scenic Byways, USDA
Forest Service: Deschutes National Forest

〉 I have always worked ever since I started as an undergraduate. I interned in a series of offices and found what out what scale of office I liked to be in, so that was a really great value.

Thomas Oslund, FASLA, FAAR
Principal, oslund.and.assoc.

〉 My first summer I worked for a private design/build firm, which gave me a lot of practice and helped me become aware of how design/build operates. I also worked for a public agency; I did an internship for the Forest Service one summer. That helped me to understand the role of the landscape architect in a public agency. It also gave me a little more practice on a larger-scale project. I think with design, like anything, you get better the more you practice.

Nancy D. Rottle, RLA, ASLA
Associate Professor, Department of Landscape Architecture,
University of Washington

〉 After my third year I took 16 months off school and I was able to dive into a real-world work experience. The role of that extended internship was definitely the clincher for me to stay in this profession, affording me a solid understanding about the field prior to graduation.

Todd Kohli, RLA, ASLA
Co-Managing Director, Senior Director, EDAW San Francisco

〉 Penn's summer field ecology, which we did at Litchfield (Connecticut) was absolutely fantastic. We had five weeks with top-notch foresters, ecologists, soil scientist, hydrologists, and landscape architects. Walking through the landscape and learning about the interaction between geology and soils and plants and water and human activities, and understanding and reading the landscape: To me that was invaluable.

Jose Alminana, ASLA
Principal, Andropogon Associates, Ltd.

〉 Internships are huge. My second one, with Carol Johnson and Associates in Cambridge, was great. I'd come to work everyday and see the big models and the beautiful drawings; and walking around the studios, I was like, man, this is landscape architecture. That internship really cemented it for me; until that point I had a really abstract notion of what landscape architecture was about.

Kofi Boone, ASLA
Assistant Professor, Department of Landscape Architecture,
North Carolina State University

Professional Licensure

All critical professions that interact with the public, such as doctors, lawyers, architects, and engineers, require legal certification, called a license, to practice. Every state is entrusted with the duty to protect the public's health, safety, and welfare. Because the work that landscape architects do is quite complex, and if done improperly could cause great harm, landscape architects are licensed in the name of consumer protection. Licensure is required in 49 American states, 2 Canadian provinces, and 1 U.S. territory, to ensure that the work performed by a landscape architect will not have an adverse impact on the public or the environment.

Landscape architecture, like many of the professions just listed, is a service-based profession. This means the product—the design work—cannot be examined before the work is performed and completed (i.e., you cannot test-drive what a landscape architect does before it is purchased). In service-based professions it is difficult for the general public to ascertain whether a practitioner is competent. Holding a license signifies formal recognition that an individual has demonstrated sufficient knowledge, skills, and abilities to practice without endangering the public. A license conveys legal and professional responsibilities and privileges.

Most people who become landscape architects do so because they want to make a positive difference in the world. Many landscape architects feel they have a special responsibility to be stewards of the land and to create places of meaning for people. To reach goals such as those for an individual, and for the profession as a whole, designers must become licensed to have the legal right to practice and perform landscape architectural work. Holding a license to practice landscape architecture also confers professional status and credibility, which advances parity with allied building professionals, such as architects and engineers. All allied building professionals must achieve licensure to perform their practice; therefore, if landscape architects want equal respect for their work, they too must become licensed professionals.

The first profession to be licensed was the medical field, in 1872. In 1953, California became the first state to license landscape architects. There are two main types of licensure laws: Title Acts and Practice Acts. The Title Act provides weaker consumer protection since someone can perform the work of a landscape architect as long as he or she does not call him- or herself a landscape architect. The majority of license laws are Practice Acts. These laws regulate those who can practice and perform the work of landscape architecture, and restrict the use of the title "landscape architect" to those who have a current license.

LICENSURE REQUIREMENTS

There are three main steps to becoming a professional landscape architect. The first is completing a formal education at an accredited program. A list of schools accredited to offer landscape architecture degrees is included at the end of this chapter. The second step is obtaining professional work experience under the supervision of a licensed landscape architect. Step three is taking and passing the

Grading plan for Shortlidge Mall on Penn State's University Park Campus. Courtesy of Lager Raabe Skafte Landscape Architects, Inc.

Landscape Architects Registration Exam (LARE). Once licensed, many states require that profession-als keep current in the field through taking continuing education classes to maintain their license. Although there is some variation in the educational and experience requirement components, all licensing laws require an individual to pass the national exam (LARE).

Until they become licensed new graduates cannot legally be called landscape architects, so they are often referred to as *apprentices*, *landscape designers, or intern landscape architects*. It is wise for early-career professionals to get a wide range of experience to gain further knowledge and skills needed for the licensure exam. Apprentices must perform their work under the supervision of a licensed landscape architect. All work, such as drawings and specifications, must be signed and sealed by the licensed landscape architect, who will take legal responsibility for the work.

The licensure laws vary by state and province, but typically a minimum of two to three years of professional work experience, supervised by a licensed landscape architect, is required to be eligi-ble to take the LARE. If someone does not have an accredited landscape architecture degree, some states and provinces will allow a person to take the LARE if he or she has a minimum of 12 years of work experience under the supervision of a licensed landscape architect.

THE LANDSCAPE ARCHITECTS REGISTRATION EXAM (LARE)

The licensure of professionals is regulated by state-appointed registration boards. Each board is a government agency and is completely independent. Since licensure occurs at the state level, and there are no national regulations, the boards are responsible for establishing and enforcing licensure laws. Over the years, however, boards have collectively recognized that they address similar issues, no matter their location. Striving for efficiencies led to a standardization of exam requirements. This means the Landscape Architects Registration Exam (LARE) is the same for every jurisdiction. It was also recognized that this standardization would help facilitate practice for professionals who perform work in more than one state. Professionals can take and pass the exam in one state and then seek reciprocity in other states. Due to these similarities, most registration boards are members of the Council of Landscape Architects Registration Boards (CLARB). This nonprofit association was formed to promote the sharing of information among member boards regarding the licensure of landscape architects and related issues.[4]

The Landscape Architects Registration Exam (LARE) covers knowledge and skills required to practice, as revealed in a 2005 Job Analysis Study conducted by CLARB. Tasks and skills deemed to be critical to the protection of the public's health, safety, and welfare are the main components of the exam. The LARE comprises these five main areas of professional practice:

Section A. Project and Construction Administration

Section B. Inventory, Analysis, and Program Development

Section C. Site Design

Section D. Design and Construction Documentation

Section E. Grading, Drainage, and Stormwater Management

Some states require the passage of additional exam sections, such as irrigation design or plant materials. Three sections, A, B, and D, are multiple-choice questions and are administered on a computer. Two of the sections, C and E, require a graphic response; typically, an 11×17-inch hand-drafted solution.[5]

The exam is now offered several times a year, depending on the jurisdiction. Typically, the graphic response sections can be taken in December, and the multiple-choice sections in March and September. The CLARB Web site provides the most up-to-date information about exam timing and locations. The goal is to ascertain a threshold of minimum competency to practice without endangering the public, thus, the LARE is a pass/fail exam. Sections may be taken and passed individually, but one cannot become licensed until all five sections have been passed.

The following, excerpted from CLARB's 2007 guide to the LARE's updated content, summarizes the topics covered in each exam section and their percentage value to the overall score.[6]

LARE TEST INFORMATION

SECTION A. PROJECT AND CONSTRUCTION ADMINISTRATION

Landscape architects must understand construction contracts and the responsibilities of various parties under such contracts, and their responsibilities during construction observation, and processes for assessing and reviewing projects or plans after they are complete.

Communication (20 percent)

Standards of Practice (23 percent)

Contract Administration (17 percent)

Construction Evaluation (20 percent)

Construction Practices (20 percent)

SECTION B. INVENTORY, ANALYSIS, AND PROGRAM DEVELOPMENT

Landscape architects must know how to define a problem through the understanding of the client's intentions and needs, determine project user values through focus groups and surveys, and define the project goals and objectives. Landscape architects are also required to understand how and where to gather information for a project and how to analyze that information to make design decisions. They must understand how to analyze the relationships of all of the project elements and formulate the project requirements.

Problem Definition (11 percent)

Inventory (29 percent)

Analysis (36 percent)

Programming (24 percent)

SECTION C. SITE DESIGN

Four Vignette Problems

Landscape architects are expected to develop site or land use plans that take into consideration the off-site and on-site influences to development. Landscape architects must consider various codes, consultant studies, and principles of sustainability when creating a site design. They should be able to evaluate the design solutions of others and possess the ability to create alternative solutions to a problem.

SECTION D. DESIGN AND CONSTRUCTION DOCUMENTATION

Landscape architects must be able to refine the preferred solution to a problem and prepare plans and contract documents to ensure the project can be built correctly. A landscape architect must have knowledge of design principles, resource conservation, graphic communication, construction documentation, and materials and methods of construction, to ensure the project is completed in a safe manner.

Design Principles (16 percent)

Resource Conservation and Management (18 percent)

Graphic Communication (8 percent)

Construction Documentation (20 percent)

Materials and Methods of Construction (38 percent)

SECTION E. GRADING, DRAINAGE, AND STORMWATER MANAGEMENT

Four Vignette Problems

Landscape architects are required to manipulate landforms to convey runoff, meet design requirements, and minimize environmental impact. Landscape architects are also expected to evaluate the impact of their decisions on existing off-site conditions and develop strategies for water conservation and preservation of land resources.

CONTINUING EDUCATION

Passage of the LARE exam signifies competency to practice at the time the exam was administered; however, the world in which landscape architects work is ever changing, and the types of projects landscape architects are engaged in are becoming increasingly complex. Additionally, landscape architects, by their nature, are curious and seek to constantly improve upon their skills toward professional advancement. For all these reasons it is deemed critical that landscape architects engage in furthering their understanding of the field by participating in continuing education. The sharing of expertise and ideas by attending classes and conferences is a proven way to advance not only individuals but the profession itself.

The continuing education requirements to maintain an active license to practice are not isolated to the landscape architecture profession. Most licensed professionals, such as architects and engineers, are required to demonstrate that their understanding of their profession and the issues critical to maintaining public health, safety, and welfare is current. The issue of professional development through continuing education is fluid, and requirements vary by jurisdiction. One thing is clear: This topic will only gain in importance as landscape architects continue to advocate for a greater role in the professional building and development community.

Schools Offering Accredited (or Certificate) Programs

This list is current as of the publication date of this book. For updated information, contact the American Society of Landscape Architects at www.asla.org/schools.aspx.

Note the following delineations:

MLA= Graduate degree

BLA or BSLA= Undergraduate degree

Candidacy = Program in process of becoming accredited

Pre-Candidacy = Program plans to be in candidacy shortly after book's publication date

Certificate = Not a degree

Alabama

Auburn University
MLA Program
Landscape Architecture, School of Architecture
104 Dudley Hall
Auburn, AL 36849-5316
www.landarch.auburn.edu

Alaska

None

Arizona

Arizona State University
BSLA Program
Landscape Architecture Program, School of Architecture and Landscape Architecture
PO Box 871605
Tempe, AZ 85287-1605
http://design.asu.edu/sala/program.shtml

The Art Center Design College

BLA Program (Candidacy)

2525 N. Country Club Road

Tucson, AZ 85716

www.theartcenter.edu/programs/PROGmenu.
html

University of Arizona

MLA Program

School of Landscape Architecture, College of
Architecture and Landscape Architecture

PO Box 210444

Tucson, AZ 85721-0044

http://capla.arizona.edu/landscape

Arkansas

University of Arkansas

BLA Program

Department of Landscape Architecture, School
of Architecture

230 Memorial Hall

Fayetteville, AR 72701

http://architecture.uark.edu/larch

California

California Polytechnic State University, San Luis Obispo

BLA Program

Landscape Architecture Department, College of
Architecture and Environmental Design

Building 034, Room 251

San Luis Obispo, CA 93407

http://landarch.calpoly.edu/larc

California State Polytechnic University, Pomona

BSLA Program/MLA Program

Department of Landscape Architecture, College
of Environmental Design

3801 West Temple Avenue

Pomona, CA 91768

www.csupomona.edu/~la

University of California–Berkeley

MLA Program

Department of Landscape Architecture, College
of Environmental Design

202 Wurster Hall

Berkeley, CA 94720-2000

www-laep.ced.berkeley.edu/laep/index.html

University of California–Davis

BSLA Program

Landscape Architecture Program, Department of
Environmental Design

College of Agricultural and Environmental
Sciences

One Shields Avenue, 142 Walker Hall

Davis, CA 95616-8585

http://lda.ucdavis.edu

University of California–Los Angeles

Certified by State of California Architects Board

Certificate in Landscape Architecture

UCLA Extension, Department of the Arts

10995 Le Conte Avenue #414

Los Angeles, CA 90024

www.uclaextension.edu/landarch

University of Southern California

MLA Program (Candidacy)

Graduate Studies in Landscape Architecture,
School of Architecture

Robert Y. Time Research Center, Room 339

Los Angeles, CA 90089-0291

http://arch.usc.edu/Programs/
GraduateDegreesandCertificates/
MasterofLandscapeArchitecture

Colorado

Colorado State University
BSLA Program
Program in Landscape Architecture
Department of Horticulture and Landscape
Architecture, College of Agricultural Sciences
111 Shepardson Building
Fort Collins, CO 80523
www.colostate.edu/Depts/LArch

University of Colorado–Denver
MLA Program
Landscape Architecture Program, College of
Architecture and Planning
Campus Box 126
PO Box 173364
Denver, CO 80217
www.cudenver.edu/Academics/Colleges/
ArchitecturePlanning/programs/masters/MLA/
Pages/mla.aspx

Connecticut

University of Connecticut
BSLA Program
Landscape Architecture Program, College of
Agriculture and Natural Resources
1376 Storrs Road, U-4067
Storrs, CT 06269-4067
http://plantscience.uconn.edu/la.html

Delaware

None

District of Columbia

None

Florida

Florida A&M University
MLA Program
Graduate Program in Landscape Architecture
1936 S Martin Luther King Boulevard
Tallahassee, FL 32307
www.famusoa.net/degrees/grad/mlarch/prog-
desc

Florida International University
BLA Program (Candidacy)/MLA Program
Graduate Program in Landscape Architecture,
School of Architecture
University Park Campus
Miami, FL 33199
www.fiu.edu/~soa/land_architecture.htm

University of Florida
BLA Program/MLA Program
Department of Landscape Architecture, College
of Design Construction and Planning
336 Architecture Building
PO Box 115704-5704
Gainesville, FL 32611
www.dcp.ufl.edu/landscape

Georgia

University of Georgia
BLA Program/MLA Program
Program in Landscape Architecture, College
of Environment and Design, School of
Environmental Design
609 Caldwell Hall
Athens, GA 30602-1845
www.ced.uga.edu

Hawaii

None

Idaho

University of Idaho
BLA Program
Landscape Architecture Department, College of
Letters, Arts & Social Sciences
PO Box 442481
Moscow, ID 83844-2481
www.caa.uidaho.edu/larch

Illinois

Illinois Institute of Technology
MLA Program (Pre-Candidacy)
College of Architecture
3360 S. State Street
Chicago, IL 60616-3793
www.iit.edu/arch/programs/graduate

University of Illinois
BLA Program/MLA Program
Department of Landscape Architecture, College
of Fine and Applied Arts
101 Buell Hall MC 620, 611 Taft Drive
Champaign, IL 61820
www.landarch.uiuc.edu

Indiana

Ball State University
BLA Program/MLA Program
Department of Landscape Architecture, College
of Architecture and Planning
Muncie, IN 47306
www.bsu.edu/landscape

Purdue University
BSLA Program
Landscape Architecture Program, Department of
Horticulture and Landscape Architecture
625 Agriculture Mall Drive

West Lafayette, IN 47907-2010
www.hort.purdue.edu/hort/landarch/landarch.
shtml

Iowa

Iowa State University
BLA Program
Department of Landscape Architecture
College of Design, Room 146
Ames, IA 50011
www.design.iastate.edu/LA

Kansas

Kansas State University
BLA Program (through 2010)/MLA Program
Department of Landscape Architecture/
Regional and Community Planning, College of
Architecture, Planning and Design
302 Seaton Hall
Manhattan, KS 66506-2909
www.capd.k-state.edu/prospective-students/
introduction

Kentucky

University of Kentucky
BSLA Program
Department of Landscape Architecture
S305 Agriculture Science North
Lexington, KY 40546-0091
www.uky.edu/Agriculture/LA

Louisiana

Louisiana State University
BLA Program/MLA Program
Robert Reich School of Landscape Architecture
302 Design Building
Baton Rouge, LA 70803-7020
www.design.lsu.edu/la.htm

Maine

None

Maryland

Morgan State University

MLA Program

Graduate Program in Landscape Architecture

Montebello Complex, Room B107

2201 Argonne Drive

Baltimore, MD 21251

www.morgan.edu/academics/IAP/landscape_
home.html

University of Maryland

BLA Program/MLA Program (Candidacy)

Landscape Architecture Program, Department of
Plant Science and Landscape Architecture

2102 Plant Sciences Building

College Park, MD 20742

www.larch.umd.edu

Massachusetts

Boston Architectural College

BLA Program (Candidacy)

Program Director for Landscape Architecture,
Boston Architectural College, Room 210

320 Newbury Street

Boston, MA 02115

www.the-bac.edu/x271.xml

Harvard University

MLA Program

Department of Landscape Architecture,
Graduate School of Design

409 Gund Hall, 48 Quincy Street

Cambridge, MA 02138

www.gsd.harvard.edu

University of Massachusetts

BSLA Program/MLA Program

Department of Landscape Architecture and
Regional Planning

Hills North 109

Amherst, MA 01003

www.umass.edu/larp/index.html

Michigan

Michigan State University

BLA Program

Landscape Architecture Program, School of
Planning, Design, and Construction

East Lansing, MI 48824-1221

www.spdc.msu.edu/la

University of Michigan

MLA Program/PhD Program

Landscape Architecture Program, School of
Natural Resources and Environment

2502 Dana Hall

Ann Arbor, MI 48109

www.snre.umich.edu//la

Minnesota

University of Minnesota

MLA Program

Department of Landscape Architecture

89 Church Street, SE, 144 Rapson Hall

Minneapolis, MN 55455

http://landarch.cdes.umn.edu

Mississippi

Mississippi State University

BLA Program/MLA Program

Department of Landscape Architecture, College
of Agriculture and Life Sciences

PO Box 9725

Mississippi State, MS 39762-9725

www.lalc.msstate.edu

Missouri

Washington University in St. Louis
MLA Program (Pre-Candidacy)
The Sam Fox School of Design & Visual Arts,
Graduate School of Architecture & Urban Design
One Brookings Drive
St. Louis, MO 63130
http://samfoxschool.wustl.edu

Montana

None

Nebraska

University of Nebraska–Lincoln
BLA Program (Pre-Candidacy)
College of Architecture, Landscape Architecture
Program
210 Architecture Hall
Lincoln NE 68588-0106
http://landscapearchitecture.unl.edu

Nevada

University of Nevada–Las Vegas
BLA Program
Department of Landscape Architecture and
Planning
4505 Maryland Parkway, Box 45018
Las Vegas, NV 89154
http://architecture.unlv.edu/landscape.htm

New Hampshire

None

New Jersey

Rutgers–The State University of New Jersey
BSLA Program
Department of Landscape Architecture, Cook
College

93 Lipman Drive
New Brunswick, NJ 08901-8524
www.landarch.rutgers.edu

New Mexico

University of New Mexico
MLA Program
Landscape Architecture Program, School of
Architecture and Planning
2414 Central Avenue, SE
Albuquerque, NM 87131-1226
http://saap.unm.edu

New York

Cornell University
BSLA Program/MLA Program
Landscape Architecture Department
440 Kennedy Hall
Ithaca, NY 14853
www.landscape.cornell.edu

State University of New York
BLA Program/MLA Program
Faculty of Landscape Architecture, College of
Environmental Science and Forestry
1 Forestry Drive
Syracuse, NY 13210-2787
www.esf.edu/la

The City College of New York
MLA Program (Candidacy)
Urban Landscape Architecture, School of
Architecture Urban Design and Landscape
Architecture
138th Street and Convent Avenue
New York, NY 10031
www1.ccny.cuny.edu/prospective/architecture

North Carolina

North Carolina A&T State University

BSLA Program

Landscape Architecture Program

231 Carver Hall

Greensboro, NC 27411

www.ag.ncat.edu/academics/natres/landarch/
index.html

North Carolina State University

BLA Program/MLA Program

Landscape Architecture Department, College of
Design

PO Box 7701

Raleigh, NC 27695-7701

http://ncsudesign.org/content

North Dakota

North Dakota State University

BLA Program

Department of Architecture and Landscape
Architecture

PO Box 5285, S.U. Station

Fargo, ND 58105-5285

http://ala.ndsu.edu/landscape_architecture

Ohio

Ohio State University

BSLA Program/MLA Program

Landscape Architecture Section, Austin E.
Knowlton School of Architecture

275 West Woodruff Avenue

Columbus, OH 43210-1138

http://knowlton.osu.edu

Oklahoma

Oklahoma State University

BLA Program

Landscape Architecture Program

360 AGH

Stillwater, OK 74078-6027

www.hortla.okstate.edu

University of Oklahoma

MLA Program

Landscape Architecture Program

Gould Hall, Room 162

Norman, OK 73019-0265

http://la.coa.ou.edu

Oregon

University of Oregon

BLA Program/MLA Program

Department of Landscape Architecture, School
of Architecture and Allied Arts

Eugene, OR 97403-5234

http://landarch.uoregon.edu

Pennsylvania

Chatham University

MLA Program

Landscape Architecture/Landscape Studies
Program

Woodland Road

Pittsburgh, PA 15232

www.chatham.edu/departments/artdesign/
graduate/landscapearch/index.cfm

Pennsylvania State University

BLA Program/MLA Program (Candidacy)

Department of Landscape Architecture

121 Stuckeman Family Building

University Park, PA 16802-1912

www.larch.psu.edu

Philadelphia University

BLA Program (Candidacy)

Landscape Architecture Program, School of
Architecture

Smith House

Philadelphia, PA 19144

www.philau.edu/architecture

Temple University

BSLA Program

Department of Landscape Architecture and
Horticulture

580 Meetinghouse Road

Ambler, PA 19002-3994

www.temple.edu/ambler/la-hort

University of Pennsylvania

MLA Program

Department of Landscape Architecture, School
of Design

119 Meyerson Hall, 210 South 34th Street

Philadelphia, PA 19104-6311

www.design.upenn.edu/new/larp/index.php

Rhode Island

Rhode Island School of Design

MLA Program

Department of Landscape Architecture

231 South Main Street

Providence, RI 02903

www.risd.edu/graduate_landscape.cfm

University of Rhode Island

BLA Program

Landscape Architecture Program

Rodman Hall, Room 201

94 West Alumni Avenue

Kingston, RI 02881

www.uri.edu/cels/lar

South Carolina

Clemson University

BLA Program/MLA Program (Candidacy)

Department of Planning and Landscape
Architecture, College of Architecture, Arts and
Humanities

163 Lee Hall, PO Box 340511

Clemson, SC 29634-0511

www.clemson.edu/caah/landscapearchitecture

South Dakota

None

Tennessee

University of Tennessee

MLA Program (Pre-Candidacy)

Graduate Program in Landscape Architecture,
College of Architecture + Design

1715 Volunteer Boulevard

Knoxville, TN 37996

www.arch.utk.edu/acedemic/larch.html

Texas

Texas A&M University

BLA Program/MLA Program

Department of Landscape Architecture and
Urban Planning, College of Architecture

3112 Langford Architecture Center

College Station, TX 77843-3137

http://archone.tamu.edu/LAUP

Texas Tech University

BLA Program/MLA Program

Department of Landscape Architecture, College
of Agricultural Sciences and Natural Resources

Box 42121

Lubbock, TX 79409-2121

www.larc.ttu.edu

The University of Texas–Arlington
MLA Program
Pat D. Taylor, ASLA, Director
PO Box 19108
Arlington, TX 76019-0108
www.uta.edu/architecture/academic/grad/
academic_grad_land.htm

The University of Texas, Austin
MLA Program
Graduate Program in Landscape Architecture,
School of Architecture
1 University Station B7500
Austin, TX 78712-0222
http://soa.utexas.edu

Utah

Utah State University
BLA Program/MLA Program
Department of Landscape Architecture and
Environmental Planning, College of Humanities,
Arts and Social Sciences
Logan, UT 84322-4005
http://laep.usu.edu

Vermont

None

Virginia

University of Virginia
MLA Program
Department of Architecture and Landscape
Architecture, School of Architecture
PO Box 400122
Charlottesville, VA 22904-4122
www.arch.virginia.edu/landscape

Virginia Polytechnic Institute & State University
BLA Program/MLA Program
Landscape Architecture Program, School of
Architecture + Design
121 Burruss Hall–0190
Blacksburg, VA 24061
http://archdesign.vt.edu/landscape-architecture

Washington

University of Washington
BLA Program/MLA Program
Department of Landscape Architecture, College
of Architecture and Urban Planning
348 Gould Hall, Box 355734
Seattle, WA 98195-5734
www.caup.washington.edu/larch

Washington State University
BLA Program
Department of Horticulture and Landscape
Architecture, College of Agriculture and Home
Economics
Johnson Hall 149
Pullman, WA 99164-6414
http://hortla.wsu.edu

West Virginia

West Virginia University
BSLA Program
Landscape Architecture Program, Division
of Resource Management, Davis College of
Agriculture, Forestry and Consumer Sciences
PO Box 6108
Morgantown, WV 26506-6108
www.caf.wvu.edu/resm/la/index.html

Wisconsin

University of Wisconsin–Madison
BSLA Program/MLA (not accredited)
Department of Landscape Architecture, School
of Natural Resources, College of Agricultural
and Life Sciences
1450 Linden Drive
Madison, WI 53706
www.la.wisc.edu

Wyoming

None

Canada

University of British Columbia
MLA Program
Landscape Architecture Program, School of
Architecture and Landscape Architecture,
Faculty of Applied Science
389-2357 Main Mall
Vancouver, BC V6T 1Z4
www.sala.ubc.ca

University of Guelph
BLA Program/MLA Program
School of Environmental Design and Rural
Development
Guelph, Ontario N1G 2W1
www.uoguelph.ca/sedrd/LA

University of Manitoba
MLA Program
Department of Landscape Architecture, Faculty
of Architecture
Winnipeg, Manitoba R3T 2N2
www.umanitoba.ca/faculties/architecture/pro-
grams/landarchitecture

University of Montreal
BLA Program
École d'architecture de paysage
2940 Chemin de la Côte Ste-Catherine, Bureau
4055-1
Montréal, QC H3T 1B9
www.apa.umontreal.ca

University of Toronto
MLA Program
Landscape Architecture Program, John H.
Daniels Faculty of Architecture, Landscape, and
Design
230 College Street
Toronto, Ontario M5T 1R2
www.daniels.utoronto.ca/programs/master_of_
landscape_architecture

Related

Northern Alberta Institute of Technology
Two-year diploma, not accredited
Landscape Architecture Technology
11762-106 Street
Edmonton, Alberta T5G 2R1
www.nait.ca/program_home_15713.htm

APPENDIX A

Resources

LANDSCAPE ARCHITECTURE ORGANIZATIONS

American Society of Landscape Architects (ASLA)
636 Eye Street NW
Washington, DC 20001-3736
888-999-2752
www.asla.org

Canadian Society of Landscape Architects (CSLA)
PO Box 13594
Ottawa, ON, K2K 1X61
866-781-9799
http://csla.ca/site

Council of Educators in Landscape Architecture (CELA)
PO Box 7506
Edmond, OK 73083-7506
405-330-4150
www.thecela.org

Council of Landscape Architectural Registration Boards (CLARB)
3949 Pender Drive, Suite 120
Fairfax, VA 22030
571-432-0332
www.clarb.org

Cultural Landscape Foundation
1909 Q Street NW, Second Floor
Washington DC 20009
202-483-0553
www.tclf.org

International Federation of Landscape Architects (IFLA)
www.iflaonline.org
Contact information is via elected officers. Consult the IFLA Web site for up-to-date information.

Landscape Architecture Accreditation Council (LAAC)
c/o Canadian Society of Landscape Architects
PO Box 13594
Ottawa, ON, K2K 1X6
866-781-9799
http://csla.ca/site/index.php?q=en/node/13

Landscape Architecture Canada Foundation (LACF)
c/o CSLA, P.O. Box 13594
Ottawa, ON, K2K 1X61
866 781-9799
http://csla.ca/site/?q=en/node/9

Landscape Architecture Foundation (LAF)
818 18th Street NW, Suite 810
Washington, DC 20006
202-331-7070
www.lafoundation.org

Landscape Architectural Accreditation Board (LAAB)
636 Eye Street NW
Washington, DC 20001
www.asla.org/AccreditationLAAB.aspx

The Landscape Institute (the Royal Chartered body for landscape architects in the United Kingdom)
33 Great Portland Street
London, W1W 8QG
www.landscapeinstitute.org
Student-Related Resources

Alpha Rho Chi (Co-educational Architecture and Allied Arts Fraternity)
PO Box 3131
Memphis, TN 38173
www.alpharhochi.org

LABASH (Annual International Student Landscape Architecture Conference)

www.asla.org/MeetingAndEventLanding.aspx
The location of the LABASH Conference, first held in 1970, moves to a different school each year. Go to the ASLA Web site for this year's location.

Sigma Lambda Alpha (National Landscape Architecture Honor Society)

c/o Texas Tech University, Department of Landscape Architecture
Box 42121
Lubbock, TX 79409-2121

ALLIED ORGANIZATIONS

Design | Planning

Active Living by Design
University of North Carolina at Chapel Hill
School of Public Health
400 Market Street, Suite 205
Chapel Hill, NC 27516-4028
919-843-2523
www.activelivingbydesign.org

American Association of State Highway and Transportation Officials (AASHTO)
444 North Capitol Street N.W., Suite 249
Washington, DC 20001
202-624-5800
www.transportation.org

American Institute of Architects (AIA)
1735 New York Ave. NW
Washington, DC 20006-5292
800-242-3837

American Planning Association (APA)
122 S. Michigan Ave., Suite 1600
Chicago, IL 60603
312-431-9100
www.planning.org

American Society of Civil Engineers (ASCE), Washington Office
101 Constitution Avenue NW, Suite 375 East
Washington, DC 20001

800-548-ASCE (2723) ext. 7850
www.asce.org

Architects / Designers / Planners for Social Responsibility (ADPSR)
PO Box 9126
Berkeley, CA 94709
510-845-1000
www.ADPSR.org

Association of American Geographers
1710 Sixteenth Street NW
Washington, DC 20009-3198
202-234-1450
www.aag.org

Association of Collegiate Schools of Planning (ACSP)
6311 Mallard Trace
Tallahassee, FL 32312
850-385-2054
www.acsp.org

Association for Community Design
c/o Boston Society of Architects
52 Broad Street
Boston MA, 02109-4301
www.communitydesign.org/About.htm

Congress for the New Urbanism (CNU)
The Marquette Building
140 S. Dearborn Street, Suite 310
Chicago, IL 60603
312-551-7300
www.cnu.org

Institute of Transportation Engineers
1099 14th Street NW, Suite 300 West
Washington, DC 20005-3438
202-289-0222
www.ite.org

Leadership in Energy and Environmental Design (LEED)
www.usgbc.org/leed
Planners Network
106 West Sibley Hall

Cornell University
Ithaca, NY 14853
607-254-8890
www.plannersnetwork.org

Society for College and University Planning
339 East Liberty, Suite 300
Ann Arbor, MI 48104
734-998-7832
www.scup.org

Urban Land Institute
1025 Thomas Jefferson Street, NW Suite 500 West
Washington, DC 20007
202-624-7000
www.uli.org

U.S. Green Building Council (USGBC)
1800 Massachusetts Avenue NW, Suite 300
Washington, DC 20036
800-795-1747
www.usgbc.org

Cultural | Historic

Alliance for Historic Landscape Preservation (AHLP)
www.ahlp.org/docs/about.html
Contact information is via board officers. Consult the
AHLP Web site for up-to-date information.

Historic American Landscape Survey (HALS)
Heritage Documentation Programs
National Park Service, Department of the Interior
1201 Eye Street NW (2270), Seventh Floor
Washington, DC 20005
202-354-2135
www.nps.gov/hdp/hals/index.htm

Historic Roads
Paul Daniel Marriott & Associates
3140 Wisconsin Avenue NW , Suite 804
Washington, DC 20016
www.historicroads.org

International Council on Monuments and Sites (ICOMOS)
ICOMOS International Secretariat
49-51, rue de la Fédération
75015 Paris, France
www.icomos.org

Library of American Landscape History (LALH)
PO Box 1323
Amherst, MA 01004-1323
413-549-4860
www.lalh.org

National Trust for Historic Preservation
1785 Massachusetts Ave. NW
Washington, DC 20036-2117
800-944-6847
www.preservationnation.org

Environment | Ecology

American Fisheries Society
5410 Grosvenor Lane
Bethesda, MD 20814
301-897-8616
www.fisheries.org

American Society of Consulting Arborists
9707 Key West Avenue, Suite 100
Rockville, MD 20850
301-947-0483
www.asca-consultants.org

Ecological Society of America
1990 M Street NW, Suite 700
Washington, DC 20036
202-833-8773
www.esa.org

International Society of Arboriculture
PO Box 3129
Champaign, IL 61826-3129
888-472-8733
www.isa-arbor.com

Society for Ecological Restoration International
285 West 18th Street, Suite 1
Tucson, AZ 85701
520-622-5485
www.ser.org

Society of Wetland Scientists
1313 Dolley Madison Boulevard, Suite 402
McLean, VA 22101
703-790-1745
www.sws.org

Soil and Water Conservation Society
945 SW Ankeny Road
Ankeny, IA 50023-9723
515-289-2331
www.swcs.org

Construction

American Nursery & Landscape Association
1000 Vermont Avenue NW, Suite 300
Washington, DC 20005-4915
202-789-2900
www.anla.org

Construction Specifications Institute (CSI)
99 Canal Center Plaza, Suite 300
Alexandria, VA 22314-1588
800-689-2900
www.csinet.org

Professional Landcare Network (PLANET)
950 Herndon Parkway, Suite 450
Herndon, VA 20170
703-736-9666
www.landcarenetwork.org
PLANET includes landscape contractors.

Recreation | Parks

American Public Garden Association (APGA)
100 West 10th Street, Suite 614
Wilmington, DE 19801
302-655-7100
www.publicgardens.org

American Society of Golf Course Architects (ASGCA)
125 N Executive Drive
Brookfield, WI 53005
262-786-5960
www.asgca.org

City Parks Alliance
1111 16th Street NW, Suite 310
Washington, DC 20036
202-223-9111
www.cityparksalliance.org

National Association for Olmsted Parks (NAOP)
1111 16th Street NW, Suite 310
Washington, DC 20036
866-666-6905
www.olmsted.org

National Recreation and Park Association
22377 Belmont Ridge Rd.
Ashburn, VA 20148
703-858-0784
www.nrpa.org

National Therapeutic Recreation Society (NTRS)
www.nrpa.org/content/default
.aspx?documentId=956
The NTRS is a branch of the National Recreation and Park Association.

Service Organizations

ACE Mentor Program of America
400 Main Street, Suite 600
Stamford, CT 06901
203-323-0020
www.acementor.org

AmeriCorps
1201 New York Avenue NW
Washington, DC 20525
202-606-5000
www.AmeriCorps.org

Architects without Borders
www.awb.iohome.net
Design Corps
302 Jefferson Street, Suite 250
Raleigh, NC 27605
919-828-0048
www.designcorps.org

Habitat for Humanity International
1-800-422-4828 (1-800-HABITAT)
www.habitat.org

Peace Corps
Paul D. Coverdell Peace Corps Headquarters
1111 20th Street NW
Washington, DC 20526
800-424-8580
www.peacecorps.gov

APPENDIX B

Selected References

BOOKS

Alanen, Arnold, and Robert Melnick, eds. 2000. *Preserving Cultural Landscapes in America*. Baltimore: Johns Hopkins University Press.

Alexander, Christopher. 1997. *A Pattern Language: Towns, Buildings, Construction*. New York: Oxford University Press.

American Planning Association. 2006. *Planning and Urban Design Standards*. Hoboken, NJ: John Wiley & Sons, Inc.

Amidon, Jane. 2005. Michael Van Valkenburgh Associates: Allegheny Riverfront Park. *Source Books in Landscape Architecture*. New York: Princeton Architectural Press.

———. 2006. *Ken Smith Landscape Architects/ Urban Projects*. New York: Princeton Architectural Press.

———. 2006. *Peter Walker and Partners: Nasher Sculpture Center Garden: Source Books in Landscape Architecture*. New York: Princeton Architectural Press.

Amidon, Jane, and Dan Kiley. 1999. *Dan Kiley: The Complete Works of America's Master Landscape Architect*. Boston: Bulfinch Press.

Barnett, Jonathan. 2003. *Redesigning Cities: Principles, Practice, Implementation*. Chicago: Planners Press.

Beardsley, John. 2006. *Earthworks and Beyond*. New York: Abbeville Press.

Booth, Norman K. 1989. *Basic Elements of Landscape Architectural Design*. Project Heights, IL: Waveland Press.

Bruegmann, Robert. 2005. *Sprawl: A Compact History*. Chicago: University of Chicago Press.

Calkins, Meg. 2008. *Materials for Sustainable Sites: A Complete Guide to the Evaluation, Selection, and Use of Sustainable Construction Materials*. Hoboken, NJ: John Wiley & Sons, Inc.

Carr, Ethan. 1999. *Wilderness by Design: Landscape Architecture and the National Park Service*. Lincoln, NE: University of Nebraska Press.

Conan, Michel. 2000. *Environmentalism in Landscape Architecture*. Washington, DC: Dumbarton Oaks Research Library and Collection.

Corner, James. 1999. *Recovering Landscape: Essays in Contemporary Landscape Architecture*. New York: Princeton Architectural Press.

Cullen, Gordon. 1971. *The Concise Townscape*. New York: Van Nostrand Reinhold Co.

Czerniak, Julia, and Georges Hargreaves. 2007. *Large Parks*. New York: Princeton Architectural Press.

Dee, Catherine. 2001. *Form and Fabric in Landscape Architecture: A Visual Introduction*. New York: Spon Press.

Dramstad, Wenche, James Olson, and Richard Forman. 1996. *Landscape Ecology Principles in Landscape Architecture and Land-Use Planning*. Washington, DC: Island Press.

Dreiseitl, Herbert. 2005. *New Waterscapes: Planning, Building and Designing with Water*. Boston: Birkhäuser.

Fabos, Julius Gy, and Jack Ahern. 1996. *Greenways: The Beginning of an International Movement*. Amsterdam: Elsevier Science.

Farr, Douglas. 2008. *Sustainable Urbanism: Urban Design with Nature*. Hoboken, NJ: John Wiley & Sons, Inc.

Flint McClelland, Linda. 1998. *Building the National Parks: Historic Landscape Design and Construction*. Baltimore: John Hopkins University Press.

Forman, Richard T. 1995. *Land Mosaics: The Ecology of Landscapes and Regions*. Cambridge; New York: Cambridge University Press.

France, Robert. 2008. *Handbook of Regenerative Landscape Design*. Boca Raton, FL: CRC Press.

Francis, Mark, and Randolph T. Hester. 1990. *The Meaning of Gardens*. Cambridge, MA: MIT Press.

Frankel, Felice, and Jory Johnson. 1991. *Modern Landscape Architecture: Redefining the Garden*. New York: Abbeville Press.

Girling, Cynthia, and Kenneth I. Helphand. 1996. *Yard, Street, Park: The Design of Suburban Open Space*. New York: John Wiley & Sons, Inc.

Hargreaves, George. 1998. *Designed Landscape Forum I*. Washington, DC: Spacemaker Press.

Harris, Charles, and Nicholas Dines. 1997. *Time-Saver Standards for Landscape Architecture*, 2nd ed. New York: McGraw-Hill Professional.

Hester, Randolph T. 2006. *Design for Ecological Democracy*. Cambridge, MA: MIT Press.

Hiss, Tony. 1991. *The Experience of Place: A New Way of Looking at and Dealing with Our Radically Changing Cities and Countryside*. New York: Random House, Vintage Books.

Holling, C.S. 1978. *Adaptive Environmental Assessment and Management*. New York: John Wiley & Sons, Inc.

Hood, Walter. 1997. *Urban Diaries*. Washington, DC: Spacemaker Press.

Hough, Michael. 1992. *Out of Place: Restoring Identity to the Regional Landscape*. New Haven, CT: Yale University Press.

———. 2004. *Cities and natural process: a basis for sustainability*. London: Routledge.

Jackson, John Brickerhoff. 1986. *Discovering the Vernacular Landscape*. New Haven, CT: Yale University Press.

Jacobs, Allan B. 1995. *Great Streets*. Cambridge, MA: MIT Press.

Jacobs, Jane. 1993. *The Death and Life of Great American Cities*. New York: Modern Library.

Jellicoe, Geoffrey, and Susan Jellicoe. 1995. *The Landscape of Man: Shaping the Environment from Prehistory to the Present Day*, 3rd ed. London: Thames & Hudson.

Johnson, Bart R., and Kristina Hill. 2002 *Ecology and Design: Frameworks for Learning*. Washington, DC: Island Press.

Keeney, Gavin. 2000. *On the Nature of Things: Contemporary American Landscape Architecture*. Boston: Birkhäuser.

Kirkwood, Niall. 2004. *Weathering and Durability in Landscape Architecture*. Hoboken, NJ: John Wiley & Sons, Inc.

———. 1999. *The Art of Landscape Detail: Fundamentals, Practices, and Case Studies*. New York: John Wiley & Sons, Inc.

Lawson, Laura. 2005. *City Bountiful: A Century of Community Gardening in America*. Berkeley, CA: University of California Press.

Leopold, Aldo. 1949. *A Sand County Almanac*. New York: Ballentine Books.

Longstreth, Richard, ed. 2008. *Cultural Landscapes: Balancing Nature and Heritage in Preservation Practice*. Minneapolis, MN: University of Minnesota Press.

Losantos, Agata, Daniela Santos Quartino, Bridget Vranckx; translation: Martin Douch. 2007. *Urban Landscape: New Tendencies, New Resources, New Solutions*. Barcelona: Loft Publications.

Louv, Richard. 2008. *The Last Child in the Woods: Rescuing Children from Nature Deficit Disorder*. Chapel Hill, NC: Algonquin Books of Chapel Hill.

Lyle, John Tillman. 1996. *Regenerative Design for Sustainable Development*. New York: John Wiley & Sons, Inc.

Lynch, Kevin. 1960. *The Image of the City*. Cambridge, MA: Technology Press.

Lynch, Kevin, and Gary Hack. 1984. *Site Planning*, 3rd ed. Cambridge, MA: MIT Press.

Mann, William A. 1993. *Landscape Architecture: An Illustrated History in Timelines, Site Plans, and Biography*. New York: John Wiley & Sons, Inc.

Marcus, Clare Cooper, and Marni Barnes. 1999. *Healing Gardens: Therapeutic Benefits and Design Recommendations*. New York: John Wiley & Sons, Inc.

McHarg, Ian. 1995. *Design with Nature*. New York: John Wiley & Sons, Inc.

Meinig, Donald W., ed. 1979. *The Interpretation of Ordinary Landscapes: Geographical Essays*. New York: Oxford University Press.

Moore, Charles, Bill Mitchell, and William Turnbull. 1988. *The Poetics of Gardens*. Cambridge, MA: MIT Press.

Motloch, John L. 2000. *Introduction to Landscape Design,* 2nd ed. New York: John Wiley & Sons, Inc.

Nassauer, Joan Iverson. 1997. *Placing Nature: Culture and Landscape Ecology*. Washington, DC: Island Press.

Ndubisi, Forster. 2002. *Ecological Planning: A Historical and Comparative Synthesis*. Baltimore: Johns Hopkins University Press.

Newton, Norman T. 1971. *Design on the Land: The Development of Landscape Architecture*. Cambridge, MA: Belknap Press.

Norberg–Schulz, Christian. 1980. *Genius Loci: Toward a Phenomenology of Nature*. New York: Rizzoli.

Odum, Eugene. 1997. *Ecology: A Bridge between Science and Society*. Sunderland, MA: Sinauer Associates.

Odum, Martha, and Eugene Odum. 2000. *Essence of Place*. Athens, GA: Georgia Museum of Art.

Olin, Laurie. 1996. *Transforming the Common Place: Selections from Laurie Olin's Sketchbooks*. Cambridge, MA: Harvard University Graduate School of Design.

Orr, David. 2004. *The Nature of Design*. New York: Oxford University Press.

Potteiger, Matthew, and Jamie Purinton. 1998. *Landscape Narratives: Design Practices for Telling Stories*. New York: John Wiley & Sons, Inc.

Pregill, Philip, and Nancy Volkman. 1999. *Landscapes in History: Design and Planning in the Eastern and Western Tradition*. New York: John Wiley & Sons, Inc.

Rogers, Walter. 1996. *The Professional Practice of Landscape Architecture: A Complete Guide to Starting and Running Your Own Firm*. New York: John Wiley & Sons, Inc.

Rowe, Peter. 1991. *Making a Middle Landscape*. Cambridge, MA: MIT Press.

Sharky, Bruce. 1994. *Ready, Set, Practice: Elements of Landscape Architecture Professional Practice*. New York: John Wiley & Sons, Inc.

Simo, Melanie Louise. 1999. *100 Years of Landscape Architecture: Some Patterns of a Century*. Washington, DC: Spacemaker Press.

Simonds, John Ormsbee, and Barry Starke. 2006. *Landscape Architecture*, 4th ed. New York: McGraw-Hill.

Spens, Michael. 2003. *Modern Landscape*. New York: Phaidon Press Limited.

Spirn, Anne Whiston. 1984. *The Granite Garden*. New York: Basic Books Inc.

———. 1998. *The Language of Landscape*. New Haven, CT: Yale University Press.

Steiner, Frederick R. 2000. *The Living Landscape: An Ecological Approach to Landscape Planning*. New York: McGraw-Hill Professional.

Strom, Steven, and Kurt Nathan, Jake Woland, and David Lamm. 2004. *Site Engineering for Landscape Architects,* 4th ed. Hoboken, NJ: John Wiley & Sons, Inc.

Swaffield, Simon. 2002. *Theory in Landscape Architecture: A Reader*. Philadelphia: University of Pennsylvania.

Thayer, Robert. 1993. *Gray World, Green Heart: Technology, Nature, and the Sustainable Landscape*. New York: John Wiley & Sons, Inc.

Thompson, J. William, and Kim Sorvig. 2007. *Sustainable Landscape Construction: A Guide to Green Building Outdoors, Second Edition*. Washington, DC: Island Press.

Thompson, George F., and Frederick R. Steiner, eds. 1997. *Ecological Design and Planning*. New York: John Wiley & Sons, Inc.

Tiberghien, Gilles. 1995. *Land Art*. New York: Princeton Architectural Press.

Trancik, Roger. 1986. *Finding Lost Space: Theories of Urban Design*. New York: John Wiley & Sons, Inc.

Treib, Marc, ed. 2002. *The Architecture of Landscape, 1940–1960*. Philadelphia, PA: University of Pennsylvania Press.

———. 1994. *Modern Landscape Architecture: A Critical Review*. Cambridge, MA: MIT Press.

Tufte, Edward R. 1990. *Envisioning Information*. Cheshire, CT: Graphics Press.

Untermann, Richard K. 1996. *Principles and Practices of Grading, Drainage, and Road Alignment: An Ecological Approach*. New York: Prentice Hall Professional Technical Reference.

van Sweden, James. 2003. *Gardening with Nature*. New York: Watson–Guptill.

Waldheim, Charles, ed. 2006. *The Landscape Urbanism Reader*. New York: Princeton Architectural Press.

Walker, Peter, and Melano Simo. 1994. *Invisible Gardens*. Cambridge, MA: MIT Press.

Watts, May Thielgaard. 1975. *Reading the Landscape of America*. New York: MacMillan.

Weilacher, Udo. 1996. *Between Landscape Architecture and Land Art*. Boston: Birkhäuser.

Whyte, William H. 2001. *The Social Life of Small Urban Spaces*. New York: Project for Public Spaces Inc.

Wilson, Edward O. 1986. *Biophilia*. Cambridge, MA: Harvard University Press.

PERIODICALS

Domus: www.domusweb.it/home.cfm

Dwell: www.dwell.com

Ecological Restoration: A publication for the University of Wisconsin–Madison Arboretum, published by the University of Wisconsin Press; www.ecologicalrestoration.info

Garden Design Magazine: www.gardendesign.com

Green Places Journal: A publication of the Landscape Design Trust; www.landscape.co.uk/greenplaces/journal

Journal of Landscape Architecture: The journal of the European Council of Landscape Architecture Schools (ECLAS); www.info-jola.de

Journal of Urban Design: www.tandf.co.uk/journals/titles/13574809.asp

Landscape Architecture Magazine: The magazine of the American Society of Landscape Architects (ASLA); www.asla.org/nonmembers/lam.cfm

Landscape Australia: Official magazine of the Australian Institute of Landscape Architects (AILA); www.aila.org.au/landscapeaustralia

Landscape Journal Design, Planning and Management of the Land: The official journal of the Council of Educators in Landscape Architecture (CELA); http://lj.uwpress.org

Landscape Review: An Asia–Pacific journal of landscape architecture

Landscape and Urban Planning: An International Journal of Landscape Ecology, Planning and Design; www.elsevier.com

Restoration Ecology: The Journal of the Society for Ecological Restoration International; www.wiley.com/bw/journal.asp?ref=1061-2971

Topos: The International Review of Landscape Architecture and Urban Design; www.topos.de

Urban Land Magazine: An Urban Land Institute publication; www.uli.org/ResearchAndPublications/Magazines/UrbanLand.aspx

VIEW: Annual publication of the Library of American Landscape History; www.lalh.org/view.html

Professionals and Students Interviewed for This Book

Jose Alminana, ASLA
Principal, Andropogon Associates, Ltd.
Philadelphia, Pennsylvania

Gerdo Aquino, ASLA
Managing Principal, SWA Group
Los Angeles, California

Edward L. Blake, Jr.
Founding Principal, The Landscape Studio
Hattiesburg, Mississippi

Jacob Blue, MS, RLA, ASLA
Landscape Architect/Ecological Designer,
Applied Ecological Services, Inc.
Brodhead, Wisconsin

Frederick R. Bonci, RLA, ASLA
Founding Principal, LaQuatra Bonci Associates
Pittsburgh, Pennsylvania

Kofi Boone, ASLA
Assistant Professor, Department of Landscape
Architecture, North Carolina State University
Raleigh, North Carolina

Ignacio Bunster–Ossa, ASLA, LEED AP
Principal, Wallace Roberts & Todd, LLC
Philadelphia, Pennsylvania

Jim Burnett, FASLA
President, The Office of James Burnett
Houston, Texas; Solana Beach, California

Kevin Campion, ASLA
Senior Associate, Graham Landscape
Architecture
Annapolis, Maryland

Jeffrey K. Carbo, FASLA
Principal, Jeffrey Carbo Landscape Architects
Alexandria, Louisiana

Stephen Carter, ASLA
BRAC NEPA Support Team, U.S. Army Corps of
Engineers
Mobile, Alabama

Joanne Cody, ASLA
Senior Landscape Architect, National Park
Service, Denver Service Center
Lakewood, Colorado

Karen Coffman, RLA
NPDES Program Coordinator, Maryland State
Highway Administration, Highway Hydraulics
Division
Baltimore, Maryland

Kurt Culbertson, FASLA
Chairman of the Board, Design Workshop
Aspen, Colorado

Julia Czerniak
Principal, CLEAR
Syracuse, New York
Director, UPSTATE: A Center for Design,
Research, and Real Estate
Associate Professor of Architecture, Syracuse
University

Barbara Deutsch, ASLA, ISA
Associate Director, BioRegional North America
(One Planet Communities)
Washington, DC

Mike Faha, ASLA, LEED AP
Founding Principal, GreenWorks, PC
Portland, Oregon

Eddie George, ASLA
Founding Principal, The Edge Group
Columbus, Ohio, Nashville, Tennessee

Jennifer Guthrie, RLA, ASLA
Director, Gustafson Guthrie Nichol Ltd.
Seattle, Washington

Robin Lee Gyorgyfalvy, ASLA
Director of Interpretive Services & Scenic Byways,
USDA Forest Service: Deschutes National Forest
Bend, Oregon

Devin Hefferon
Landscape Designer, Michael Van Valkenburgh
Associates, Inc.
Cambridge, Massachusetts

Douglas Hoerr, FASLA
Partner, Hoerr Schaudt Landscape Architects
Chicago, Illinois

Mark Johnson, FASLA
Founding Principal and President, Civitas, Inc.
Denver, Colorado

Elizabeth Kennedy, ASLA
Principal, EKLA Studio
Brooklyn, New York

Mikyoung Kim
Principal, mikyoung kim design
Brookline, Massachusetts

John Koepke
Associate Professor, Department of Landscape
Architecture , University of Minnesota
Minneapolis, Minnesota

Todd Kohli, RLA, ASLA
Co-Managing Director, Senior Director, EDAW
San Francisco, California

Roy Kraynyk
Executive Director, Allegheny Land Trust
Sewickley, Pennsylvania

Dawn Kroh, RLA
President, Green 3, LLC
Indianapolis, Indiana

Stephanie Landregan, ASLA
Chief of Landscape Architecture, Mountains
Recreation & Conservation Authority
Los Angeles, California

Tom Liptan, ASLA
City of Portland Bureau of Environmental
Services, Sustainable Stormwater Management
Program
Portland, Oregon

Patricia O'Donnell, FASLA, AICP
Principal, Heritage Landscapes, Preservation
Landscape Architects & Planners
Charlotte, Vermont

Thomas Oslund, FASLA, FAAR
Principal, oslund.and.assoc.
Minneapolis, Minnesota

Chris Reed
Principal, StoSS
Boston, Massachusetts

Nancy D. Rottle, RLA, ASLA
Associate Professor, Department of Landscape
Architecture; Director, Green Futures Research
and Design Lab, University of Washington
Seattle, Washington

Mario Schjetnan, FASLA
Founding Partner, Grupo de Diseno Urbano
Colonia Condesa, México

Gary Scott, FASLA
2010 President of ASLA; Director West Des
Moines Parks & Recreation Department
West Des Moines, Iowa

Nathan Scott
Landscape Designer, Mahan Rykiel Associates
Baltimore, Maryland

Juanita D. Shearer–Swink, FASLA
Project Manager, Triangle Transit
Research Triangle Park, North Carolina

Jim Sipes, ASLA
Senior Associate, EDAW
Atlanta, Georgia

Douglas C. Smith, ASLA
Chief Operating Officer, EDSA
Fort Lauderdale, Florida

Frederick R. Steiner, PhD, FASLA
Dean, School of Architecture, University of Texas
Austin, Texas

Emmanuel Thingue, RLA
Senior Landscape Architect, New York City
Department of Parks and Recreation
Flushing Meadows–Corona Park, New York

Robert B. Tilson, FASLA
President, Tilson Group
Vienna, Virginia

Cindy Tyler
Principal, Terra Design Studios
Pittsburgh, Pennsylvania

Meredith Upchurch, ASLA
Green Infrastructure Designer, Casey Trees
Endowment Fund
Washington, DC

Ruben L. Valenzuela, RLA
Principal, Terrano
Tempe, Arizona

James van Sweden, FASLA
Founding Principal, Oehme, van Sweden &
Associates, Inc.
Washington, DC

Scott S. Weinberg, FASLA
Associate Dean and Professor, College of
Environment and Design, University of Georgia
Athens, Georgia

Students

Stephanie Bailey
Candidate, Master of Landscape Architecture,
Department of Landscape Architecture,
University of Oregon
Eugene, Oregon

Brittany Bourgault
Undergraduate Candidate, Department of
Landscape Architecture, University of Florida
Gainesville, Florida

Tabitha Harkin
Candidate, Master of Landscape Architecture,
College of Environmental Design, California
State Polytechnic University
Pomona, California

Tim Joice
Candidate, Master of Landscape Architecture,
Department Landscape Architecture, Penn State
University
University Park, Pennsylvania

Nick Meldrum
Undergraduate Candidate, Department of
Landscape Architecture and Environmental
Planning, Utah State University
Logan, Utah

Mallory Richardson
Undergraduate Candidate, Department of
Planning and Landscape, Architecture, Clemson
University
Clemson, South Carolina

Ian Scherling
Non-Baccalaureate Undergraduate MLA
Candidate, Department of Landscape
Architecture/Regional and Community Planning,
Kansas State University
Manhattan, Kansas

Melinda Alice Stockmann
Candidate, Master of Landscape Architecture,
Department of Landscape Architecture, SUNY
College of Environmental Science and Forestry
(ESF)
Syracuse, New York

CHAPTER NOTES

Chapter 1

1. McHarg, Ian L., and Frederick R. Steiner. 1998. *To Heal the Earth: Selected Writings of Ian L. McHarg.* Washington, DC: Island Press, p. 192.

2. Mayell, Hillary. 2002. "Human 'Footprint' Seen on 83 Percent of Earth's Land," *National Geographic News.* Retrieved October 21, 2008, from http://news.nationalgeographic.com/news/2002/10/1025_021025_HumanFootprint.html.

3. *What Is Landscape Architecture?* 2007. Washington, DC: American Society of Landscape Architects. Retrieved October 30, 2008, from www.asla.org/uploadedFiles/CMS/Government_Affairs/Member_Advocacy_Tools/2007landscape_architecture.pdf.

4. Newton, Norman T. 1971. *Design on the Land.* Cambridge, MA: Belknap Press, p. 221.

5. Rybczynski, Witold. 1999. *A Clearing in the Distance.* New York: Scribner, p. 271.

6. Karson, Robin. 2008. "A New Angle on the Country Place Era," *View.* Amherst, MA: Library of American Landscape History, Vol. 8, p. 5.

7. Ibid., p. 5.

8. Newton, *Design on the Land,* p. 535.

9. Karson, "New Angle," p. 9.

Chapter 2

1. Malin, Nadav. July 2007. Case Study: Sidwell Friends Middle School. "Academic Achievement: A School Expansion in Our Nation's Capitol

Introduces a Wetland to a Dense Urban Site," *GreenSource.* Retrieved February 6, 2008 from http://greensource.construction.com/projects/0707_sidwell.asp.

2. Ogden, Michael. June 2005. "Stormwater and Wastewater Treatment and Reuse," *Building Safety Journal,* pp. 36–39.

3. Middle School Green Building. Sidwell Friends School. Retrieved August 18, 2008, from www.sidwell.edu/about_sfs/greenbuilding_ms.asp.

4. Alminana, Jose. February 22, 2008. In-person interview. Andropogon Associates, Philadelphia, Pennsylvania.

5. Green Buildings. Sidwell Friends School. Retrieved August 18, 2008, from www.sidwell.edu/about_sfs/greenbuilding.asp.

6. ASLA 2007 Professional Awards. Retrieved July 10, 2008, from www.asla.org/awards/2007/07winners/207_msp.html.

7. "About the Center." 2006 Retrieved July 10, 2008, from www.mesaartscenter.org/ContributeDocuments/MACFactSheet_2006.pdf.

8. ASLA 2007 Professional Awards. Retrieved July 10, 2008, from www.asla.org/awards/2007/07winners/207_msp.html.

9. Ibid.

10. Ibid.

11. Ibid.

12. Lurie Garden. Millenium Park, Chicago. Retrieved July 10, 2008 from www.millenniumpark.org/artandarchitecture/lurie_garden.html.

13. GRHC Green Roof Award write-up. Retrieved July 10, 2008, from www.greenroofs.org/washington/index.php?page=millenium.

14. ASLA 2008 Professional Awards. Retrieved July 10, 2008, from www.asla.org/awards/2008/08winners/441.html.

15. Ibid.

16. Lurie Garden Design Narrative. Millennium Park. *CityofChicago.org.* Retrieved September 28, 2008, from http://egov.cityofchicago.org/city/

webportal/portalContentItemAction.do?contentOI
D=536908544&contenTypeName=COC_EDITORIA
L&topChannelName=SubAgency&channelId=0&e
ntityName=Millennium+Park&deptMainCategoryO
ID=-536887892&blockName=Millennium+Park%
2FLurie+Garden%2Fl+Want+To.

17. ASLA 2008 Professional Awards, www.asla.org/
awards/2008/08winners/441.html.

18. Ibid.

19. Ulam, Alex. November 2008. "The Park IKEA Built,"
Landscape Architecture Magazine, 98, No. 11,
p. 116.

20. Byles, Jeff. September 3, 2008. "Erie Basin Park,"
The Architect's Newspaper. Retrieved November
22, 2008, from www.archpaper.com/e-board_rev
.asp?News_ID=2763&PagePosition=10.

21. Ulam, "The Park IKEA Built," p. 111.

22. Byles, "Erie Basin Park."

23. Ulam, "The Park IKEA Built," pp. 110–117.

24. Lee Weintraub Profile, NYSCLA. 2008. Retrieved
November 23, 2008, from www.nyscla.org/db/
nyscla_details.php?id=97.

25. Lee Weintraub Profile, FASLA. September 21,
2006. Landscape Online.com. Retrieved November
25, 2008, from www.landscapeonline.com/
research/article/7814.

26. Ulam, "The Park IKEA Built," p. 113.

27. Ibid.

28. Ibid, p. 115.

29. Brady, Sheila A. October 28, 2008. Email interview
with Oehme, van Sweden & Associates, Inc.,
Washington, DC.

30. Ibid.

31. ASLA 2008 Professional Awards. Retrieved
September 9, 2008, from www.asla.org/
awards/2008/08winners/254.html.

32. Brady, "Email interview."

33. Ibid.

34. ASLA 2008 Professional Awards, www.asla.org/
awards/2008/08winners/254.html.

35. Ibid.

36. Ibid.

37. Brady, "Email interview."

38. Ibid.

39. 2007 CPRA Awards and Recognition Program.
CPRA E-News. 2007. Retrieved November 25,
2008, from www.cpra.ca/UserFiles/File/EN/
sitePdfs/newsE-News/2007ENGFallEdition.pdf.

40. Metro Skate Park. Space2place. 2008. Retrieved
September 9, 2008, www.space2place.com/
public_bonsor.html.

41. Ibid.

42. Ibid.

43. Use of EcoSmart Concrete for the Metro Skate
Park—Burnaby, BC. Space2Place. 2004. Retrieved
November 25, 2008, from www.ecosmartconcrete
.com/kbase/filedocs/csrmetro_design.pdf.

44. Hinton Eco–Industrial Park—Statement of
Qualifications. Space2Place. 2006. Retrieved
November 25, 2008, from www.ecoindustrial.ca/
hinton/pdfs/roster/Space2Place.pdf.

45. Curran, Patrick. August 14, 2008. Telephone
interview. SWA Group, Los Angeles, California.

46. ASLA 2008 Professional Awards. Retrieved
September 4, 2008, from www.asla.org/
awards/2008/08winners/108.html.

47. ASLA 2007 Professional Awards. Retrieved
September 9, 2008, from www.asla.org/
awards/2007/07winners/506_nna.html.

48. NE Siskiyou Green Street Project Report. 2005.
Retrieved November 23, 2008, from www.
portlandonline.com/Bes/index
.cfm?a=78299&c=45386.

49. ASLA 2007 Professional Awards, www.asla.org/
awards/2007/07winners/506_nna.html.

50. "NE Siskiyou Green Street Project Report."

51. Ibid.

52. ASLA 2007 Professional Awards, www.asla.org/
awards/2007/07winners/506_nna.html.

53. "NE Siskiyou Green Street Project Report."

54. ASLA 2007 Professional Awards, www.asla.org/
awards/2007/07winners/506_nna.html.

55. Jordan, Scott. September 11, 2008. Email
interview with Civitas, Inc.

56. Ibid.

57. Viani, Lisa Owens. August 2007. "The Feel of a
Watershed—The Cedar River Watershed Education
Center teaches by sensory experience. Should it
do more?" in *Landscape Architecture Magazine,*
97, no 8, p. 34.

58. Ibid., pp. 24–39.

59. Ibid., pp. 24–39.

60. Ibid., pp. 24–39.

61. Ibid., p. 27.

62. 2004 ASLA Professional Awards. Retrieved
September 10, 2008, from www.asla.org/
awards/2004/04winners/entry441.html.

63. Ballentine, Jane. September 11, 2003. "The Louisville Zoo Wins Coveted AZA Exhibit Award." Retrieved October 27, 2008, from www.aza.org/HonorsAwards/Exh_LouisvilleZoo.

64. Sawyer, Jeff. October 17, 2008. Telephone interview. CLR Design, Philadelphia, Pennsylvania.

65. CLR Design. Retrieved October 22, 2008, from http://clrdesign.com.

Chapter 3

1. "Landscape Architects." December 18, 2007. *Occupational Outlook Handbook, 2008–09 Edition*. Bureau of Labor Statistics, U.S. Department of Labor. Retrieved January 22, 2009, from www.bls.gov/oco/ocos039.htm#emply.

2. Showcase Projects: Washington's Landing. "About the URA, Urban Redevelopment Authority of Pittsburgh." Retrieved October 31, 2008, from www.ura.org/showcaseProjects_washLanding.html.

3. Putaro, Sarah M., and Kathryn A. Weisbrod. August 24, 1998. Site Information. Carnegie Mellon University. Retrieved October 31, 2008, from www.ce.cmu.edu/Brownfields/NSF/sites/Washland/INFO.htm.

4. HGTV "Brownfields." Retrieved September 14, 2008, from www.hgtv.com/rm-products-trade-shows/brownfields/index.html.

5. Putaro, "Site Information" (Aesthetics subsection)

6. LaQuatra Bonci Web site. Retrieved September 14, 2008, from www.laquatrabonci.com/portfolio/portfolio_main.php?view=project&id=7&folder=2

7. Washington's Landing Web site. Accessed September 14, 2008, from www.washingtonslanding.info.

8. Mays, Vernon. June 1998. "La Transformacion," in *Landscape Architecture Magazine,* vol 88, pp. 75–97.

9. El Conquistador Resort and Country Club, Project Data Sheet. EDSA. Retrieved October 27, 2008, from www.edsaplan.com/upload/project_doc/17_El_Conquistador_Resort_and_Country_Club.pdf.

10. "Landscape Architects," *Occupational Outlook Handbook, 2008–09 Edition*.

11. ASLA 2007 Professional Awards. Retrieved July 10, 2008, from www.asla.org/awards/2007/07winners/161_nps.html.

12. Ibid.

13. Ibid.

14. "Existing Greenways: Natural Resources." 2007. New England Greenway Vision Plan. Retrieved January 22, 2009, from www.umass.edu/greenway/Ma/ma-frame-exist.html.

15. Koepke, John. September 23, 2008, Telephone interview. University of Minnesota.

16. 2008 ASLA Community Service Honor Award: The Hills Project. ASLA. Retrieved January 18, 2009, from www.asla.org/awards/2008/studentawards/052.html.

17. Ibid.

18. Lee, Brian. January 24, 2009. Email interview.

19. "2008 ASLA Community Service Honor Award."

20. Ibid.

21. University of Kentucky: Department of Landscape Architecture. 2008. "The Hills Project." University of Kentucky. Retrieved January 18, 2009, from www.nkapc.org/Hills/Presentation_1.pdf.

22. Lee, Brian. September 19, 2008. "UK Landscape Architecture Students Win International Award." University of Kentucky: College of Agriculture: Ag News. Retrieved January 18, 2009, from www.ca.uky.edu/NEWS/?c=n&d=206.

23. "2008 ASLA Community Service Honor Award."

24. Lee, "Email interview."

25. "2008 ASLA Community Service Honor Award."

26. Ibid.

27. Balderrama, Anthony. 2008. "Resume Blunders That Will Keep You from Getting Hired." *CareerBuilder.com*. Retrieved July 28, 2008, from www.cnn.com/2008/LIVING/worklife/03/19/cb.resume.blunders/index.html.

28. Portfolio. Dictionary.com. *Online Etymology Dictionary*. Douglas Harper, Historian. 2001. Retrieved November 2, 2008, from http://dictionary.reference.com/browse/portfolio.

29. National Employment Matrix: Employment by Industry, Occupation, and Percent Distribution, 2006–2016, 17–1012 Landscape Architects. Retrieved January 10, 2009, from ftp://ftp.bls.gov/pub/special.requests/ep/ind-occ.matrix/occ_pdf/occ_17-1012.pdf.

30. Job Outlook–Landscape Architects. December 18, 2007. *Occupational Outlook Handbook, 2008–09 Edition*. Bureau of Labor Statistics, U.S. Department of Labor. Retrieved September 25, 2008, from www.bls.gov/oco/ocos039.htm#outlook.

31. Pollack, Peter, Chair, ASLA Council on Education. April 2007. "Growing the Profession—A White Paper," p. 2.

32. Pollack, ibid., p. 3.

33. 2008 ASLA Graduating Students Study. August 2008, pp. 7, 16. Retrieved January 10, 2009, from www.asla.org/uploadedFiles/CMS/Education/Career_Discovery/2008ASLAGraduatingStudents Report0.7.pdf.

34. Earnings–Landscape Architects. December 18, 2007. *Occupational Outlook Handbook, 2008–09 Edition*. Bureau of Labor Statistics, U.S. Department of Labor. Retrieved January 10, 2009, from www.bls.gov/oco/ocos039. htm#earnings.

35. Pollack, "Growing the Profession," p. 2.

36. Leighton, Ron. January 12, 2009. ASLA Education Director. Email correspondence.

37. 2008 ASLA Graduating Students Study, p. 3.

38. Cahill–Aylward, Susan. January 12, 2009. ASLA Managing Director Information and Professional Practice. Email correspondence.

39. 2008 ASLA Graduating Students Study, p. 3.

40. About Us—American Society of Landscape Architects. 2008. Retrieved January 10, 2009, from www.asla.org/AboutJoin.aspx.

41. About—Canadian Society of Landscape Architects. Retrieved January 10, 2009, from http://csla.ca/site/index.php?q=en/node.

42. Membership—Join/Renew, American Society of Landscape Architects. 2008. Retrieved January 10, 2009, from www.asla.org/JoinRenew.aspx.

43. CSLA Membership—Canadian Society of Landscape Architects. Retrieved January 10, 2009, from http://csla.ca/site/index.php?q=en/node/494.

44. ASLA Code of Professional Ethics, as amended April 27, 2007. Retrieved January 10, 2009, from www.asla.org/uploadedFiles/CMS/About__Join/Leadership/Leadership_Handbook/Ethics/CODEPRO.pdf.

Chapter 4

1. Wescoat, James L. Jr., and Douglas M. Johnston, eds. 2008. *Places of power: Political Economies of Landscape Change*. Dordrecht ; London: Springer, p. 197.

2. "Give Us Green… But Make It Fashionable: Cotton Incorporated Releases New Consumer Ad Campaign." Release Date: Tuesday, June 10, 2008. Retrieved October 24, 2008, from www.cottoninc.com/pressreleases/?articleID=468.

3. "Future Needs of Land Design Professions." Landscape Architecture Foundation. Accessed October 24, 2008, from www.lafoundation.org/landscapefutures/initiative.aspx.

4. "Shifting Population Patterns," in *The State of World Population 1999. 6 billion: A Time for Choices*. United Nations Population Fund. Retrieved October 28, 2008, from www.unfpa.org/swp/1999/pressumary1.htm.

5. Herlitz, Jeff. August/September 2008. "Our Imperiled Oceans and Coasts," in *Planning*. Chicago: American Planning Association, 74, no. 8, p. 46.

6. Nodvin, Steven C. September 12, 2008. "Global Warming," in *The Encyclopedia of Earth*. Retrieved October 25, 2008, from www.eoearth.org/article/Global_warming.

7. "Carbon Sequestration R&D Overview." September 19, 2007. U.S. Department of Energy, Fossil Energy Office of Communications. Retrieved October 25, 2008, from http://fossil.energy.gov/sequestration/overview.html.

8. "Terrestrial Sequestration Research." August 1, 2005. U.S. Department of Energy, Fossil Energy Office of Communications. Retrieved October 25, 2008, from http://fossil.energy.gov/sequestration/terrestrial/index.html.

9. "About Green Hour." 2008. The National Wildlife Federation. Retrieved October 25, 2008, from http://greenhour.org/section/about#FAQ.

10. Louv, Richard. 2006. *Last Child in the Woods*. Chapel Hill, NC: Algonquin Books, p. 34.

11. Kaplan, Rachel. 1998. *With People in Mind: Design and Management of Everyday Nature*. Washington, DC: Island Press, pp. 68, 76.

12. "Human Well-being." 2007. Sustainable Sites Initiative. Retrieved October 26, 2008, from www.sustainablesites.org/human.html.

13. Kuo, Frances E. May 2003. "The Role of Arboriculture in a Healthy Social Ecology," in *Journal of Arboriculture, 29*, no. 3, pp. 149–155.

14. "Background," *Pennsylvania Strategies, Codes, and People Environments.* 2003. The Pennsylvania State University. Retrieved October 25, 2008, from www.pennscapes.psu.edu.

15. Daily, Gretchen C., Susan Alexander, Paul R. Ehrlich, Larry Goulder, Jane Lubchenco, Pamela A. Matson, Harold A. Mooney, Sandra Postel, Stephen H. Schneider, David Tilman, George M. Woodwell. *Ecosystem Services: Benefits Supplied to Human Societies by Natural Ecosystems. Issues in Ecology,* "Ecosystem Services: Benefits Supplied to Human Societies by Natural Ecosystems," No. 2, Spring, 1997, Ecological Society of America. Retrieved October 26, 2008, from www.ecology.org/biod/ value/EcosystemServices.html.

16. "Benefits," *Plant-it 2020.* Retrieved October 25, 2008, from www.plantit2020.org/benefits.html.

17. "History," Sustainable Sites Initiative. 2007. Retrieved October 26, 2008, from www .sustainablesites.org/history.html.

18. Pink, Daniel. 2005. *A Whole New Mind: Why Right-Brainers Will Rule the Future.* New York: Riverhead Books, p. 2.

19. Huitt, W. 2007. "Success in the Conceptual Age: Another Paradigm Shift." Paper delivered at the 32nd Annual Meeting of the Georgia Educational Research Association, October 26. Retrieved October 27, 2008, from http://chiron.valdosta. edu/whuitt/papers/conceptual_age_s.doc.

20. Pink, *A Whole New Mind,* p. 245.

21. "Top Ten Cubicle-Free Jobs: Landscape Architect." May 2008. *Outside Magazine.* Retrieved September 25, 2008, from http://outside.away. com/outside/culture/200805/ten-cubicle-free-jobs-landscape-architect.html.

22. Nemko, Marty. December 19, 2007. "Best Careers 2008," in *U.S. News & World Report.* Retrieved September 25, 2008, from www.usnews. com/features/business/best-careers/best-careers-2008.html.

23. ———. December 19, 2007. "How the Best Careers Were Selected," in *U.S. News & World Report.* Retrieved September 25, 2008, from www.usnews.com/articles/business/best-careers/2007/12/19/how-the-best-careers-were-selected.html.

24. "Job Outlook—Landscape Architects." December 18, 2007. *Occupational Outlook Handbook, 2008–09 Edition.* Bureau of Labor Statistics, U.S. Department of Labor. Retrieved September 25, 2008, from www.bls.gov/oco/ocos039. htm#outlook.

25. Orland, Brian. November 2006. "The 0.1 Percent Dilemma," in *Landscape Architecture Magazine,* 96, no. 11, p. 88.

26. Green Futures Research and Design Lab. University of Washington. Retrieved September 2, 2008, from http://greenfutures.washington.edu/projects.php.

Chapter 5

1. 2008 CLARB Member Board Roster. 2008. Fairfax, VA: Council of Landscape Architectural Registration Boards. Retrieved December 6, 2008, from www.clarb.org/documents/BDroster.pdf.

2. Landscape Architecture Merit Badge. Boy Scouts of America. Retrieved December 6, 2008, from www.boyscouttrail.com/boy-scouts/meritbadges/ landscapearchitecture.asp.

3. "Linking Girls to the Land." September 22, 2008. U.S. Environmental Protection Agency. Retrieved December 6, 2008, from www.epa.gov/ linkinggirls.

4. Rankin, Matthew (ed.) 2000. *The Road to Licensure and Beyond.* Fairfax, VA: Council of Landscape Architectural Registration Boards, p. 26.

5. "Structure and Specifications." Fairfax, VA: Council of Landscape Architectural Registration Boards. Retrieved January 24, 2009, from www.clarb.org/ Pages/Exams_About.asp?target=fo.

6. "The Landscape Architect Registration Examination (LARE) Content Guide." November 2007. Fairfax, VA: Council of Landscape Architectural Registration Boards. Retrieved January 24, 2009, from www.clarb.org/documents /2007contentguidenewAspecs.pdf.

INDEX